Research for Development

The series Research for Development serves as a vehicle for the presentation and dissemination of complex research and multidisciplinary projects. The published work is dedicated to fostering a high degree of innovation and to the sophisticated demonstration of new techniques or methods.

The aim of the Research for Development series is to promote well-balanced sustainable growth. This might take the form of measurable social and economic outcomes, in addition to environmental benefits, or improved efficiency in the use of resources; it might also involve an original mix of intervention schemes.

Research for Development focuses on the following topics and disciplines:

Urban regeneration and infrastructure, Info-mobility, transport, and logistics, Environment and the land, Cultural heritage and landscape, Energy, Innovation in processes and technologies, Applications of chemistry, materials, and nanotechnologies, Material science and biotechnology solutions, Physics results and related applications and aerospace, Ongoing training and continuing education.

Fondazione Politecnico di Milano collaborates as a special co-partner in this series by suggesting themes and evaluating proposals for new volumes. Research for Development addresses researchers, advanced graduate students, and policy and decision-makers around the world in government, industry, and civil society.

THE SERIES IS INDEXED IN SCOPUS

More information about this series at http://www.springer.com/series/13084

Giuseppe Andreoni · Cinzia Mambretti
Editors

Digital Health Technology for Better Aging

A multidisciplinary approach

Springer

Editors
Giuseppe Andreoni
Department of Design
Polytechnic University of Milan
Milan, Italy

Cinzia Mambretti
Polytechnic University of Milan
Milan, Italy

ISSN 2198-7300 ISSN 2198-7319 (electronic)
Research for Development
ISBN 978-3-030-72662-1 ISBN 978-3-030-72663-8 (eBook)
https://doi.org/10.1007/978-3-030-72663-8

This Springer imprint is published by the registered company Springer Nature Switzerland AG
The registered company address is: Gewerbestrasse 11, 6330 Cham, Switzerland

Preface

Interview with Irina Kalderon Libal, Representative of European Commission, DG Communications Networks, Contents and Technology

Ageing presents one of the greatest social and economic challenges of the twenty-first century. In most EU countries, people born today can expect to live beyond the age of 80: 6 more years, on average. According to the WHO, the 10% rise in doctor and nurse numbers seen in Europe over the last decade is unlikely to be enough to cover the needs of ageing populations. Physicians are also getting older, with nearly one in three aged over 55. Structural demographic changes like these force national health systems to adapt, so they can continue to provide adequate and affordable care. This is where digital technology can help to increase efficiency, bring innovation, improve people's quality of life as well as encourage healthy living.

Well-designed technology empowers people and keeps them independent and mobile. The elderly should not be afraid of technology but help design the right technologies in support of their real needs.

The European Commission recognises that Europe needs to face the challenges imposed by demographic change, increasing care demand and personnel shortage in care, further digitisation of our society. Several answers in response of these societal challenges are possible, but in every answer smart technology will be an essential element.

The European Commission is investing in digital technology for active and healthy ageing and stimulate European collaboration to further unlock the huge potential of this emerging market and make sure that digital innovation for active and healthy ageing is making a difference to Europeans' lives.

There is already very good work is ongoing on many Active and Healthy Ageing (AHA) topics, such as independent living, age-friendly environments, smart home and smart city concepts. European health and care system owners, policymakers, research funders, researchers, developers and innovators in this field have already worked together under different umbrellas, focusing on solutions for a sustainable health and care system of Europe. The TO-REACH project has already delivered a member state and associated country supported strategic research agenda on how to identify more effective and sustainable ways to organise, manage, finance and deliver high quality care to European citizens. The "Active and Assisted Living" programme (AAL) has for many years successfully provided bottom up ICT-based innovation opportunities and solutions for the ageing society. The European Innovation Partnership on Active and Healthy Ageing (EIP-AHA) strengthened EU research and innovation. It brought together all the relevant actors at EU, national and regional levels across different policy areas to handle societal challenges and involved all the innovation chain levels. The Joint Programming Initiative More years better life (JPI MYBL) consolidates more than 15 countries to enhance coordination and collaboration between European and national research programs related to demographic change.

The SAPEA report[1] 1 on „Transforming the Future of Ageing" (2019) states that in view of the current numbers of older adults in Europe (in 2016, there were 98 million people in the EU aged 65 and older) and taking into consideration that the life expectancy of the next generation of older adults is likely to surpass their parents, two strategies can be proposed:

(1) Promoting healthy lifestyles over the life course, as well as detecting and modifying early and mid-life risk factors of impaired function and chronic diseases with the aim of delaying age-related disability;
(2) Providing more appropriate health and social care for the aged EU population by offering integrated and holistic care in all-age community and health and care facilities.

The report also stresses that both approaches must consider that technology will revolutionise care delivery systems in thge next future and that an adequate number of skilled professionals is essential.

Decision-makers at national, regional or service level therefore need to explore solutions to ensure that they can continue to provide accessible health care that is of high quality, responsive, affordable and financially sustainable by taking into account the existing challenges on globalisation and technological development, demographic, climate and environmental changes as well as changes in the political and social landscape.

Under the future Horizon Europe, the European Commission and the Member States are currently working on a new partnership focusing on Health Systems Transformation. Building on the experiences from Horizon 2020, the new partnership will be able to provide evidence for innovative solutions that support cost-effective and fiscally sustainable health and care policies, and best practices. It will build knowledge on the conditions for transferability and up-scaling of innovative solutions across and within EU countries, develop and test a mechanism to support diffusion of innovative solutions, unleash unmet needs of citizens and health and care systems.

---

[1] https://www.sapea.info/topics/ageing/.

The European Commission has already invested in very successful projects to advance the digital transformation in health and care. The Work Programme 2018–20 of Horizon 2020 allocates EUR 400M in this area. The next step now is to manage to bring these results to the market and promote a large-scale deployment of these digital solutions, in order to benefit EU citizens and find economically sustainable business models. The Commission will encourage closer cooperation between regional and national authorities to stimulate the development of the health technology sector. This will include supporting start-ups and small and medium size enterprises. It will also entail promoting cooperation between public authorities and other stakeholders committed to promoting shared or mutually recognised principles for validating and certifying digital solutions for adoption in health systems (for instance, mHealth and independent living).

The Commission will help Member States and regional authorities develop their capacity to engage in this transformation and receive technical assistance. It will also facilitate investment opportunities in Member States and regions to leverage public and private investment for the large-scale deployment of digitally enabled, integrated person-centred care.

Under Horizon Europe, the Commission and the Member States are currently developing a newly proposed co-funded Partnership: "Transforming Health and Care Systems". It will focus on improving health and care models in an ageing, data-driven and digital society, shifting to holistic health promotion and person-centred care approaches through health policy and health systems research (applied for the production and up-scaling of policy and service innovations that are transposable across health systems).

The co-funded partnership proposal is merging different existing initiatives in (digital) health by pooling knowledge and resources of the Active and Assistive Living Programme (AAL, Art. 185), European Innovation Partnership on Active & Healthy Ageing (EIP-AHA), Joint Programming Initiative (JPI) "More Years, Better Lives" and the Blueprint for Digital Innovation in Health and Care.

It is very important that EU citizens can trust such innovative digital solutions and can embrace them without fear. Their acceptance and take-up by individuals depend on public perception of these aspects.

Here, there are a number of EU rules, notably the General Data Protection Regulation (GDPR) and the ePrivacy Directive, which provide the strongest safeguards of trustworthiness (i.e. voluntary approach, data minimisation, time limitation) for such apps to operate widely and accurately.

In addition, the large volume and sensitivity of the data that is processed require robust cybersecurity measures to mitigate the risk to security and of data breaches that could have the devastating effect on the trust of public. The EU supports Member States such as via the EU framework for cybersecurity as set out in the Directive on Security of network and information systems (NIS).

The European Union is regularly implementing the GDPR and Cybersecurity regulations and takes reinforcement measures whenever it is necessary. Ensuring users' trust in our digitised systems requires an effective consideration of the legal framework by providers of digital and online services. However, cybersecurity and data protection are not the only factors influencing users' trust in our digitised systems. Providers of such services should ensure quality, relevant and continuous service, as well as transparency.

Milan, Italy

Giuseppe Andreoni
Cinzia Mambretti

Contents

Older Persons in Europe 2020: Needs and Challenges for an Interdisciplinary Polytechnic Approach

Cinzia Mambretti and Giuseppe Andreoni

Abstract Ageing population is a fact in the European countries. How to improve the quality of life and sustain healthy ageing is one of the big challenges that deserve to be addressed considering the several and different aspects of life. But a person is a complex system and the last decades' approach demonstrated that, even if general or cluster medicine reached good results, the new barriers to overcome are ad hoc solutions, tailored to the single to improve wellbeing and preserve decline. The Personalised Medicine call, SC1-PM-15-2017 Personalised coaching for well-being and care of people as they age, under the Horizon 2020 program, aims at developing and validating new ICT based approaches for empowering and motivating people. This section will introduce the reader to the European scenario, the challenge and the research and innovation action promoted under personalised medicine and the specific call.

1 Ageing in Europe 2020

Ageing of the population is a challenge in most of the westerns' countries. How to effectively manage this change in the demographic composition is a priority in Europe and also worldwide. The recent publication of the Green paper from the European Commission highlights some topic and challenges to be tackled in the coming years to face this important social responsibility [1]. In particular, technological, clinical, cognitive and social guidelines are suggested through fostering solidarity and responsibility between generations.

Birth rate is regularly decreasing while life expectancy at birth is more than 80 years old. Longer life doesn't implicitly mean healthy life for the whole period, but to postpone at last as we can the physical and psychological decline is one

C. Mambretti (✉)
Fondazione Politecnico di Milano, Piazza Leonardo Da Vinci 32, 20129 Milan, Italy
e-mail: cinzia.mambretti@fondazione.polimi.it

G. Andreoni
Department of Design, Politecnico di Milano, Milan, Italy

G. Andreoni and C. Mambretti (eds.), *Digital Health Technology for Better Aging*, Research for Development, https://doi.org/10.1007/978-3-030-72663-8_1

of the main challenges of the modern society. We are experiencing an unexpected and growing pressure to the National Healthcare Systems, not only to respond to emergency as the Covid-19 is forcing the systems, but also in the normal time and its day by day activities.

The Eurostat Statistics on population development confirms an Ageing Europe. The trend shows significantly increase of elderly aged 65+ in the EU-27, rising from 90.5 million at the beginning of 2019 to reach 129.8 million by 2050.

Those aged 75–84 years are projected to expand by 56.1%, while the number of people aged 65–74 years is projected to increase by 16.6%. By contrast, the latest projections suggest that there will be 13.5% fewer people aged less than 55 years living in the EU-27 by 2050.

The following Fig. 1 shows the estimated decrease of population aged 65 and the increase of the elderly.

The European Commission 2018 Ageing Report states that EU is moving from 3.3 working age people for every person aged over 65 to only 2 working-age people in the next 50 years. In fact, the old-age dependency ratio, defined as number of people 65+/number of people aged between 15 and 64 is projected to increase from 29.6% in 2016 to 51.2 in 2070. On the other hand, this increasing of population age is a significant challenge for the society of the future considering the total costs of public spending is expected to increase of 1.7% points of the GDP between 2016 and 2070. The public costs include pensions, education, unemployment benefit, but healthcare and long-term care are responsible of the higher impact. The increased demand of

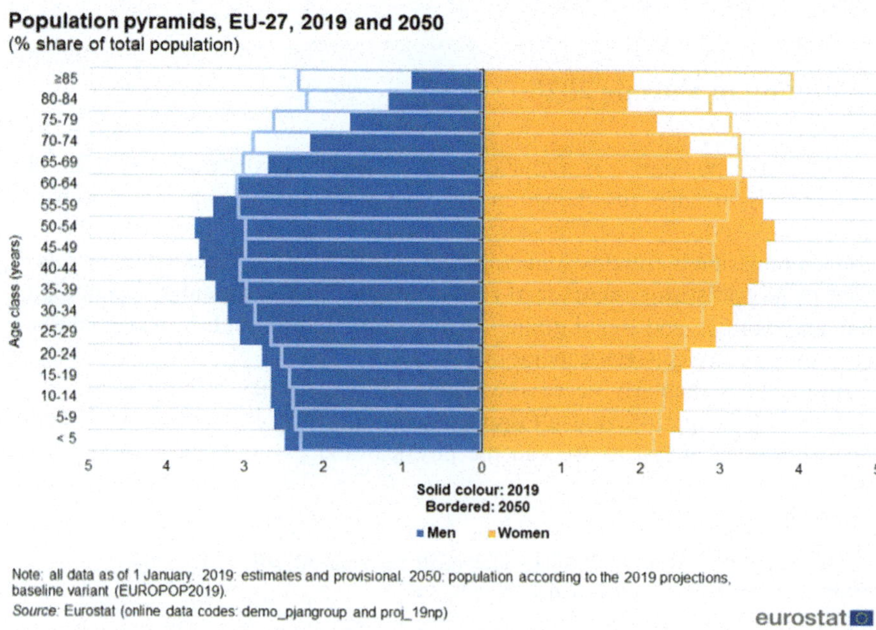

Fig. 1 Change of demographic composition 2019–2050

care services and the decreased availability of healthcare professionals could bring the system to the collapse. Unfortunately, during the recent and still ongoing Covid-19 emergency most of the European countries are experiencing an acceleration on this trend due to the rapidly spread-out of the disease, especially among elderly, thus realizing that is not only necessary to introduce adequate adjustment to reduce the burden of the system, but that innovation is required to effectively manage the change of people approach to their self-wellbeing. Social, demographic, economic and financial policies are basic bricks toward a sustainable society. In this scenario, the healthcare system plays an important role in the promotion and actively support of empowerment of patient and people, guiding them toward correct lifestyles and wellbeing, in other words toward "Healthy Ageing" [2, 3]. The digital transformation and the emerging and fast growth of the so called "Silver Economy" have paved the way for a big change in the elderly from cure to care. Nowadays information runs at light speed through the new tele-communication technologies, is available and easy usable, allows older people to be more careful about their health status than their predecessors. This trend can only increase in the next elderly generation. Furthermore, they are economically independent and discretely digital educated to welcome the ICT/IoT new era. The social, economic, and infrastructural environment is ready to allow for the digital innovation of healthcare system, that now can leverage upon these multiple factors and opportunities.

Technologically speaking the time is mature but experience still demonstrates high barriers to disrupt into practice. Usability and acceptance are often at core of failures.

Eurostat statistics about ageing in Europe shows how different is the scenario across countries, however, considering all the concurrent aspects of wellbeing in the human being, European overall medium is always below 50%:

- 45.6% practice regularly physical activity (Fig. 2),
- 19.2% interacts every day with friends and relatives, but it raises to 35.6% considering once per week frequency. Besides, considering friends instead of family, they become 10.9% and 36.1% respectively (Fig. 3).

Nutrition is as well a notorious dilemma, as weight problems are fast increasing in Europe and estimates counts 66% of overweight people in the 65–74 age range. While overweight is at the top of the iceberg, others malnutrition problems afflict elderly introducing other type of health risks, e.g. low calcium intake and related risks of bone fractures, or low proteins levels and muscle mass decrease.

Data demonstrate that there is room for improvements in all these areas. The person should be considered as a whole, healthy food and physical activity for the body, but also right social activity, cognitive and psychological wellbeing for the mind. Complex and interrelated connections of effort and accomplishment rather than just a diet and exercise.

While ICT is handy to catch the challenge, on the other hand, digital skills drop as the age increase: in the 65–74 ageing range, the Eu28 counts on 25% of population able to use basic digital technology, and 34% able to participate in social networks (Facebook, Twitter) (Fig. 4).

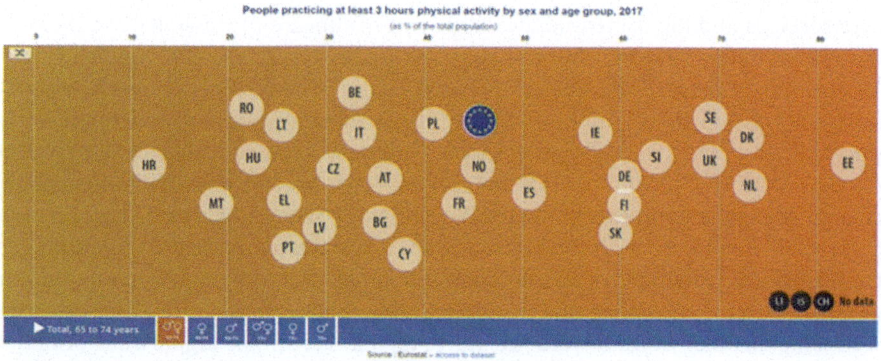

Fig. 2 Eurostat data about physical activity among elderly, 2017

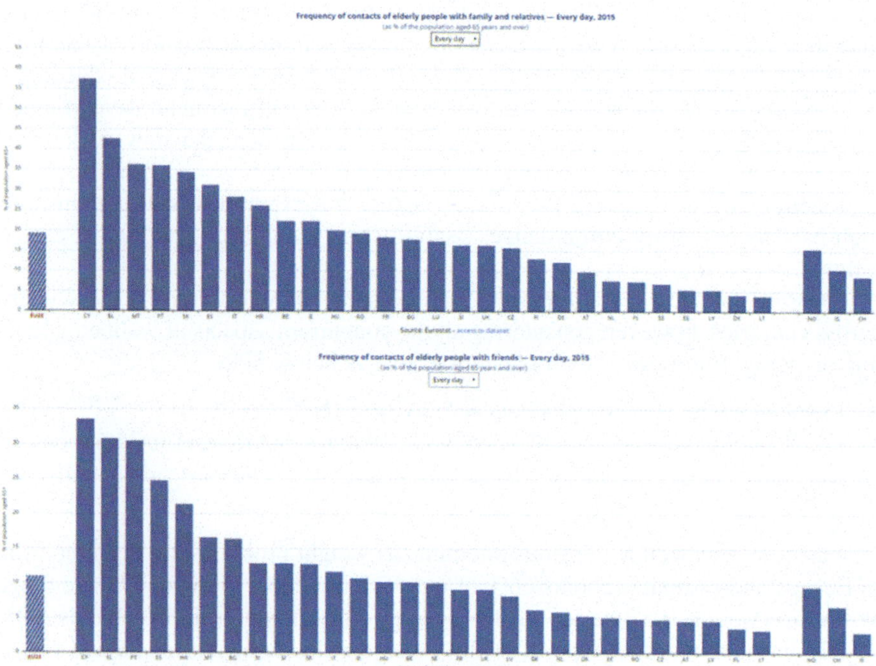

Fig. 3 Eurostat data about social life among elderly, 2015

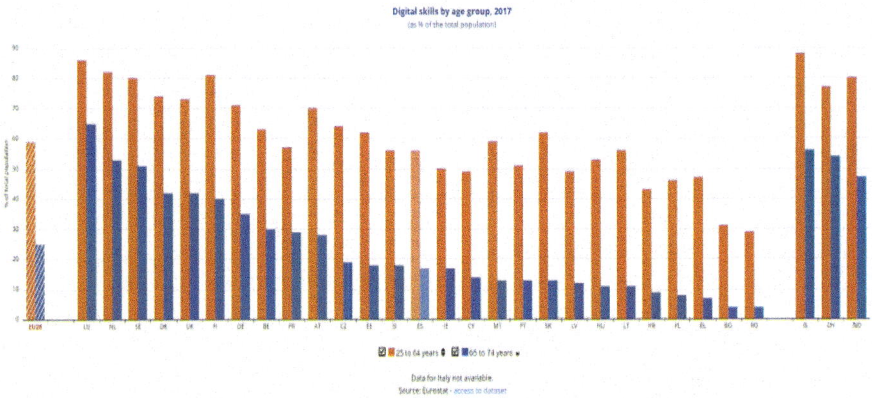

Fig. 4 Digital skills by age in Europe, 2017

2 Status, Needs and Challenges for the Design and Implementation of Effective Active Healthy Ageing Solutions

As defined by WHO, "Active and Healthy Ageing (AHA) is the process of optimizing opportunities for health, participation and security in order to enhance quality of life as people age. It applies to both individuals and population groups. 'Health' refers to physical, mental and social wellbeing. 'Active' refers to continuing participation in social, economic, cultural, spiritual and civic affairs, not just the simple ability to be physically active or to participate in the labour".

For this joint individual and community vision, AHA is a complex topic and very variable according to the different perspectives and "ambitions" of single end-users and opportunities/services offered by the social environment.

It is individually complex because AHA it is multifactorial: by including the concepts of health and wellbeing, it comprehends all the dimensions of people: physiological, physical, functional, nutritional, cognitive, psychological and social (at familiar and friends circle).

For this reason, to support the main goal of AHA to have a meaningful quality of life in the very personal consideration, i.e. singularly considered and based on the lifestyle, activities, inclusion and participation into his/her own social environment and relationships, it means that all the solutions/services should be greatly modular to support personalized interventions.

The societal challenge of identifying and providing innovative solutions to improve the health and quality of life of on older people is crucial also at higher level, i.e. in supporting the long-term sustainability and efficiency of health and social care systems.

Ageing is a natural process, during which some weakening of functions is shown but some and specific countermeasures could be adopted. Two main priorities are identifiable: stay in a stable healthy functional state or improve the personal condition according to specific therapeutic pathways. This health strategies for over 65 population were taken and explored also within the frame of the NESTORE project.

According to these, two main relevant product-service systems: a) technologies and related services for the early diagnosis and detection of health issues in the corresponding domain (physical, physiological, psychological, cognitive and social), b) solutions for the monitoring and follow-up chronic conditions that however allow a good and fully independent living.

The first set of solutions are related to safety and vital monitoring so that we can call prevention and emergency services. Specific categories of systems can be the personal alarm devices; falls detection devices; activity monitoring devices; and wearable technology [4–6].

The second category of systems and related services includes several telemonitoring solutions, the internet of things (IoT) technology together with mobile Apps have greatly populated in these last years.

In the past several years, advancements have been made in technology specifically developed for monitoring the movement and activity of older adults in their homes. Today, the current state of technologies includes wearable technology, unobtrusive monitoring like environmental sensing and several devices dedicated to specific measurements of dedicated parameters, like arterial blood pressure, pulse oximetry, blood sugar, weight and body composition through bio-impedance technique, that are the most common and used systems [4–7].

New advances in health devices added solutions for measuring and practising visual acuity, gamified memory apps, health logging, medicine reminders and new solutions implementing Artificial Intelligence (AI) to provide voice enabled solutions, that were just at the embryonal stage at the beginning of the PM-15 Horizon 2020 call (where the NESTORE project operates in) in 2017 and now they are existing AI and consumer tech solutions such as Alexa and Google home.

Indeed, these tangible personal assistants could become a promising tool to aid the elderly in their day-to-day lives.

Technology is continuously changing and advancing, its validity, reliability, and cost-effectiveness is rapidly improving also thanks and in light of the new regulatory framework introduced by the recent Medical Device Regulation 745/2017. There are many issues of standardization, design and ethical considerations that need to be addressed before advances can be made with these technologies so that these patients can be remotely monitored, supported, and coached towards a better quality of life or care services [7].

New applications of technology may be of great benefit to help the older adult live safely in their home and city environment, but the native analogue generation the European and worldwide elderly belong to has demonstrated several troubles in training and using these technologies.

The development and design of these system is too often technologically driven more than user driven so impacting their acceptability. The adoption of multidisciplinary approaches to development of solutions would be ideal to combine the technology with users' perspective including also the social and clinical application and evaluation. A more intuitive and natural interface design is still a strong demand for a full adoption and consequently, exploitation. Literature highlights that the reason for non-acceptance of health technologies is complex. Authors have cited confidence, the stigmatizing aesthetics of products, meaningfulness of technology in the broader context of the persons' life, ease of use and integration into everyday routines as important factors.

But usability and acceptance of technology is only a first step of a long pathway: motivation and engagement. For achieving healthy aging success is needed a strong and continuous commitment by all user but specifically the target population that is elderly people and a good personalization capability in light of the consideration that not all seniors have the same motivations and behaviours. Therefore, motivation and engagement are representing both the strategies and the challenges to be pursed. On this aspect recent studies focused on behavioural models and methods and strategies to implement effective interventions in medicine both for prevention and for treatment practice depends on successful behaviour change interventions. This requires an appropriate method for characterising interventions and linking them to an analysis of the targeted behaviour able to exploit users' needs, thoughts, and preferences.

The most recent theories refer to the involvement of these three essential conditions: capability, opportunity, and motivation (from what the term the 'COM-B system' is derived). This forms the hub of a 'behaviour change wheel' (BCW) around which are positioned the nine intervention functions aimed at addressing deficits in one or more of these conditions; around this are placed seven categories of policy that could enable those interventions to occur [8]. Another approach is based on the mechanisms of health behaviour change in persons with chronic illness or disability called the Health Action Process Approach (HAPA) [9]. Risk perception, outcome expectancies, and task self-efficacy are seen as predisposing factors in the goal-setting (motivational) phase, whereas planning, action control, and maintenance/recovery self-efficacy are regarded as being influential in the subsequent goal-pursuit (volitional) phase. It is important to set a limited number of manageable goals, to establish a more trusting relationship by listening (in this sense voice assistants are an interesting tool), and to encourage use of technology overcoming the traditional attitude to be resistant to technology as in the past.

For all these reasons, a more comprehensive and integrated approach is needed in the design phase.

3 A Polytechnic Approach to Design of Intuitive and Integrated AHA Services: The NESTORE Case Study

A strong need and an urgent demand to enhance the use and uptake of these technologies for AHA services is still present in all European countries. This requires a more integrated and multidisciplinary vision in design and implementing technology and its related service. A possible solution is the early adoption of co-design methods to enhance acceptance and usability. This is what we implemented in the frame of the NESTORE project.

NESTORE project was conceived to overcome the limitations of current solutions and will be used as an example of successful multidisciplinary approach. NESTORE addresses healthy older people and covers five key dimensions of wellbeing with an integrated approach, leveraging on the participatory design of the solution.

NESTORE that, as the mythological Nestor, can give advice to older people so that they can maintain their wellbeing and their independence at home, based on experience and on understanding the current situation. The experience of the modern NESTORE is based on well-grounded psychological and behavioral theories in conjunction with relevant knowhow on the ageing process, while the current situation is understood on the basis of a comprehensive sensors' system able to monitor the different key parameters. An intelligent system, based on a cloud and leveraging Decision Support logics, delivers "advise and coaching", which are offered via the companion, embodied in a smart phone or an intelligent tangible object, according to the user's preferences and interests. Only in this perspective Healthy ageing can really become the optimisation of "opportunities for good health, so that older people can take an active part in society and enjoy an independent and high quality of life".[1]

In light of these considerations—and remembering that ageing is a multidimensional and multidirectional process involving the social, economic, physical, psychological and cognitive spheres and that all these characteristics of a person and its context are strongly interconnected-, this book describes the multidisciplinary approach needed to tackle an emerging and urgent societal challenge: ageing better. In the era of mHealth and mobile technology, of virtual assistants and social design, this book describes the participation of the polytechnic know-how (specifically Design and Engineering) added with social sciences and medicine, to the design of a novel system for coaching towards healthy behaviors to achieve a better quality of life. The proposed comprehensive overview is divided into five sections for a better reading.

Section 1 ("Designing mHealth solutions for better ageing: clinical and methodological perspective") is dedicated to highlight the challenges in (co)designing products and digital systems for the elderly, both from the design perspective and the related methodologies, but also from the "clinical" point of view (where physical, physiological, nutritional, cognitive and social factors need to be tackled for a comprehensive approach of the human).

Starting from these needs and requirements, Sect. 2: ("Technology applied to solutions for Healthy ageing") makes a survey of the most recent technologies (ICT and specifically mHealth digital services, wearables and smart objects, IoT, WoT, AI and DSS, serious gaming, data privacy and protection, cloud computing, and big data analysis). As actual example, we describe the solutions designed and adopted in the NESTORE project, a EU funded initiative related to the design and implementation

[1] EuroHealthNet, https://www.healthyageing.eu/.

of digital solutions for healthy aging. An insight on the interoperability issues and key challenge for the implementation of services and future standards is included.

So that, Sect. 3 ("Lifestyle improvement and virtual coaching and ICT services in the human domains through friendly technology") presents the translation of the scientific findings and know-how into strategies and algorithms towards a personalized recommendation system for healthy behaviors. These coaching activity is delivered through novel technologies: conversational agents and chat-bot, virtual assistants and interactive technologies for emotion recognition and sustaining user engagement. These examples represent the current state-of-art.

But how to measure the impact of such systems? Sect. 4 ("Innovation impact measured in subjective (usability and experience), social (community level) and business (companies and institutions) opportunities") is dedicated to this aspect presenting a model of social ROI and impact assessment of services dedicated to healthy ageing. Management Engineering and Design collaborated in the definition of a new model integrating Usability and Technology Acceptance to be applied in this novel era of digital services for elderly. This opens the door to the exploitation of such systems into the Silver Economy domain. Strategies and theoretical business models are here presented.

But exploitation should proprietarily consider the new vision and regulatory frame dedicated to Privacy and Data Protection. These aspects are treated in Sect. 5 ("Aspects of Ethics and Data Management in healthy ageing digital services") providing not only a general statement of the regulation recently entered into force but, above all, a vision of "privacy by design" and design tools to match these requirements not simply from a legal point of view but in a subject-centred approach. This is the real Ethical and Responsible Research and Innovation.

The last section, "Sect. 6: From research to action: what's next?", introduces the common frame built with other project at European level to share experiences and good practices so to be proactive towards a better policy making in this field and to draw new trajectories for a brighter future in this research line. EU representatives from the EU DG Communications Networks, Contents and Technology are giving the vision of this framework and the expected evolution of the policies at international level.

References

1. Green Paper on Ageing. Fostering solidarity and responsibility between generations. EU Commission, January 27, 2021.
2. Schwarzer, R. (1992). Self-efficacy in the adoption and maintenance of health behaviors: Theoretical approaches and a new model. In R. Schwarzer (Ed.), *Self-efficacy: Thought control of action* (pp. 2176–2242). Washington, DC: Hemisphere.
3. Sniehotta, F. F., Schwarzer, R., Scholz, U., & Schüz, B. (2005). Action planning and coping planning for long-term lifestyle change: Theory and assessment. *European Journal of Social Psychology, 35,* 565–576.

4. Wagner, F., Basran, J., & Bello-Haas, V. D. (2012). A review of monitoring technology for use with older adults. *Journal of Geriatric Physical Therapy, 35*(1), 28–34. https://doi.org/10.1519/JPT.0b013e318224aa23.
5. Pigini, L., Bovi, G., Panzarino, C., Gower, V., Ferratini, M., Andreoni, G., et al. (2017). Pilot test of a new personal health system integrating environmental and wearable sensors for telemonitoring and care of elderly people at home (SMARTA Project). *Gerontology, 63*(3), 281–286. 0304-324X. Karger Publishers.
6. Rivolta, M. W., Perego, P., Andreoni, G., Ferrarin, M., Baroni, G., Galzio, C., et al. (2016). A new personalized health system: The SMARTA project. In P. Perego, G. Andreoni, & G. Rizzo (Eds.), *Wireless mobile communication and healthcare. MobiHealth 2016*. Lecture Notes of the Institute for Computer Sciences, Social Informatics and Telecommunications Engineering (Vol. 192, pp. 375–380). Cham: Springer. https://doi.org/10.1007/978-3-319-58877-3_13. Print ISBN 978-3-319-58876-6. Online ISBN 978-3-319-58877-3.
7. Karunanithi, M. (2007). Monitoring technology for the elderly patient. *Expert Review of Medical Devices, 4*(2), 267–277. https://doi.org/10.1586/17434440.4.2.267 PMID: 17359231.
8. Michie, S., van Stralen, M. M., & West, R. (2011). The behaviour change wheel: A new method for characterising and designing behaviour change interventions. *Implementation Sci, 6*, 42. https://doi.org/10.1186/1748-5908-6-42.
9. Schwarzer, R., Lippke, S., & Luszczynska, A. (2011). Mechanisms of health behavior change in persons with chronic illness or disability: The health action process approach (HAPA). *Rehabilitation Psychology, 56*(3), 161–170. https://doi.org/10.1037/a0024509.

Designing mHealth Solutions for Better Ageing: Clinical and Methodological Perspective

The Multi-domain Coaching Approach to Counteract Ageing Decline

A. Mastropietro, C. Röecke, S. Porcelli, J. M. Del Bas, Sabrina Guye, Lucia Tarro, G. Manferdelli, and G. Rizzo

Abstract Based on the international guidelines on healthy lifestyles for older adults in different well-being domains, this chapter describes the general approach of personalized coaching proposed in NESTORE by the domain experts involved in the project. The coaching domains that are the basis of the NESTORE virtual coach include physical activity, nutrition, cognition and social behaviour. Each domain, although maintaining its peculiar characteristics and specific aspects, present a common personalization pathway, based on the actual status of the users. The coaching design approach used in NESTORE includes the identification of domain-specific targets and pathways to deal with the critical aspects of ageing. The personalization of the coaching plans is based on initialization/assessment variables that are gathered by the NESTORE system.

A. Mastropietro (✉) · S. Porcelli · G. Manferdelli · G. Rizzo
Institute of Biomedical Technologies, National Research Council, Via Fratelli Cervi 93, 20090 Segrate, Milan, Italy
e-mail: alfonso.mastropietro@itb.cnr.it

C. Röecke · S. Guye
University Research Priority Program "Dynamics of Healthy Aging", University of Zurich, Zurich, Switzerland

J. M. Del Bas · L. Tarro
Eurecat, Centre Tecnològic de Catalunya, Unitat de Nutrició i Salut, Reus, Spain

L. Tarro
Universitat Rovira i Virgili, Facultat de Medicina i Ciències de la Salut, Functional Nutrition, Oxidation, and Cardiovascular Diseases Group (NFOC-Salut), Reus, Spain

G. Manferdelli
Institute of Sport Sciences, University of Lausanne, Lausanne, Switzerland

G. Andreoni and C. Mambretti (eds.), *Digital Health Technology for Better Aging*, Research for Development, https://doi.org/10.1007/978-3-030-72663-8_2

1 Introduction

Ageing is a multi-dimensional and multi-factorial process since it involves strongly interconnected spheres (social, economic, physical, psychological, cognitive) that characterize and define the person. Crucial factors that affect wellbeing are: physiological status and physical activity behaviour, nutrition, cognitive capabilities, mental wellbeing, and social interaction.

Ageing is often characterized by motor function impairments, associated with generalized loss of skeletal muscle mass and strength (i.e., sarcopenia), that may have a detrimental impact on the ability to perform daily-life activities and may result in reduced independence and self-confidence. Physical activity is the most effective intervention to counteract skeletal muscle impairment and aerobic and anaerobic physical activities should be combined to retain or improve their cardiovascular fitness, muscle strength and overall balance.

Furthermore, ageing involves a decay of the metabolic flexibility often resulting in altered absorption of nutrients associated with decreased capacity in detoxifying by-products. The whole metabolism is more sensitive to unbalanced diets and suboptimal nutrition. Therefore, a balanced diet together with optimal dietary patterns is key to maintain the whole body homeostasis and to overcome the naturally occurring physiological decline of the person.

Ageing is also related to cognitive decline, one of the most worrying age-related changes. In particular, fluid abilities show an average decline throughout adulthood, with a faster decline late in life. Cognitive training interventions are known to be successful in improving the trained abilities.

Other important aspects are the preservation of mental wellbeing and the social capital provided by older people. The quality of the social contacts and the availability of emotionally meaningful social relations is an important factor to consider for better wellbeing. There is evidence that voluntary work, as well as the educational and social activity group interventions, can improve mental health and prevent social isolation and loneliness among older people.

Considering the complexity of the ageing process, a multi-domain approach (meaning at least 2 domains) was adopted in most of the virtual coaches proposed so far, however, only a few of them had a holistic approach [1].

The NESTORE Virtual Coach was developed with a multi-domain holistic approach and its guidelines, which were the basic principles for the development of the system, were defined according to the recent scientific literature.

Based on the experts' recommendations, each target domain (Physical Activity, Nutrition, Cognitive and Mental Status and Social Behaviour) was implemented in different intervention areas providing a complete set of coaching guidelines for counteracting the physiological decline occurring with ageing.

For each domain, the recommendations are described as well as the effects/benefits of correct adherence to the guidelines. Moreover, the behaviours and the related coaching strategies, which should be followed to reach specific targets, are defined taking into account the variables composing the NESTORE Model of Healthy

Ageing [2]. For each intervention area, different pathways are introduced to either retain/maintain or improve the specific behaviours.

Concerning the Physical Activity domain, the NESTORE coaching plans are focused on (1) *Aerobic/Endurance*, (2) *Strength/Resistance*, (3) *Flexibility* and (4) *Balance* training to retain or improve physical user's performance in all these areas.

Regarding the Nutrition domain, the NESTORE coaching plans are focused on: (1) *Body Weight management*, with a weight maintenance diet when the user status is satisfying or a dietary intervention to achieve optimal body weight; (2) *Body Composition management* to retain or improve body composition; (3) *Healthy Diet*, aimed at monitoring the user habits and suggesting dietary habits modification if needed.

The NESTORE coaching plans related to Cognitive Status are focused on (1) *Executive Functioning and Working Memory* through traditional cognitive training to retain or improve the users' abilities; (2) Overall *Cognitive Status* using video games and productive intellectual engagement interventions to retain/improve the overall cognitive skills.

Finally, the NESTORE coaching plans involving Social Behaviour are focused on (1) *Social Skills* through ICT solutions for Social Networking; (2) *Social Contact* through Befriending to retain/improve opportunities for socialization; (3) *Social Support* employing a plethora of coaching activities (e.g. home visits, animal-assisted therapy, etc.); (4) *Social Cognition* using various therapeutic approaches (e.g. reminiscence therapy, cognitive behavioural therapy). Each of these interventions is aimed at retaining/improving specific personal skills/abilities.

The guidelines included in the chapter are the basis to develop the NESTORE coaching plans. In particular, the training activities and recommendations were personalized, when necessary, taking into account the user's status and behaviour, by the definition of specific rules for the initialization and adaptation of the coaching system and personalized activities; moreover, the definition and the technological implementation of the specific coaching activities, as suggested and provided by the NESTORE virtual coach, will be deeply defined and implemented, also taking into account user preferences and capacities.

2 General Framework for the Design of the NESTORE Coaching Plans

The NESTORE coaching plans were designed and developed based on a general framework that was then adopted in each coaching domain. The approach is composed of two different pathways based on different target behaviours that depend on the initial characteristics of the users. In particular, NESTORE can propose to the users a ***specific target*** depending on whether the user must retain or improve his/her abilities/skills. Each pathway is associated with specific coaching plans that

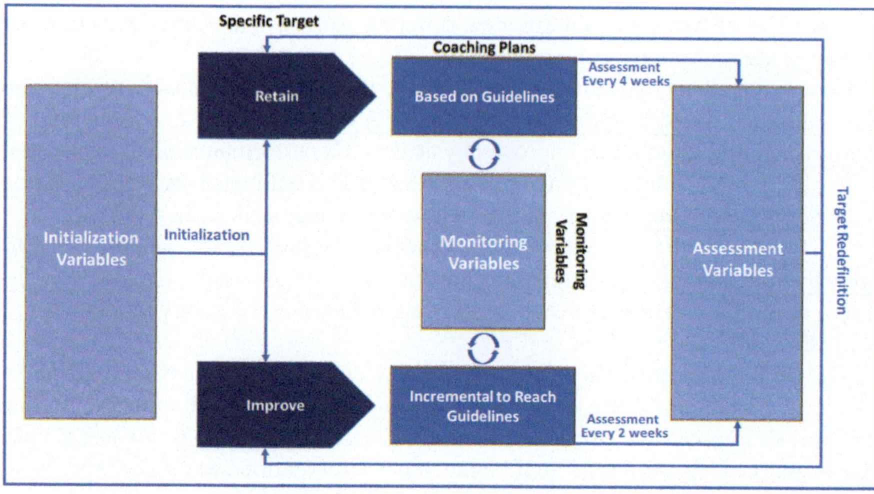

Fig. 1 Schematic representation of the approach used in NESTORE to design the coaching plans in different domains

meet the reference guidelines, in the case of "retain", or are designed with an incremental approach to progressively meet the guidelines prescription during the training duration, in the case of "improve".

The coaching plans are personalized based on the characteristics of the users through ***initialization variables*** that are collected before the intervention start and are used to guide the users towards the best pathway. During the intervention period, ***monitoring variables*** can be collected using the NESTORE monitoring system to provide feedback to the users for improving motivation and engagement and to further adapt the coaching activity.

After a period of 2 or 4 weeks, the user's performances are re-evaluated and the ***assessment variables***, which are usually the same as the monitoring variables, are collected. The specific target can be therefore modified according to the evolution of users' performances.

Figure 1 shows a representative scheme containing all the components of the proposed approach. In the next paragraphs, the peculiar features of each coaching domain are described and the specific information to personalize the coaching plans, such as target and variables, are defined.

3 Physical Activity

There is strong evidence that regular physical activity produces considerable and extensive health benefits in both adults aged 18–64 and in older adults aged 65 and above [3]. In some cases, the evidence of health benefits is strongest in older adults because the outcomes related to inactivity are more common in this group of persons [4].

The scientific evidence for adults aged >65 years demonstrates that, compared to less active individuals, persons who are more active have:

- lower mortality-rates, coronary heart disease, hypertension, stroke, type 2 diabetes, colon cancer and breast cancer;
- a better cardiorespiratory and muscular fitness;
- healthier body mass and composition;
- more favorable biomarker profile for the prevention of cardiovascular disease, type 2 diabetes and the enhancement of bone health;
- lower rate of cognitive decline;
- reduced susceptibility to falls;
- improved aspects of mental well-being such as self-esteem and mood.

Therefore, participation in a regular exercise training program is a cost-effective intervention with proven benefits to improve health, postpone physical decline, and prevent/treat chronic diseases in older adults [5]. Since deconditioning, low muscle tone, and/or low functional capacity contribute to poor health outcomes and low quality of life, the American College of Sports Medicine's (ACSM) recommends that older adults engage in a combination of aerobic/endurance, strength/resistance, flexibility, and balance training to promote and maintain health [6, 7].

The recommended amount of physical activity is usually designed in a systematic and individualized manner in terms of the Frequency, Intensity, Time, Type, Volume, and Progression, known as the FITT-VP principle (Table 1).

To improve a person's aerobic capacity, it is important to prescribe exercises that predominantly involve the cardio-respiratory system and can be performed at an appropriate intensity to achieve a training effect [8]. For example, walking on a treadmill or outdoors, running or cycling allow to adequately personalize the effort by easily adapting the exercise intensity.

Regarding strength training, multi-joint and single-joint exercises are recommended for all fitness levels. Training opposing muscle groups (e.g., abdominals and lumbar extensors, quadriceps and hamstrings) is also important to prevent muscular imbalances [9].

Different types of stretching techniques are beneficial when applied correctly and at the right time during an exercise session. For this purpose, static and dynamic stretching are proposed in NESTORE.

Finally, exercises that improve perceptual-motor skills should be included in the balance component of the exercise prescription. Examples include walking with different gait patterns or variable walking speeds, negotiating obstacle courses, performing exercises on compliant or moving surfaces or without vision [10].

The NESTORE coach of physical activity is based on 4 Targets, one for each subdomain, as listed in Table 2. Each goal must be achieved by specific exercises to improve/retain aerobic/endurance, strength/resistance, flexibility and balance performance of the users. The pathways of the cardio-respiratory and the strength-power target are personalized according to the assessment variables (modified 6-min

Table 1 ACSM's physical activity recommendations to individualized training program following the FITT-VP principle [5–7]

FITT-VP principle	ACSM's Recommendations
Frequency	≥5 days per week (d/wk) for moderate-intensity aerobic exercise (or ≥3 d/wk for vigorous-intensity aerobic exercise, or 3 to 5 d/wk for a combination of moderate- and vigorous-intensity exercise) supplemented by resistance exercise ≥2 d/wk and flexibility exercise ≥2 d/wk. Balance (neuromotor) training is also recommended 2 to 3 d/wk
Intensity	On a scale of 0–10 for the level of physical exertion, 5–6 for moderate-intensity aerobic exercise, 7–8 for vigorous-intensity aerobic exercise, and 6–7 for resistance exercise
Time	A minimum of 30 min or up to 60 min per day (m/d) for moderate-intensity aerobic exercise or at least 20–30 m/d for vigorous-intensity aerobic exercise. As for resistance exercise, the amount of time depends on the number of repetitions and type of exercise, as well as the recovery time needed by each person. The time of flexibility and balance exercises should be at least 20 m/d
Type	Emphasis should be placed on aerobic activities that do not impose excessive orthopedic stress, such as walking. Resistance training may supplement as an adjuvant to aerobic training and should consist of 8–10 different exercises targeting the major muscle groups. Flexibility exercises should involve both limbs and trunk muscles and request to hold the position from 30 to 60 s. Balance training should involve progressively difficult postures that gradually reduce the base of support
Volume	It should correspond to a total of 150 min per week (m/wk) of moderate-intensity exercise or 75 m/wk of combined moderate- and vigorous-intensity exercise
Progression	The components of a complete exercise prescription including recommendations about the four subdomains may be increased, as tolerated, to achieve the recommended volume. Progression may be individualized based on tolerance and preference in a conservative manner

Table 2 Summary of relevant characteristics of physical activity coaching

Target	Intervention type	Assessment variables	Monitoring variables
Retain/Improve cardio-respiratory fitness	Aerobic/Endurance exercises	Modified 6-min walking test	Total Quality of Recovery scale, TQR Borg scale, RPE
Retain/Improve strength-power	Strength/Resistance exercises	Modified 30 s. Chair rise test	Borg scale, RPE
Retain/Improve flexibility	Flexibility exercises	Not available in NESTORE	Not available in NESTORE
Retain/Improve balance	Balance exercises	Not available in NESTORE	Not available in NESTORE

walking test, mod6MWT and modified 30-s chair rise test, mod30sCRT) whereas monitoring variables are collected to evaluate the recovery (Total Quality of Recovery Scale, TQR) and fatigue of the users (Borg Scale, RPE).

4 Nutrition

Ageing is associated with some changes in body weight and body composition that can affect wellbeing such as loss of muscle mass [11]. Moreover, aging is associated with malnutrition [12] and paradoxically, with overweight and obesity status [13, 14], both linked to poor quality of life, poor wellbeing and an increased mortality risk [15, 16].

Body weight management, body composition (body fat mass and muscle mass) and diet should be the principal aspects to take into account in older adults' wellbeing.

The recommendations for **body weight management** are mainly based on the use of a **combination of nutrient and calorie-dense foods and exercise** to gradually increase or decrease their BMI, ideally using resistance training to increase muscle mass to prevent sarcopenia [17]. Another important point is that **body composition** has facilities to increase fat mass and decrease muscle. Regarding **body fat mass,** according to evidence, a caloric restriction of approximately 500–800 kcal less, providing also an adequate protein intake (estimated in 1 g/kg body weight/day) plus exercise, is related to a weight loss of about 10% of Body Weight, which is accompanied by a reduction of fat mass and lean mass [18]. Regarding **body muscle mass**, it is estimated that muscle mass decreases by 1–2% annually [19] which can decline autonomy and develop sarcopenia, and it is associated with frailty status and increasing considerably the risk of falls and fractures in older people.

Moreover, there are **nutritional requirements** for older adults. Following the conclusions of the Scientific Opinion on Dietary References Values (DRV) for the energy of the EFSA Panel on Dietetics Products, Nutrition and Allergies [20], the average energy needs for elderly people are listed in Table 3.

Macronutrients: According to the different sources macronutrients recommendations in older adults do not vary considerably in their distribution in comparison to the general population:

Table 3 Summary of average requirement (AR) for energy for older adults. REE, resting energy expenditure; PAL, physical activity level

Age (Years)		REE (Kcal/day)	AR at PAL = 1.4	AR at PAL = 1.6	AR at PAL = 1.8	AR at PAL = 2.0
Men	60–69	1,433	2,006	2,293	2,603	2,890
	70–79	1,433	1,982	2,269	2,555	2,842
Women	60–69	1,170	1,624	1,863	2,102	2,317
	70–79	1,146	1,624	1,839	2,078	2,300

(a) 50–60% of the total energy intake as **carbohydrates**: a **minimum of 130 g/day** as complex carbohydrates and limiting simple sugars [21] and fiber: 25–40 day/fibre [22–24].
(b) 25–35% of the total energy intake as **fat**: the monounsaturated fats and the ω-3 polyunsaturated fats are considered key nutrients in the elderly where saturated fats should **not represent >10% of the total energy intake and cholesterol <200 mg/day** [25].
(c) 15–20% of the total energy intake as **protein**: no consensus about protein intake but the population reference intake proposed (PRI) is **among 0.83 g/kg/day to 1.2 g/kg/day** for maintenance of the muscle mass [26, 27].

Micronutrients: Older adults are characterized by a complex and multi-causal decline of body metabolism and systemic function. Micronutrients (vitamins and minerals) are necessary to prevent or delay the onset of age-related diseases. Each micronutrient has a different and important role in the health of people, i.e. iron which its deficits develop anemia [28].

The following Table 4 summarizes the specific requirements of micronutrient depending on sources:

The NESTORE coach of nutrition domain is based on 4 pathways focusing to tackle the most prevalent health problems of elderly people presented before: (1) loss of muscle mass, (2) overweight and obesity; (3) underweight, or (4) not follow a healthy diet, nutritional recommendations were designed (Table 5).

For each pathway, there are recommendations for minimum and maximum consumption per food group. Table 6 summarizes the food group recommendations by pathways.

Table 4 Summary of vitamins and minerals requirements for older adults

Vitamins	B6 (mg/d)		B9 (μg/d)		B12 (μg/d)		C (mg/d)		A (μg/d)		E (mg/d)		D (μg/d)	
	♂	♀	♂	♀	♂	♀	♂	♀	♂	♀	♂	♀	♂	♀
EFSA	**1.7**	**1.6**	330	330	4	4	**110**	**95**	**750**	**650**	**13**	**11**	*15*	*15*
FESNAD	*	*	300	300	2	2	70	70	700	600	15	15	7.5	7.5
NNC	**1.8**	**1.5**	**300**	**300**	**2.8**	**2.8**	**75**	**75**	**900**	**700**	**10**	**8**	**20**	**20**
SINU	**1.7**	**1.5**	**400**	**400**	**2.4**	**2.4**	**105**	**85**	**700**	**600**	13	12	**15**	**15**
Food and Nutrition Board (IOM)	**1.7**	**1.5**	**400**	**400**	**2.4**	**2.4**	**90**	**75**	**900**	**700**	**15**	**15**	**15**	**15**

Minerals	Sodium (g)	Iron (mg/d)		Calcium (mg/d)		Zinc (mg/d)		Selenium (μg/d)		Magnesium (mg/d)	
	♂/♀	♂	♀	♂	♀	♂	♀	♂	♀	♂	♀
EFSA	*	**11**	**11**	**950**	**950**	**9.4–16.3**	**7.5–12.7**	*70*	*70*	*350*	*300*
FESNAD	1.3	10	10	1000	1000	10	7	55	55	350	320
NNC	*	**9**	**9**	**1200**	**1200**	**9**	**7**	**60**	**50**	**350**	**280**
SINU	1.1	**10**	**10**	**1000**	**1200**	**11**	**8**	**55**	**55**	**240**	**240**
Food and Nutrition Board (IOM)	1.3	**8**	**8**	**1000**	**1200**	**11**	**8**	**55**	**55**	**420**	**320**

*No Dietary Reference Intake (DRI) has still been defined. Population Reference Intake (PRI) is represented in bold type. Adequate intake (AI) values are expressed in *italic*. Dietary Reference Intake values are represented underlined. EFSA, European food safety authority (EFSA, 2017); FESNAD, Federación española de sociedades de nutrición, alimentación y dietética (FESNAD, 2010); NNC, Netherlands nutrition centre (NNC, 2014); SINU, Societá Italiana di Nutrizione Umana (SINU, 2012); IOM, Institute of Medicine US (IOM, 2011)

Table 5 NESTORE targets for nutrition domain

Pathways	Recommendations
Increase muscle mass	**Energy**: Caloric needs according to body weight maintenance **Protein**: 1–1.2 g/Kg body weight/day protein **Food patterns**: Increase meal frequency with a combination of protein and calorie-dense foods
Decrease body fat mass	**Energy**: Reduction in 500–750 kcal (from TEE) **Protein**: 1–1.2 g/Kg weight/day protein **Food patterns**: Low-caloric density foods, reduction of high-sugar and high-fat rich foods, an increase of fibre intake
Gain body weight	**Energy**: Increase of 500 to 750 kcal/day (to TEE) **Protein**: 1.2–1.6 g/kg/day weight/day protein **Food patterns**: Increase meal frequency with a combination of protein and calorie-dense foods
Achieve a healthy diet	**Energy**: Caloric needs according to body weight maintenance **Food patterns**: healthy food recommendations

Table 6 Summary of relevant characteristics of the nutrition domain by pathways

Target	Increase muscle mass		Achieve a healthy diet		Gain body weight		Decrease body fat mass	
Food group	Min	Max	Min	Max	Min	Max	Min	Max
Cold cuts and pates	–	2/w	–	1/w	–	2/w	–	1/w
Dairy products	3/d	5/d	3/d	4/d	3/d	5/d	2/d	4/d
Eggs	3/w	–	2/w	4/w	2/w	4/w	2/w	4/w
Fish and seafood	3/w	5/w	2/w	4/w	2/w	4/w	2/w	4/w
Fruits			3	–			3	–
Grains and potatoes			3 p/d	6 ps/d	5 p/d	7 ps/d	3 p/d	5 ps/d
Legumes	2/w	5/w	2 p/w	5 p/w	2 p/w	5 p/w	2 p/w	5 p/w
Nuts	3 ps/w	1 p/d	1 p/w	1 p/d	3 ps/w	1 p/d	1 p/w	1 p/d
Oil			2 s/d	3 s/d	2–3 s/d	3–4 s/d	1 s/d	2–3 s/d
Read meat	1/w	2/w	0/w	1/w	1/w	2/w	0/w	1/w
Salt			–	5 g/d	–	5 g/d	–	5 g/d
Salty snacks			–	1 w	–	1 w	–	1 w
Sweets pastries and cookies			–	1 w			–	1 w
Vegetables			2	–			2	–
White meat	3/w	5/w	2	4	2	5	2	4

w: week; d: day; p: portion; s: spoon; g: grams

5 Cognitive Status and Social Behaviour

The maintenance of cognitive functioning is of key importance to most individuals [29]. It is thus not surprising to witness a strong focus on cognitive training interventions in the literature [30]. Findings indicate that both structured and unstructured lifestyle-based interventions can be successful to improve performance in the trained areas, with small effects also in terms of transfer to other (non-trained) areas of cognitive functioning [31]. General recommendations tend to encompass mentally stimulating activities that go beyond the cognitive domain and encompass physical activity, social engagement and nutrition as well [32, 33] (see Tables 7 and 8).

Most interventions in the social domain focus on improvements of social contact quantity and quality as they strongly aim to reduce loneliness (i.e., improve social integration and social contacts). The rate of success of these interventions in reducing loneliness is mixed, however [34, 35].

In NESTORE we include social coaching pathways nonetheless, given the importance of social relations for well-being and health [36, 37], and we based the coaching pathways on meta-analytic evidence on various intervention types and successes [38]: (a) improving social skills, (b) increasing opportunities for social contact, (c) enhancing social support, and (d) addressing maladaptive social cognition. All of the four yielded significant effects for loneliness reductions, with the largest effects found for those approaches that addressed a change in maladaptive social cognition. However, aiming to improve social cognition and enhancing social support primarily focus on clinical subgroups and settings, and are least suited within the NESTORE context. Therefore, the social coaching pathways in NESTORE focus primarily on increasing individuals' opportunities for social contacts and improving social skills by way of encouraging unstructured leisure activities in an explicitly social setting that follow the very general recommendations to promote meaningful social engagement [39] (see Tables 9 and 10).

Table 7 General recommendations for cognitive health

Domain	Recommendation
Brain stimulation	Challenge the way you think, learn new skills
Combination of mental and physical	Engage in activities that incorporate mental and physical exercise
Social engagement with greater purpose	Seek out social engagement and purpose (e.g., volunteering, mentoring) in mentally-stimulating activities
Diet	Eat a Mediterranean diet
Sleep	Sleep right (i.e., in a restorative way)

Table 8 Summary of relevant characteristics of cognitive coaching

Target	Intervention type	Assessment variables during training	Monitoring variables
Retain/Improve executive functioning: Training of executive functioning Training of and transfer to fluid intelligence and everyday performance	Traditional structured cognitive training	Numerical working memory, digit Span backwards, self-reported everyday memory failures	For all training targets: Trail making test A & B N-back Digit span backwards Numerical updating Berlin intelligence structure test Digit symbol substitution test Cognitive failure questionnaire In addition: activity enjoyment and perceived difficulty
Retain/Improve overall cognitive status: Training of and transfer to multiple cognitive functioning domains and everyday performance	Multidomain cognitive training/serious game (video game) training	Performance accuracy in three domains: spatial ability, inhibition, sensorimotor performance	
Retain/Improve overall cognitive status: Training of and transfer to fluid intelligence and everyday performance	Productive intellectual engagement	Engagement in Selected Everyday Activities	

Table 9 Examples of general recommendations to promote meaningful social engagement

1. Focus on social relations you enjoy the most
2. If you feel lonely, try to make new connections by seeking opportunities to engage with others
3. Try to keep a circle of friends, family, or neighbors with whom you can exchange ideas, thoughts, concerns and practical matters and who can also help or encourage you
4. Try to have at least one trustworthy and reliable confidant
5. Help others informally or through an organization
6. Add a new relationship or social activity by placing yourself in everyday contexts where you can meet and interact with others
7. Be active and challenge yourself to try out organized clubs, courses, interest groups, etc.
8. If you see barriers to interacting with people (i.e., mobility restrictions, neighborhood safety issues), see if you can ask someone to assist in making connections

6 Conclusions

This chapter introduced the main characteristics of the design of specific coaching plans that can be considered the heart of the NESTORE virtual coach. The holistic approach as well as the personalization strategies that are embedded in the system

Table 10 Summary of relevant characteristics of social coaching

Target	Intervention type	Assessment variables during coaching	Monitoring variables
Retain/Improve opportunities for social contact	Befriending, taking up new social activities	Number and types of social interactions, loneliness	De Jong Gierveld loneliness scale Lubben social network scale 6
Retain/Improve social skills	Integrated into befriending, taking up new social activities (i.e., engage in conversations and social interactions and thus practice social skills)	Number and types of social interactions, loneliness	Loneliness Social integration
Retain/Improve social support	Home visits, animal-assisted support, educational classes, psychosocial counseling	Not available in NESTORE	Berlin social support scales
Retain/Improve social cognition	Counseling concerning awareness of feelings, reminiscence therapy, cognitive behavioral therapy	Not available in NESTORE	Not available in NESTORE

for most of the coaching domains can be considered the strength of NESTORE and can serve as a reference for other projects having the same focus. In the following chapters, more details regarding the development of the coaching activities in each specific domain will be described.

References

1. El Kamali, M., Angelini, L., Caon, M., Carrino, F., Röcke, C., Guye, S., …, & Mugellini, E. (2020). *Virtual coaches for older adults' wellbeing: A systematic review.* IEEE Access.
2. Mastropietro, A., Röecke, C., Porcelli, S., del Bas, J., Boquè, N., Maldonado, L. F., & Rizzo, G. (2018, July). Multi-domain model of healthy ageing: The experience of the H2020 NESTORE project. In *Italian forum of ambient assisted living* (pp. 13–21). Springer, Cham.
3. Brown, M., & Holloszy, J. O. (1991). Effects of a low intensity exercise program on selected physical performance characteristics of 60-to 71-year olds. *Aging Clinical and Experimental Research, 3*(2), 129–139.
4. World Health Organization. (2010). *Recommended population levels of physical activity for health.* Global recommendations on physical activity for health (pp. 15–34).
5. Zaleski, A. L., Taylor, B. A., Panza, G. A., et al. (2016). Coming of age: Considerations in the prescription of exercise for older adults. *Methodist Debakey Cardiovascular Journal, 12*(2), 98–104. https://doi.org/10.14797/mdcj-12-2-98.
6. Chodzko-Zajko, W. J., Proctor, D. N., et al. (2009). American College of Sports Medicine position stand. Exercise and physical activity for older adults. *Medicine & Science in Sports & Exercise, 41*(7), 1510–1530.

7. Pescatello, L., Arena, R., Riebe, D., & Thompson, P. (2013). *ACSM's guidelines for exercise testing and prescription* (9th ed.). Baltimore, ML: Lippincott Williams & Wilkins.
8. Nelson, M. E., Rejeski, W. J., Blair, S. N., Duncan, P. W., Judge, J. O., King, A. C., et al. (2007). Physical activity and public health in older adults: recommendation from the American college of Sports Medicine and the American Heart Association. *Medicine & Science in Sports & Exercise, 39*(8), 1435–1445.
9. Schlicht, J., Camaione, D. N., & Owen, S. V. (2001). Effect of intense strength training on standing balance, walking speed, and sit-to-stand performance in older adults. *The Journals of Gerontology Series A: Biological Sciences and Medical Sciences, 56*(5), M281–M286.
10. Sullivan, G. M., & Pomidor, A. K. (Eds.). (2015). *Exercise for aging adults: A guide for practitioners*. Springer.
11. Ticinesi, A., Lauretani, F., Milani, C., Nouvenne, A., Tana, C., Del Rio, D., …, & Meschi, T. (2017). Aging gut microbiota at the cross-road between nutrition, physical frailty, and sarcopenia: is there a gut–muscle axis? *Nutrients, 9*(12), 1303.
12. Streicher, M., van Zwienen-Pot, J., Bardon, L., Nagel, G., Teh, R., Meisinger, C., …, & Denkinger, M. (2018). Determinants of incident malnutrition in community-dwelling older adults: A MaNuEL multicohort meta-analysis. *Journal of the American Geriatrics Society, 66*(12), 2335–2343.
13. Eurostat. (2018). *Overweight and obesity—BMI statistics—Statistics explained*. http://ec.europa.eu/eurostat/statistics-explained/index.php/Overweight_and_obesity_-_BMI_statistics.
14. Mathus-Vliegen, E. M., Basdevant, A., Finer, N., Hainer, V., Hauner, H., Micic, D., …, & Toplak, H. (2012). Prevalence, pathophysiology, health consequences and treatment options of obesity in the elderly: A guideline. *Obesity facts, 5*(3), 460–483.
15. Osher, E., & Stern, N. (2009). Obesity in elderly subjects: In sheep's clothing perhaps, but still a wolf! *Diabetes Care, 32*(suppl 2), S398–S402.
16. Gentile, S., Lacroix, O., Durand, A. C., Cretel, E., Alazia, M., Sambuc, R., et al. (2013). Malnutrition: A highly predictive risk factor of short-term mortality in elderly presenting to the emergency department. *The Journal of Nutrition, Health & Aging, 17*(4), 290–294.
17. Morley, J. E. (2015). *Nutrition in older adults, an issue of clinics in geriatric medicine, e-book* (Vol. 31, No. 3). Elsevier Health Sciences.
18. Waters, D. L., Ward, A. L., & Villareal, D. T. (2013). Weight loss in obese adults 65 years and older: A review of the controversy. *Experimental Gerontology, 48*(10), 1054–1061.
19. Papa, E. V., Dong, X., & Hassan, M. (2017). Skeletal muscle function deficits in the elderly: Current perspectives on resistance training. *Journal of Nature and Science, 3*(1).
20. EFSA Panel on Dietetic Products, Nutrition and Allergies (NDA). (2013). Scientific opinion on dietary reference values for energy. *EFSA Journal, 11*(1), 3005.
21. Brouns, F. (2015). WHO guideline. *Agro FOOD Industry Hi Tech, 26,* 34–36.
22. EFSA Panel on Dietetic Products, Nutrition and Allergies (NDA). (2011). Scientific Opinion on the substantiation of health claims related to oat and barley grain fibre and increase in faecal bulk (ID 819, 822) pursuant to Article 13 (1) of Regulation (EC) No 1924/2006. *EFSA Journal, 9*(6), 2249.
23. FESNAD. (2010). Ingestas dietéticas de referencia (IDR) para la población española.
24. Berendsen, A., Santoro, A., Pini, E., Cevenini, E., Ostan, R., Pietruszka, B., …, & Fairweather-Tait, S. (2014). Reprint of: A parallel randomized trial on the effect of a healthful diet on inflammageing and its consequences in European elderly people: Design of the NU-AGE dietary intervention study. *Mechanisms of Ageing and Development, 136*, 14–21.
25. Ros, E., López-Miranda, J., Picó, C., Rubio, M. Á., Babio, N., Sala-Vila, A., …, & Gil Hernández, A. (2015). Consenso sobre las grasas y aceites en la alimentación de la población española adulta: postura de la Federación Española de Sociedades de Alimentación, Nutrición y Dietética (FESNAD). *Nutricion hospitalaria, 32*(2), 435–477.
26. EFSA Panel on Dietetic Products, Nutrition, and Allergies (NDA). (2010). Scientific opinion on principles for deriving and applying dietary reference values. *EFSA Journal, 8*(3), 1458.
27. Pedersen, A. N., & Cederholm, T. (2014). Health effects of protein intake in healthy elderly populations: A systematic literature review. *Food & Nutrition Research, 58*(1), 23364.

28. Ward, R. J., Zucca, F. A., Duyn, J. H., Crichton, R. R., & Zecca, L. (2014). The role of iron in brain ageing and neurodegenerative disorders. *The Lancet Neurology, 13*(10), 1045–1060.
29. Lawton, M. P., Moss, M., Hoffman, C., Grant, R., Ten Have, T., & Kleban, M. H. (1999). Health, valuation of life, and the wish to live. *The Gerontologist, 39*(4), 406–416. https://doi.org/10.1093/geront/39.4.406.
30. Guye, S., Röcke, C., Mérillat, S., von Bastian, C. C., & Martin, M. (2016). Adult lifespan. In T. Strobach & J. Karbach (Eds.), *Cognitive training*. Springer, Cham. https://doi.org/10.1007/978-3-319-42662-4_5.
31. Guye, S., Röcke, C., Mérillat, S., von Bastian, C. C., & Martin, M. (2016). Plasticity in different age groups: Adult lifespan. In T. Strobach & J. Karbach (Eds.), *Cognitive training: An overview of features and applications* (pp. 45–55). Berlin: Springer.
32. Global Council on Brain Health. (2017). *Engage your brain: GCBH recommendations on cognitively stimulating activities*. www.GlobalCouncilOnBrainHealth.org.
33. NIA. (2020). https://www.nia.nih.gov/health/cognitive-health-and-older-adults.
34. Coll-Planas, L., Nyqvist, F., Puig, T., Urrútia, G., Solà, I., & Monteserín, R. (2016). Social capital interventions targeting older people and their impact on health: A systematic review. *Journal of Epidemiology and Community Health*, jech-2016.
35. Findlay, R. A. (2003). Interventions to reduce social isolation amongst older people: Where is the evidence? *Ageing & Society, 23*(5), 647–658.
36. House, J. S., Landis, K. R., & Umberson, D. (1988). Social relationships and health. *Science, 241*(4865), 540–545.
37. Seeman, T. E. (1996). Social ties and health: The benefits of social integration. *Annals of Epidemiology, 6*(5), 442–451.
38. Masi, C. M., Chen, H. Y., Hawkley, L. C., & Cacioppo, J. T. (2011). A meta-analysis of interventions to reduce loneliness. *Personality and Social Psychology Review, 15*(3), 219–266.
39. Global Council on Brain Health. (2017). *The brain and social connectedness: GCBH recommendations on social engagement and brain health*. www.GlobalCouncilOnBrainHealth.org.

Found in Translation: Innovative Methods of Co-design in the Development of Digital Systems for Promoting Healthy Aging

Paul Chamberlain, Claire Craig, and Nick Dulake

Abstract This chapter describes the Design Research contribution to the NESTORE Horizon 2020 project, which adopted a participatory design research method, called 'exhibition in a box', developed by the authors which is predicated on 'thinking through things'. Over 100 older people across four countries participated in the study, which sought to develop a virtual digital coach to support active ageing. We discuss themes that arose relating to the barriers and enablers to engagement with technology as identified by participants within the study. It critically reflects on the strengths and challenges of the co-design methodology. The methodological approach followed in NESTORE provides for users to be involved in the design of the solution throughout the project duration and permeates the work of all the work-packages. The reason for non-acceptance of health technologies is complex and the context where the technologies will operate and how they relate to the end users' lives are key factors to uptake and utilization. Researchers have suggested that the poor design of many devices and subsequent non-uptake may be directly attributed to the failure of technologists to engage end users and elicit understanding of their requirements. To date few studies have articulated how this might be achieved.

Keywords Design · Co-design · Design for health · Health technology

1 Introduction

The authors have a strong track record in the area of co-design. Chamberlain and Craig are co-directors of Lab4Living, an interdisciplinary research group at Sheffield Hallam University (SHU) based on a collaborative community of researchers in design, healthcare and creative practice. The focus of Lab4Living is to work in partnership with end users to develop products, services and interventions that promote dignity and enhance quality of life by applying design skills and methods to identify and formulate questions, build understanding and create solutions. Key to this work

P. Chamberlain (✉) · C. Craig · N. Dulake
Lab4Living, Sheffield Hallam University, Cantor Building, 153 Arundel Street, Sheffield S1 2NU, UK
e-mail: p.m.chamberlain@shu.ac.uk

G. Andreoni and C. Mambretti (eds.), *Digital Health Technology for Better Aging*, Research for Development, https://doi.org/10.1007/978-3-030-72663-8_3

is working in collaboration with people who use products and services recognising their inherent strengths and knowledge based on their personal and professional experiences.

Declining mortality rates mean higher life expectancies globally. In 2015 there were 901 million people aged 60 years and over worldwide. By 2050 it will have increased to 2.1 billion or 21.3% of the global population [8]. This ageing population and the resultant pressure on healthcare capacity and changing roles and expectations are driving demand for innovative solutions to support independence at home for people living with long term conditions and disability. Digital technologies are being seen as a way to respond to these challenges and as a consequence the way in which medical and healthcare is delivered is being transformed [9].

Much of the focus of technology to date has been on medical device development with a particular emphasis on products that measure to record data relating to physical functioning (e.g. blood pressure, heart rate, pulse-oxygen). However, more recently there has been an increased recognition of the link between social isolation, loneliness and reduced life expectancy [3, 11] and this has led to a growing emphasis on policies to address the social dimension of health.

Alongside these changes, a paradigm shift has occurred within health that places greater emphasis on self-management and health promotion. Here responsibility is given to the individual to recognize and manage the symptoms of their condition [12]. Approaches that support a more pro-active approach and that do not rely on health and social care services are being promoted globally. Models of healthy and active ageing with a focus on the multi-stage life are replacing previous conceptualizations of ageing predicated on decline and withdrawal from society. Within this new paradigm technology can play a key role in offering integrated solutions to promote on-going engagement in meaningful activity and promote community connectedness.

Whilst technology can potentially have a significant impact on health and well-being, to date the uptake of digital health technologies has been problematic in a number of wide-scale studies [17]. Literature highlights that the reason for non-acceptance is complex. Authors have cited confidence, the stigmatizing aesthetics of products, meaningfulness of technology in the broader context of the persons' life, ease of use and integration into everyday routines as important factors [2, 10, 15, 16].

1.1 Aims of the Research

Novel Empowering Solutions and Technologies for Older People to Retain Everyday Life Activities (NESTORE) is a Horizon 2020 funded project focusing on a technological innovation to enable individuals to engage in health promoting activities as they age. The innovation is conceptualized as a 'friend, a companion and coach' seeking to valorize the capabilities of the older person, to recognize and support them in maximizing their abilities and to experience mental, physical and cognitive wellbeing. NESTORE is intended to promote choice, to educate, to signpost to opportunities, to connect individuals to community facilities and resources and to promote on-going social connectedness throughout the life-course. The system is not a medical device. Rather, it seeks to promote wellbeing through enabling the person to identify and reflect on current lifestyle choices and to access opportunities to engage in meaningful health promoting activities. To develop a solution fit for purpose it is therefore necessary to build understanding of what end users identify as being meaningful and the qualities and characteristics the technology needs to possess. The role of the design set within the context of this project was to better understand the broader physical and social environments in which services and technologies will operate and how they relate to the contexts of the end-user. The aim then was that these insights would be communicated to the technologists in the development of the end product. The methodological approach followed in NESTORE provided for users to be involved in the design and development of the solution throughout the project duration.

The Consortium responsible for undertaking the research comprises of sixteen partners from eight European countries. Research expertise included: design, health (psychology, medicine, nutrition), engineering, business and technology. These partners span Higher Education Institutions and Industry. The overall study is divided into 4 distinct phases. Phase one of the research utilizes participatory research methods and is focused on developing cultural and behavioural insights related to technology, initially in the United Kingdom. Phase two extends and develops this participatory methodology to focus on the materiality, interaction and usability issues related to the NESTORE system. Co-design groups in the Netherlands, Italy and Spain extend these cultural insights and test the transferability of the methodology. Phase three of the study then supports the development of prototypes and product through an iterative co-design process. Phase four of the research comprises of a pilot study with over 60 participants across Italy, the Netherlands and Spain.

1.2 Methods of Engagement

There is widespread support for the fact that recipients or users of products and services should be involved in some way in their creation and there is a body of literature in support of the value of participatory and co-design. Arnstein's ladder of citizen participation [1] describes levels of citizen engagement in planning processes that can usefully be applied to participatory and co-design. However too often participatory engagement doesn't extend beyond the level of tokenism as presented in Arnstein's ladder (Fig. 1).

Participatory methods are centred on the principle that participant engagement can provide value throughout research planning and implementation, yielding findings that directly reflect on a community's needs and perceptions. Participants are given an active role, allowing them to shape the direction and methods of the research itself. Multiple benefits are associated with the use of participatory methods including developing collaborative and productive partnerships with participants, providing

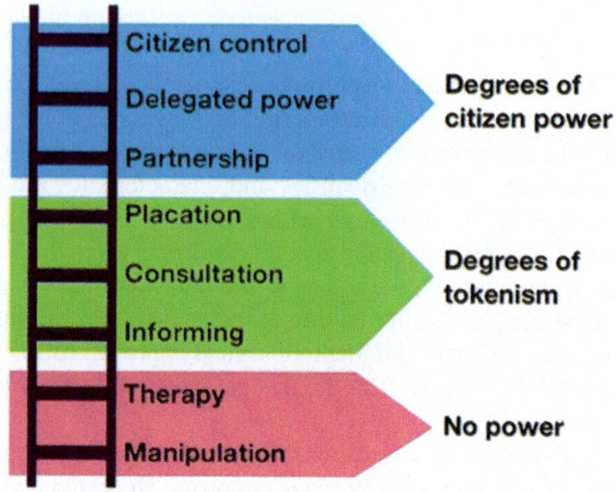

Fig. 1 Arnstein's ladder of citizen participation 1969

participants with a voice and harnessing participant engagement to stimulate positive change and the design of better products.

Within our study, co-design was defined as creativity of designers and people not trained in design working together in the design development process. From the outset of the research it was envisaged that as the project evolved multiple levels of engagement and participation would occur. For instance, in the earlier stages of the research, individuals would be actively involved in the co-design of the products whilst at other points participants would play more of a role in providing feedback and reflections on the products being developed. The overall study design followed the UK Design Council's Double Diamond with the initial phases of the research interrogating the requirements of the product by adopting a more exploratory approach, asking questions, conceptualizing possibilities rather than offering solutions (Fig. 2).

2 Design of the Research

The research was structured into four phases to align with the Double Diamond model (Fig. 3) The first of these phases to explore the problem space was undertaken in the United Kingdom. Community living older people were invited to engage in a co-design process to build understanding of user requirements of the technology, identify factors that promote and inhibit use and explore potential contexts where technologies would be used. An older expert group was recruited to help analyse the data collected.

Phase two of the research was then undertaken in the partner countries of Spain, Italy and the Netherlands. The same co-design methodology was used with groups of community living older people in these countries with the addition that themes

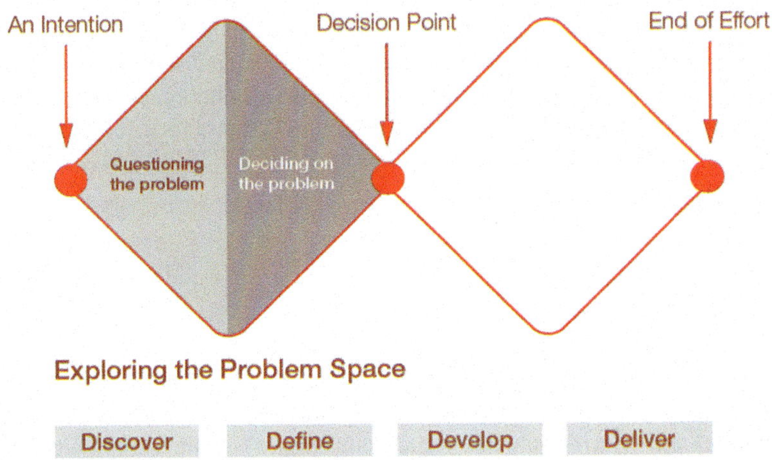

Fig. 2 Design Council (UK) double diamond

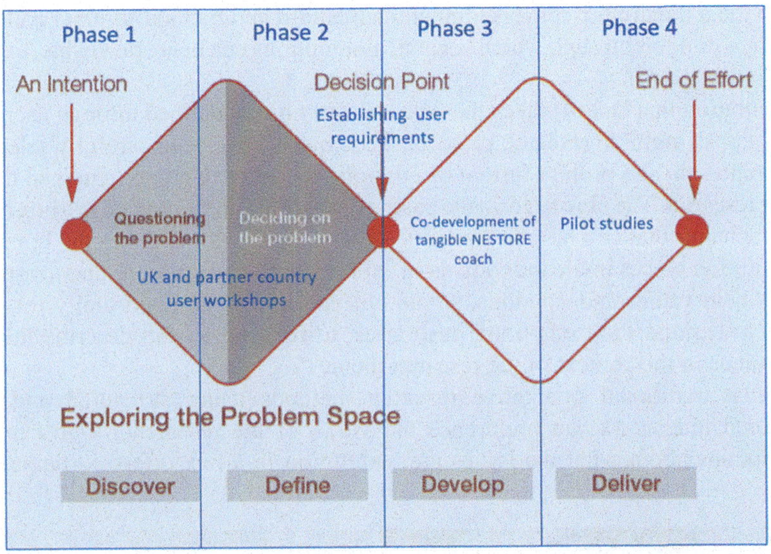

Fig. 3 NESTORE co-design activity mapped onto Design Council's (UK) double diamond

from the first phase of the study were shared to build understanding of the potential for transferability. The aims of this phase were to build understanding of the similarities/differences in requirements of older people in these countries that would determine user requirements for the NESTORE system and in the context of the double diamond model arrive at the decision point. The expert older group from the UK and members of AGE Platform Europe were integral to this process.

Phase three, the development of the research, involved how the user requirements established through phase one and two could be translated into tangible solutions with the technologist. This again was conducted in collaboration with the older expert group though a series of co-design workshops. Phase four, the delivery phase of the process, would involve the pilot studies to test the NESTORE system in context with older users in the Netherlands, Italy and Spain.

3 Methods

Co-design methods in NESTORE drew on an existing body of work developed by the authors [4, 6, 7] which used objects and artefacts as methods to stimulate and scaffold thinking, offering valuable vehicles through which the complexities of lives can be understood. The concept of exhibition is embedded within the culture of art and design and has a long history as a form of gathering employed to prompt academic discourse. Exhibition as a research vehicle is often used by the authors to provide a theatre for conversation and a medium and method for data collection, creating a conduit through which societal assumptions can be made visible, explored and challenged [5].

Exhibition in a box [4] takes the form of nine objects defined through user workshops across multiple research projects. The objects have been carefully selected to code, represent and prompt further discussion on themes that have emerged through earlier research. The objects form the basis of an exhibition, contained in a box (Fig. 4) á la Duchamp that can be transported to diverse environs including the home. Just as exhibition pieces invite individuals to express ideas and opinions and to articulate deeply held values and opinions, so the objects provide an opportunity for participants to express their emotional responses, to respond to and describe things of importance in the context of the research theme.

Whilst traditional qualitative research methods using structured and semi-structured interviews can preference the views of the researcher who can make assumptions about what the issues are, exhibition in a box offers participants the

Fig. 4 Exhibition in a box

space to reflect, discuss, explore and define the questions that reflect their priorities. The objects offer scaffolds for communication because at one and the same time they are both concrete and abstract.

4 The Study

4.1 *Phase One*

The aim of the study was to build understanding of user requirements of the NESTORE technology and the factors that promote and inhibit use. In addition to explore potential contexts of where the NESTORE technologies might be used.

Ethical approval for the study was granted from Sheffield Hallam University's Ethics Committee in October 2017. Between October 2017—January 2018 a convenience sample of 82 older user representatives were recruited from organizations across the city of Sheffield, in the north of England, to participate in a series of NESTORE co-design workshops. Inclusion criteria for the study were that participants should be community living older people aged 50 and over; individuals able to give informed consent; people who had some degree of familiarity with the use of technology (reflecting future groups of people who may use NESTORE).

Workshops were facilitated across a number of different venues including community centres, people's homes, and the user-laboratory space within the University. It is important to consider the diverse environments that NESTORE might be used. Consequently, workshops were held in a variety of contexts, for instance where people might work, meet socially or in the home. The context of delivery of the workshop sometimes impacted on the conversations that were elicited and, participants could relate their experiences to objects and surroundings. Each workshop lasted on average between one and two hours and comprised of between four and eight participants, facilitated by a combination of two of the authors. The workshops began with a general introduction from the research team and an invitation for participants to share (verbally) activities they engaged in and found meaningful, with a particular focus on hobbies or leisure. Exhibition in a box was then introduced and participants were invited, in turn, to select and use the object to explore their ideas further (this might relate to the object's form, its sensory quality or a more metaphorical use). This was shared with the broader group. Participants were then invited to share associations that came to mind when they heard the word technology. Again, the critical artefacts were used to explore and interrogate these themes further. With permission, each workshop was audio-recorded and then transcribed.

4.2 User Workshop Findings

A number of strengths in relation to the exhibition in a box method were identified. The objects transcended boundaries of culture, language and age and whilst the objects remained unchanging the associations they prompted and the stories they elicited were dynamic and ever changing. Across the various workshop/focus groups different objects elicited the same themes of conversation. Particularly powerful were the keys which very much related to security and the dice which participants used to talk about parity of access. Participants shared rich descriptions of their attitudes towards and experiences of technology and a depth of information was offered within the first few minutes of the workshop beginning. Older people expressed appreciation of the tangibility of the objects and their sensory qualities, acting as a physical prompt. The method also enabled individuals to achieve some distance when sharing more personal stories by 'speaking through the objects' or using the objects metaphorically. Rather than being dependent on fixed interview schedules whereby the researcher had pre-defined questions the method very much preferenced the views of participants. This is integral to the co-design process. Individuals participating in the workshops expressed enjoyment of the experience and reflected on their learning and the new insights they had gained through the process. This positive experience led to an expressed interest in participating in other elements of the study.

The workshop was structured into two parts where the 'exhibition in a box' was used to prompt discussion on personal interests and attitudes to technology. The following topics and issues emerged.

4.2.1 Meaningful Activities

Hobbies and activities

The range of hobbies and activities people described as being important was broad and included for example; listening to music, cooking, playing instruments, walking, gardening, drawing, art, creative writing, golf, cricket, football, and engaging in cultural pursuits such as reading, visiting museums and galleries. Older participants were more likely to talk about the importance of spirituality and faith and a number of individuals described the importance of attending church in relation to their emotional and spiritual wellbeing. Interestingly because a number of participants were still in employment, the value of work was described in some depth as an area which offered structure to the day, a role and a sense of identity. There was recognition, particularly amongst participants in the 50–60 year age bracket, of the need to keep physically well and to engage in health promoting activities. This was identified as a motivation to engage in a range of pursuits although it was also acknowledged that healthy lifestyle choices could be difficult.

Physical activity

Physical wellbeing was regarded as important and a number of participants engaged in a range of exercise including running and walking. However, exercise was not seen only in terms of physical wellbeing but also as offering an opportunity for relaxation and for the maintenance of mental wellbeing. Access to outside space and spending time outside was seen as key particularly as people grew older. The social dimension of exercise was a motivating factor—participants found purpose when being with friends or pets.

Social dimension of activity

Socialising and engaging in activities with other people were a significant theme that ran throughout all workshops. Participants spoke of the importance and value of interacting with family, engaging in intergenerational activity and of being with others. Friendship and socialising were seen as key to maintaining good mental wellbeing. At times individuals spoke of the social dimension of the activity being the motivating factor and at other times keeping connected and spending time with friends became an end in itself.

Creative activities

A significant theme that arose during the workshops was the value that participants placed on creative activities and in attending cultural events. Creativity was regarded as an outlet for self-expression, a way to reflect and to make sense of situations. Creativity was also seen as a form of problem solving, as a way to identify and to think about solutions. The idea of making something tangible and of engaging with physical materials in the creation of new things was linked closely to legacy and of the act of creating and making a mark that would live beyond the participants' lifetime. Across all workshops individuals identified creativity, art, writing and drawing as ways of keeping mentally and cognitively well and as a way to retain a sense of curiosity and new learning. For a number of individuals it offered a sense of balance and was key to emotional wellbeing.

Factors that promote engagement

Some factors that promoted and maximised engagement were also identified in this phase of the study. Individuals were more likely to engage in health promoting activities if they were part of a routine, particularly if they were in full or part-time employment. Participants spoke of the importance of the social element of activities as a motivating factor, particularly if they could be undertaken with friends and family. Having a sense of challenge or a goal to work towards was also seen as being important particularly in terms of creating a sense of achievement.

Barriers to engagement

Across all the workshops, participants also spoke of barriers to engagement. Lack of encouragement or reward was a theme that led some to disengage from activity, particularly when participants were seeking to learn something new. Lack of confidence and the challenge of taking the first step was also a theme that emerged across workshops. When people felt coerced or that they did not have a choice but to participate this acted as a barrier to engagement and continued engagement in the activity. However, by far the greatest barrier to engagement in meaningful activity was lack of time and financial resources. Within the demographic of this research a significant number of participants were of the so called 'sandwich generation' caring for children or even grandchildren and for elderly parents. Time was at a premium and the notion of engaging in any form of activity outside of work or caring roles was felt by a number of participants to be impossible.

4.2.2 Perceptions of Technology

Perceptions of technology were broad and individuals described and identified this in a number of ways. The most common association was with digital technology: smartphone, computers, wires, cables, phones. A small number of people spoke about technology more generally including aeroplanes, cars, kettles and household objects and a couple of participants offered more philosophical definitions linked to time and place:

> So technology is essentially the stuff that has just been developed or is being developed and we're just trying to get to grips with it. So everything… watches were technology at one point, just as (telephone) landlines – we don't call landlines technology now, because they're just landlines.

Digital technologies were seen as mechanisms through which to access information, and to offer vehicles and opportunities for new learning and to connect to interests. At the same time individuals framed technology as having potential detrimental affects on health and posing a threat to the present way of life.

With the exception of four or five individuals, everyone had access to a smartphone or tablet computer and this was the most common device described. Attitudes to and responses to technology across all the workshops were polarised. On the one hand, the strengths and potential of technology to be an enabler was recognised, particularly in helping individuals to overcome challenges such as dyslexia. Digital technology was also seen as a mechanism through which to access information quickly, to provide a vehicle through which it was possible to access opportunities, learn new things and to connect to interests (such as exhibitions and to book travel and accommodation). For some people advances were seen as a good thing, particularly when it had a clear function that enabled participation in meaningful activity. On the other hand the same technologies were seen as a threat to present way of life. Terms such as 'good' and 'evil', 'frustration', 'fear' were used. A number of participants described technology as being 'dull' and 'uninteresting' particularly in relation to digital technology.

Barriers to engagement

Barriers to engaging in technology included the speed of change leading to challenges in new learning at a point of cognitive decline, questions relating to privacy and trust in terms of who is able to access and use the data generated and the reliability of the technology and the information and readings created. Prohibitive costs and lack of technological infrastructures were also seen as challenges.

4.2.3 Design Considerations

Design considerations which were identified as supporting engagement and adoption included the potential for personalization, portability, durability and considerations in relation to ergonomics. Features that promoted control and the building of self-efficacy were also valued. An aesthetic that was fit for purpose, as according to Dieter Rams 'good design is aesthetic' [14]. A visual language that expresses reliability and durability, for example, was identified as an important aspect in the design of NESTORE.

Above all it was necessary to consider how technology relates to other elements of the person's life and how it fits with self-concept and value system. Specific design considerations identified by individuals participating in the study are described as follows: The ability to personalize the technology was by far the most desirable design consideration expressed in this element of the research. This was seen as a way to counter the uniformity of existing technology and to enable participants to create a sense of identity and ownership. If personalization and the ability to adapt and shape the technology reflected the owners personality then the opposite was true in relation to the operation of digital devices. Participants identified the need above all for consistency in design, in the symbols used on controls across products. These characteristics both align with and validate existing usability guidelines for IT systems [13].

Portability was another design consideration. Older people in our study enjoyed travel and pursuits in the locality and did not want to be tied to the home or to a particular room in the house. Within this, size and weight were both factors.

Participants valued design features to promote control and self-efficacy. Individuals were, for instance, clear that not being dependent on others to update the device or change batteries should be a consideration especially if the aim of the technology was to increase self-efficacy. Participants also appreciated the choice and option to have time to disconnect from technology and there was much discussion about feelings in relation to using systems that were completely automated. There were mixed views in terms of whether devices should have multiple functions or whether a single piece of technology should have a single function.

One unexpected theme that emerged during this phase of the research was discussion the workshops relating to the potential negative impact technology may have on health. Concern was expressed as to whether a focus on measurement of health behaviours (pedometers, step counters) could result in the focus being on the behaviour rather than the activity itself. Technology was also seen as both being as addictive and as a gateway to websites that might provide dangerous to individuals vulnerable to addictive behaviours, feeding addictions such as online gambling and pornography. However, the greatest perceived threat regarding technology in relation to mental health was in the breakdown of relationships and the ensuing isolation.

4.2.4 Data Analysis Phase One

Transcriptions of the user workshops were shared with a group of ten older people in the UK who formed an older expert group for NESTORE (Fig. 5). During a one-day workshop these individuals were engaged in a process of identifying the main themes from the overall data collection and identifying the most important factors in relation to considerations and user requirements of NESTORE. These were; Privacy, Empowerment, Fits my life, Personalization, Cost, Freedom, Ergonomics, Reliability, Observation, Connectedness, Security, Infrastructure, Being social, Engaging, Keeping active.

4.3 Phase Two

A similar methodology was adopted in workshops with older people in each of the partner countries, Milan (Italy), Barcelona (Spain), Delft (the Netherlands). The

Fig. 5 Older expert group UK

Fig. 6 Co-design workshops (Delft, Milan, Barcelona)

objective of conducting user workshops in the Netherlands, Italy and Spain was to identify if the findings from the workshops in the UK aligned with communities in other countries. Nominated members of the country partner NESTORE team facilitated each workshop. All took part in earlier briefing meetings with the UK team prior to the workshop and workshops were delivered in the local language. The UK team was present and contributed to the workshop with translation support. A convenience sample of 30 older people across the three countries took part in this phase of the research (Fig. 6).

Workshop participants engaged in the thinking through things method with exhibition in a box sharing their personal insights into what is meaningful in their lives and their opinions and relationships with technology. The second part of the workshop focused on the priorities and characteristics identified from the user workshops conducted in the UK. Participants were collectively asked to reflect on each of these and whether they agreed or disagreed with their validity in the context of what NESTORE should consider in its development and application. In addition the participants were asked if there were any themes they felt were missing from the list.

4.3.1 Findings

Findings from phase one of the study were found to be congruent across countries with a few minor differences mainly concerning the politics of how NESTORE might be appropriated (distributed through current health systems and regulations) and a call for NESTORE to be underpinned by research. There were no significant cultural differences however it was noted that climate and environment should be carefully considered in how it might impact on lifestyles. Participants, and in particular the group from Italy, discussed a concern for the ethical dimension and sustainability of technology in terms of resource and rare minerals. The workshops were conducted during the winter period with extreme cold weather in the UK and the Netherlands in contrast with mild pleasant weather in Italy and Spain. This has significant bearing on the ability for people to engage in outdoor activities.

4.4 Analysis of Phase One and Two

Following the workshops in Milan (Italy), Barcelona (Spain), Delft (the Netherlands) and in collaboration with the older expert group, the user requirements identified in phase one and shared in phase two were further refined and focused on three broad themes; TRUST, FITS MY LIFE and COST.

TRUST

Privacy/security/reliability of NESTORE
The system's management of data is transparent. Users are aware of where data goes and how it is used. The user has control over their privacy settings (in a usable manner and who has access to the data)
Health related data is accurate and can be viewed in real time by users of the system
Users have the capacity to turn off analytics (on/off switch)
The system will translate health data into contextualised user centred feedback appropriate to its audience
The system should be robust and withstand everyday use
The system should not compromise or effect other health technologies of the user (e.g. pace maker)
Charging requirements should not interfere with lifestyle
Software updates should not alienate access.

FITS MY LIFE

Responsiveness of the system to reflect the needs and preferences of the end user including considerations of ergonomics
Interface should be clear, concise and elegant with the opportunities for manual customisation by the user reflecting their own preferences and style
The visual interface (e.g. icons) should be easily recognisable, provide consistent look and feel
Single sign in (log in once rather than multiple times)
The system should provide a creative user-friendly solution for log in and resource access
Users settings should be remembered throughout the platform
When the user changes the interface settings the interface should be updated immediately and continuously
Resources should be accessible and usable by all users of the system. Features should include interaction modes for touch and voice alongside high visibility settings appropriate to personal needs (e.g. high contrast for people with visual impairments etc.) and language settings/options. Language should be clear and meet the needs of individuals with varied literacy skills
The system should be responsive and adapt itself to the environment and user needs

The system should have the capacity to be used beyond the user's physical home environment.

COST

Affordability
NESTORE should be scalable (e.g. inclusive core features with option to purchase additional functionality)
Costs should not be prohibitive to the specified user group.

5 Transferability of User Requirements to Technologists

Phase one and two of the research concluded the *discover* and *define* stage phase of the double diamond model that established the user requirements for the NESTORE system, the *decision* point. Often this is the point in the design process where the co-design concludes and the development and delivery phase of the double diamond model is conducted by other partner stakeholders. The intersection of the double diamond becomes the transactional point of where an exchange of knowledge takes place. However, it is at this point where key insights can be lost in translation and consequently this research programme ensured collaborative engagement through further co-design activity continued between the design research team, the older expert group and the technologists. This was to ensure the user requirements identified in phase one and two, the exploratory phase of the double diamond, were interpreted thoughtfully and creatively. Consequently, a set of creative tools was developed by the design researchers to facilitate a further series of co-design workshops.

5.1 Digital Probes

The aim of this workshop was to build understanding of design features of current digital interfaces participants find helpful/unhelpful. A digital probe methodology was used where participants were provided with a 'probes pack' created by the authors that included a disposable film camera, a tick/cross counter disc, and an instruction booklet (Fig. 7). Each participant was invited to place counters with either a tick or a cross by particular technology interfaces they found particularly helpful or unhelpful and record with the camera. It was stressed that participants should make comment on the interface of technology rather than the activity associated with the technology. For example, watching television might be enjoyable but the interface not.

Photographs were printed and the results were shared and discussed within the workshop (Fig. 8)

Multiple themes emerged through the workshop in relation to the design facets of existing technologies. Participants commented on the number of digital technologies

Fig. 7 Digital probe pack and instructions for use

Fig. 8 Analysis of digital probes

they regularly interacted with and again questions were raised on the ethics of technology in relation to privacy and the sharing of data. In some instances comments were contradictory.

Within the expert by experience group, negative characteristics of existing technologies included:

The need to have multiple controls to operate digital technologies (for example multiple controls to operate television, DVD player etc.)
Interfaces with buttons requiring multiple hits to scroll through different functions. For example, setting digital timers
The intrusiveness of many of the audio-qualities of technology ('indistinct bleeps and piercing sounds')
Feeling tied to technology—an inability to get away from it
Participants spoke of valuing particular types of digital technology but struggling with the interfaces (e.g. small numbers, symbols on buttons that are not uniform and which wear away over time)
There were also questions raised by the group in relation to installation and the need to have clearer instructions in relation to how to use systems
Poor cable management
Restrictions in portability were raised by women who often do not have pockets in clothing.

Positive characteristics of existing technological interfaces included;

Easy access to information (internet)
Voice activated. e.g. Siri, Alexa
Convenience of portability (iPhone)
Gestural control (light switches).

There were mixed responses from the group with respect to multi-function products. Some people liked to have many functions in one device (e.g. smart phone) however others commented that they often use only a fraction of the functionality on many devices and stressed a desire to choose or customise would be preferable.

The group felt that one of the challenges is that often interfaces are designed without full consultation with end users and there was a sense that the technologists who are designing systems and products do not know enough about the end user. It was therefore decided to create a series of films to communicate to the technologists who the end user of NESTORE might be. This aligned well with the user personas developed by others in the consortium.

5.2 Personas

Over the course of four weeks the expert by experience group created a series of four films in partnership with the design researchers (Fig. 9). The aim of the films was to bring life to existing personas and to support the technologists in understanding the audience NESTORE would reach.

Whilst the technologists found the films of great interest, feedback was that it was difficult to relate the overall technology design requirements to such a diverse group within the NESTORE project team and that a system of more simplified personas was preferred. This led to the iterative development of a series of personas (Fig. 10)

Fig. 9 Screen shots of 'users' lives' videos

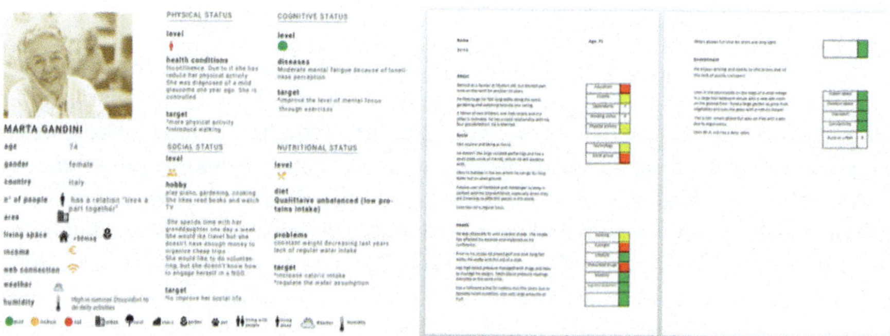

Fig. 10 Examples of personas (potential NESTORE users)

developed in collaboration with the project partners and informed by the expert by experience group. This prompted critical discussion concerned with the target user for NESTORE and establishing 'inclusion' criteria based on socio-economic profile and health condition. It was generally felt that NESTORE should be inclusive as possible and provide facility for potential users at the lower end of the socio-economic scale. However, recognising the resource and timeframe of the project it was determined NESTORE might have to be developed in a staged approach providing varying formats and functionality to be able to target diverse social groups. In addition it was felt NESTORE would not target users with chronic health conditions, where users should seek expert medical help, although it could provide additional healthy lifestyle support. However, NESTORE will include those with physiological decline as they age that lead to minor chronic conditions.

NESTORE is to support improved health and is conceptualised as a coach rather than a doctor. Whereas a doctor might instruct you to take action, a coach should be supportive to help progress the things deemed important from the user's perspective. Consequently, if NESTORE is conceptualised as a coach it also might need a persona that would be considered in the design of the tangible coach.

5.3 Pathways

User perspectives that have emerged through the workshops to date indicate the NESTORE system could potentially be complex both in the diverse content it needs to offer and the different ways people might wish to access this content. For the NESTORE team to collectively and conceptually understand how the system might operate to facilitate the diverse needs of users, it was decided to apply an analogue approach through the use of physical pathway cards to enable the expert by experience to map their pathways.

A set of pathway cards was co-designed with the older expert group to visually present scenarios of use based on a user's profile, their needs/requirements and activities. For instance, NESTORE would need to understand who the user is, male or female, and maybe whether the system is being used by an individual or a couple. NESTORE needs to understand the intent of the user as to whether they wish or choose to improve their health and engage in familiar activities, or whether there is recognition that a behaviour change is needed and they will need a motivational and suggestive prompt. The range of activities to support healthy life may be offered and suggested through the NESTORE system but there may be a requirement for users to pro-actively inform the system of activities linked to their interests (a two-way approach). The systems intelligence may learn user preferences in time. The pathways need to be clear to users for them to understand options and how they will easily navigate their way to achieving their goal.

Based on the example scenarios the expert by experience group were tasked with creating pathways based on their own profile, motivation, activities and interests (Fig. 11). The pathway cards helped the group systematically think through and visually map options and decision points. The expert by experience group worked in pairs in the spirit of co-design.

The pathway cards (Fig. 12) provided an important co-design tool and tangible interface to ensure NESTORE partners from different Work packages adopted a collective and coherent understanding of the complex variables presented by the NESTORE system.

Fig. 11 Expert by experience group creating pathways through real life scenarios

5.4 *Co-designing the Tangible Coach*

The NESTORE user requirements established in phase one and two of this co-design research programme were developed and translated through further co-design activity between the design research team, the older expert group and the technologists. A series of user scenarios developed by the older experts translated the user requirements into tangible systems and product concepts drawing on the data gathered from the digital probe activity set against the NESTORE user personas.

An iterative process of product design development incorporating interactive features were presented to the expert older group for feedback during as the development phase progressed. The design research team were equipped with the design and technical skills to realise tangible interpretation emerging for the co-design sessions (Fig. 13). While the design research team focused on realising the user experience aspects of the design the technologists focused on the coding, visual recognition and voice activation features. What was critical was a common understanding between the design researchers and the technologists of the underpinning technological platforms that NESTORE would be based.

The tangible coach (Fig. 14) would be one of the central physical interfaces of the NESTORE system to be tested as part of the pilot studies in the final phase four and delivery phase of the research programme.

Fig. 12 NESTORE system pathway cards

6 Discussion and Conclusion

This research study aimed to inform the design and development of NESTORE a digital platform and tangible interface which seeks to promote wellbeing through enabling the person to identify and reflect on current lifestyle choices and to access opportunities to engage in meaningful health promoting activities. In response to an ageing population and growing pressures on health services digital technologies are seen as a solution to these challenges. However, there is to date limited uptake of health technologies with literature suggesting lack of user engagement being a

Fig. 13 Co-design of NESTORE tangible coach

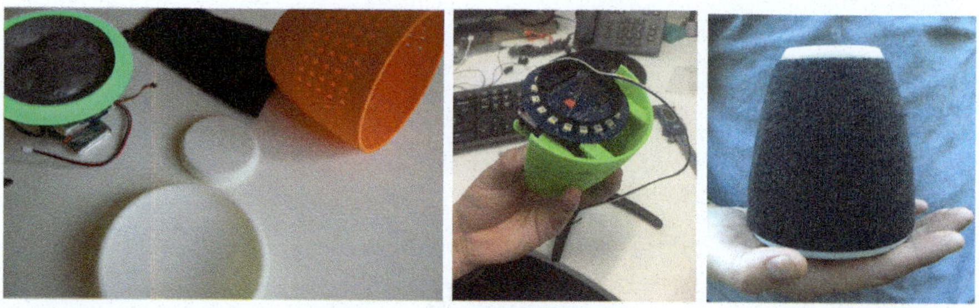

Fig. 14 Prototyping of tangible coach

significant reason for this. Whilst the literature is clear in terms of the importance of involving end users from the beginning of the design process in collective imagining, few case studies exist of ways to accomplish this. Traditional qualitative research methods using structured and semi-structured interviews can preference the views of the researcher who can make assumptions about what the issues are. This can be particularly challenging when seeking to imagine facets of products that have yet to be created. Within this study, exhibition in a box provided a tangible tool to offer participants a space to reflect, discuss, explore and begin to envision the qualities and characteristics NESTORE might need to possess. Finding ways to involve people authentically within research is important and exhibition in a box offers a useful method for engagement where researcher and participant enter a space on equal terms and individuals are literally able to think and talk through things.

To ensure commitment and buy-in from participants in co-design activities, it is important creative approaches are adopted to ensure it a positive experience for them. An important aspect of this research was the creative development of tools to support the co-design activity. Exhibition in a box, the pathway cards and the digital probe pack were central to the methodology and present transferable tools that could be applied in other co-design research contexts. Participants in this research programme shared rich descriptions of their experiences of and relationship with technology, and older people expressed appreciation of the tangibility of the objects and their sensory qualities, acting as a physical prompt. They also expressed enjoyment of the experience and reflected on their learning and the new insights they had gained through the process. This positive experience led to an expressed interest in participating in other elements of the study.

Co-design design activity can be applied to the Design Council's double diamond model at any stage of the discover, define, develop and deliver phases of the process. This research programme significantly embedded co-design that included participation from end users throughout all phases of the process. When involving multiple partners and diverse communities in research projects there are many stages of the process where knowledge and information can be lost in translation. Critical in this international research programme was the articulation and sharing of the research findings from the UK across multiple EU country partners and then interpreting their contributions. Translating the user requirements to the technologists was another critical point where contrasting disciplinary cultures could present opportunity for misunderstanding and misinterpretation. In this research study, the design research team, the older expert group and technologists provided a consistent team throughout the process while engaging older people across diverse international communities to minimise barriers to exchanging knowledge and ideas.

Designers bring a broad set of skill sets to co-design activity. Critical in this programme of research was the creative and technical understanding of the design research team who were able to facilitate the creative abstract conversations in the exploratory phase, tangibly interpret and realise conceptual ideas through the development phase and, importantly, present technically viable prototypes to the technologists. The co-design research led by the authors delivered through the NESTORE project presents co-design tools and a methodology that has been important in engaging end users that might increase the uptake and adoption of the system. The tools and methodology also provide a transferable model that can be applied in other research context to ensure end users have a voice and more likely to help shape the future health services and products that are fit for purpose.

References

1. Arnstein, S. R. (1969). A ladder of citizen participation. *Journal of the American Planning Association, 35*(4), 216–224. Retrieved June 12, 2010, from https://doi.org/10.1080/01944366908977225. hdl:11250/2444598.
2. Bentley, C., Powell, L., Orrell, A., & Mountain, G. (2014). Addressing design and suitability barriers to telecare use: Has anything changed? *Technology and Disability, 26*(4), 221–235.
3. Bhatti, A. B., & Haq, A. (2017, January 24). The pathophysiology of perceived social isolation: Effects on health and mortality. *Cureus*. https://doi.org/10.7759/cureus.994.
4. Chamberlain, P., & Craig, C. (2013). Engaging design, methods for collective creativity, human-computer interaction. In *Human-centred design approaches, methods, tools, and environments* (Vol. 8004, pp. 22–31). Lecture Notes in Computer Science.

5. Chamberlain, P., & Craig, C. (2019). *HOSPITAbLe—Critical design and the domestication of healthcare*. figshare. Journal contribution. https://doi.org/10.6084/m9.figshare.4746952.v1.
6. Chamberlain, P., & Roddis, J. (2003). Making sense. *The Design Journal, 6*(1). Ashgate Publications Ltd. England. ISBN 0-7546-0910.
7. Chamberlain, P., & Yoxall, A. (2012). Of mice and men. *The Role of Interactive Exhibitions as Research Tools for Inclusive Design, 15*(1), 57–78. Ashgate Publications.
8. DESA. (2017). *World population prospects, key findings and advance tables*. New York: United Nations.
9. EU. (2018). *The silver economy: Luxembourg*. Publications Office of the European Union.
10. Hanson, V. L. (2010). Influencing technology adoption of older adults. *Interacting with Computers, 22*, 502–509.
11. Holt-Lundstad, J., Sith, T. B., Baker, M., Harris, T., & Stephenson, D. (2015). Loneliness and social Isolation as risk factors for mortality: A meta-analytic review. *Perspectives on Psychological Science, 10*(2), 227–237.
12. Lorig, K., & Holman, H. (2004). Patient self-management: A key to effectiveness and efficiency in care of chronic diseases. *Public Health Report, 119*(3), 239–243.
13. Rajanen, (Marghescu), D. (2009). *Usability evaluation of information systems: A review of five international standards*. https://doi.org/10.1007/978-0-387-68772-8_11.
14. Rosenfield, K. (2012, January 9). Dieter Rams 10 principles of "Good Design". *ArchDaily*. Retrieved June 19, 2019 from https://www.archdaily.com/198583/dieter-rams-10-principles-of-%25e2%2580%259cgood-design%25e2%2580%259d/. ISSN 0719-8884.
15. Sligo, J., Gauld, R., Roberts, V., & Villa, L. (2017). A literature review for large-scale health information system project planning, implementation and evaluation. *International Journal of Medical Informatics, 97*, 86–97.
16. Standing, C., Standing, S., McDermott, M., Gururajan, R., & Kiani Mavi, R. (2018). The paradoxes of telehealth: A review of the literature 2000–2015. *Systems Research and Behavioural Science, 35*, 90–101.
17. Steventon, A., et al. (2012). Effect of telehealth on use of secondary care and mortality: Findings from the whole system demonstrator cluster randomised trial. *British Medical Journal*, 344.

Technology Applied to Solutions for Healthy Ageing

Monitoring in the Physical Domain to Support Active Ageing

E. Denna, M. Civiello, S. Porcelli, A. Crivello, F. Mavilia, and Filippo Palumbo

Abstract Monitoring system have been customized to collect data and to analyse several aspects of the users' life, the reason of this custom solution came from the needs to join physical activity of the user, life usage, social interaction and mind activities, all these features are not present in standard devices all together, so we arrived to a new system architecture where the monitoring system is the first front end versus the user. This chapter describes the general monitoring system architecture and provides insight into the contribution and role of sensors. Such sensing solutions are not only designed to match the needs and requirements of the user but also to reduce intrusiveness and usage complexity. By doing so the system is designed around the life of its users and maximizes the effectiveness of data collection. Example from NESTORE project are taken as reference.

1 Design Requirements and Guidelines

The monitoring system has been designed according to some precise requirements coming from different workshops that took place in different sites, with several champion users. Due to the target users characteristics, workshops led to identify some basic user needs: the monitoring system needed to be composed by not invasive devices, with a user friendly interface and easy to be used, and at the same time able to collect several data to track different activities of the user and some of his/her biometric parameters.

Keeping in mind the physical requirements and the user design requirements coming from the workshop, the monitoring system resulted to be composed by 6

E. Denna (✉) · M. Civiello
Flex Design Medical S.r.l., Via Ernesto Breda 176, 20126 Milan, Italy
e-mail: enrico.denna@flex.com

S. Porcelli
Institute of Biomedical Technologies, National Research Council, Segrate, Milan, Italy

A. Crivello · F. Mavilia · F. Palumbo
Institute of Information Science and Technologies, National Research Council, Pisa, Italy

G. Andreoni and C. Mambretti (eds.), *Digital Health Technology for Better Aging*, Research for Development, https://doi.org/10.1007/978-3-030-72663-8_4

Fig. 1 Graphic representation of Nestore wearable and environmental monitoring system

devices, each one able to satisfy one or more requirements and to always meet the user requirements:

The wristband is Bluetooth 4.2 connected with the apps in the user smartphone, while the beacons are Bluetooth 4.2 connected to the wristband itself, so all the data of these devices are transferred to the app on the smartphone, while the sleep monitor and the smart scale are Wi-Fi connected by the user router, transferring data directly to the cloud.

The monitoring system architecture is represented in the following figure (Fig. 1).

The user smartphone and tangible interface complete the set of devices used by the Nestore user and they are present in his house. User smartphone is used also to take pictures of food and beverages consumed by the user to track his/her nutrition consumption and habits. This additional operation is considered part of the monitoring system, while the tangible interface is not.

From all the variables present in the Table 1, a final group of variables will be monitored during specific test exercises the user will be asked to complete at identified moments. The required exercises are:

- 6 min walking test
- 30-s Chair Raise Test.

During these tests, several variables will be monitored to obtain precise information to be analysed and described in the table below (Table 2):

All these data are transferred to the cloud where algorithms will process and elaborate to provide lifestyle suggestions to the user.

The following figures better depict the wearable wristband and environmental monitoring system components (Figs. 2, 3, 4, 5 and 6):

Table 1 Devices of the Nestore monitoring system

Device	Physical requirements	Technical requirements	User requirement
Wearable wristband  	Continuous monitoring of variables: Steps Distance Activity recognition Sedentariness Stairs Energy expenditure Data report: Start/stop time and duration Exercise intensity Target heart rate Cardio-respiratory score Peak heart rate Post exercise heart rate recovery Activity energy expenditure Total steps Total distance Difference in altitude Data as time series: Timestamp with time zone info Steps Cadence Distance Exercise heart rate Grade	Battery level	The wearable wristband looks like a common smartwatch for fitness monitoring, so it doesn't' look like a medical device. The user interface is based on a colour LCD display with few simple and big icons and fonts, reporting essential information. The feedback to the user is given by a motor vibrator inside the wearable and user interaction is granted with a single multifunction button. The battery recharging operation is managed by a wireless charging station provided as accessory
Environmental beacons   	User activities inside his/her home	RSSI Battery level Motion detection House temperature	Devices attached in the user house that don't limit or interfere with the normal life of the user in his/her house. No user interface and feedback are present, the battery is expected to last 1 year

(continued)

Table 1 (continued)

Device	Physical requirements	Technical requirements	User requirement
Social beacons 	Social interaction activities	RSSI Battery Level	Devices provided to user friends and relatives. They look like a common keychain. No user interface and feedback are present, the battery is expected to last 1 year
Sleep monitor 	Sleep duration Sleep quality		Transparent to the user because it is attached and powered under his/her bed, so no battery recharging operation is required to the user It is Wi-Fi connected to the user router
Smart scale 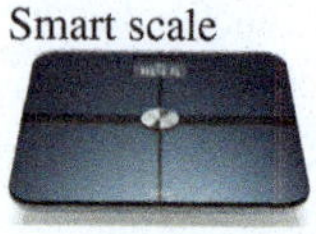	Weight Body mass	Wi-Fi and battery indicators are provided by the display of the scale	It is a commercial scale powered by commercial batteries and Wi-Fi connected to the user router

In the following paragraphs the single physical devices will be analysed from a more technical point of view.

2 Wearable Wristband Architecture Overview

The wearable is designed as a bracelet. In the present section, there is a description of its technical implementation examined according to the Industrial Design and Mechanical, Hardware and Firmware engineering structure.

The wearable has the following features (Fig. 7).

Table 2 Variables of the test exercises

Test exercise	Variables
6 min walking test	Data report: Start/stop time Peak heart rate Post exercise heart rate recovery Activity energy expenditure Total steps Total distance Difference in altitude Data as time series: Timestamp with time zone info Steps Cadence Distance Exercise heart rate Grade
30-s chair raise test	Data report: Start/stop time Peak heart rate Post exercise heart rate recovery Activity energy expenditure Total repetitions Data as time series: Timestamp with time zone info Acceleration Repetition Pressure

Fig. 2 Wearable device: to be worn daily, to monitor basic vital parameters (i.e.: Heart Rate, energy expenditure, steps count etc.) and to provide the first user interface

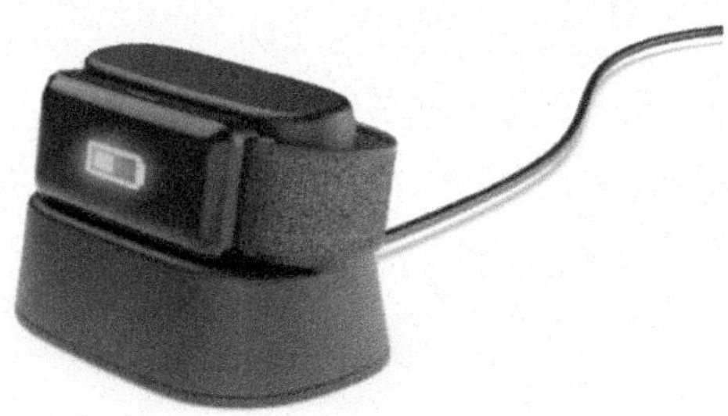

Fig. 3 Ad-hoc charging station for the wearable device: the device is suitable to wireless charge the wearable device. Design and functionalities have been realized to optimize the usage

Fig. 4 Social (black) beacons and Environmental (white) beacons: devices suitable to monitor respectively the user social interactions and the user in-house habits during daily life activities. They provide two environmental parameters: house temperature and humidity

Fig. 5 Off-the-shelf smart scale (https://www.withings.com/uk/en/body-plus): the device is able to measure not only the weight of the user, but also additional useful data such as muscle, bone and fat mass and body water. The device is Wi.FI connected directly to the Cloud

Fig.6 Off-the-shelf sleep monitoring sensor: the device can monitor the user sleep activity and quality mapping movements during the sleep. The device is Wi.FI connected directly to the Cloud (https://www.murata.com/en-eu/products/sensor/accel/sca10h_11h/sca11h)

Feature	Solution
Body position	Wrist
Sensors	Accelerometer, Barometer, PPG
Form Factor	Wrist-band
User Interface	Button, TFT display,Motor vibrator
Connectivity	BTLE
Power	Rechargeable battery

Fig.7 Wearable device features

2.1 *Industrial Design and User Interface Solution*

During the workshops conducted in the first period of the project, users expressed a clear preference for a small and discreet wristband that could be well integrated with people's lifestyles and existing accessories, with a minimal and simplified UI.

The wristband design respects the following characteristics:

- **DISCREET**. During the workshops conducted, users expressed concerns that people might label and stigmatize them when noticing them wearing a strange new device or a device that looked like medical. The wristband should, therefore, have a sober aesthetic that doesn't catch people's attention.

Designers examined some possible solutions like:

- hiding the UI when not in use, for instance by using a lens or a particular material or finish on top of the display.
- simple and approachable overall shape, not too styled or characterized.
- neutral or desaturated colours
- In alternative, disguise the wristband as something else, such as a generic bracelet or fashion/sport accessory.

Finally, a simple and linear black case was designed and ad-hoc produced, in order to seem sober and not out of the ordinary design language of the most known smart watches/wristbands actually present on the market.

- **EASY TO WEAR**. As elderly people develop dexterity problems the more they grow old, particular attention should be given to the strap design, in order to guarantee a quick and effortless operation.

Possible solutions examined were:

- prioritizing simplified locking mechanism that does not require high accuracy of movements such as Velcro or magnetic attachments.
- Potentially explore a closed-loop design that doesn't require feeding the strap through small elements etc.
- Minimize the number of steps of the overall operation.

For these purposes, an ultra-light, soft and magnetic bracelet has been chosen as the best solution.

- **EASY TO MANAGE**. From the user workshops, it was clear that elderly develop strong habits that are hard to change. The solution should adapt to their routines rather than disrupt them. Particular attention should be therefore given to the charging experience, a key aspect in the wearable usage that, if not designed well, could negatively affect the overall experience or even lead to discontinuity in usage. Cleanability is another key aspect that shall be well addressed.

The possible solutions were:

- Create a solution that feels natural and requires little to no attention from the user, such as a docking, to be positioned on the bedside that wirelessly charges the wristband overnight.
- Consider using magnetic attachments between the two elements to aid positioning and provide a quality feeling.
- Easy separation of wristband body and bands could also aid cleanability (potentially in the washing machine) which in terms will result in higher user acceptance.

For these purposes, an ad-hoc charging station was designed and produced. The station is simple and intuitive to use, and a magnetic alignment system has been inserted to avoid any mistake in the positioning of the bracelet onto the station. Thus, the user is guided, by the magnetic alignment system, to get the right position of the wearable onto the station.

Furthermore, an easy and intuitive UI has been designed, in order to adapt to what users already utilize every day with their smartphones.

- **COMFORTABLE & COMFORTING**. Many users tend to dislike wearable devices the more they grow old: during the workshops, many mentioned not even wearing classic watches because uncomfortable or having to wear one because someone dear gifted them. The solution should therefore well integrate with their lifestyle and routines, as well as be physically ergonomic and enjoyable to wear.

The possible solutions identified were:

- using softer and 'warmer' materials for the wristband body, such as textile or PU,
- having an organic and ergonomic shape that well adapts to the user's wrists.
- Particular attention shall be given to balancing the tightness of the wristband necessary to properly monitor heartbeat related variables and the comfort expected by the users.

Given the impediments identified with textile and PU wristbands (excessively thick and uncomfortable to be worn with a single hand), Flex selected a metallic wristband with a magnetic clasp that firmly stacks without any effort required to the user.

- **CUSTOMIZABLE**. Healthy elderly people are still quite active socially and give much importance to their look and public image. Moreover, as Nestore users will be of both sexes and different cultures, the wristband shall be able to adapt and be personalized based on individual tastes and needs. Being able to customize elements of the User interface could also be a highly appreciated feature that could make users feel more understood and valued as individuals.

Possible solutions:

- offering swappable bands that could be picked at the moment of purchase or offering a few variants as main to allow choice based on the occasion or need. This approach will also simplify maintenance and be expandable for future updates.
- allowing, through the smartphone APP, to customize the wearable UI both visually as well as in terms of haptic/sound feedbacks.

For these purposes, Flex selected a standard size (20 mm) for the wristband alignment to the wearable case. The users are free to change their wristbands with every off-the-shelf wristband that respect that standard measure.

- **SIMPLE & EMOTIONAL UI**. During the workshops, most users expressed preferences for a coach with a friendly and supportive personality, someone that understands them and motivate them with positive messages rather than stressing their misbehaviours and leverage on a sense of guilt. Moreover, users were not particularly fond on receiving complex information on the wristband (whose small form factor also would pose serious problems on the readability of the messages due to the natural decay of eyesight). The User interface shall, therefore, be simplified displaying less information in a clear way and adopt a more emotional tone of voice that could be perceived as more motivating and natural by non-technical users.

The possible solutions identified were:

- prioritize simple human language over technical stats
- leverage on haptic feedbacks to communicate simple messages through different patterns without having to look at the device.
- Communicate activities progress in a visual way through progress bars or circles or even colours.
- Utilize icons and visuals to provide context to the messages.
- Minimize user interactions avoiding the need to press buttons to trigger activities.

For these purposes Flex identified the usage of a vibramotor as both helpful and discreet. It lets the user receiving feedbacks without requiring any user active interaction.

2.2 Technology Selection

The data collection solution involves a selection of the suitable technology for the Nestore application. There are several sensors to be selected for the scope according the available alternatives.

Starting from the wristband device, the proper technology to be used for heart rate monitoring is the Photoplethysmography (PPG) that is an uncomplicated and inexpensive optical measurement method. PPG is a non-invasive technology that uses a light source and a photodetector at the surface of skin to measure the volumetric variations of blood circulation. A more precise method is the ECG monitoring based on electrical pulse sensor, but this system is more used in medical application and even if it is possible to reduce the number of the electrodes, the user should attach the electrodes to his skin by some wires, resulting in an uncomfortable solution.

The physical movements of the user including step and climb are normally obtained by a combination of accelerometer and precise barometer that combine movement and ligth air pressure difference. The feature in the technology is mainly given by the algorithms used that shall consider and filter false movements and increase the precision of the measure. Some of these algorithms, like fall detection, step count and climbing measurement shall be calibrated and personalized around the hardware designed. Of course, also the Nestore algorithm of the device have been tuned to obtain the desired accuracy.

The other functionalities of wristband are implemented with standard technologies for wireless connection and user interface: Bluetooth communication, vibramotor, colour LCD and wireless charger.

The technologies used for beacon is mainly related to the proximity sensing, used either for the social than for the environmental. There are several options for proximity detection from optical solution, microwave, ultrasound or magnetic sensors. Due to the Bluetooth connection already implemented in the wristband, Nestore leverages on the RSSI of the Bluetooth protocol to detect the proximity between the beacon and the wristband.

Sleep monitoring and Smart scale are commercial solutions selected for Nestore according the requirements of not invasiveness.

In the following chapters a detailed technical description of the device implementations will be presented.

2.3 Wristband Mechanical Description

This section describes the mechanical implementation of the wearable wristband device and his accessories.

Mechanical dimensions have been chosen in order to design and produce a case with a display and one button to get the simplest user interface, to respect the user requirements expressed during the Workshop user study. The charging base is designed with Renesas proprietary low power wireless technology, to meet miniaturizing and power budget efficiency needs. Renesas uses circa 100 mW instead of 5 W consumed by a standard C or WMA protocols.

The bracelet consists of a rigid part containing and protecting the electronics components and a soft and adjustable bracelet for maximum wearability comfort guaranteeing the correct positioning and therefore the correct functioning of the PPG sensor.

Compatibly with the mandatory electronics components, Flex designed and produced the smallest and most comfortable dimensions possible. The PPG sensor protrudes of 1.5 mm, to guarantee the correct positioning and functioning (Fig. 8).

The bracelet case is made of biocompatible plastic materials (polycarbonate) and was produced with injection moulding technology.

Injection moulding is an industrial production process in which a plastic material is melted and injected under high pressure into a closed mould, which is opened after solidification of the manufactured article. Usually injection moulding is a suitable process for a high volume of production; nevertheless, in this case, with a limited production quantity, was selected because it ensures high quality of the parts in respect to other technical solutions (e.g.: 3D printing).

Concerning the rigid part of the bracelet: since the PPG sensor needs to be glued on the plastic case, Flex chose a polycarbonate material to guarantee the tightness between the two parts. This choice was supported, furthermore, by the good mechanical properties of the polycarbonate.

The wristband is metallic with a magnetic clasp and it was chosen to ensure the best comfortability and wearability easiness (Fig. 9).

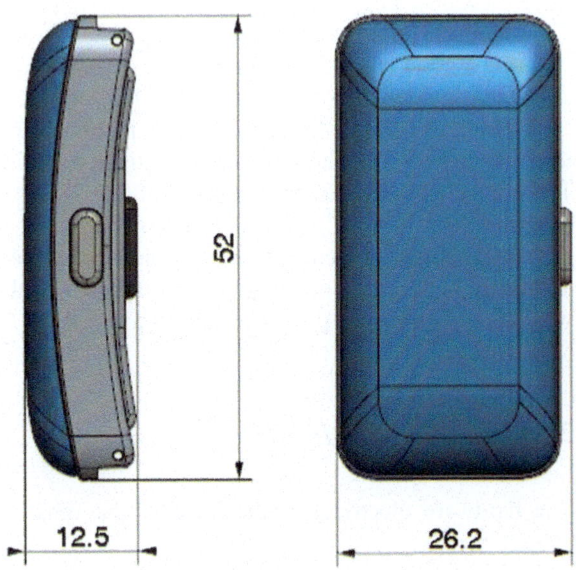

Fig. 8 Wearable case CAD file view

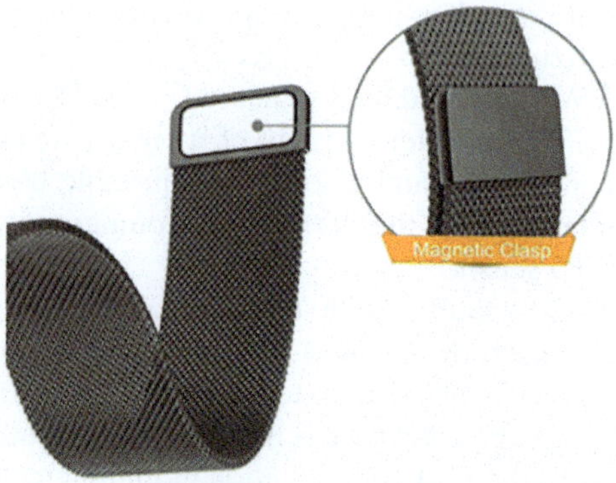

Fig. 9 Metallic bracelet clasp detail

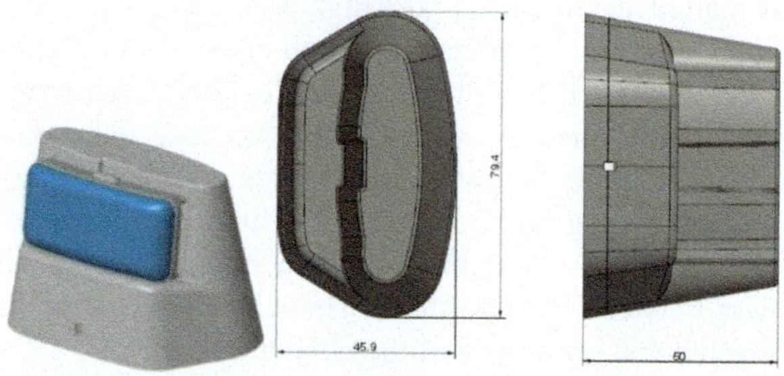

Fig. 10 Charging station CAD files view

2.4 *Mechanical Drawing for Charging Station*

The approach for the construction of the loader was to keep small dimensions and ensuring a good solidity to keep the charger and device during charging in position and avoid accidental drops. The charger has a micro USB interface (Fig. 10).

As gathered during the requirements identification phase, the mechanical team, in collaboration with the ID team, investigated the idea of an error-proof interface. The main goal was to identify a solution that avoids misplacing the device onto the station.

A magnetic alignment system was inserted in both the case and the station. The alignment between the magnets guides the user to place the wearable in the correct way, thus ensuring the proper recharging.

2.5 *Hardware Solution*

The hardware electrical architecture of the wristband is described in the block diagram below:

To monitor all the required variables, the electronics is equipped with three sensors:

- A Valencell module (Benchmark wrist 1.2) implementing the Heart Rate and PPG function
- A 3-axis accelerometer (LIS3DH—ST) suitable for step count, distance and exercise detection
- A barometer (ICP-10100—TDK) providing useful information for floor climbing and exercise, combined with accelerometer information.
  The user interface is composed of two main elements:
- A colour TFT display that is used for an easy user interface, and can also be versatile and upgradable to provide even more complex information too, if required in the future
- A vibro-motor, common in all wearable devices and smartphones or smartwatches that can provide haptic feedbacks (Fig. 11).

- One mechanical button that can be used for power on–off and for general interactions

The communication with the router and with the other smart accessories is done by a customized BTLE interface with an integrated antenna. All the logic functions are managed by a microprocessor CC2640R2F of Texas Instrument that leverages on a Serial NAND to store and buffer the data to be transmitted via BTLE.

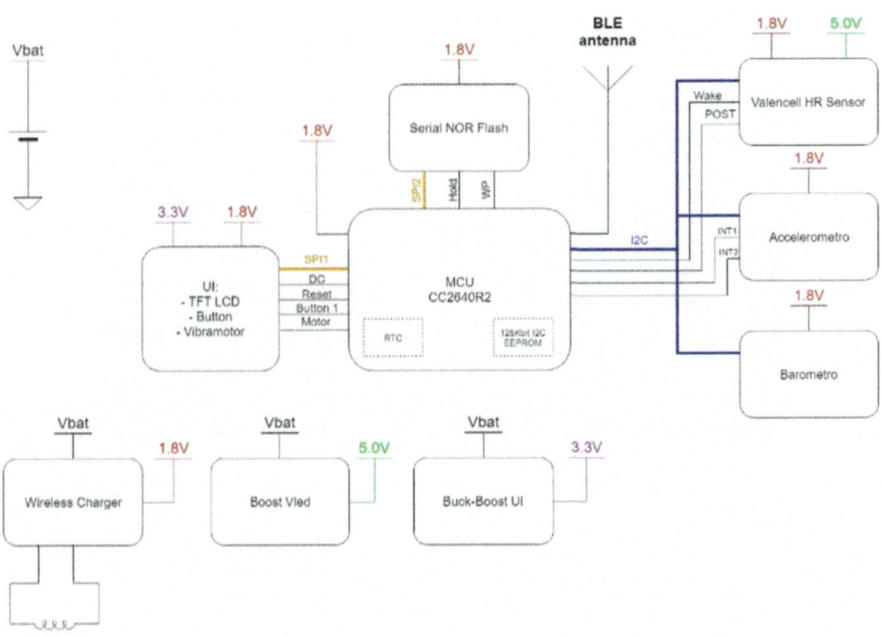

Fig. 11 Block diagram of wearable electrical architecture

The wristband is powered by a rechargeable battery of Li+ polymer in the order 95mAh. The recharging operation is realized with a couple of TX-RX device of Renesas where the TX is inside an external docking station powered by a standard wall adapter with micro-USB connector, typical for mobile applications and easy to use.

The battery duration esteem is based on the Nestore user scenario. It has been necessary to make some assumptions about the time the users might spend in performing usual daily activities. The table below summarizes the number of hours daily spent for different purposes (Fig. 12)

The following graph describes the power budget computation based on the composition estimation of the power consumption. The actual battery duration is around 1 day of usage, around 20 h, depending on the utilization (Figs. 13 and 14).

Day time division	Hours
Sleep hours	7 h
Physical Activity hours	2 h
Wake-up hours	15 h

Fig. 12 Use case scenario for a standard daily utilization of the wearable device

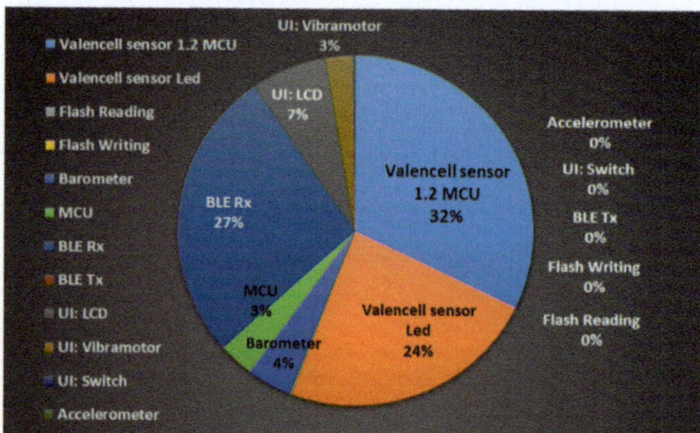

Fig. 13 Graphical representations of components percentage power consumption distribution

		Worst case	Best case	Actual status
Heart rate sensor		Always on during the day; disabled during sleep time	Always on during the physical activity. During the other hours of the day: 30 seconds on and 30 seconds off; when the device is not worn or in charge	1 minute on and 2 minutes off during the utilization. Disabled when the device is not worn or in charge
Flash	Writing	Writing any 265 bytes of data, corresponding to 0.5ms any 5 seconds	Writing any 265 bytes of data, corresponding to 0.5ms any 5 seconds	Range considered: from 6 to 9 times a day. Disabled when the device is not worn or in charge
	Reading	3times per day during synchronization; total read byte 3.1 Mbyte, esteem reading time: 6 seconds	3 times per day during synchronization; total read byte 3.1 Mbyte, esteem reading time: 6 seconds	Range considered: from 6 to 9 times a day. Disabled when the device is not worn or in charge
Barometer		Always on during the day; disabled when the device is not worn or in charge	Always on during the day; disabled when the device is not worn or in charge	Always on when the device is worn. Disabled when the device is not worn or in charge
MCU		Normally in sleep mode, it wakesup to Collect, store, process transmit sensor data and visualize information on the screen	Normally in sleep mode, it wakesup to Collect, store, process transmit sensor data and visualize information on the screen	Normally in sleep mode, it wakesup to Collect, store, process transmit sensor data and visualize information on the screen
BLE	TX	3 times per day to transmit data from flash memory during synchronization	3 times per day to transmit data from flash memory during synchronization	The range actually considered: from 6 to 9 times a day. Disabled when the device is not worn or in charge
	RX	400 ms any 2 seconds to receive data from beacons	220 ms any 3 seconds to receive data from beacons	330 ms for each BLE transmission channel (3 in total) every 3 seconds. Total: 990ms
UI	LCD	Overall 10 minutes on per day	Overall 10 minutes on per day	Overall 10 minutes on per day
	Vibro-motor	Overall 1 minute on per day	Overall 1 minute on per day	Overall 1 minute on per day
	Switch	Overall 2 minutes on per day	Overall 2 minutes on per day	Overall 2 minutes on per day

Fig. 14 Power consumption analysis

2.6 *Charging Station*

Here following the block diagram of the charging station used to wirelessly recharge the wearable device (Fig. 15).

All the hardware architecture is based on Renesas TX board working on 175 kHz power less than 1 W and an off-the-shelf coil to couple with the RX. A LED is present

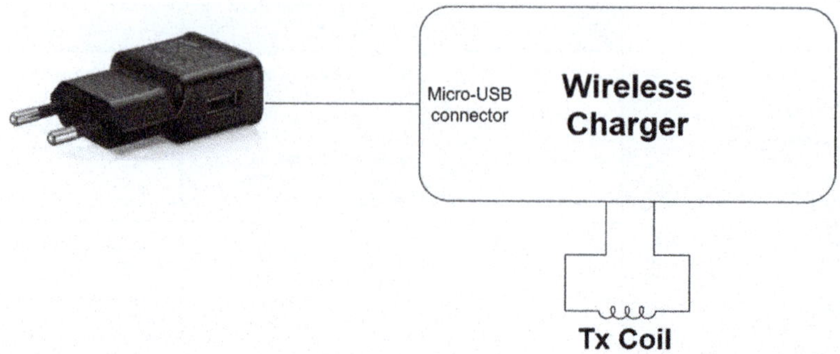

Fig. 15 Charging station block diagram

to indicate the charger activity. The connection to the main power is realized by a standard wall-plug adapter with a standard USB cable with micro connector.

3 Environmental Sensors for Physical Activity

The NESTORE environmental monitoring system is an ensemble of wireless sensors able to sense the variables indicated by the domain experts. Furthermore, it has the aim of detecting the interaction of the user with his circle of friends and caregivers and the environment itself, while monitoring the status of the environment, in terms of indoor thermal comfort. For this reasons, we call *environmental* device any sensor deployed in the user's vital space, while *wearable* the wristband worn by the user during his daily activities.

In order to build the integrated NESTORE environmental monitoring system, we first performed a technology selection to satisfy not only the requirements coming from the domain experts related to the user profile (to cover as much variables as possible), but also the ones coming from the co-design activities in terms of unobtrusiveness. The integrated system should be unobtrusive under diverse perspectives: (R1) user interaction—the user should not wear additional sensors or explicitly interact with the environmental device; (R2) number of device—the user's living environment should not be filled with lot of visible devices; (R3) installation and maintenance—it should be easy to deploy and maintain the device without additional effort from the user.

We focus now on the environmental technologies used to cover the variable indicated by the medical experts of NESTORE, in terms of: sleep monitoring [1, 2], weight monitoring [3], indoor user's behaviour and environmental status monitoring [4–6], and social interaction detection [7–9].

Figure 16 shows the ensemble of devices and technologies chosen to build the NESTORE environmental monitoring system.

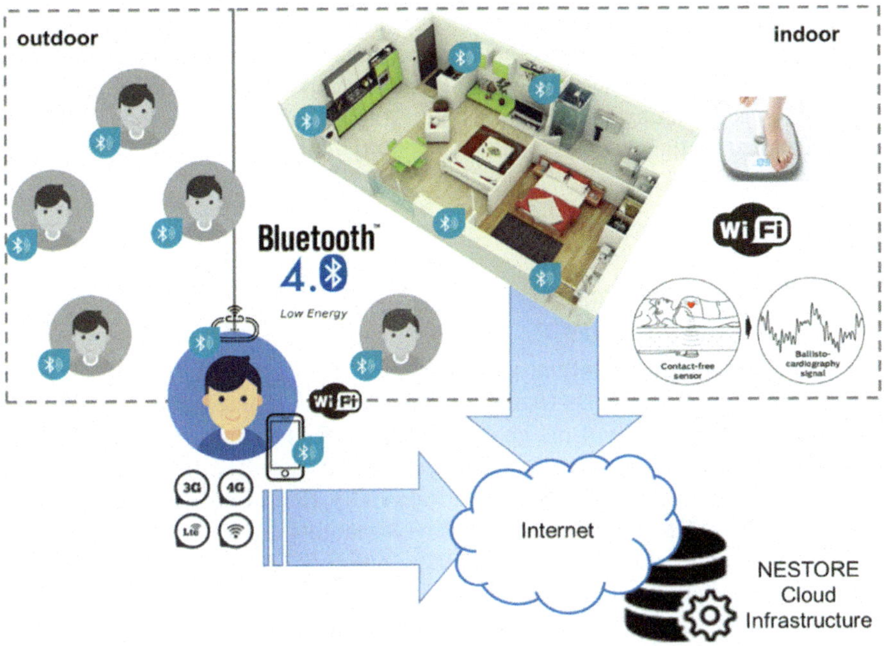

Fig. 16 The technologies used in the NESTORE environmental monitoring system

3.1 BLE Beacons

The Bluetooth Low Energy (BLE) beacons are emitters that periodically send beacons (called advertisements in BLE) with a specific rate and power. They are received by other BLE devices located nearby (e.g., the NESTORE wristband). When the receiver hears a beacon, it estimates the Received Signal Strength Indicator (RSSI), a value expressed in a decibel scale (dbm), which can be related to the distance of the receiver from the transmitter.

The set of NESTORE devices based on BLE connectivity is composed by the wristband, a charging station, and five social and five environmental beacons. The choice of BLE allows us to provide different kind of services to the user with the same devices (i.e., social interaction detection, indoor behavioural index, and indoor thermal comfort) using the inherent capabilities offered by this technology. We exploit the characteristics of the BLE technology in terms of type of customizable BLE messages (the BLE devices embed different sensors like accelerometers, humidity and temperature sensors, which information is transmitted in the advertisement's payload) and possibility to infer proximity using the Received Signal Strength of the received BLE advertisements.

Besides the social interaction and indoor thermal comfort detection, in the physical activity domain, we use BLE beacons for unsupervised user habits detection. By monitoring the activation of the sensors embedded in the BLE beacons, indicating the opening/closing of doors and room occupation of the user during his time spent at home, it is possible to retrieve heterogeneous and multivariate time-series over long periods. These time-series are used to learn recurrent behaviours of the user in her/his daily activities by analysing the time variations of several parameters like the room occupied by the user and qualitative activity level. More details can be found in [10].

3.2 *Ballistocardiography*

Despite being used commonly in sleep medicine, the term "sleep quality" has not been rigorously defined [11]. Usually it refers to well defined questions in dedicated questionnaires. One of the goals of NESTORE is to find a measurable sleep quality index starting from sleep related physiological characteristics. The main variables influencing sleep quality are Heart Rate (HR), Heart Rate Variability (HRV), Respiratory Rate (RR), and Respiratory Rate Variability (RRV).

From a technological point of view, there are very few ways to monitor sleep quality, among them we find polysomnography (PSG), actigraphy [2], and ballistocardiography (BCG). Being one of the main requirements of the NESTORE system its unobtrusiveness, we easily chose BCG as best candidate.

Ballistocardiography is a method for the measurement of the mechanical forces originated from the body [12]. This phenomenon was first studied in 1877 by Gordon and further investigated through the 1900s century. However, BCG was not accurate enough for medical use until recent improvements in the signal processing methods. The new ways to assess BCG signal have produced reliable results when compared with the traditional ECG measurements [13].

The rationale behind the performed sensor selection is the possibility to collect data without an explicit interaction of the user with 3rd party applications or the device itself. For this reasons, among the possible BCG solutions available on the market, we have chosen a device able to transmit data over WiFI (in order to not have a dedicate application on the user's smartphone) and that allows us to gather data with available open API. The cost has also been kept in mind. We also performed a preliminary study about their usability and performance. From the usability point of view, we considered how the device is installed, if the user has to manually start and stop the data collection and how he can view his own data. These considerations lead to the choice of the Murata SCA11H (https://www.murata.com/en-eu/products/sensor/accel/sca10h_11h/sca11h) sensor, also because it allows to design our own user interface to be integrated in the NESTORE dashboard. Also the performance analysis confirmed the Murata SCA11H as the best candidate, being the sensor that instead of providing an already aggregated and usually unreliable information about user's sleep quality it collect a more rich set of raw data, like HR, HRV, RR, and RRV.

3.3 *Smart Scale*

In order to collect information about the user's body composition, we integrated in the NESTORE system a smart scale able to detect the variables indicated by the domain experts (e.g., weight, percentage of fat mass, percentage of muscle mass, percentage of water, percentage of bone mass). All of the considered devices uses Bioelectrical Impedance Analysis (BIA) to calculate the body composition [14]. BIA actually determines the electrical impedance, or opposition to the flow of an electric current through body tissues which can then be used to estimate total body water (TBW), which can be used to estimate fat-free body mass and, by difference with body weight, body fat.

For the selection of the best candidate smart scale solution we considered the easiness of installation and use (no need to manually synchronize a mobile app and the device after a weighing), but also the availability of APIs to gather the collected data. For these reasons, we choose Withings Body+. It has been chosen on the basis of the availability of open APIs provided by the Withings development community. It comes with a full specification and documentation available on a dedicated website: https://developer.withings.com/oauth2/.

4 Firmware Solution

The wearable device is an embedded system that must have real-time performances and execute a lot of different tasks:

- It acquires data from different sensors, manages their data and stores them in a dedicated flash memory
- It executes different integrated algorithms to compute elaborated data starting from the sensor raw data
- It manages the Bluetooth Low Energy connections
- It manages the receiving of advertising messages of beacons devices
- It manages the bi-directional communication with the smartphone for data exchange
- It provides the user with feedback using a display and a motor-vibrator
- It responds to the user input (button pressing).

Generally, the best firmware solution for embedded devices that require pre-emption consists of using a RTOS (Real-Time Operating System). This approach permits to write an application characterized by different tasks clearly defined and prioritized. The tasks division and prioritization can greatly enhance the system's real-time performance, the modularity and portability of the code. Furthermore, many RTOS generally have some middleware stacks already implemented and the RTOS approach is often suggested when the system needs to integrate a Bluetooth Low Energy protocol for optimizing all operations.

Therefore, the design of an RTOS based firmware solution resulted appropriate for the Nestore wearable device development.

The FW application of the wearable device is divided into different tasks by functionality:

- Sensors task: It manages the peripherals on which the sensors are connected, the sensors initialization, the sensor reading procedure and the communication termination. Furthermore, it manages the algorithms that elaborate raw data coming from the sensors and orchestrates the general configuration, operation and power management of the system
- Flash task: It manages the data storing in the embedded non-volatile memory
- Bluetooth task: It manages the Bluetooth Low Energy communication
- User Interface task: It manages the feedback to the user driving the motor-vibrator and the display.

The wearable device covers two different Bluetooth roles to communicate with beacons and with the user smartphone.

4.1 For the Beacons

The wearable shall be a "BLE-observer", while the beacons shall act as "BLE-broadcaster":

the beacons advertise their specific data in broadcast permitting to every BLE device in scanning mode in the near area to receive their advertisement messages. The wearable going in receiving status scans for these advertising messages catching the beacons information without establishing a connection with them.

4.2 For the Smartphone

The wearable shall be a "BLE-peripheral", while the smartphone shall act as "BLE-central": the wearable advertises its presence like the beacons. When receiving the advertisement, the smartphone sends a scan request to the wearable. The wearable responds with a scan response.

This process is called "device discovery": the smartphone and the wearable start sharing a bi-directional connection. When the connection is established, the wearable functions as a slave exposing its services and characteristics to the user smartphone.

4.3 Data Management

Data collected by the wearable come both from its embedded sensors and from the beacons.

These data are elaborated and buffered by the sensor manager and then stored in the flash memory. The elaborated data can also be sent by the sensor manager to the UI task to give feedback to the user using vibration patterns and/or displaying texts and images on the screen (Figs. 17 and 18).

The data are read from the flash memory by the flash manager and sent through BLE to the user smartphone.

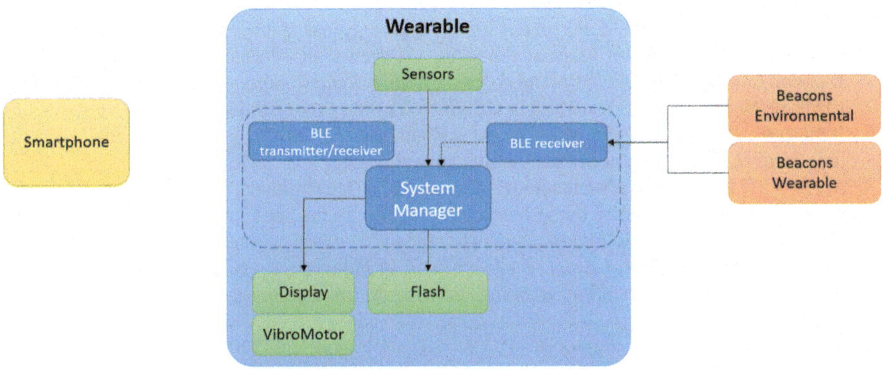

Fig. 17 Schematic of the wearable data collection process

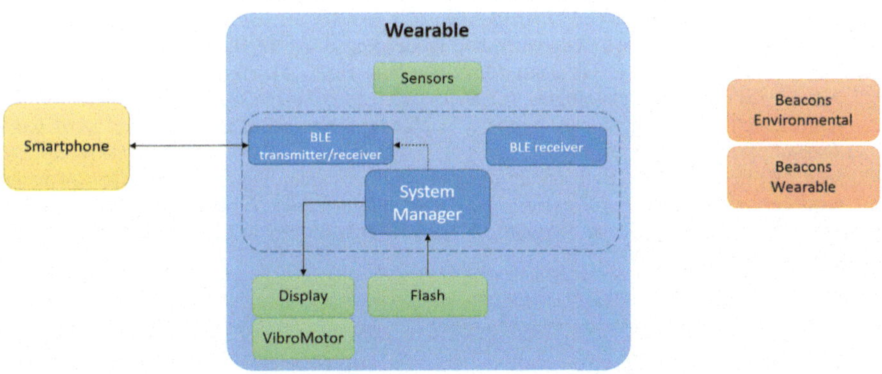

Fig. 18 Schematic of the wearable data transmission process

References

1. Crivello A., Palumbo, F., Barsocchi, P., La Rosa, D., Scarselli, F., & Bianchini, M. (2019). Understanding human sleep behaviour by machine learning. In *Cognitive infocommunications, theory and applications* (pp. 227–252). Springer.
2. Alfeo, A. L., Barsocchi, P., Cimino, M. G., La Rosa, D., Palumbo, F., & Vaglini, G. (2018). Sleep behavior assessment via smartwatch and stigmergic receptive fields. *Personal and Ubiquitous Computing, 22*(2), 227–243.
3. Bacciu, D., Chessa, S., Gallicchio, C., Micheli, A., Pedrelli, L., Ferro, E., et al. (2017). A learning system for automatic berg balance scale score estimation. *Engineering Applications of Artificial Intelligence, 66,* 60–74.
4. Barsocchi, P., Crivello, A., Girolami, M., Mavilia, F., & Palumbo, F. (2017). Occupancy detection by multi-power bluetooth low energy beaconing. In *2017 International Conference on Indoor Positioning and Indoor Navigation (IPIN)* (pp. 1–6). IEEE.
5. Palumbo, F., La Rosa, D., & Ferro, E. (2016). Stigmergy-based long-term monitoring of indoor users mobility in ambient assisted living environments: the doremi project approach. In S. Bandini, G. Cortellessa, & F. Palumbo (Eds.), *Artificial intelligence for ambient assisted living (AI*AAL.it)* (pp. 18–32). No. 1803 in CEUR Workshop Proceedings—AI*IA Series, Aachen.
6. Barsocchi, P., Crivello, A., Mavilia, F., & Palumbo, F. (2017). Energy and environmental long-term monitoring system for inhabitants' well-being.
7. Mavilia, F., Palumbo, F., Barsocchi, P., Chessa, S., & Girolami, M. (2019). Remote detection of indoor human proximity using bluetooth low energy beacons. In *2019 15th International Conference on Intelligent Environments (IE)* (pp. 1–6). IEEE.
8. Baronti, P., Barsocchi, P., Chessa, S., Mavilia, F., & Palumbo, F. (2018). Indoor bluetooth low energy dataset for localization, tracking, occupancy, and social interaction. *Sensors, 18*(12), 4462.
9. Crivello, A., Mavilia, F., Barsocchi, P., Ferro, E., & Palumbo, F. (2018). Detecting occupancy and social interaction via energy and environmental monitoring. *International Journal of Sensor Networks, 27*(1), 61–69.
10. Palumbo, F., Baronti, P., Crivello, A., Furfari, F., Girolami, M., Mavilia, F., et al. (2019). Exploiting BLE beacons capabilities in the NESTORE monitoring system. In S. Bandini, G. Cortellessa, & F. Palumbo (Eds.), *Artificial intelligence for ambient assisted living (AI*AAL.it)* (pp. 66–84). No. 2559 in CEUR Workshop Proceedings—AI*IA Series, Aachen.
11. Crivello, A., Barsocchi, P., Girolami, M., & Palumbo, F. (2019). The meaning of sleep quality: A survey of available technologies. *IEEE Access, 7,* 167374–167390.
12. Pollock, P. (1957). Ballistocardiography: A clinical review. *Canadian Medical Association Journal, 76.*
13. Inan, O., et al. (2015). Ballistocardiography and seismocardiography: A review of recent advances. *IEEE Journal of Biomedical and Health Informatics, 19*(4), 1414–1427.
14. Schmidt, A., Döring, T., & Sylveste, A. (2011). Innovations in Ubicomp Products. *IEEE Pervasive Computing, 10*(4), 6.

Nutritional Monitoring in Older People Prevention Services

Bhalaji Nagarajan, Rupali Khatun, Marc Bolaños, Eduardo Aguilar, Leonardo Angelini, Mira El Kamali, Elena Mugellini, Omar Abou Khaled, Noemi Boqué, Lucia Tarro, and Petia Radeva

Abstract Nutritional monitoring is an important aspect of providing a healthy lifestyle and smarter food consumption. Food recognition is a key task in nutrition monitoring applications especially of interest for older people suffering from malnutrition and unhealthy eating. In order to ease the problem of food intake monitoring, recent health apps involve Artificial Intelligence algorithms for food image analysis. Food recognition is a highly challenging task as the dishes could be composed of mixed types, it could have a lower inter-class variance and also the number of dishes to be recognized is quite higher. In this chapter, we present an in-depth analysis and insights into the development of a nutritional monitoring system that would act as a Key Performance Indicator for the older people food intake monitoring. This system is aimed at providing a convenient food logging environment that would assist older people and their relatives as well as geriatrists in monitoring and maintaining the healthy daily dietary nutritional needs.

Keywords Intake monitoring · Food recognition · Nutrition analysis

---

B. Nagarajan (✉) · R. Khatun · M. Bolaños · E. Aguilar · P. Radeva
Departament de Matemàtiques i Informàtica, Universitat de Barcelona, Gran via de les Corts Catalanes 585, 08007 Barcelona, Spain
e-mail: bhalaji.nagarajan@ub.edu

E. Aguilar
Departamento de Ingeniería de Sistemas y Computación, Universidad Catolica del Norte, Antofagasta, Chile

L. Angelini · M. El Kamali · E. Mugellini · O. A. Khaled
HumanTech Institute, University of Applied Sciences Western Switzerland, Delémont, Switzerland

N. Boqué · L. Tarro
Unitat de Nutriciò Salut, Eurecat, Centre Tecnològic de Catalunya, Reus, Spain

L. Tarro
Functional Nutrition, Oxidation, and Cardiovasular Diseases Group (NFOC-Salut), Facultat de Medicina i Ciències de la Salut, Universitat Rovira i Virgili, Reus, Spain

P. Radeva
Computer Vision Center, Cerdanyola (Barcelona), Spain

G. Andreoni and C. Mambretti (eds.), *Digital Health Technology for Better Aging*, Research for Development, https://doi.org/10.1007/978-3-030-72663-8_5

1 Introduction

'Population-aging', the increasing median age of a population, is expected to be one of the major social transformations of the twenty-first century. The impact of population-aging is increased elderly representation in the overall age structure of a country or a region [84]. As per the World Population Prospects of 2019 [24], the percentage of people over 65 will increase from 9% in 2019 to 16% in 2050 and the number of people aged over 80 is projected to rise from 143 million in 2019 to 426 million in 2050. This shift in aging has become a point of consideration in the attitudes, policies and practices of the government bodies from the start of the decade [96]. Longer lifespan can be attributed towards the improvements in health care, greater social support and more social contacts [52]. However, this does not always relate to better individual health than the previous generations.

Majority of people in this group show lack of good health and this trend can be largely associated with increase in chronic physical illness such as diabetes, hypertension and cardiovascular problems [21]. Most of the elderly suffer from more than one health condition. People with multiple chronic conditions are at a higher risk of fluctuations in the daily functioning [46]. 'Happy aging' is an approach to examine the physical and psychological factors such a way to offer well-defined diagnostic approaches to the aged. Following this paradigm, the current healthcare systems are designed such a way that they allow affordable access to services and introduce clinical focus of care for the older people [74]. Ambient Intelligence—the integration of several assistive technologies such as smart-phone applications, wearable devices and sensors, helps in monitoring the person's well-being remotely [6]. Healthcare systems range from collecting vital signs, monitoring food habits, analyzing behavioural patterns such as sleep habits, and so on.

The NESTORE project [8] is a personalized coaching system for the elderly, aimed at providing better everyday practices and activities. The well-being is maintained in four major domains: physical activity, nutrition, mental well-being and social life. Nutritional patterns play an important role in managing the well-being of an individual. Change of food patterns lead to nutrient losses which affects the health directly. Deficient eating habits introduce serious health issues in elders, in addition to higher rate of mortality [68]. In recent times, there has been considerable research, focused at precisely monitoring the nutritional patterns of aged. Daily eating habits are recorded and are analyzed for various patterns so as to keep the food intake at recommended levels. Food intake monitoring helps the professionals to gather essential information such as the number of vitamins, minerals and other substances that were taken by the person, which in turn allows them to detect nutritional problems.

The traditional approach to monitor the food intake is by maintaining a food journal. The users write down the food items every time they consume their food [20]. Paper-based food diaries are often troublesome to carry and the user tends to feel embarrassed in a social settings [33, 34]. There is a need for self-motivation for regular recording and owing to the difficulty many users tend to fall off from recording [80]. Also for better analysis, long term intake records are very important.

However, with tedious recording process, the users provide no information or partial information for certain logs [87]. It is very difficult to obtain meaningful insights with long food journals. The other challenge is to record the nutritional composition in these journals, which is close to impossible for most of the cases. These difficulties were addressed using 3-Day Food Diaries and Food Frequency Questionnaires (FFQ) [27, 51, 71]. FFQs were helpful that they required the users to answer specific details [79]. They are helpful in understanding various food patterns for a shorter duration. However, they are still tedious in the long term and the same issues with paper-based journals were recurring.

The turn of the millennium offered several advancements in the technology front, the most noteworthy one is the growth of mobile devices. The devices tend to become smarter and one of the highly impacted area is the mobile health [70]. With more and more smarter and self-tracking devices, user behaviour tracking, such as activity monitoring, sleep pattern analysis and nutrition monitoring became more and more easier [25, 85]. Several smartphone-based health apps have been available in the market such as MyFitnessPal,[1] LoseIt[2] and Fooducate[3] [13]. These apps allowed the users to search for the food information against a food database and along with the portion sizes, the apps would provide the nutrient information. Even though these smartphone-based apps eased the paper based process, still it was laborious to enter the details and compute the daily goals [29]. These apps still possessed other issues such as inaccurate portion size estimates, wrong entries and not finding food items from the existing food database. These constraints stop the users from continuously using the apps. By 2014, it was estimated that only 3% of 190,000 downloads of a food-journal app resulted in a person using it for more than one week [32].

The more recent health apps started using photo-based journals [19]. The new generation health apps allow the users to capture the food images and provide quantitative and qualitative assessment of the food intake. Several challenges still exist with continuous and automated food journal systems. User fatigue, inaccurate food databases, custom meal entries, mood and sensory input of the users are some of the common issues that any food journal faces [102]. With the evolution of deep learning and its success in image recognition tasks [5], food logging is taking greater strides in offering ease of use services to the users. In today's scientific community, food Computing as a research problem has gained a lot of research significance [64]. Automated food recognition is vital to any food journal because it is able to tackle the above listed challenges. The user is able to snap a picture and get the nutrition information automatically registered. However, food image recognition is a very complex computer vision task, due to the nature of images [98]. Food images are often mixed or composed of many items in a single platter, and also they have high intra-class variance and low inter-class variance. Although, these challenges exist in food images, new advancements in the deep learning paradigm allow the underlying algorithms to get over them.

---

[1] https://www.myfitnesspal.com/.

[2] https://www.loseit.com/.

[3] https://www.fooducate.com/.

As more and more health apps come to the market, the need to have faster and more convenient solutions are in demand. With this trend and need for better food recognition services, we present LogMeal,[4] a deep learning based food image recognition system, that is available as an API service for different front-end applications such as mobile devices and web applications. Various deep learning models are trained for different food recognition tasks at different levels of complexity and the models are available for inferencing at the back-end server. We also provide information regarding the dataset that was collected to train the models. LogMeal offers the nutritional services in the NESTORE platform. The users of NESTORE record various aspects of their daily activities and for nutritional monitoring, they take pictures of the food during each intake and the LogMeal APIs are used to detect the food class and offer the standard nutritional information to the user. LogMeal works across different cuisines and is able to detect close to 850 dishes. The images were all crawled from public web search results and were carefully annotated for different tasks. In this chapter, we present an overview of the LogMeal system and its integration with the NESTORE platform. We also present the validation schemes used to analyse the model performance. The rest of this chapter is organized as follows. We present the related works in Sect. 2. We discuss the system architecture in Sect. 3 and the details of the dataset in Sect. 4. We show the system validation in Sect. 5, followed by conclusions in the last section.

2 Related Works

In this section, we present the most recent relevant literature related to the nutrition monitoring systems. We also show the latest research in the field of food recognition, which is the core to several of those food monitoring systems.

2.1 Nutrition Monitoring Systems

Nutrition monitoring is done by systematically collecting information of various factors that affect the daily food composition. It is aimed at providing a balanced lifestyle overcoming both undernourishment and overeating. The recent nutrition monitoring applications rely on one or a combination of the three methods [7].

(1) Image-based, (2) Eating Action Unit-based [10, 88, 95] and (3) Biochemical methods [53, 73]. With the increased flooding of images shared on social media and different cooking inspired web sites such as Yummly[5] and Allrecipes,[6] it has been possible to gather a wide variety of food images. This fact coupled with the success

[4]http://logmeal.es/.

[5]https://www.yummly.com/.

[6]https://www.allrecipes.com/.

of deep neural networks, has made it possible for automated food recognition in the food monitoring applications. Android-based food recognition has been a widely accepted solution, which works a health awareness indicator showing the nutritional contents and having daily goals [72]. These apps combine various data analytics strategies and often are used as a tracking system that is also remotely monitored by medical institutions to adjust the intake in accordance with various heath conditions [67].

The common tasks in any food monitoring application are: (1) Food recognition, (2) Ingredient analysis and (3) Volume estimation. Equally important to food recognition is the ingredient analysis. This offers a different set of challenges such as invisible ingredients, the ingredients are often transformed during cooking and the uneven distribution of each ingredient in various dishes [55]. The common approach is to use the cooking instructions to detect the ingredients using a deep network [81]. Recent studies are devoted in understanding the relationship between the food classes and ingredients and exploit this mutual information to estimate nutritional facts [14, 65]. Volume estimation is even more complex since it has to rely on single view settings to recognize the amount of contents in the image [61]. Using fixed size reference objects [26] helps to estimate the volumes, but it is still a difficult task in real-world scenario. Another common approach is to rely on multi-view reconstruction techniques [22, 104]. The recent depth sensing smartphones also help in estimating the volume of food intake [36], but it is not a prevalent solution during the change in hardware which is costlier than changing software tools. To tackle this, most of the recent applications rely on human-in-the-loop to help removing the uncertainty in predictions. Getting consent from users, by asking the users to confirm volumes of food are some of the approaches that the recent apps rely on. However, with more and more research in the automated application domains, the users have less input to the systems in comparison with the past applications.

Conventionally food and nutrient recognition is performed using only food images, however using multi-modal interactions is also gaining importance. Adding the context to the images such as the location of the image taken, has been instrumental in providing more precise nutritional information [60]. Geo-context is useful in exploiting the information such as menus of restaurants which helps in discarding unlikely categories [35]. Combining information from wearable systems also assists the applications to generate more distant patterns in terms of nutrition monitoring [42].

Food intake monitoring is widely used in applications for different domains ranging from common physical conditions such as weight loss management [76] to specific clinical conditions such as Gestinal diabetes [77], dialysis treatments [57], bariatric surgery [28], to name a few. In spite of numerous developments, nutrient and calorie estimation are still a challenging problem in automated diet monitoring. A through evaluation of mobile-based food recognition systems has always been performed [49] by different groups to find various shortcomings in the current systems. The most important challenge in any automated food monitoring system is with the performance of the recognition algorithms. Food recognition algorithms, though popular, are still highly complex being a very active area of research.

2.2 Food Recognition

Food recognition algorithms have been central to intelligent health applications such as in dietary management, food perception, food recommendation and food health analysis [64]. Deep learning has its fair share of success in the high performance of these food recognition algorithm. With more and more advancements in the architectures of neural networks, more advanced food recognition tasks are carried out, such as in GoogLeNet [100], Network-In-Networks [93], Inception V3 [30], ResNet50 [67], Ensemble NN [69], Wide Residual Networks [58], and CleanNet [54]. The base architecture was modified to enhance the learning task, such as in NutriNet [62], a modified AlexNet architecture.

The earlier networks relied on benchmark datasets which were confined to a smaller cuisine or a representation with less number of classes and images. With the explosion of images in different social platforms, recent datasets involve a large number of food images [16, 47]. The datasets have become more and more fine-grained in nature, which require more advancements in the algorithms. With the increased computational capabilities, using ensemble of various models is a common approach [1, 75, 94]. Different voting schemes were used in different ensemble methods to boost the performance [94]. Fusion of a slice network and a residual network have been effective [58] in increasing the recognition performance. An integration of local and flat classifiers has also shown to improve the classification performance [3]. Preceding the classification with a detection network is another common approach [63]. Faster R-CNN based detection was carried out for finding the candidate regions before using a classification network [44]. The more recent architectures rely on using teacher-student learning network [103], knowledge distillation [37], attention network [65], prototypical networks [86] and incremental learning [91] for food recognition.

Solving the food recognition as a multi-class problem has a main practical difficulty, that is, most of the platters in the real world are multi-labeled, i.e. more than one food class is present in the image. Therefore, there is a need to look at the food recognition as a multi-label problem. Detecting candidate regions and classifying them using the co-occurrence relationship between candidate classes [59] are a common approach used in multi-labeled datasets. Another general approach is to detect the location of food and then recognize each class in the image [9]. Multi-task based learning methods are also proposed when treating multi-label food images [2, 105]. Using multiple semantic features from ingredient recognition and recipe modelling tasks into food recognition produces better performance with lower parameters [56]. Multi-scale region based multi-label classifier [99] was used to boost the recognition performance. Segmentation networks have also been used to identify the different regions of food in images before recognizing the class [82]. Region proposals have been used to detect the candidate regions before classification, which has improved the recall rate [4, 83].

Single- and multi-label food recognition is showing great promise with the amount of new research outcomes using deep learning. This would in turn help the automated food intake monitoring applications more accurate and have less human effort in logging the daily food intake. In this current work, we introduce one such food recognition system, LogMeal, that is integrated into the NESTORE platform for nutrition monitoring benefits. LogMeal relies heavily on deep learning based solutions for various food detection tasks.

3 LogMeal—A Food Intake Monitoring Tool Integrated in the NESTORE Platform

In this section, we show the overall architecture of the LogMeal system, the various components that are available in the system and also how it is integrated into the NESTORE platform.

The LogMeal system can be visualized as a two-phased environment: The development environment and the production environment, where the development of models is offline and the production is an online entity where the system is deployed as a RESTful web service accessible via HTTP/HTTPS protocol.

3.1 Production Environment

The front-end of the client is platform and language independent where the APIs can be accessed using a web application or as a mobile application. At the backend, python along with Flask[7] framework was used to program the RESTful APIs in order to receive and service the user requests. It is also responsible to redirect the user requests to the inferencing engine, where the trained models are used to predict/classify the food images. The inferencing engine is written using Keras framework with Tensorflow backend and the inferences are performed in a GPU mode. The communication between the API calls and the inferencing models are carried out using Redis[8] queries. The back end server has MySQL database to manage the user profiles and recognition information. The server is equipped to handle multiple requests and perform inferences at the same time. The entire production ecosystem is hosted in the Google Cloud distributed infrastructure. The production environment is equipped with several API services for user profile management and for the food recognition tasks, where the food recognition APIs are realized using different semantic levels.

Semantic Levels Food recognition in LogMeal is achieved at different semantic levels ranging from 1 to 5. In the system, each level is achieved using a separate deep learning model. The semantic levels for food detection can be ordered as food types

[7]https://www.fullstackpython.com/flask.html.

[8]https://redis.io/.

detection, food group detection, dish recognition, ingredient information and nutritional analysis, where food types detection is at level 1 and the nutritional analysis is at level 5.

Food type detection is the highest level of detection that is performed using the LogMeal system. The model trained on this task is used to detect if the picture contains a single dish, combo dish (picture contains more than one dishes which are clearly distinguishable), drink, ingredient (raw vegetable or fruit), sauce or non food. The next level of detection is the food group detection. Here the models are trained to detect the most common food groups following the classical structure of recommended daily intake groups. The detected food is classified as one of the following: Meat (red and white meat), dessert, dairy, fish, seafood (food with animals with shells like clams and prawns), rice, fruit, pasta, vegetables, bread, fried food, egg and soup.

The third level is the dish recognition—both single and combo dish recognition is performed in this semantic level. In the single dish recognition, a total of 800+ dishes are recognized. The dishes broadly cover different cuisines such as Spanish, French, Italian, Dutch, Chinese and Japanese. For the combo dishes, the classes do not fall under a particular food group or cuisine and the food items are more general. The total number of dishes that are recognized using the combo model is 75.

In next two semantic levels are the ingredients information and the nutrient composition. For the ingredient information, the dishes are first identified from the images and using the cooking recipe, the ingredients are provided along with specific quantities. The total number of ingredients range close to 790 and the list is prepared with the assistance of expert dietitians. Using the ingredient information, the nutrition information is provided. The system is able to provide 42 nutritional indicators such as carbs, cholesterol, calcium and so on.

3.2 Development Environment

The development environment of LogMeal is performed offline, where we train each of the food recognition models as an individual entity. In recent years, it is a well established practice in deep learning to use the weights trained on large datasets such as ImageNet [23] to initialize the networks for different tasks and has been very effective in training [41]. Using pre-trained nets to initialize the weights work better than training networks from scratch [50]. Using this success, we use pre-trained ImageNet models and fine tune them on our food dataset for various recognition tasks.

During the course of the development stages, we have trained different base architectures such as ResNet [31], Inception [90], InceptionResnet [89], ResNeXt [101], SENet [39], DenseNet [40] and EfficientNet [92]. We have used standard approaches for data augmentation such as rotation, random crop, etc. We performed several experiments on the base architectures to find the optimal hyperparameters and image sizes for each task. The food type detection, food group detection, single dish recognition tasks are multi-class in nature whereas combo dish recognition task is multi-label in nature. For each of the food type, a separate model is trained. The loss functions and the metrics were adjusted accordingly as per the nature of the task. The development environment is a continuous process, where we update the models based on the advancements in the training process, new loss functions and different base architectures.

3.3 LogMeal Integration into NESTORE

The food recognition APIs of LogMeal is integrated into the NESTORE platform through a mobile application called as NESTORE e-coach. LogMeal APIs are used in monitoring the nutritional aspect of the elder people. An overview of the workflow between NESTORE and LogMeal is shown in Fig. 1.

Nutrition monitoring is an important activity in the NESTORE e-coach. The users keep track of food they consume by taking a picture using the mobile app. The image is passed to the LogMeal production environment through the service request. Initially, the food type is identified by the type classifier and is sent back to the user. The user has an option to confirm the predicted type or select the correct type. Based on the selection, the classes are recognized using the corresponding model. The user is presented with the most probable classes and is allowed to confirm the prediction. The nutrition information for standard portion sizes is provided to the user based on the class confirmation. Although the predictions and the nutrition information can be automatically logged, the human-in-loop is an important step. Since the nutritional monitoring is done regularly to help the users better with their lifestyle, it is important to not have false negatives of the inferencing models. If the user does not find the correct class in the list provided by the app, he/she has an option to manually enter the

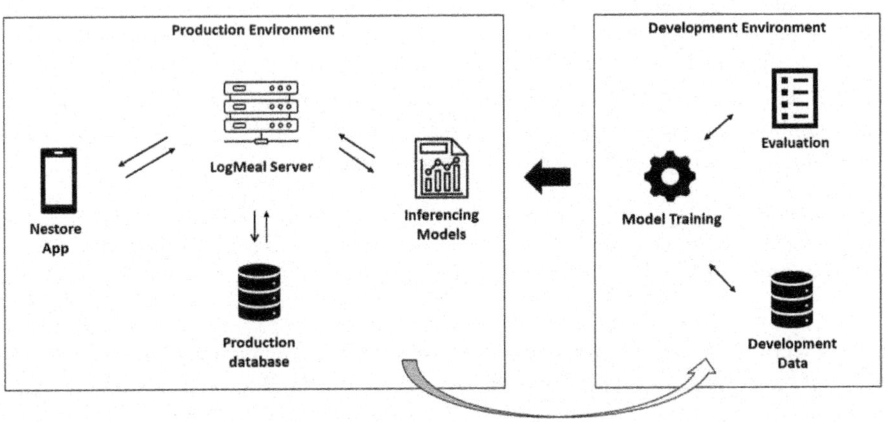

Fig. 1 LogMeal integration into NESTORE

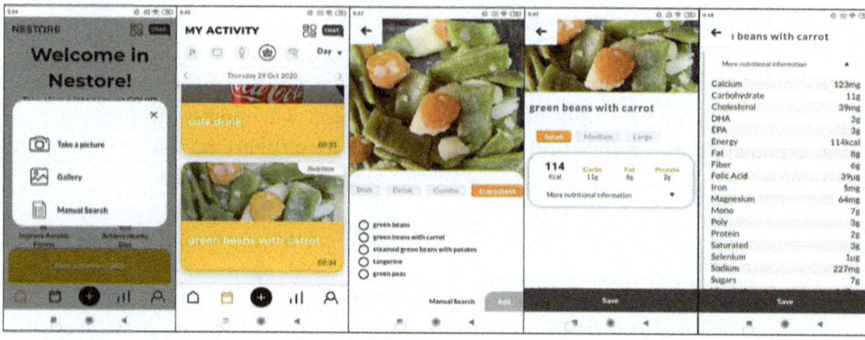

Fig. 2 NESTORE app showing food intake monitoring

food class. The user selections are recorded by the LogMeal server for monitoring the performance of the system in real world, which will in turn help improve the performance of the models and also to improve the datasets for new classes.

NESTORE e-coach Figure 2 shows the nutrition monitoring in the NESTORE app. The user has the option of taking the picture or using an already taken picture to log the intake. Once the food image is added, the app shows the food types with the prediction highlighted and it provides the top 5 predicted classes based on the type identified. The user selects the correct prediction and the app responds with the nutritional information based on standard portion sizes. If the user does not find the prediction matching to the image, he/she can also perform the food search manually. The corresponding nutrition information and an educational message about the matched food type is shown to the user. The app constantly records the user logs, such information would be useful for health care professionals to view the dietary patterns and adjust the nutrition intake. The user can also log his/her food through a chatbot, with a similar interaction flow to the one depicted for the app. The app allows the user keeping track of the entered food, showing the taken photos in a calendar view. Moreover, several charts are available in order to monitor the nutrient intake, with special focus on Calcium, Vitamin D, Vitamin B12, Omega-3 intake, which are particularly relevant for older adults. The app provides also information about calorie intake and the energy balance in respect to energy consumption estimated by the system, allowing for a better weight management.

4 Constructing LogMeal Food Dataset

In this section, we first compare the existing food datasets and then show the importance of collecting our dataset. We briefly present the annotation procedure and also show the different classes of data that have been collected.

4.1 Public Food Datasets

Despite its great applications, food recognition faces a lot of challenge mainly because of its lack of large dataset, presence of huge intra-class variation, hard to capture discriminative details [66] and improper annotation or presence of noisy labels in dataset.

One of the earliest food dataset [45] contains only 50 different food categories mostly Japanese food and the images are collected from the web. Later on in a subsequent work this food dataset has been enlarged to 85 food categories [38]. UECFOOD-100 a public dataset [48], which contains more than 9,000 images of 100 food different categories. Food101 dataset is one of the most popular foodrelated data we used [11], which contains 101,000 images with 101 categories. Chen et al.[14] introduced the Vireo Food-172 dataset from 172 Chinese food categories. Recently, ISIA Food-500 was introduced which consists of 399,726 food items [66]. Each item includes the food name and food images. There are totally 500 kinds of different food dishes.

These datasets (Table 1) lack of diversity and do not coverage the wide range of food categories and images present which leads to shallow algorithms for food recognition.

We hence introduce a new data set of 800+ different categories with 1,348,507 number of images, including cuisine like Spanish, French, Italian, Dutch, Chinese, Japanese, etc. We have categorised this dataset into three different types such as Food Type (for example Fig. 4), Group food and Single Dish (for example Fig. 5). This

Table 1 Summary of available datasets for food recognition

Dataset	Images	Categories	Coverage
PFID [15]	4,545	101	Japanese
UEC Food100 [48]	14,361	100	Japanese
UEC Food256 [59]	25,088	256	Japanese
ETHZ Food-101 [11]	101,000	101	Western
UPMC Food-101 [97]	90,840	101	Western
UNIMIB2015 [17]	2,000	15	Misc
UNIMIB2016 [18]	1,027	73	Misc
MAFood-121 [2]	21,175	121	Western
ChineseFoodNet [16]	192,000	208	Chinese
Vireo Food-172 [14]	110,241	172	Chinese
KenyanFood13 [43]	8,174	13	Kenyan
Sushi-50 [78]	3,963	50	Japanese
FoodX-251 [47]	158,846	251	Misc
ISIA Food-200 [66]	197,323	200	Misc
ISIA Food-500 [66]	399,726	500	Misc.
Our	1,348,507	800+	Misc.

dataset increases diversity, large volume and cover a large number of different types of food.

4.2 Food Hierarchy

In the Food Type category we have types like—Ingredients, Sauce, Food, Drinks and Non-food and we have collected the images accordingly (Fig. 3).

Food: contains mainly prepared/cooked food or elaborated dish (e.g. steak, spaghetti bolognese, caesar salad, etc.). More than 620 in total different categories of food are present in our dataset.

Fig. 3 Some samples from our food dataset. First row shows different food images, second row—drink images, third row—different ingredient images, fourth row—different sauce images, sixth row—different combo/group food images present in our dataset

Fig. 4 Food types: first row shows **a** food image and **b** ingredient image. Second row shows **c** drink image and **d** sauce image

Drink: contains any kind of drink (e.g. water, orange juice, beer, etc.) more than 35 in total different categories of drinks are present in our drink dataset.

Ingredients: category contains any type of fruit or raw/individual vegetable (e.g. apple, eggplant, banana, etc.). More than 110 in total different categories of ingredients are present in our dataset.

Sauce: contains prepared sauce or sauce-like food (e.g. soy sauce, mayonnaise, ketchup, apple etc.). More than 20 in total different categories and more than 5 k images in total of sauces are present in our dataset.

Combo-dish: contains combination of dish or combo-dish composed of several individual and clearly distinguishable elements in a single plate called combodish (Fig. 5).

Non food: images were collected from the web as well as during cleaning the dataset where we have run a binary classifier to filter out all the non food images. In the Single dish dataset we only have those images where there is only one type of food present, where as in Group food data set we have food images which contain multiple foods together or combo-plate images.

Regarding the food categories, we have used:

- Meat: any kind of white or red meat.
- Dessert: dishes usually eaten as dessert.
- Dairy products: products derived from dairy, like milk or yogurt.
- Seafood: products derived from animals with shells like clams or prawns.
- Rice: rice or products that can contain rice.

Fig. 5 Single food (left) and group food (right)

- Fruit: any kind of cooked or fresh fruit.
- Noodles/pasta: all types of Italian pasta or Asian noodles.
- Vegetables: either cooked or raw vegetable products.
- Fish: fish and fish-derived products.
- Bread: all kinds of bread and grain-like products.
- Fried food: any food that was fried during its cooking procedure.t
- Egg: that contains a relevant amount of egg.
- Soup: dish in the form of soup, which has a large portion of liquid.

4.3 The Dataset Construction

To create a broad highly diverse food dataset first we have created a food category list keeping the concept of "Lists of foods by ingredient from Wikipedia, as well as the food groups of Wikipedia. Along with Wikipedia we have went through multiple other website to obtain large number of food category. After collecting the images we have removed the redundant categories.

We have crawled food images from various search engines i.e.: Google, Bing, Yahoo, DuckDuckGo etc. We have used some particular Key or Search term such as "Food", "Dish", "cuisine" etc. As we have collected these food images from different search engines so there was a high chance of collecting same image repeatedly, to remove those repeated image we have used duplication detection method. For cleaning the dataset we have run a binary classifier to check for food vs non food and filtered out all the non food images. After image collection we have annotated by professional annotators as well as we built our own annotation tool, and validated all the annotated images very carefully to get rid of Noise label or wrongly labelled data.

Even after collecting a lot of data from the web as well as combining publicly present datasets, there were still many food categories with few number of images. To enlarge those categories or dataset we have translated the name of those food into different languages, such as French, Italian, Dutch etc., and crawled the images respectively. Finally we came up with a 800+ categories with 1,348,507 number of large diverse food dataset.

To create this dataset, we have also combined other public datasets to increase the variety of images. ETHZ Food-101 (western dishes), VireoFood-172 (eastern dishes), MAFood-121 and UECFOOD-100 are some of the datasets that are added to the LogMeal dataset.

LogMeal Annotation Tool Logmeal has created its own annotation tool to label collected datasets efficiently by means of crowd-sourcing. It is a web based tool so the users have to go to the particular image labeling website and need to validate themselves by username and password. Once they are inside they will find a set of job assigned to them. The jobs will contain around 1000 images each. Annotators have to Investigate the visual appearance of all the dishes/ingredients that appear in the tab menu next to the displayed image and decide if the image appearing on screen is a "combo-plate" or not. If it is not a combo-plate or the image is not clear (blurry, deformed, etc.), or the annotator does not know how to label it, he/she should press the discard image button located at the bottom side of the annotation tool.

If the image is a combo-plate, it should be assigned all labels as food appears in the picture on the screen. In the annotation tool label tray located underneath the image where the annotator can see the selected annotation for any particular image and if a label is not selected for the current dish, it will not be displayed there. If none of the labels applies to the current image, it should be discarded by pressing "Discard Image" button. To remove a label the user should press the 'X' or "Discard" button attached to it (for example Fig. 6).

For faster annotation, Logmeal tool also has a search bar in the labeling website. By clicking on it the annotator will be able to enable the search mode, which reduces the amount of clicks needed to add/remove labels (see Fig. 6). Once the search bar is focused (by clicking on it) a shortcut cheat sheet will appear. While in this mode,

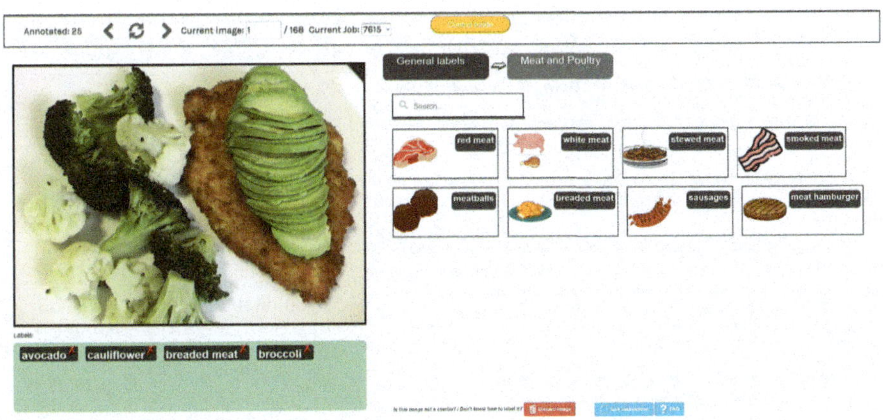

Fig. 6 LogMeal annotation tool

the user can type the name of the label he/she wants to add, and it will automatically search for the most similar labels compared to the text entered. The result on top of the list will always be highlighted. In order to select an element from the list which is not located at the top he/she can use the "up" and "down" arrows in order to change the selected item. If the user adds a label by mistake, he/she can press the "CTRL + BACKSPACE" in order to remove the last label from the list of added classes.

4.4 Nutritional Food Composition of Recipes

Given the high number of recipes collected for LogMeal, in order to determine the nutritional composition, we decided to use an international food composition table which provides information on the average nutritional composition of food, that was Ciqual food composition table. Ciqual has nutritional information of a large amount of food such as calories information and macro-and micro-nutrients (by 100 g): carbohydrates (specifying all types of sugar), proteins, fats (specifying all types of fats), vitamins and minerals.

For each recipe, a total of the nutritional information of each ingredient, using the common and recommended portion size for each food, was calculated. Moreover, the fat absorption for each cooking type was taking account at the final weight of the recipe (see Table 2).

Consequently, the total energy and macro-/micro-nutrients information were detailed for each recipe in relation to the Ciqual table food composition. Some examples of traditional recipes can be seen in Table 3.

Table 2 Nutritional food composition

Type of cooking	Percentage of absorbed fat
Microwave/Boiled	0%
Papillote	2%
Grill/Oven	5%
Fried	7%
Sautéed	8%
Stew	10%
Roast	12%
Covered (only flour)	7% flour + 17% oil
Covered (bread)	7% bread + 5% egg + 17% oil
Sofrito	5% onion + 7% tomato + 6% oil

Table 3 Traditional recipes of LogMeal

Dish	Ingredients	Total weight
Catalan spinach	43.0 g raisins, 25 g pine nuts, 180.0 g, spinach, 14.5 g olive oil, 3.0 g garlic, 0.7 g salt, 0.3 g pepper 168.0 g	266.5 g
Baked Brussels sprouts	Brussels sprouts, 8.4 g olive oil, 0.5 salt, 0.5 g black pepper	177.4 g

4.5 Nationality

We have collected food images as per different Nationality Spanish, French, Italian, Dutch, Chinese, Japanese, Greek, Asian, Mexican, Korean, Indian, Vietnamese, Philippines etc.

4.6 API Images

Other than collecting food images from different web platforms we also have collected images from our day to day life (university cafeteria, different restaurant's, homemade food by mobile camera) and then we have annotated all those images by professional annotators, which helped us to crate a huge diverse food dataset. We also have used all the images collected by LogMeal api for food recognition (see Table 4 to know number of images per category).

5 System Validation

In this section, we show the validation of LogMeal with respect to the development phase, where we evaluate against the validation set of our dataset. We also show the real-time validation of LogMeal in the NESTORE platform using the collected feedback from the users.

Table 4 Image distribution

Category	Number of images
Food	511,469
Ingredients	73,324
Drinks	16,857
Sauces	5,624
Combo dish	9,538
Non-food	731,695

5.1 Performance Insights During Development

We use two different evaluation metrics depending on the type of recognition tasks. We use accuracy as a metric to evaluate the models dealing with multi-class datasets and we use F1-Score to evaluate the models with multi-label datasets. We present both Top-1 accuracy and Top-5 accuracy to show the model performance. Top-1 accuracy is the conventional accuracy where the highest probable class is matched with the target label. Top-5 accuracy is measured when the target label is matched in the top 5 probable predictions. We also show the Top-1 Balanced Accuracy of the models. Balanced accuracy [12] is measured as the average of the proportion corrects of each class individually and it is a useful metric in dealing with imbalanced classes. Table 5 shows the validation performance of different recognition models.

High top-5 accuracy shows that most of the miss-classifications in the models would be within the high confusing classes. High number of classes in the dataset results in more fine-grained classes. The high intra-class variance can also be attributed to the low performing classes. It is also quite possible that the user is unable to recognize the difference between the high confusing classes. Similar top-1 accuracy and top-1 balanced accuracy show that the models are able to overcome the imbalanced nature of the datasets.

Figure 7 shows some samples that were wrongly classified by the recognition models. The common reasons for wrong classification are not having sufficient training samples for that particular class or completely unknown class. Another reason has been with orientation and count of the food items in a single image. The

Table 5 Performance of various models on the validation data

Model type	Architecture	Top-1 accuracy	Top-5 accuracy	Top-1 balanced
Food type	InceptionResnetV2	0.92	1.00	0.90
Sauces	InceptionResnetV2	0.73	0.96	0.68
Drinks	InceptionResnetV2	0.75	0.94	0.70
Ingredients	InceptionResnetV2	0.80	0.93	0.79
Single dish	InceptionResnetV2	0.67	0.87	0.64
Combo dish	Resnet50	0.704 (F1-Score)		

Fig. 7 Some samples showing miss-classifications of the recognition models. The reasons for wrongly classification are (from the left) too many dishes (**a**, **b**), not available in training set (**c**, **d**), and being very different form of class from the dataset (**e**)

multi-label food recognition model is unable to predict the classes correctly when there is no so much information from the picture. The hardest problems are the ones where the image is completely home-made. The network would not have learnt such representation and therefore fails to recognize the food.

As explained earlier, the development of models is continued with the view of improving model performance based on the following questions: (1) Is the performance showing short comings in the training strategies? (2) Is the false classifications due to the fine grained nature of the classes? (3) Is the performance reflecting the dataset that is used for training? The feedback that is recorded by the server is used to analyse the datasets and models based on these questions. By monitoring the pattern of miss-classifications, it is possible to increase the diversity of the images and the classes thereby making the models more robust over iterations.

5.2 Performance Insights During Production

To analyse the performance of models with data from the wild, we use the recorded food images. An expert is used to annotate the images and the overall system is evaluated against the annotations. This is a highly expensive approach as it is very difficult for the expert to annotate the labels from a high number of possible classes. This process is performed periodically to test the performance of the system. Another easier approach is to use the user feedback. Table 6 shows the overall system performance. Top-1 accuracy is the highest probable dish suggested to the user. Single-click accuracy is the accuracy of the types plus the top 5 predictions shown to the user. Double-click accuracy is the accuracy of the initial 6 options shown to the user along with the new 5 predictions that are shown after the user changes the type of the food.

From the results, it can be seen that the models could meet difficulties when recognizing food in the wild. There are several factors that can be attributed to the worse performance of the system in comparison with the validation data of our dataset.

- It is possible that the annotations are of high quality and the wild data is of a different quality. The more obvious difference would be in the distribution of the data. Bias has been an active research in deep learning and it is possible that the model suffers from various bias factors.
- Another common problem would be because of the lack of training data for that particular class. Since the dataset is imbalanced, there is a chance that the classes have insufficient data.

Table 6 Accuracy of LogMeal in NESTORE platform

Top-1	Single-click	Double-click
44.74	74.66	67.52

- Incomplete pictures, poorly illuminated images, unknown food classes are other possible reasons. Although unknown food classes are easily studied based on the user feedback and are easy to include in the next revision of the dataset, the other problems are close to impossible to rectify.
- Since the results are calculated based on user feedback, it is possible that the feedback is not correct.
- Some food classes might be still be missing from the database.

The possible reasons presented above are not an exhaustive list. There could be more reasons that are affecting the performance of the system in real time. On a general analysis, the validation is a continuous process as per the real world performance is considered and the system would undergo several iterations based on the study of the feedback and is continually improved.

6 Conclusions

NESTORE platform is aimed at providing personalized coaching based on the needs and preferences of the aged people using various activities. Nutrition monitoring is an important part of maintaining well-being in NESTORE and LogMeal is used to provide automatic food recognition and food logging. The system consists of various deep learning models trained for various food recognition tasks.

The dataset is composed of a wide variety of food classes and a diverse collection of cuisines. We have trained various models with different parameters to get the best performing model. The models are used for inferencing in a web server application. We have shown different validation strategies which are performed continually to develop both the datasets and the models. The LogMeal system is available as an API service and is integrated into the NESTORE e-coach mobile app. We have presented the analysis that is done using the real-world setting. Food intake monitoring is very important for people suffering with chronic ailments and are equally important for elder people. LogMeal integrated into NESTORE helps the aged to achieve a healthier lifestyle with continuous support.

Acknowledgements This work was partially funded by TIN2018-095232-B-C21, SGR-2017 1742, NESTORE project of the European Commission Horizon 2020 programme (Grant no. 769643), GreenHabit EIT Digital and Validithi EIT Health program and CERCA Programme/Generalitat de Catalunya. We acknowledge the support of NVIDIA Corporation with the donation of Titan Xp GPUs.

References

1. Aguilar, E., Bolaños, M., & Radeva, P. (2017). Food recognition using fusion of classifiers based on cnns. In *International Conference on Image Analysis and Processing* (pp. 213–224). Springer.
2. Aguilar, E., Bolaños, M., & Radeva, P. (2019). Regularized uncertainty-based multi-task learning model for food analysis. *Journal of Visual Communication and Image Representation, 60*, 360–370.
3. Aguilar, E., & Radeva, P. (2020). Uncertainty-aware integration of local and flat classifiers for food recognition. *Pattern Recognition Letters, 136*, 237–243.
4. Aguilar, E., Remeseiro, B., Bolaños, M., & Radeva, P. (2018). Grab, pay, and eat: Semantic food detection for smart restaurants. *IEEE Transactions on Multimedia, 20*(12), 3266–3275.
5. Ahmad, J., Farman, H., & Jan, Z. (2019). Deep learning methods and applications. In *Deep learning: Convergence to big data analytics* (pp. 31–42). Springer.
6. Al-Khafajiy, M., Baker, T., Chalmers, C., Asim, M., Kolivand, H., Fahim, M., et al. (2019). Remote health monitoring of elderly through wearable sensors. *Multimedia Tools and Applications, 78*(17), 24681–24706.
7. Alshurafa, N., Lin, A. W., Zhu, F., Ghaffari, R., Hester, J., Delp, E., et al. (2019). Counting bites with bits: Expert workshop addressing calorie and macronutrient intake monitoring. *Journal of medical Internet research, 21*(12), e14904.
8. Angelini, L., Mugellini, E., Khaled, O. A., C. Röcke, Guye, S., Porcelli, S., Mastropietro, A., Rizzo, G., Boqué, N., Bas, J. M. d., et al. (2019). The nestore e-coach: Accompanying older adults through a personalized pathway to wellbeing. In *Proceedings of the 12th ACM International Conference on Pervasive Technologies Related to Assistive Environments* (pp. 620–628).
9. Anzawa, M., Amano, S., Yamakata, Y., Motonaga, K., Kamei, A., & Aizawa, K. (2019). Recognition of multiple food items in a single photo for use in a buffet-style restaurant. *IEICE Transactions on Information and Systems, 102*(2), 410–414.
10. Bi, S., Wang, T., Davenport, E., Peterson, R., Halter, R., Sorber, J., & Kotz, D. (2017). Toward a wearable sensor for eating detection. In *Proceedings of the 2017 Workshop on Wearable Systems and Applications* (pp. 17–22).
11. Bossard, L., Guillaumin, M., & Van Gool, L. (2014). Food-101–mining discriminative components with random forests. In *European Conference on Computer Vision* (pp. 446–461). Springer.
12. Brodersen, K. H., Ong, C. S., Stephan, K. E., & Buhmann, J. M. (2010). The balanced accuracy and its posterior distribution. In *2010 20th International Conference on Pattern Recognition* (pp. 3121–3124). IEEE.
13. Bruno, V., & Silva Resende, C. J. (2017). A survey on automated food monitoring and dietary management systems. *Journal of Health & Medical Informatics, 8*(3).
14. Chen, J., & Ngo, C.-W. (2016). Deep-based ingredient recognition for cooking recipe retrieval. In *Proceedings of the 24th ACM International Conference on Multimedia* (pp. 32–41).
15. Chen, M., Dhingra, K., Wu, W., Yang, L., Sukthankar, R., & Yang, J. (2009). Pfid: Pittsburgh fast-food image dataset. In *2009 16th IEEE International Conference on Image Processing (ICIP)* (pp. 289–292). IEEE.
16. Chen, X., Zhou, H., Zhu, Y., & Diao, L. (2017). *Chinesefoodnet: A large-scale image dataset for chinese food recognition*. arXiv:1705.02743.
17. Ciocca, G., Napoletano, P., & Schettini, R. (2015). Food recognition and leftover estimation for daily diet monitoring. In *International Conference on Image Analysis and Processing* (pp. 334–341). Springer.
18. Ciocca, G., Napoletano, P., & Schettini, R. (2016). Food recognition: A new dataset, experiments, and results. *IEEE Journal of Biomedical and Health Informatics, 21*(3), 588–598.
19. Cordeiro, F., Bales, E., Cherry, E., & Fogarty, J. (2015). Rethinking the mobile food journal: Exploring opportunities for lightweight photo-based capture. In *Proceedings of the 33rd Annual ACM Conference on Human Factors in Computing Systems* (pp. 3207–3216).

20. Cox, A. M., McKinney, P., & Goodale, P. (2017). Food logging: An information literacy perspective. *Aslib Journal of Information Management*.
21. Daskalopoulou, C., Stubbs, B., Kralj, C., Koukounari, A., Prince, M., & Prina, A. M. (2017). Physical activity and healthy ageing: A systematic review and meta-analysis of longitudinal cohort studies. *Ageing Research Reviews, 38*, 6–17.
22. Dehais, J., Anthimopoulos, M., Shevchik, S., & Mougiakakou, S. (2016). Two-view 3d reconstruction for food volume estimation. *IEEE Transactions on Multimedia, 19*(5), 1090–1099.
23. Deng, J., Dong, W., Socher, R., Li, L.-J., Li, K., & Fei-Fei, L. (2009). Imagenet: A large-scale hierarchical image database. In *2009 IEEE Conference on Computer Vision and Pattern Recognition* (pp. 248–255). IEEE.
24. Desa, U. (2019). *World population prospects 2019: Highlights*. New York (US): United Nations Department for Economic and Social Affairs.
25. Doumit, R., Long, J., Kazandjian, C., Gharibeh, N., Karam, L., Song, H., et al. (2016). Effects of recording food intake using cell phone camera pictures on energy intake and food choice. *Worldviews on Evidence-Based Nursing, 13*(3), 216–223.
26. Ege, T., Ando, Y., Tanno, R., Shimoda, W., & Yanai, K. (2019). Image-based estimation of real food size for accurate food calorie estimation. In *2019 IEEE Conference on Multimedia Information Processing and Retrieval (MIPR)* (pp. 274–279). IEEE.
27. El Kinany, K., Garcia-Larsen, V., Khalis, M., Deoula, M. M. S., Benslimane, A., Ibrahim, A., et al. (2018). Adaptation and validation of a food frequency questionnaire (ffq) to assess dietary intake in moroccan adults. *Nutrition Journal, 17*(1), 61.
28. Elvin-Walsh, L., Ferguson, M., & Collins, P. F. (2018). Nutritional monitoring of patients post-bariatric surgery: Implications for smartphone applications. *Journal of Human Nutrition & Dietetics, 31*(1), 141–148.
29. Goyal, S., Liu, Q., Tajul-Arifin, K., Awan, W., Wadhwa, B., & Liu, Z. (2017). I ate this: A photo-based food journaling system with expert feedback. arXiv:1702.05957.
30. Hassannejad, S. H., Matrella, G., Ciampolini, P., De Munari, I., Mordonini, M., & Cagnoni. (2016). Food image recognition using very deep convolutional networks. In *Proceedings of the 2nd International Workshop on Multimedia Assisted Dietary Management* (pp. 41–49).
31. He, K., Zhang, X., Ren, S., & Sun, J. (2016). Deep residual learning for image recognition. In *Proceedings of the IEEE Conference on Computer Vision and Pattern Recognition* (pp. 770–778).
32. Helander, E., Kaipainen, K., Korhonen, I., & Wansink, B. (2014). Factors related to sustained use of a free mobile app for dietary self-monitoring with photography and peer feedback: Retrospective cohort study. *Journal of Medical Internet Research, 16*(4), e109.
33. Herman, C. P. (2015). The social facilitation of eating. A review. *Appetite, 86*, 61–73.
34. Herman, C. P., Roth, D. A., & Polivy, J. (2003). Effects of the presence of others on food intake: A normative interpretation. *Psychological Bulletin, 129*(6), 873.
35. Herranz, L., Jiang, S., & Xu, R. (2016). Modeling restaurant context for food recognition. *IEEE Transactions on Multimedia, 19*(2), 430–440.
36. Herzig, D., Nakas, C. T., Stalder, J., Kosinski, C., Laesser, C., Dehais, J., et al. (2020). Volumetric food quantification using computer vision on a depth-sensing smartphone: Preclinical study. *JMIR mHealth and uHealth, 8*(3), e15294.
37. Hinton, G., Vinyals, O., & Dean, J. (2015). *Distilling the knowledge in a neural network*. arXiv:1503.02531.
38. Hoashi, H., Joutou, T., & Yanai, K. (2010). Image recognition of 85 food categories by feature fusion. In *2010 IEEE International Symposium on Multimedia* (pp. 296–301). IEEE.
39. Hu, J., Shen, L., & Sun, G. (2018). Squeeze-and-excitation networks. In *Proceedings of the IEEE Conference on Computer Vision and Pattern Recognition* (pp. 7132–7141).
40. Huang, G., Liu, Z., Van Der Maaten, L., & Weinberger, K. Q. (2017). Densely connected convolutional networks. In *Proceedings of the IEEE Conference on Computer Vision and Pattern Recognition* (pp. 4700–4708).

41. Huh, M., Agrawal, P., & Efros, A. A. (2016). *What makes imagenet good for transfer learning?* arXiv:1608.08614.
42. Hussain, G., Maheshwari, M. K., Memon, M. L., Jabbar, M. S., & Javed, K. (2019). A cnn based automated activity and food recognition using wearable sensor for preventive healthcare. *Electronics, 8*(12), 1425.
43. Jalal, M., Wang, K., Jefferson, S., Zheng, Y., Nsoesie, E. O., & Betke, M. (2019). Scraping social media photos posted in kenya and elsewhere to detect and analyze food types. In *Proceedings of the 5th International Workshop on Multimedia Assisted Dietary Management* (pp. 50–59).
44. Jiang, L., Qiu, B., Liu, X., Huang, C., & Lin, K. (2020). Deepfood: Food image analysis and dietary assessment via deep model. *IEEE Access, 8,* 47477–47489.
45. Joutou, T., & Yanai, K. (2009). A food image recognition system with multiple kernel learning. In *2009 16th IEEE International Conference on Image Processing (ICIP)* (pp. 285–288). IEEE.
46. Kalid, N., Zaidan, A., Zaidan, B., Salman, O. H., Hashim, M., Albahri, O., & Al-bahri, A. (2018). Based on real time remote health monitoring systems: A new approach for prioritization "large scales data" patients with chronic heart diseases using body sensors and communication technology. *Journal of Medical Systems, 42*(4), 69.
47. Kaur, P., Sikka, K., Wang, W., Belongie, S., & Divakaran, A. (2019). *Foodx-251: A dataset for fine-grained food classification.* arXiv:1907.06167.
48. Kawano, Y., & Yanai, K. (2013). Real-time mobile food recognition system. In *Proceedings of the IEEE Conference on Computer Vision and Pattern Recognition Workshops* (pp. 1–7).
49. Knez, S., & Šajn, L. (2020). Food object recognition using a mobile device: Evaluation of currently implemented systems. *Trends in Food Science & Technology.*
50. Kornblith, S., Shlens, J., & Le, Q. V. (2019). Do better imagenet models transfer better? In *Proceedings of the IEEE Conference on Computer Vision and Pattern Recognition* (pp. 2661–2671).
51. Labonté, M.-È., Cyr, A., Baril-Gravel, L., Royer, M., & Lamarche, B. (2012). Validity and reproducibility of a web-based, self-administered food frequency questionnaire. *European Journal of Clinical Nutrition, 66*(2), 166–173.
52. Laurino, M., Alfì, G., Billeci, L., Bortone, I., Buzzigoli, E., Cecchi, A., Del Ry, S., Gastaldelli, A., Lai, E., Morales, M. A., et al. (2020). Healthy aging: The intecman project. *Aging Clinical and Experimental Research* (pp. 1–5).
53. Lee, T. H., Choi, T. K., Lee, Y. B., Cho, H. R., Ghaffari, R., Wang, L., et al. (2016). A graphene-based electrochemical device with thermoresponsive microneedles for diabetes monitoring and therapy. *Nature Nanotechnology, 11*(6), 566–572.
54. Lee, K.-H., He, X., Zhang, L., & Yang, L. (2018). Cleannet: Transfer learning for scalable image classifier training with label noise. In *Proceedings of the IEEE Conference on Computer Vision and Pattern Recognition* (pp. 5447–5456).
55. Li, J., Han, F., Guerrero, R., & Pavlovic, V. (2020). *Picture-to-amount (pita): Predicting relative ingredient amounts from food images.* arXiv:2010.08727.
56. Liang, H., Wen, G., Hu, Y., Luo, M., Yang, P., & Xu, Y. (2020). Mvanet: Multi-tasks guided multi-view attention network for chinese food recognition. *IEEE Transactions on Multimedia.*
57. Lim, J.-H., Ibrahim, I., Syahrul, J., Zabil, M. H. M., Zakaria, N. F., Daud, Z. A. M., et al. (2020). Limitations of existing dialysis diet apps in promoting user engagement and patient self-management: Quantitative content analysis study. *JMIR mHealth and uHealth, 8*(6), e13808.
58. Martinel, N., Foresti, G. L., & Micheloni, C. (2018). Wide-slice residual networks for food recognition. In *2018 IEEE Winter Conference on Applications of Computer Vision (WACV)* (pp. 567–576). IEEE.
59. Matsuda, Y., & Yanai, K. (2012). Multiple-food recognition considering co-occurrence employing manifold ranking. In *Proceedings of the 21st International Conference on Pattern Recognition (ICPR2012)* (pp. 2017–2020). IEEE.

60. Merler, M., Wu, H., Uceda-Sosa, R., Nguyen, Q.-B., & Smith, J. R. (2016). Snap, eat, repeat: A food recognition engine for dietary logging. In *Proceedings of the 2nd International Workshop on Multimedia Assisted Dietary Management* (pp. 31–40).
61. Meyers, A., Johnston, N., Rathod, V., Korattikara, A., Gorban, A., Silberman, N., Guadarrama, S., Papandreou, G., Huang, J., & Murphy, K. P. (2015). Im2calories: Towards an automated mobile vision food diary. In *Proceedings of the IEEE International Conference on Computer Vision* (pp. 1233–1241).
62. Mezgec, S., & Seljak, B. K. (2019). Using deep learning for food and beverage image recognition. In *2019 IEEE International Conference on Big Data (Big Data)* (pp. 5149–5151). IEEE.
63. Miasnikov, E., & Savchenko, A. (2020). Detection and recognition of food in photo galleries for analysis of user preferences. In *International Conference on Image Analysis and Recognition* (pp. 83–94). Springer.
64. Min, W., Jiang, S., Liu, L., Rui, Y., & Jain, R. (2019). A survey on food computing. *ACM Computing Surveys (CSUR), 52*(5), 1–36.
65. Min, W., Liu, L., Luo, Z., & Jiang, S. (2019). Ingredient-guided cascaded multi-attention network for food recognition. In *Proceedings of the 27th ACM International Conference on Multimedia* (pp. 1331–1339).
66. Min, W., Liu, L., Wang, Z., Luo, Z., Wei, X., Wei, X., & Jiang, S. (2020). Isia food-500: A dataset for large-scale food recognition via stacked global-local attention network. In *Proceedings of the 28th ACM International Conference on Multimedia* (pp. 393–401).
67. Ming, Z.-Y., Chen, J., Cao, Y., Forde, C., Ngo, C.-W., & Chua, T. S. (2018). Food photo recognition for dietary tracking: System and experiment. In *International Conference on Multimedia Modeling* (pp. 129–141). Springer.
68. Moguel, E., Berrocal, J., & García-Alonso, J. (2019). Systematic literature review of food-intake monitoring in an aging population. *Sensors, 19*(15), 3265.
69. Nag, N., Pandey, V., & Jain, R. (2017). Health multimedia: Lifestyle recommendations based on diverse observations. In *Proceedings of the 2017 ACM on International Conference on Multimedia Retrieval* (pp. 99–106).
70. Nilsen, W., Kumar, S., Shar, A., Varoquiers, C., Wiley, T., Riley, W. T., et al. (2012). Advancing the science of mhealth. *Journal of health communication, 17*(sup1), 5–10.
71. Noor Hafizah, Y., Ang, L. C., Yap, F., Nurul Najwa, W., Cheah, W. L., Ruzita, A. T., Jumuddin, F. A., Koh, D., Lee, J. A. C., Essau, C. A., et al. (2019). Validity and reliability of a food frequency questionnaire (ffq) to assess dietary intake of preschool children. *International Journal of Environmental Research and Public Health, 16*(23), 4722.
72. Ocay, A. B., Fernandez, J. M., & Palaoag, T. D. (2017). Nutritrack: Android-based food recognition app for nutrition awareness. In *2017 3rd IEEE International Conference on Computer and Communications (ICCC)* (pp. 2099–2104). IEEE.
73. Oncescu, V., O'Dell, D., & Erickson, D. (2013). Smartphone based health accessory for colorimetric detection of biomarkers in sweat and saliva. *Lab on a Chip, 13*(16), 3232–3238.
74. Organization, W. H., et al. (2017). *Global strategy and action plan on ageing and health.*
75. Pandey, P., Deepthi, A., Mandal, B., & Puhan, N. B. (2017). Foodnet: Recognizing foods using ensemble of deep networks. *IEEE Signal Processing Letters, 24*(12), 1758–1762.
76. Payne, J. E., Turk, M. T., Kalarchian, M. A., & Pellegrini, C. A. (2018). Defining adherence to dietary self-monitoring using a mobile app: A narrative review. *Journal of the Academy of Nutrition and Dietetics, 118*(11), 2094–2119.
77. Pustozerov, E., Chernykh, V. Y., Popova, P., Vasyukova, E., Tkachuk, A., & Yuldashev, Z. (2020). Health monitoring system for patients with gestational diabetes mellitus based on nutrition diaries and fitness bracelets. *BioMedical Engineering, 53*(5), 305–308.
78. Qiu, J., Lo, F. P. W., Sun, Y., Wang, S., & Lo, B. (2019). *Mining discriminative food regions for accurate food recognition.*
79. Reščič, N., Valenčič, E., Mlinarič, E., Seljak, B. K., & Luštrek, M. (2019). Mobile nutrition monitoring for well-being. In *Adjunct Proceedings of the 2019 ACM International Joint Conference on Pervasive and Ubiquitous Computing and Proceedings of the 2019 ACM International Symposium on Wearable Computers* (pp. 1194–1197).

80. Sahoo, D., Hao, W., Ke, S., Xiongwei, W., Le, H., Achananuparp, P., Lim, E.-P., & Hoi, S. C. (2019). Foodai: Food image recognition via deep learning for smart food logging. In *Proceedings of the 25th ACM SIGKDD International Conference on Knowledge Discovery & Data Mining* (pp. 2260–2268).
81. Salvador, A., Drozdzal, M., Giro-i Nieto, X., & Romero, A. (2019). Inverse cooking: Recipe generation from food images. In *Proceedings of the IEEE Conference on Computer Vision and Pattern Recognition* (pp. 10453–10462).
82. Shimoda, W., & Yanai, K. (2015). Cnn-based food image segmentation without pixel-wise annotation. In *International Conference on Image Analysis and Processing* (pp. 449–457). Springer.
83. Shimoda, W., & Yanai, K. (2016). Foodness proposal for multiple food detection by training of single food images. In *Proceedings of the 2nd International Workshop on Multimedia Assisted Dietary Management* (pp. 13–21).
84. Shrestha, L. B. (2000). Population aging in developing countries: The elderly populations of developing countries are now growing more rapidly than those in industrialized nations, thanks to health advances and declining fertility rates. *Health Affairs, 19*(3), 204–212.
85. Solanas, A., Patsakis, C., Conti, M., Vlachos, I. S., Ramos, V., Falcone, F., Postolache, O., Pérez-Martínez, P. A., Di Pietro, R., Perrea, D. N., et al. (2014). Smart health: A context-aware health paradigm within smart cities. *IEEE Communications Magazine, 52*(8), 74–81.
86. Song, G., Tao, Z., Huang, X., Cao, G., Liu, W., & Yang, L. (2020). Hybrid attention-based prototypical network for unfamiliar restaurant food image few-shot recognition. *IEEE Access, 8*, 14893–14900.
87. Stumbo, P. J. (2013). New technology in dietary assessment: A review of digital methods in improving food record accuracy. *Proceedings of the Nutrition Society, 72*(1), 70–76.
88. Sundaravadivel, P., Kesavan, K., Kesavan, L., Mohanty, S. P., Kougianos, E., & Ganapathiraju, M. (2018). Smart-log: An automated, predictive nutrition monitoring system for infants through the iot. In *2018 IEEE International Conference on Consumer Electronics (ICCE)* (pp. 1–4). IEEE.
89. Szegedy, C., Ioffe, S., Vanhoucke, V., & Alemi, A. A. (2017). Inception-v4, inception resnet and the impact of residual connections on learning. In *Thirty-First AAAI Conference on Artificial Intelligence.*
90. Szegedy, C., Vanhoucke, V., Ioffe, S., Shlens, J., & Wojna, Z. (2016). Rethinking the inception architecture for computer vision. In *Proceedings of the IEEE Conference on Computer Vision and Pattern Recognition* (pp. 2818–2826).
91. Tahir, G. A., & Loo, C. K. (2020). An open-ended continual learning for food recognition using class incremental extreme learning machines. *IEEE Access, 8*, 82328–82346.
92. Tan, M., & Le, Q. V. (2019). *Efficientnet: Rethinking model scaling for convolutional neural networks*. arXiv:1905.11946.
93. Tanno, R., Okamoto, K., & Yanai, K. (2016). Deepfoodcam: A dcnn-based real-time mobile food recognition system. In *Proceedings of the 2nd International Workshop on Multimedia Assisted Dietary Management* (p. 89).
94. Tasci, E. (2020). Voting combinations-based ensemble of fine-tuned convolutional neural networks for food image recognition. *Multimedia Tools and Applications*, 1–22.
95. Thong, Y. J., Nguyen, T., Zhang, Q., Karunanithi, M., & Yu, L. (2017). Predicting food nutrition facts using pocket-size near-infrared sensor. In *2017 39th Annual International Conference of the IEEE Engineering in Medicine and Biology Society (EMBC)* (pp. 742–745). IEEE.
96. UN, P. D. (2002). *Madrid international plan of action on ageing*. Second World Assembly on Ageing, Madrid, Spain.
97. Wang, X., Kumar, D., Thome, N., Cord, M., & Precioso, F. (2015). Recipe recognition with large multimodal food dataset. In *2015 IEEE International Conference on Multimedia & Expo Workshops (ICMEW)* (pp. 1–6). IEEE.
98. Wang, Y., Chen, J.-j., Ngo, C.-W., Chua, T.-S., Zuo, W., & Ming, Z. (2019). Mixed dish recognition through multi-label learning. In *Proceedings of the 11th Workshop on Multimedia for Cooking and Eating Activities* (pp. 1–8).

99. Wang, Y., Chen, J.-j., Ngo, C.-W., Chua, T.-S., Zuo, W., & Ming, Z. (2019). Mixed dish recognition through multi-label learning. In *Proceedings of the 11th Workshop on Multimedia for Cooking and Eating Activities*, CEA '19 (pp. 1–8). New York, NY, USA: Association for Computing Machinery.
100. Wu, H., Merler, M., Uceda-Sosa, R., & Smith, J. R. (2016). Learning to make better mistakes: Semantics-aware visual food recognition. In *Proceedings of the 24th ACM International Conference on Multimedia* (pp. 172–176).
101. Xie, S., Girshick, R., Dollár, P., Tu, Z., & He, K. (2017). Aggregated residual transformations for deep neural networks. In *Proceedings of the IEEE Conference on Computer Vision and Pattern Recognition* (pp. 1492–1500).
102. Zhang, Y., & Parker, A. G. (2020). Eat4thought: A design of food journaling. In *Extended Abstracts of the 2020 CHI Conference on Human Factors in Computing Systems* (pp. 1–8).
103. Zhao, H., Yap, K.-H., Kot, A. C., & Duan, L. (2020). Jdnet: A joint-learning distilled network for mobile visual food recognition. *IEEE Journal of Selected Topics in Signal Processing*.
104. Zheng, X., Gong, Y., Lei, Q., Yao, R., & Yin, Q. (2018). Multi-view model contour matching based food volume estimation. In *International Conference on Applied Human Factors and Ergonomics* (pp. 85–93). Springer.
105. Zhou, B., Khosla, A., Lapedriza, A., Oliva, A., & Torralba, A. (2016). Learning deep features for discriminative localization. In *Proceedings of the IEEE Conference on Computer Vision and Pattern Recognition* (pp. 2921–2929).

Social Behaviour and Cognitive Monitoring in Healthy Ageing

Christina Röcke, Sabrina Guye, Michele Girolami, and I. Kniestedt

Abstract Social integration is a key predictor of health in later life, as is cognitive functioning. This chapter describes the evidence related to levels of and interventions on social integration and cognitive functioning for older adults and outlines how this evidence was translated into the personalized coaching approach in NESTORE in both of these domains. From the technological side, social beacons are used to obtain objective contact measures for users' local social networks and thus complement self-report information on social interactions beyond face-to-face contacts. In the cognitive domain, a serious game involving a multidomain cognitive training was developed on the basis of evidence-based game and training principles.

1 Introduction

Social participation, that is having a social network of close others available to draw upon in good and bad times represents a strong correlator and predictor of physical and mental health as well as survival [11, 24, 33].

The social networks of older adults tend to be overall smaller than during midlife and young adulthood, but the number of emotionally close other persons remains fairly stable until old age on average [14, 15] and the availability of social support also tends to be maintained [12]. Consistent with the notion that emotionally close others remain available in the networks from young up to old age, certain social relationship types show greater changes than others. For instance, the family network shows stability from adolescence/young adulthood to old age, whereas the friendship

C. Röcke (✉) · S. Guye
University of Zurich, University Research Priority Program "Dynamics of Healthy Aging", Andreasstrasse 15, Box 2, C8050 Zurich, Switzerland
e-mail: christina.roecke@uzh.ch

M. Girolami
National Council of Research, ISTI-CNR, Pisa, Italy

I. Kniestedt
Technical University Delft, Delft, Netherlands

G. Andreoni and C. Mambretti (eds.), *Digital Health Technology for Better Aging*, Research for Development, https://doi.org/10.1007/978-3-030-72663-8_6

and personal network show decreases into old age and networks with co-workers or neighbours play an important role only in defined periods during the life span [9]. Social and emotional functioning shows reliable interplay. Older adults tend to report greater satisfaction with their networks than younger adults [9] and they report fewer negative social interactions than their younger counterparts [6].

With the rise of experience sampling and ambulatory assessment methods and designs in psychological research, including lifespan developmental and ageing research (e.g., [8, 23, 34], there have been novel ways of examining social integration more in terms of a behaviour and fluctuating experience and not only as a stable person characteristic and over long-term time spans using survey questionnaires that tap the general/typical or retrospective status of the social network and social support exchanges as well as leisure activities including those that involve social interactions (e.g., [25]). Much of this research is conducted in young adult samples (e.g., [16, 23]). Older adults have been shown to report fewer interpersonal stressors than middle-aged and younger adults and also that they felt less stressed in reaction to the tensions that occurred than young adults [7, 10]. Older adults, compared to younger age groups, have also been found to report more interpersonal tensions with spouses than with children, unlike younger age-groups which may be due to the fact that older adults' children have likely moved out from home and even further away, so there is less room for tension. In line with the expectation that lifelong experience in dealing with emotional situations, older adults have also been found to show more passive constructive (e.g., do noting) behaviour in response to tensions than middle-aged and younger adults, and less arguing than the younger adults [7].

Many interventions in the social domain do not target older adults [12]. Of those that do explicitly have the older population in mind, many have a strong focus on decreasing or preventing loneliness and aim on improving social skills, enhancing social support, increasing opportunities for social interaction and social cognitive training [27]. These target domains reflect theoretical models of loneliness that propose an individual difference concept such that lonely and non-lonely individuals approach and appraise social encounters differently, including more sceptical and negative perceptions of and during interactions and behaviours that are more likely to lead to rejection on the side of the lonely persons [cf. 27]. Many loneliness interventions thus intend to increase the quantity and quality of relationships. To date, there is mixed evidence on the success of social network interventions in later life (e.g., [13]). The general coaching approach in the social well-being domain in NESTORE is described in more detail in chapter "The Multi-domain Coaching Approach to Counteract Ageing Decline".

Cognition is among the most widely studied domains in the ageing literature. Despite the possible stereotype and assumption of prevailing losses, cognitive functioning does not show uniform decline as people age. Much in line with lifespan theoretical notion of multidirectional development [1], two components of cognitive functioning can be differentiated and show distinct trajectories of age-related change: whereas fluid abilities such as processing speed and working memory tend to decline with increasing age, crystallized abilities such as vocabulary, knowledge,

Table 1 Self-report social monitoring variables and instruments

Construct	Measurement instrument
Social well-being status (Baseline, Posttest)	
Loneliness	De Jong Gierveld loneliness scale
Social integration with family and friends	Lubben social network scale 6
Perceived social support	Berlin social support scales
Social well-being in daily life	
Social interactions (Frequency, Type)	Single items from experience sampling literature
Social and emotional loneliness	Single items from De Jong Gierveld loneliness scale

and autobiographical memory tend to increase or be maintained [22, 32]. Overall, in addition to the broad distinction between fluid and crystallized cognitive abilities, there is quite some complexity and heterogeneity in trajectories of stability and change across cognitive domains [21].

In NESTORE, we assessed status and daily life performance in the social and cognitive domains using standard instruments and employed coaching in both of these domains with evidence-based structured and unstructured tasks.

2 Monitoring of Social Behaviour in NESTORE

2.1 Self-reported Social Integration and Behaviour

In NESTORE, the social status and behaviour of the users are assessed both at baseline and post test, as well as in daily life during the coaching phase, using various standard questionnaires that focus on measuring social and emotional loneliness and the degree of social integration with family and friends. Furthermore, we assess received and provided social support as an additional outcome variable related to social well-being. Table 1 provides and overview of the social network constructs assessed within NESTORE and the respective measurement instruments.

2.2 Sensor-Based Social Behaviour Assessments

Understanding the way people interact raises a number of challenges. As reported in the previous section, the NESTORE project implements self-report tools for the social integration with the goal of collecting subjective feedbacks from the end-users during the pilot sites. This approach is undoubtful a first required step for a better comprehension of the social attitude of people, while following the NESTORE pathways. The data collected can provide a first outlook of the amount and of the quality of the social interactions. However, such approach can be complemented with a second method based on the objective measurement of the features characterizing of the social context. To this end, we describe the monitoring and analytics tools designed for monitoring interactions among subjects involved in the NESTORE pilot sites with sensing-based devices.

The pervasive diffusion of mobile sensing technologies opens to a new era for experiments and initiatives devoted to revealing the ties binding people. A tie between two individuals is the result of several factors combined together, such as the time spent in proximity, emotional intensity, use of gestures and verbal communication [19], such factors ultimately determine the strength of a tie [26]. The NESTORE project focuses on one of such sociological markers, namely proximity, as a necessary condition for a face-to-face social interaction. Determining the proximity between two or more individuals refers to the possibility of detecting, with sensing technologies, those users who are nearby. As originally proposed by Edwad T. Hall in 1963 with the term proxemics, interactions among people, generally, happen in the so-called social space, a virtual radius surrounding us ranging from 1 to 3.5 m approximately. Of course, such range can vary according to numerous factors: obstacles, crowded environments, personal attitude etc. nevertheless we argue that it represents a reference distance to be considered for detecting people in the nearby.

Proximity can be detected by assuming that a personal device, e.g., a smartphone, smartwatch or a tag, acts as proxy for the person. More specifically, we aim at detecting the proximity between user's devices with proximity-based sensing technologies. To this purpose, we adopted the Bluetooth Low Energy technology as a cheap and effective solution for the identification of devices at a given distance. We briefly report the main features of the NESTORE kit adopted for the proximity detection, we refer to chapters "Monitoring in the Physical Domain to Support Active Ageing", "Nutritional Monitoring in Older People Prevention Services" and "Building Trust and Companionship in e-Coaching Through Embodiment" and to [30] for an in-depth description of the hardware design. The kit is composed by two elements: a receiver and an emitter, as reported in Fig. 1. The receiver is the NESTORE wristband, described in chapter "Monitoring in the Physical Domain to Support Active Ageing", able to receive, store and upload short messages broadcasted by the emitting devices. The emitter is a Bluetooth tag that periodically propagates messages with a given advertisement rate and at a given power of emission. Since the emitter is configured to broadcast messages at a given power, the receiver can listen for such messages only at a given distance from the emitter. As a result, messages are recorded only from devices at a given proximity. The receiver stores some information about the messages it receives, the timestamp, the id of the message and the received signal strength indicator (RSSI) as a measurement of the quality of the messages. The higher the RSSI, the closer the emitting device. The relationship between RSSI and distance holds in outdoor environments under a specific condition [3]: without the presence of obstacles in-between the emitter and the receiver and without any kind of wireless interferences. Differently, in indoor environments, the strength-distance

Fig. 1 The NESTORE kit for detecting proximity between users

relationship might not hold because obstacles, multi-path fading, interferences and human bodies can alter the quality of the signals [2]. Both the emitter and the receiver have been designed to operate continuously without the explicit user intervention.

The emitter devices are assigned only to the primary NESTORE users, namely the individuals recruited according to the selection criteria defined for the purpose of the pilot studies. The NESTORE user is required to wear the NESTORE wristband all day and to recharge it periodically. The receiving devices are assigned to the user's local circle, namely a set of 5 people (friends/relatives/caregivers/neighbours) identified by every NESTORE user (see Fig. 1). The members of the local circle are required to bring the emitter devices every time she/he visits the NESTORE user. To serve this purpose the emitter device is a simple tag that can be locked to the key-ring or put in the pocket.

As a result, the NESTORE user's devices keep track of all the messages propagated by devices of the local circle. The data set obtained enables to analyse such messages and to estimate the proximity between the user and a member of her/his local circle, such information is used to measure two key metrics: the amount of interactions between every NESTORE user with her/his local circle and the duration of such contacts.

The SID algorithm [2] is used to detect the proximity between devices (emitter and receiver). SID has been designed for a Cloud-based environment. In particular, the SID algorithm runs periodically on a virtual machine of the NESTORE Cloud, performing the following two steps: (i) Extract for each NESTORE user the data collected from the receiver device, (ii) Analysing the messages and detecting the proximity between all pairs of devices (emitter and receiver). The first operation consists of extracting the messages received from a no-SQL storage unit, while the second operation consists of analysing the time series of the messages. The proximity detection exploits two features: the rate of messages lost and the RSSI of the messages received. More specifically, the lower the number of messages sent and the higher the RSSI of the messages received, the higher the probability for a pair of devices to be in proximity. Such analysis is performed for each of the NESTORE users once per day. The metrics computed are, in turn, uploaded to the NESTORE ZivaCare system providing data to the NESTORE app. Figure 2 reports an example of the user interfaces designed for the NESTORE users.

The app reports the number and the duration of the interactions with the members of the local circle. It is worth to notice that the design of the user interface has been developed considering two key aspects:

- To avoid any kind of evaluation about the amount and duration of the interactions;
- To provide simple and intuitive data, easily comprehensible for the NESTORE users.

Concerning the first aspect, it is out of the scope of this project to provide a qualitative assessment of the interactions, rather we aim to demonstrate the possibility of automatically inferring the existence of a social interaction by exploiting sensing devices based on commercial and massively available technologies (e.g., Bluetooth Low Energy protocol). Concerning the second aspect, we did not introduce not-intuitive metrics, as they might dissuade the end-users to keep using the

Fig. 2 The local circle metrics available within the NESTORE app

application and hence reduce the motivation during the pilot study. Finally, we argue that the information reported to the NESTORE users (number and duration of the interactions) play the role of an incentive mechanism for the project adherence as they provide a tool to self-monitor one's own trajectory and evolution week after week.

The proximity technologies employed with the NESTORE project are now extremely diffused, as the recent COVID-19 pandemic demonstrated the effectiveness of tracing apps based on the proximity detection. However, we argue that for a better and more accurate identification of ties binding people it is required to mix multiple sources of information: speech, body orientation, and gesture. The combination of them even more helps to identify the explicit voluntariness of interaction for a dyad (pair of subjects). In fact, relying only on the proximity might introduce false positive interactions due to external factors not depending on the user's willingness to socialize. The NESTORE experience framed a path towards a better comprehension of the social domain with sensing technologies, and we are ready to follow it.

3 Monitoring of Cognitive Functioning in NESTORE

3.1 Assessing Cognitive Status at Baseline and Posttest

Cognitive functioning is multidimensional, encompassing various facets of fluid intelligence (i.e., more biologically driven abilities) and of cristallized intelligence (i.e., predominantely knowledge and experience-driven abilities). We thus assess multiple cognitive abilities at both baseline and posttest, and focus on key abilities for training, such as executive functioning and broader everyday cognition abilities in multi-domain approaches.

3.1.1 Trained Domains

One coaching pathways in the cognitive well-being domain focuses on a structured working memory training involving a numerical updating task that can be administered in an adaptive way such that task difficulty is continuously adapted to the current performance of an individual. To assess training gains, we assess performance in this same task at baseline and at posttest, complemented by assessements of executive functioning in two additional very standard psychometric tasks (i.e., to assess near transfer).

Table 2 Cognitive monitoring variables and instruments

Construct	Measurement instrument
Cognitive status (Baseline, Posttest)	
Task switching	Trail making test B
Working memory	N-back Digit span backwards Numerical updating
General fluid ability	Berlin intelligence structure test (BIS-4)
Processing speed	Digit symbol substitution test
Attention	Trail making test A
Everyday performance	Cognitive failure questionnaire
Cognitive performance in daily life: monitoring	
Working memory	Digit span backwards (cognitive monitoring in daily life)
Daily everyday cognitive functioning	Everyday memory failures questionnaire

3.1.2 Transfer Domains

To assess transfer to other untrained domains (i.e., far transfer), we further measure task switching, general fluid abiliy, processing speed, attention and self-reported everyday performance Table 2.

3.2 Assessing Cognitive Performance Throughout the Coaching Phase

3.2.1 Computerized Structured Cognitive Tasks

The first of two structured cognitive coaching pathways involved performance on a numerical updating task and thus train individual in the domain of working memory, a very common training domain [20]. In this task users perform arithmetic operations with two to four digits that appear in a grid presented on the smartphone screen. Individuals have to either add or subtract a number to or from those digits. After performing a total of five (easy condition used in daily life; eight operations for more difficult alternative version of task that was part of the baseline and posttest assessments) arithmetic operations individuals have to enter the final digits into each cell. When accuracy equals 0.8 or higher across one session, task difficulty is increased by one level or decreased by one level if accuracy is below 0.6, which means adding an additional cell and respective digit to the grid and total number of operations.

3.2.2 Serious Game

The second structured cognitive coaching pathway involved a so-called serious game. For many years, researchers and developers alike have worked on producing serious games designed to train the mind [28]. One of the most notable examples is Brain Age, also known as Dr. Kawashima's Brain Training [29], on the Nintendo DS. Brain training games aim to prevent cognitive decline or to measure cognitive ability [4, 17, 31, 35]. While such games have proven themselves popular with audiences, empirical evidence to their usefulness in training cognitive ability is scarce [4]. Often, these 'brain-games' focus on providing the player with puzzle-like tasks, such as crosswords and math problems. At the same time, evaluation of these games rarely goes beyond initial user responses, with long-term studies on their potential benefits lacking [18].

Pocket Odyssey, the game developed as part of the NESTORE system and based on a serious game specifically developed for healthy older adult users and indicating successful training and transfer effects [5], consists of three components. The first is the 'Ship', which functions as the main 'hub' for the player and allows access to the other parts of the game. The other parts are the 'Gym' and the 'Submarine' mini-games (see Fig. 3). The Gym game is designed for physical training and as such will not be discussed further. The Submarine game is a game for cognitive training and assessment that incorporates the tasks outlined earlier in this chapter. The first time a NESTORE user starts the game, they are welcomed by the character Nestor. He is the player's guide to the game. In the introduction, he informs the player that he requires their help in fixing up his ship. Once Nestor has established the premise

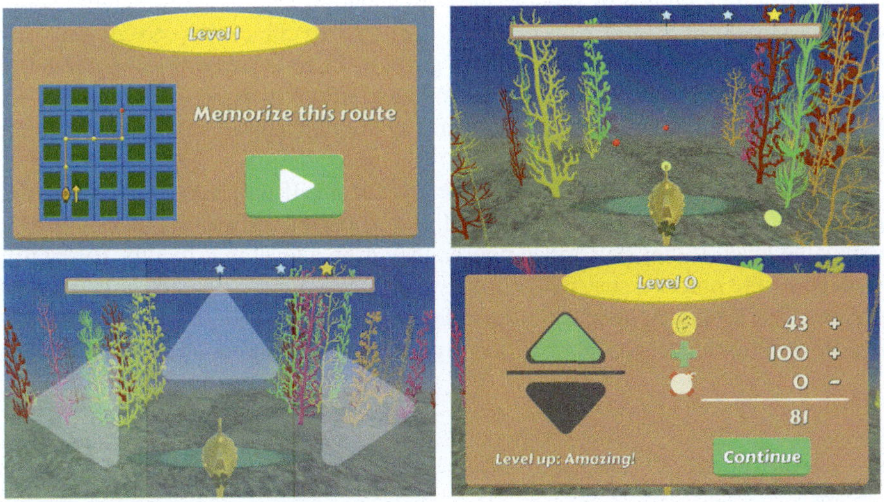

Fig. 3 Example map for a player to memorize (top left), the submarine game screen showing action radius and various pickups (top right), a player reaching a crossroads and choosing which direction the submarine will go next (bottom left), and the final scoring screen (bottom right)

of the game, he guides the player through a short tutorial that explains the basic functionality.

In the Submarine game, players are asked to memorize a route on a map with a grid. Depending on the level of difficulty, the route has a certain length and therefore requires the memorization of a number of directions to turn on each juncture. At the same time, players need to steer the submarine by tilting the mobile device so that they can collect treasure in the water, all the while avoiding bombs.

After players choose the Submarine game from the main menu, they can choose to play any of the training levels. Each of these levels introduces the player to a different aspect of the game. Playing these levels is optional and does not net the player a reward. The player starts the game by pressing the main play button. This loads the last level that the player reached. First, the player is shown a route on a map. The difficulty of the route increases with level tiers. For example, between levels 1 and 5 the player needs to complete a route with 3 junctions, while levels 45–50 consist of routes with 12 junctions. There are multiple possible layouts for the player to receive for each level. This is to improve variability and replay-ability of the game, as well as retaining challenge.

Once the player has memorized the route, they press continue. They are then presented with a 3D environment of a submarine moving through seaweed on an ocean floor. Coins and bombs may appear along the path, the frequency and ratio of which depend on the difficulty level. Players tilt their mobile device to steer the submarine left and right. The goal is to steer the submarine close to coins and collect them by tapping the screen to earn points. The player should not tap the screen when they are in range of a bomb, as this deducts points. Whenever the player reaches a junction, they need to remember in which direction the submarine will go next and confirm their choice by tapping the corresponding button on the screen. Sound effects and a score bar inform the player of whether their choice was correct, and when they collect coins or bombs. With all the game mechanics together—memorization of a route, directing the submarine, and picking up the treasure while ignoring the bombs—the submarine game tests players' spatial navigation skills, accuracy, and inhibition.

Once players finish the route, they see their score. If they score above a certain percentage, they advance to the next level. If they performed averagely, they need to replay the level. If they performed poorly, they drop a level in difficulty. Every fifth level earns the player a star, while in-between or previously cleared levels earn the player coins. Both can be used to upgrade the ship in the main screen of the game, providing a light incentive to keep playing and reaching higher levels.

4 Conclusion

In NESTORE, social and cognitive monitoring occurred within a broad battery of standardized, reliable and valid instruments at baseline and posttest as well as in daily life as part of the general daily life monitoring of individuals as well as of the coaching pathways. The battery ensures a broad range of information to be fed into the Decision Support System that allows user-specific recommendations, and also an empirically sound evaluation of coaching effectiveness in both of these key domains of psychological well-being and health.

References

1. Baltes, P. B., Staudinger, U. M., & Lindenberger, U. (1999). Lifespan psychology: Theory and application to intellectual functioning. *Annual Review of Psychology, 50*(1), 471–507.
2. Baronti, P., Girolami, M., Mavilia, F., Palumbo, F., & Luisetto, G. (2020). On the analysis of human posture for detecting social interactions with wearable devices. In *IEEE International Conference on Human-Machine Systems (ICHMS)*, Rome, Italy (pp. 1–6).
3. Barsocchi, P., Oligeri, G., & Potorti, F. (2009). Measurement-based frame error model for simulating outdoor Wi-Fi networks. *IEEE Transactions on Wireless Communications, 8*(3), 1154–1158.
4. Binder, J. C., Zöllig, J., Eschen, A., Mérillat, S., Röcke, C., Schoch, S., et al. (2015). Multi-domain training in healthy old age: Hotel Plastisse as an iPad-based serious game to systematically compare multi-domain and single-domain training. *Frontiers in Aging Neuroscience, 7*, 137.
5. Binder, J. C., Martin, M., Zöllig, J., Röcke, C., Mérillat, S., Eschen, A., et al. (2016). Multi-domain training enhances attentional control. *Psychology and Aging, 31*(4).
6. Birditt, K. S., & Fingerman, K. L. (2003). Age and gender differences in adults' descriptions of emotional reactions to interpersonal problems. *The Journals of Gerontology Series B: Psychological Sciences and Social Sciences, 58*(4), P237–P245.
7. Birditt, K. S., Fingerman, K. L., & Almeida, D. M. (2005). Age differences in exposure and reactions to interpersonal tensions: A daily diary study. *Psychology and Ageing, 20*(2), 330.
8. Brose, A., & Ebner-Priemer, U. W. (2015). Ambulatory assessment in the research on ageing: Contemporary and future applications. *Gerontology, 61*(4), 372–380.
9. Carstensen, L. L. (1992). Social and emotional patterns in adulthood: Support for socioemotional selectivity theory. *Psychology and Aging, 7*(3), 331–338.
10. Charles, S. T., Piazza, J. R., Luong, G., & Almeida, D. M. (2009). Now you see it, now you don't: Age differences in affective reactivity to social tensions. *Psychology and Ageing, 24*(3), 645.
11. Dahan-Oliel, N., Gelinas, I., & Mazer, B. (2008). Social participation in the elderly: What does the literature tell us?. *Critical Reviews™ in Physical and Rehabilitation Medicine, 20*(2).
12. Ertel, K. A., Glymour, M. M., & Berkman, L. F. (2009). Social networks and health: A life course perspective integrating observational and experimental evidence. *Journal of Social and Personal Relationships, 26*(1), 73–92.
13. Findlay, R. A. (2003). Interventions to reduce social isolation amongst older people: where is the evidence? *Ageing & Society, 23*(5), 647–658.
14. Fung, H. H., Carstensen, L. L., & Lang, F. R. (2001). Age-related patterns in social networks among European Americans and African Americans: Implications for socioemotional selectivity across the life span. *The International Journal of Ageing and Human Development, 52*(3), 185–206.
15. Fung, H. H., Stoeber, F. S., Yeung, D. Y. L., & Lang, F. R. (2008). Cultural specificity of socioemotional selectivity: Age differences in social network composition among Germans and Hong Kong Chinese. *The Journals of Gerontology Series B: Psychological Sciences and Social Sciences, 63*(3), P156–P164.
16. Gable, S. L., Gosnell, C. L., & Prok, T. (2012). Close relationships. In M. R. Mehl & T. S. Conner (Eds.), *Handbook of Research Methods for Studying Daily Life* (pp. 511–524). New York: Guilford.

17. Gamberini, L., Raya, M. A., Barresi, G., et al. (2006) Cognition, technology and games for the elderly: An introduction to ELDERGAMES project. *PsychNology Journal, 4*, 285–308.
18. Granic, I., Lobel, A., & Engels, R. C. (2014). The benefits of playing video games. *American Psychologist, 69*(66), 390–408.
19. Granovetter, M. (1983). The strength of weak ties: A network theory revisited. *Sociological Theory, 1*, 201–233.
20. Guye, S., Röcke, C., Mérillat, S., von Bastian, C. C., & Martin, M. (2016). Plasticity in different age groups: Adult lifespan. In T. Strobach & J. Karbach (Eds.), *Cognitive Training: An Overview of Features and Applications* (pp. 45–55). Berlin: Springer.
21. Hartshorne, J. K., & Germine, L. T. (2015). When does cognitive functioning peak? The asynchronous rise and fall of different cognitive abilities across the life span. *Psychological Science, 26*(4), 433–443.
22. Hedden, T., & Gabrieli, J. D. (2004). Insights into the ageing mind: A view from cognitive neuroscience. *Nature Reviews Neuroscience, 5*(2), 87.
23. Hoppmann, C. A., & Riediger, M. (2009). Ambulatory assessment in lifespan psychology: An overview of current status and new trends. *European Psychologist, 14*(2), 98–108.
24. House, J. S., Landis, K. R., & Umberson, D. (1988). Social relationships and health. *Science, 241*(4865), 540–545.
25. Jopp, D. S., & Hertzog, C. (2010). Assessing adult leisure activities: An extension of a self-report activity questionnaire. *Psychological assessment, 22*(1), 108.
26. Marsden, P. V., & Campbell, K. E. (1984). Measuring tie strength. *Social Forces, 63*(2), 482–501.
27. Masi, C. M., Chen, H. Y., Hawkley, L. C., & Cacioppo, J. T. (2011). A meta-analysis of interventions to reduce loneliness. *Personality and Social Psychology Review, 15*(3), 219–266.
28. Michael, D. R., Chen, S. L. (2005). *Serious games: Games that educate, train, and inform.* Muska & Lipman/Premier-Trade.
29. Nintendo. (2005). Brain age: Train your brain in minutes a day!
30. Palumbo, F., Crivello, A., Furfari, F., Girolami, M., Mastropietro, A., Manferdelli, G., et al. (2020). "Hi This Is NESTORE, Your Personal Assistant": Design of an integrated IoT system for a personalized coach for healthy aging. *Frontiers in Digital Health, 2*, 545949.
31. Pazzi, S., Falleri, V., Puricelli, S., et al. (2014). A serious games platform for early diagnosis of mild cognitive impairments. *Games for health* (pp. 110–113). Springer.
32. Salthouse, T. A. (2010). Selective review of cognitive ageing. *Journal of the International Neuropsychological Society, 16*(5), 754–760.
33. Seeman, T. E. (1996). Social ties and health: The benefits of social integration. *Annals of Epidemiology, 6*(5), 442–451.
34. Trull, T. J., & Ebner-Priemer, U. (2013). Ambulatory assessment. *Annual review of clinical psychology, 9*, 151–176.
35. Vasconcelos, A., Silva, P. A., Caseiro, J., Nunes, F., & Teixeira, F. (2012) Designing tablet-based games for seniors: The example of CogniPlay, a cognitive gaming platform. In *Proceedings of the 4th International Conference on Fun and Games*. ACM (pp. 1–10).
36. Wrzus, C., Hänel, M., Wagner, J., & Neyer, F. J. (2013). Social network changes and life events across the life span: a meta-analysis. *Psychological Bulletin, 139*(1), 53.

Perspective and Experiences of Decision Support Systems (DSS) and AI in Prevention and Care for Older Adults

Silvia Orte, Paula Subías-Beltrán, Eloisa Vargiu, and Felip Miralles

Abstract This chapter describes the experience with the NESTORE DSS, a software conceived to be the brain of the system, and the main collector of information, which objective is to recommend personalised and targeted activities to be performed by older adults who are willing to prevent decline. It reports on the lessons learnt and important methods of the whole process from the design to the implementation.

1 Introduction

Prevention and care for older adults, together with personal health forecast became possible with the integration of virtual models and Personal Health Systems (PHS) [1]. On the one hand, virtual models are a key added value for a PHS to represent all the important factors related to individuals' status and their context. On the other hand, a PHS is needed for the real-time categorisation of the person, and the selection of the best models that apply in a certain time, allowing the possibility of creating personalised and dynamic models. Although first experiences of PHS date back to 1990s, they have gotten a significant boost in the last decade thanks to the digitalisation of the processes, the use of smartphones and other smart devices, and the use of related technologies. Concretely, in the prevention and care field. Artificial Intelligence technologies involving the following categories have disrupted this research area:

- Behaviour change models and techniques to promote healthy habits analysing and fusing heterogeneous data on different domains as nutrition, physical activity, sleep behaviour social behaviour, and cognitive impairments.
- Expert-driven methods, such as case-based reasoning and rule-based reasoning techniques, to include the expert knowledge into profiling and recommender systems.

S. Orte (✉) · P. Subías-Beltrán · E. Vargiu · F. Miralles
Eurecat, Centre Tecnològic de Catalunya, Digital Health Unit, C/Bilbao, 72, Edifici A, 08005 Barcelona, Spain
e-mail: silvia.orte@eurecat.org

G. Andreoni and C. Mambretti (eds.), *Digital Health Technology for Better Aging*, Research for Development, https://doi.org/10.1007/978-3-030-72663-8_7

- Personalised medicine to prevent and adapt treatments based on longitudinal aggregated data.
- Virtual coach and conversational bots to support users, and communicate with them.
- Analysis and connectivity of IoT data to provide more information about the status of the user in different domains, and facilitate profiling to promote decision support and logistics.

An important field of research that most times comprehends two or more of the listed AI areas, and that recently is being included in PHSs, is the field of Decision Support Systems (DSSs), which can be defined as computerised programs that support users' decision-making activities [2]. They cope with a large list of disciplines and domains ranging from prevention and public health (e.g., NESTORE DSS) to clinical advisory in certain diseases [3]. Given that, also the target audience varies from citizens, patients and health professionals, reflecting such point on the importance of making a proper design and user experience considering the conditions and constraints of each type of final user to both design the final functionalities of the DSS and the way the results are shown. Another important categorization of DSSs is basing them on the usage and the implied models and AI techniques. In this classification, we include three types:

- DSSs that include data-driven models to support decision-making. These ones use historical data to build the models.
- DSSs that include expert-driven models to support decision-making.
- DSSs that predict future trends.

NESTORE DSS includes the above mentioned three types of techniques, and its main objective is to empower users to choose the activities they prefer to do to maintain or improve their quality of life and prevent decline. In particular, it gives the necessary tools to users to decide their wellbeing path helping older adults in choosing coaching plans by suggesting personalised recommendations based on their behaviour and preferences. This intelligent DSS makes an extensive use of Artificial Intelligence techniques to identify such behaviour (like routines, conducts, and likings) for customizing the synergy of the system and the user, and it is based on expert-driven models coming from a variety of domain expert knowledge.

In this chapter, we explain the lessons learnt while developing the NESTORE DSS. Starting from the importance of involving experts on the whole process from designing to implementing, then giving some facts about adding robustness to this kind of systems by selecting the most efficient methods, to finalise with some important facts about the actual implementation of the NESTORE DSS.

2 DSS Design in Healthcare: The Importance of Experts' Involvement

Expert-driven approaches are fundamental in the healthcare field, as they bring all the experience and knowledge into technological and automatic systems. They help end-users, health professionals, and patients to model, exploit, learn from, and create new knowledge, with the final objective of getting compiled information from more than one single professional, having into account the experiences and visions of many stakeholders in one common framework. An Expert System (ES) is a computer program that tries to emulate the experience and understanding of human expertise within a domain. Expert-driven approaches are used in the healthcare field to represent knowledge that usually comes from experts on the discipline of interest. To deal with the modelling and manipulation of this knowledge, another field of Artificial Intelligence called Knowledge Representation (KR) is usually adopted. ESs use KR to facilitate the codification of experts' experience into a knowledge base, which is the basis of any reasoning system (i.e., we can process data with this knowledge base to infer conclusions). Given the objectives of most DSSs, often focused on helping decision-makers to take decisions taking into account large volumes of information and knowledge, they often use ES and KR as inference engines.

The human knowledge can come from different domains (e.g., medical, social, technological) and can be obtained either directly through conversation with experts or previous publications in the diverse fields. However, the latter could lead to misunderstandings or out of scope results if the research group does not include researchers in the field of interest. Therefore, it is crucial to have a multidisciplinary group of people involved in the design of the algorithms of a DSS so that (a) proper knowledge, (b) past experiences, and (c) targeted literature review can be performed during the whole process of design.

In previous works [4, 5], it is described the process of involving domain experts in the design of expert-driven approaches, and the importance of involving them in the whole process: from design to validation. Thus, they are important to understand the requirements to be able to build an ad-hoc and targeted model which very much represents and adapts to real life settings and real people. In healthy ageing domain, the produced technology needs to reproduce all those active ageing guidelines marked as important for domain experts, but also other indicators that are involved in the decision-making of domain experts. A useful way to extract this information is to build use-cases together with the experts, and derive from these conversations the variables that are meaningful for them to take the decisions.

In NESTORE, this process was done in a collaborative manner, and through an iterative process. This procedure had different facets and stages, including: setting-up a group of partners per domain, identifying roles, planning the interaction, and defining, fine-tuning, and tailoring the requirements to each domain specifications. Once specifications are clear, the iterative process starts with a simple planning of a small set of algorithms and/or models to be implemented and validated, selected for being the most generalist or with a higher maturity and readiness to be implemented, and, iteratively, more algorithms are included and, therefore, evolving in new versions until the whole system is planned and ready to be internally tested. At each iteration, design modifications are modelled, and new functional capabilities are added. The validation may include all groups: technical and domain experts, who usually have no computing skills.

NESTORE is grounded in a multi-domain model [6], including physical activity, nutrition, cognitive, mental, and social aspects. It is a point of strength of the project, as it includes multidisciplinary knowledge provided by experts in each of the health domains (geriatricians, but also nutritionists, physiologists, and psychologists), structured into a model, providing an harmonised multidisciplinary expert knowledge. This helps in correctly interpreting the elder status and build an effective personalised intervention plan preserving functionality in each wellness dimension. The final NESTORE model built through this process, is aimed at providing a structured characterisation of the users, built on the expertise of the NESTORE experts (physiologists, nutritionists, psychologists, and geriatricians), able to characterise the person in terms of both status and behaviour. Based on this user definition, NESTORE describes the person considering a multi-domain model, composed of different dimensions related to well-being: Physiological Status and Physical Activity Behaviour, Nutrition, Cognitive and Mental Status, and Social Behaviour.

3 Methods to Build a Robust DSS

The foundations of the DSS are many, but one of its pillars is the usage of synthetic data (see Sect. 3.1), which has allowed us to build a robust system months before having real data thus preventing the cold-start problem. Using synthetic data has also permitted the advance of the harmonisation of resources (i.e., data, processes, ways of communicating between disparate applications), which is key to guarantee that the multiple systems that form NESTORE are integrated, thus interoperable (see Sect. 3.2). Furthermore, a little piece of the synthetic data created has been used as the default value of some later personalised variables, such as the mealtimes (see Sect. 4.3). On the whole, the DSS is an elaborated and multifaceted system that acts as a data collector and processor. This section is closed with Sect. 4.4, that presents the multiple strategies applied to analyse the ability of generalisation of the DSS.

3.1 Preventing the Cold-Start Problem

The cold start problem is a well known and well researched problem for recommender systems, and AI in general. This problem is related to recommendations for new users or novel items. In case of new users, the system does not have information about their preferences in order to make recommendations, i.e., circumstances are not yet optimal for the system to provide the best possible recommendations. A way to mitigate this uncertainty is the generation of synthetic data to (1) generate as different use-cases as possible, and (2) produce models in advance, prior to an eventual pilot.

Synthetic data is any production data applicable to a given situation that is not obtained by direct measurement [7]. It is important because it can be generated to meet specific needs or conditions that are not available in existing (real) data. This can be useful when privacy requirements restrict data availability or how it can be used as Bellovin et al. explain in [8]; or when data is needed for designing or testing any type of system but such data does not exist or is not available to the public, i.e., to represent authentic data setting a baseline for a specific problem [9, 10]; or when training data is needed for machine learning algorithms and it is not available in existing (real) data, the most well-known use cases are the lack of data to train self-driving vehicles [11] or fraud detection systems [12]. In general, synthetic data has a number of benefits:

- once the synthetic environment is ready, it is fast and cheap to generate as much data as needed;
- synthetic data can have perfectly accurate labels, including labelling that might be very expensive or impossible to obtain by hand;
- synthetic data can overcome real data usage restrictions [13].

In the healthcare domain this need for synthetic but plausible data is as imperative as anywhere else due to the high sensitivity of the data. Synthetic data is used to design health classifiers that are accurate, yet preserve people's privacy [14–18].

In order to create synthetic data, you should find real data from which to derive a model that will then be used for the generation of further synthetic data. This model should be built in a way that some relevant characteristics that describe the real data are preserved. For that purpose, a generative model, which aims at learning the true data distribution, could be built using human knowledge or in a semi-automatic manner using unsupervised machine learning techniques [10].

To create synthetic data that describes the elderly population of Europe you can draw statistics from the statistical office of the European Union, *Eurostat*,[1] which is in charge of providing high quality statistics and data on Europe. In their website you can find information about a wide range of topics, such as: household type, income and living conditions, frequency of getting together, immigration, Internet use and activities, participation in volunteer activities or active citizenship, and even body mass index, grouped by sex, age, and educational level. Extracting information from these indicators will allow you to depict the elderly population of Europe in a realistic manner.

[1] https://ec.europa.eu/eurostat.

3.2 Harmonisation and Integration

Complex multi-domain and multidisciplinary projects require the convergence of resources so they are compatible and comparable, and thus facilitate interoperable systems. When working with heterogeneous resources coming from multiple locations it is important to define an integration strategy to improve the interaction between them. The absence of the right integration strategy could give rise to system-specific and intra-system data silos, which can hinder productivity and delay results. Homogenising processes could be achieved by either standardising or harmonising. The former promotes the use of a single methodology, while the latter suggests seeking ways to integrate all disparate resources without imposing a single norm. In other words, harmonisation is a more flexible practice that can be tailored toward the needs of your organisation, as opposed to the strictness of standardisation.

NESTORE is a complex multi-domain and multidisciplinary project that encompasses more than ten different sub-systems. To assure all these sub-systems work together in a synchronised manner, we opted for harmonisation over standardisation due to its flexibility. Thus, each organisation had room for maneuver to fit their heterogeneous environment. In this manner, we guarantee exact data extraction, data integrity, and scalability.

The basis of the NESTORE's integration strategy is that all resources had to be harmonise: coaching plans, raw data (format, unit, and structure), identifiers, server access protocols, Application Programming Interfaces (APIs), Message Queuing Telemetry Transport (MQTTs), etc. In this complex system, the DSS acts as the main data collector playing as a messenger between the diverse subsystems. The DSS connects the eCoach with the rest of NESTORE sub-systems through a long list of endpoints.

3.3 AI Technologies Present in DSSs Approaches

The research landscape proposing the adoption of AI technologies to build intelligent and automatic DSS may be divided to follow in three main research lines:

- Case-Based Reasoning (CBR). It is a methodology proposing the core idea of looking at past cases to find solutions to new ones: a new clinical case is compared against a knowledge base of old ones, the most similar past case is then found and selected, the successful treatments for that case are taken as a blueprint for a new one, and finally adaptations to those treatments are made to tailor the suggestion to the peculiarities of the new case. CBR is a conceptual framework to guide DSS implementations or become the actual implementation backbone of a DSS. CBR has been adopted for delivering intelligence in healthcare systems, its applications range from headache to diabetes [19, 20].
- Rule engines. Likewise CBR, rule engines have both a long history of application in clinical practice, as they guarantee predictable outcomes due to the fact

that, traditionally, they are based on expert clinical knowledge encoded in some computer-interpretable format. This line of research usually produces software tools able to monitor clinical events so as to trigger appropriate action when specific conditions hold, regardless whether they are implemented as full-fledged workflow engines [21] or rule engines [22].
- Machine Learning (ML). This research line includes the deep learning research field, probably the most recent and the most actively exploited nowadays. The promise of letting algorithms crunch thousands of clinical cases data and get back to clinicians with a treatment plan based on empirical evidence is too alluring not to be actively pursued [23, 24]. Accordingly, a plethora of innovative approaches to DSSs and even automated diagnosis emerged in the last decade, with applications ranging from analysis of physiological signals [25] to medical imaging [26].

4 NESTORE DSS as a Whole

NESTORE DSS is an intelligent and innovative software, able to analyse the behaviour of older adults, tracking its changes and its compliance to active ageing guidelines, providing personalised pathways towards the adoption and maintenance of healthy lifestyle. For such a system to work effectively, both person's goals, and overall cognitive, physical, nutritional, and social status need a joint assessment. The profile of users' is continuously updated with daily life activities monitored using technology-based tracking systems to provide a reference frame and basis for the DSS that includes an individualised real-life approach, rather than a mere population-based approach based on maximum performance laboratory-based assessments.

NESTORE DSS personalises healthy recommendations based on experts' guidelines while detects possible declines by analysing: (1) the social interaction of each user to propose activities that will be easily adopted by each individual, and (2) monitoring daily life activities such as watching TV, cooking, housekeeping, going out with friends, taking care of grandchildren, etc. to detect any possible change while performing them.

4.1 *Target Variables and Data Sources*

All data analysis projects starts with the definition of the problem to be solved. And part of the problem definition is defining the target variables. This is the most critical step in the process that relates to the data, and more important than data preparation, missing value imputation, and the algorithm that is used to build the models. The target variables contain all the information that summarises the outcome we would like to predict, classify, or use throughout the data analysis models.

In healthy ageing projects, as NESTORE, the most important target variables are related to individual habits. In NESTORE, target variables were established as indicators related to the acquisition, evaluation, and assessment of *Pathways to well-being* in order to detect, quantify, and propose a way to change a lifestyle that is susceptible to be changed. Every pathway involves one or more behaviours to be changed and represent a major threat to health to the old people in a short- and long-term basis. Since +65 is a critical period because major physical and psychological changes occur and may derive in health decline, an adequate knowledge and tracking of good lifestyle behaviours may prevent the onset of chronic diseases. *Pathways* are therefore the main bare bones of the system and become the guidelines for defining the necessary data to monitor and extract. They address the following habits in NESTORE:

- Dietary habits. Focusing on four nutritional health problems: (1) loss of muscle mass, (2) overweight and obesity, (3) underweight, and (4) not following a healthy diet.
- Active and resting habits. Everyday life habits with respect to an active style (including not only physical activity but also sedentariness and even sleep patterns) involve several behaviours amenable to change, which are significantly associated with the risk of decline.
- Cognitive impairment, including three cognitive intervention types: (a) a traditional computer-based cognitive training intervention, (b) a video game intervention, and (c) a productive intellectual engagement intervention.
- Social interaction and inclusion, focusing on increasing individuals' opportunities for social contacts and improving social skills.

As described in previous chapters, the NESTORE system includes three main sources of information: a sensing system, applications, and contextual services that conforms the necessary points for supplying the required data for modelling the needed behaviours.

After cleaning and processing the information coming from the heterogeneous sources of data (sensors' data streams, questionnaires, and mobile applications), we generate the datasets, which become the basis of the posterior analysis. Depending on the project, datasets are only generated one time or are generated dynamically as the information arrives to our servers. After that, the objective is to extract knowledge from the datasets in order to extract metrics and indicators used by the subsequent components to infer new knowledge or to provide personalised recommendations.

Data sources in the lifestyle monitoring domain are mainly based on (a) wearables and environmental bio-sensing technologies, (b) mobile applications, and (c) questionnaires [27]. All these technologies have enabled the development of automatic systems to monitor not only outward behaviours, but also inward physiological states in humans. These monitoring systems are focused on the analysis of a broad range of indicators such as physical activity, physiological and clinical measures, habits, sleep patterns, and nutritional behaviours among others.

4.2 Architecture and Derived Workflows

The DSS has been designed and built based on the behavioural change model adopted by NESTORE: the HAPA model (chapter "Coaching Older Adults Towards a Healthier Lifestyle: Psychological and Technological Methods"). The DSS plays a role in each of the phases defined by HAPA: the *motivational phase* is used by the DSS to gather data about the users, and the *volitional phase* starts by the DSS suggesting multiple pathways to follow and lasts while the DSS sends recommendations of CEs to perform.

The algorithm infrastructure comprises unsupervised and semi-supervised algorithms for the inference of user's behavioural profile and the detection of bad behaviours. Users' trends in the five well-being dimensions are described in one single semantically annotated model (chapter "System Interoperability for Next Gen Services at Home. A Challenge/Opportunity for Integration") giving the possibility of inferring the necessary information to understand the peculiarities of each user among the other users in different scenarios thus generating the appropriate feedback. NESTORE DSS is based on a three-layer structure: (1) a short term analysis that analyses data on a daily basis; (2) a long term analysis that looks at trends and is able to detect change and adapts the coach in the long term, following the changing needs of people as they age; and (3) a combined short and long term analysis to provide a personalised mix of activities for finally sending personalised plans to the Coach when appropriate. The recognised trends are combined in the DSS with context reasoning to provide robust and recommendations. In Fig. 1, we show the DSS and the modules that helps the user to decide which activities are more convenient for them, depending on their profile, the results from questionnaires and physical activity tests, and the indicators coming from IoT system.

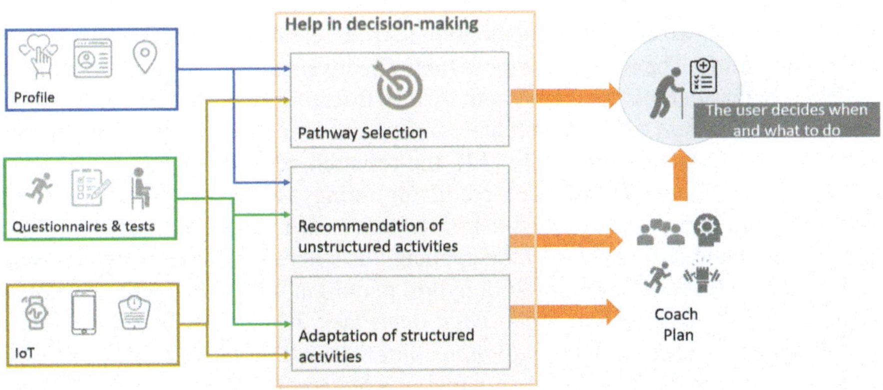

Fig. 1 The NESTORE DSS

4.3 Data Analysis Pipelines

The DSS processes the data gathered to infer behaviours and routines and recommend the most appropriate coaching plan becoming, thus, the intelligence of NESTORE. Data is gathered through numerous data sources and stored in the NESTORE cloud. Every night, the DSS processes the new data and updates its knowledge about all the active users. The DSS aims at adapting to the user's change of behaviour offering the most suitable recommendation at every time.

The data analyses that have more influence on the day-to-day communication of NESTORE are the inference of the daily meal routines, the study of the physical activities performed, and the analyses on the ratings given to the performed *coaching events* (CEs).

The daily meal routines are updated every two weeks based on the information gathered from the sleep sensor and the nutritional coaching; the two data sources are combined to infer the common wake up and sleep time, and the moments when users tend to start their meals.

The daily study of the physical activities performed is used to update the necessity of recommending unstructured CEs and to recalculate the duration of the structured training sessions.

Finally, the ratings that users give to each of the CEs they have performed is used to calculate the similarity among users and try to recommend the most appropriate CE to users based on their likings and the preferences of users that enjoy similar CEs.

4.4 Validation

There are mainly two evaluation methodologies to assess recommender systems [28]: offline and online. The former evaluates their effectiveness on a certain dataset [29]; while the latter attempts to assess them by a A/B testing [29–31]. Due to the small size of the pilots (less than 100 volunteers), we opt for an offline validation strategy.

As stated by Herlocker et al. in [32], the research community has moved from the *annotation in context* task (i.e., predicting ratings) to the *find good items* task (i.e., providing users with a ranked list of recommended items), which better corresponds to realistic settings in working applications where recommender systems are deployed. In NESTORE, we opt for a hybrid paradigm where the recommendation of pathways is categorised as a *find good items* task, while the CEs recommender system fits better under the *annotation in context* task description. This decision is made to cope with the interface design that was already in place.

The pathway recommender is assessed by *precision-based metrics*, such as the precision and the recall [33]. Both metrics capture the quality of a ranking from a slightly different angle. More specifically, precision accounts for the fraction of recommended items that are relevant, whereas recall is the fraction of the relevant items that has been recommended. The formulas of these metrics were posed by Baeza-Yates and Ribeiro-Neto in [34].

The validation of the CEs recommender system is manyfold. Both the *error* and the *precision* of the recommendations are evaluated to understand the system's performance. This strategy assumes that users rate all CEs that they execute. However, users tend to be too lazy to rate all the CEs they perform. For that reason, we end up with mostly only the so-called implicit ratings, which do not allow us to measure the ratings error because there are no ratings. We only have a value indicating whether users perform a CE or not. The implicit ratings may be called the unary ratings, which you know from Facebook's "Like" button: the rating is either positive, or unknown. On the other hand, we consider alternative performance criteria such as the *coverage* and the *diversity*. CEs coverage is analysed to test which proportion of CEs are recommended [29, 35]; and diversity is evaluated to check whether redundancy is avoided. Many definitions of diversity have been posed, such as extrapolating it from the catalogue coverage [36], or study the probability to recommend any item that the user likes [37]. Due to the characteristics of the CEs recommender system, we follow a similar approach than Zhou et al. in [38], which consists of evaluating diversity by measuring the distance between the CEs suggested per user.

5 Conclusion

The design phase is key to anticipate and mitigate the weaknesses of the system. Analysing its limitations before the start of the development phase has helped us to develop a sound system from the very beginning of the development phase. Understanding the reasons of the cold start problem was fundamental to construct the synthetic data and generate dummy models to use when not enough data was available. This comprehension empowered us to synthesise the significant variables to take into consideration as input to the recommendation system.

The creation of the synthetic data in an early phase of the project also helped us to start the debate about harmonisation guidelines quite early, which, consequently, ease the later integration between the numerous systems that form NESTORE. It is of paramount importance that all technical partners are involved when defining the harmonisation guidelines. Thus, it is ensured that development is performed in an efficient manner, and that the integration between the different modules of the systems that form NESTORE can be tested as soon as these modules are functional.

Validation of the system is crucial and should be kept in mind from the design phase. It is very important to enumerate the indicators that will help to understand the performance of the system before the start of the development phase. In this manner, the system will be constructed on a basis that will later facilitate its validation. For instance, if it is relevant to study the precision of the recommendations, it is vital that the users are encouraged to rate the activities that they perform.

All in all, DSSs are a very powerful tool to accompany users in a behavioural change process, since they can adjust to users' preferences and likings, while keeping a holistic view of how users' could reach their goals.

References

1. Schartinger, D., Miles, I., Saritas, O., Amanatidou, E., Giesecke, S., Heller-Schuh, B., et al. (2015). Personal health systems technologies: Critical issues in service innovation and diffusion. *Technology Innovation Management Review, 5*(2).
2. Arnott, D., & Pervan, G. (2005). A critical analysis of decision support systems research. *Journal of Information Technology, 20*(2), 67–87.
3. Musen, M. A., Middleton, B., & Greenes, R. A. (2014). Clinical decision-support systems. *Biomedical informatics* (pp. 643–674). Springer.
4. Ordinez, L., Santos, R., Barry, D., Firmenich, S., & S´ánchez, A. (2016). An expert-driven approach for collaborative knowledge acquisition. In *XXII Congreso Argentino de Ciencias de la Computacion (CACIC 2016).*
5. Adomavicius, G., & Tuzhilin, A. (2001). Expert-driven validation of rule-based user models in personalization applications. *Data Mining and Knowledge Discovery, 5*(1–2), 33–58.
6. Mastropietro, A., Roecke, C., Porcelli, S., del Bas, J., Boqu'è, N., Maldonado, L. F., & Rizzo, G. (2018). Multi-domain model of healthy ageing: The experience of the H2020 NESTORE project. In *Italian Forum of Ambient Assisted Living* (pp. 13–21). Springer.
7. Parker, S. (2013). *Dictionary of scientific and technical terms* (pp. 384–394).
8. Bellovin, S. M., Dutta, P. K., & Reitinger, N. (2019). Privacy and synthetic datasets. *The Stanford Technology Law Review, 22,* 1.
9. Barse, E., Kvarnstrom, H., & Johnson, E. (2003). Synthesizing test data for fraud detection systems. In *19th Annual Computer Security Applications Conference, 2003. Proceedings* (pp. 384–394). IEEE.
10. Patki, N., Wedge, R., & Veeramachaneni, K. (2016). The synthetic data vault. In *Proceedings 3rd IEEE International Conference on Data Science and Advanced Analytics, DSAA 2016* (pp. 399–410).
11. Bhandari, N. (2018). Procedural synthetic data for self-driving cars using 3D graphics. Ph.D. dissertation, Massachusetts Institute of Technology.
12. Lundin, E., Kvarnstrom, H., & Jonsson, E. (2002). A synthetic fraud data generation methodology. In *International Conference on Information and Communications Security* (pp. 265–277). Springer.
13. Kennickell, A. (1997). Multiple imputation and disclosure protection: The case of the 1995 survey of consumer finances. *Record linkage techniques* (pp. 248–267) [Online]. https://www.semanticscholar.org/paper/Multiple-Imputation-and-Disclosure-Protection-%3A-The-Kennickell/0252fd055ab1c0fdbac96d8854429a4727fe099d.
14. McLachlan, S., Dube, K., & Gallagher, T. (2016). Using the CareMap with health incidents statistics for generating the realistic synthetic electronic healthcare record. In *2016 IEEE International Conference on Healthcare Informatics (ICHI)* (pp. 439–448). IEEE.
15. Dahmen, J., & Cook, D. (2019). Synsys: A synthetic data generation system for healthcare applications. *Sensors, 19*(5), 1181.
16. Lee, N., Laine, A. F., Hu, J., Wang, F., Sun, J., & Ebadollahi, S. (2011). Mining electronic medical records to explore the linkage between healthcare resource utilization and disease severity in diabetic patients. In *2011 IEEE First International Conference on Healthcare Informatics, Imaging and Systems Biology* (pp. 250–257). IEEE.
17. Frid-Adar, M., Klang, E., Amitai, M., Goldberger, J., & Greenspan, H. (2018). Synthetic data augmentation using GAN for improved liver lesion classification. In *2018 IEEE 15th International Symposium on Biomedical Imaging (ISBI 2018)* (pp. 289–293). IEEE.

18. Shamsuddin, R., Maweu, B. M., Li, M., & Prabhakaran, B. (2018). Virtual patient model: An approach for generating synthetic healthcare time series data. In *2018 IEEE International Conference on Healthcare Informatics (ICHI)* (pp. 208–218). IEEE.
19. Yin, Z., Dong, Z., Lu, X., Yu, S., Chen, X., & Duan, H. (2015). A clinical decision support system for the diagnosis of probable migraine and probable tension-type headache based on case-based reasoning. *The Journal of Headache and Pain, 16*(1), 29.
20. El-Sappagh, S., Elmogy, M., & Riad, A. (2015). A fuzzy-ontology-oriented case-based reasoning framework for semantic diabetes diagnosis. *Artificial Intelligence in Medicine, 65*(3), 179–208.
21. Huser, V., Rasmussen, L. V., Oberg, R., & Starren, J. B. (2011). Implementation of workflow engine technology to deliver basic clinical decision support functionality. *BMC Medical Research Methodology, 11*(1), 43.
22. Kashyap, V., Morales, A., & Hongsermeier, T. (2006). On implementing clinical decision support: Achieving scalability and maintainability by combining business rules and ontologies. In *AMIA Annual Symposium Proceedings* (Vol. 2006, p. 414). American Medical Informatics Association.
23. Beam, A. L., & Kohane, I. S. (2018). Big data and machine learning in health care. *JAMA, 319*(13), 1317–1318.
24. Shickel, B., Tighe, P. J., Bihorac, A., & Rashidi, P. (2017). Deep EHR: A survey of recent advances in deep learning techniques for electronic health record (EHR) analysis. *IEEE Journal of Biomedical and Health Informatics, 22*(5), 1589–1604.
25. Faust, O., Hagiwara, Y., Hong, T. J., Lih, O. S., & Acharya, U. R. (2018). Deep learning for healthcare applications based on physiological signals: A review. *Computer Methods and Programs in Biomedicine, 161,* 1–13.
26. Fatima, M., Pasha, M., et al. (2017). Survey of machine learning algorithms for disease diagnostic. *Journal of Intelligent Learning Systems and Applications, 9*(01), 1.
27. Subías-Beltran, P., Orte, S., Vargiu, E., Palumbo, F., Angelini, L., Khaled, O. A., et al. (2019). A decision support system to propose coaching plans for seniors. In *2019 IEEE 32nd International Symposium on Computer-Based Medical Systems (CBMS)* (pp. 592–595). IEEE.
28. Gunawardana, A., & Shani, G. (2009). A survey of accuracy evaluation metrics of recommendation tasks. *Journal of Machine Learning Research, 10*(12).
29. Shani, G., & Gunawardana, A. (2011). Evaluating recommendation systems. *Recommender systems handbook* (pp. 257–297). Springer.
30. Pu, P., Chen, L., & Hu, R. (2012). Evaluating recommender systems from the user's perspective: Survey of the state of the art. *User Modeling and User-Adapted Interaction, 22*(4–5), 317–355.
31. Kohavi, R., Longbotham, R., Sommerfield, D., & Henne, R. M. (2009). Controlled experiments on the web: Survey and practical guide. *Data Mining and Knowledge Discovery, 18*(1), 140–181.
32. Herlocker, J. L., Konstan, J. A., Terveen, L. G., & Riedl, J. T. (2004). Evaluating collaborative filtering recommender systems. *ACM Transactions on Information Systems (TOIS), 22*(1), 5–53.
33. Bellogín, A. (2012). Recommender system performance evaluation and prediction: Information retrieval perspective.
34. Baeza-Yates, R., Ribeiro-Neto, B., et al. (1999). *Modern information retrieval* (Vol. 463). New York: ACM Press.
35. Ge, M., Delgado-Battenfeld, C., & Jannach, D. (2010). Beyond accuracy: Evaluating recommender systems by coverage and serendipity. In *Proceedings of the Fourth ACM Conference on Recommender Systems* (pp. 257–260).
36. Salter, J., & Antonopoulos, N. (2006). Cinemascreen recommender agent: Combining collaborative and content-based filtering. *IEEE Intelligent Systems, 21*(1), 35–41.
37. Zhang, M., & Hurley, N. (2009). Statistical modeling of diversity in top-n recommender systems. In *2009 IEEE/WIC/ACM International Joint Conference on Web Intelligence and Intelligent Agent Technology* (Vol. 1, pp. 490–497). IEEE.

38. Zhou, T., Kuscsik, Z., Liu, J.-G., Medo, M., Wakeling, J. R., & Zhang, Y.-C. (2010). Solving the apparent diversity-accuracy dilemma of recommender systems. *Proceedings of the National Academy of Sciences, 107*(10), 4511–4515.

System Interoperability for Next Gen Services at Home. A Challenge/Opportunity for Integration

Ciprian Candea, Filippo Palumbo, Michele Girolami, Daniele Segato, and Gabriela Simona Candea

Abstract Interoperability is complex non-functional requirement of any today' system, and it refers the exchanged information. Two systems must offer the possibility to exchange and use the data in order to be named "interoperable", meaning that the message sent must contain data (in a standard coded format) that can be interpreted by the system that will receive it. The next section describes the challenges encounter during the integration activities from the interoperability point of view for the next gen of systems that offer services at home.

1 Introduction

The capabilities of the NESTORE system to gather data and exchange the inferred information about the different domains of the user rely on an underlying sensing, communication and storage infrastructure that is the core of the NESTORE interoperability. From a technological point of view, cloud computing, self-learning and adaptive reasoning, multi domain unobtrusive monitoring technologies, Internet of Things, emotional computing, smart user interfaces, gamification mechanics, open ICT platform, and user-centered approach are key elements of the NESTORE solution [1]. In order to achieve the integration of this ensemble of different technologies and resources, the NESTORE system leverages a complex IoT architecture whose goal is twofold: (i) to retrieve sensing information from users; (ii) to analyze the data collected so that valuable feedback can be given to users. The NESTORE IoT architecture integrates three interconnected and complementary components essential for the e-Coaching activity: the Monitoring System, the DSS, and the Virtual Coach.

C. Candea (✉) · G. S. Candea
ROPARDO SRL, Reconstructiei Nr. 2A, 550129 Sibiu, Romania
e-mail: ciprian.candea@ropardo.ro

F. Palumbo · M. Girolami
Institute of Information Science and Technologies-CNR, Pisa, Italy

D. Segato
Neosperience Spa, Milan, Italy

G. Andreoni and C. Mambretti (eds.), *Digital Health Technology for Better Aging*, Research for Development, https://doi.org/10.1007/978-3-030-72663-8_8

These components provide a robust solution for easily adding and integrating 3rd party applications enabling the creation of next gen services at the user's home.

The underlying integrated IoT infrastructure provides the basis for building the NESTORE system as a whole. In literature, a big effort has been conducted to provide hardware and software interoperability in smart health systems. We can find two main approaches to this research goal: (i) providing an intermediate software layer to each component in the system in order to allow them to communicate and exchange information, namely a middleware; (ii) decoupling the hardware from the software, exploiting the embedded communication functionalities of the devices themselves, realizing the IoT paradigm.

Different solutions successfully exploited the middleware approach in the Ambient Assisted Living (AAL) domain. With the high number of distributed AAL systems at play on the market, each with unique requirements, the challenge lies in the need to service these disparate systems with a middleware layer that is both coherent and flexible. There is significant complexity in the management of sensor data and the derivation of contextual information, as well as in the monitoring of user activities and in locating appropriate situational services. In [2] authors address this issue focusing on the development of a scalable and context-aware framework to ease the flow between data collection and data processing. In [3] a service-oriented middleware was developed to provide access to the functionality offered by virtually any existing device, or application, in a residential setting. The proposed middleware abstracts the communication technologies involved, allowing to seemingly integrate different communication protocols, making possible the distributed cooperation of devices that were built as stand-alone products. Different projects in the smart health domain also used this kind of approach [4–6]. One of the most significant examples is provided by universAAL [7], a European research project that aims at creating an open platform and standards, which will make it technically feasible and economically viable to develop Ambient Assisted Living (AAL) solutions. It defined hardware and software infrastructure for smart environments called AAL Spaces, which enable context sharing and reasoning about activities carried out by the assisted person. AAL Services developed with the universAAL platform may be a combination of hardware, software and human resources. Tools for the development, publishing and provisioning of such services have been defined to support the whole chain of stakeholders involved in the AAL domain.

Despite the increased functionalities for deployed devices in the user's environment enabled by the middleware, this kind of approach requires additional computational and storage resources. In the last decade, we have witnessed an increased availability of simple and resource-constrained devices yet able to be connected to the Internet offering a smart sensing solution. The integration of the IoT and cloud technology is very important to have a better solution for an uninterrupted, secured, seamless, and ubiquitous framework. The complementary nature of the IoT and the could in terms of storage, processing, accessibility, security, service sharing, and components makes the convergence suitable for many applications, especially in the smart health domain [8]. Different projects embraced this vision, bringing the computational effort to the cloud. This is the case of ACTIVAGE project with its single common interoperable ACTIVAGE IoT Ecosystem Suite (AIOTES) that provides every managed user's environment with the capacity to develop standard and interoperable IoT ecosystems on top of legacy IoT platforms, or communication and data management infrastructures [9].

In NESTORE, we choose to adopt the IoT approach, including the vision of the Web of Things paradigm. REST web services are used to access the IoT system. The proposed architecture defines and implements a common strategy Application Programming Interface (API) for managing the IoT platform and for acquiring data from various devices. Through APIs, it is possible to send data from devices (e.g., sensors, mobile apps, etc.) to the cloud by Web of Things devices or gateways. Reusing and adapting patterns commonly used for the Web, we enabled the IoT architecture as Web of Things, using Web servers [10] on smart things and applying the REST architectural style [11, 12] to the physical world. The essence of REST is to focus on creating loosely coupled services on the Web so that they can be easily reused [13]. Furthermore, the NESTORE project aims at supporting the development of an ecosystem of services tailored to end-users. To this end, the NESTORE system supports the integration of its IoT/WoT platform with other strategic EU projects addressing similar objectives, as the universAAL-IoT project [14], by means of a semantic bridge.

The rest of this work is organized as follows. Section 2 shows the requirements that guided the development of the NESTORE integration infrastructure; Sect. 3 explains the core interoperable technologies as the basis of the proposed infrastructure; Sect. 4 gives insights on the challenges and opportunities given by this kind of integration.

2 Requirements of Interoperable Environments

Next generation services for domestic environments are characterized by some distinguishing features. Such features lead us to define functional and non-functional requirements. In this section, we list such requirements to be considered during the design process for the next generation of home services. For each of the requirements, we firstly describe it and then we report a short use-case clarifying its importance in real-world application scenarios.

Heterogeneous technology integration

The market of consumer devices is continuously growing. Such growth has the advantage of providing advanced hardware and software artifacts, easy to use and configure for non-expert users. However, as a drawback of such evolution, we foresee a concrete market fragmentation due to heterogeneous technologies. More specifically, vendors tend to deliver to the market vertical solutions, namely services designed to work with specific hardware and software components that, in few cases, allow mixing brands and technologies. Such vendor lock-in is possible at different technological levels. In particular, some vendors exploit the existence of open and standard initiatives by introducing customizations that break the interoperability of such initiatives. As a concrete example, we refer to the ZigBee profiles defined by the ZigBee Alliance. The idea is to define the behavior of devices adhering to a specific in different scenarios (Home automation, Industrial plant monitoring, Commercial Building Automation, Telecom Applications etc.). Such approach allows opening the market to different vendors, since the profile imposes the specification of the device itself. However, when vendors customize a profile with proprietary features not publicly released, then we observe the vendor lock-in phenomenon.

Another aspect to consider for the technology integration is the possible overlap between similar solutions. This is the case of three powerful technologies suitable for home services: ZigBee, Z-Wave, Bluetooth 5 and Wi-Fi HaLow. Such technologies present unique features, but their common target is the connectivity of low-power devices also for domestic scenarios.

In order to overcome the customization and the overlap of the existing technologies, the interoperable gateway represents a valuable approach [15]. A gateway is a hardware and software component mitigating the vendor lock-in as it allows integrating multiple technologies with an abstraction layer and pushing vendors to adhere to standards to increase the integration of their products.

Seamless Plug & Play

The possibility of extending a service with new devices or to replace existing devices is also a mandatory requirement for the next generation home services. With the term Plug & Play, we refer to the possibility of adding/removing/replacing devices at home easily by non-expert users. This is the case of a fall detection service for elderly people. Such service is supposed to detect possible falls by detecting the posture and the current location of the monitored user. The service requires some hardware devices. The higher the number of devices, the higher the accuracy of the fall detection. In this simple use-case, the final user should be able to buy and install a new device to be deployed in a different room, without the need of a maintainer or a trained user.

Achieving such a requirement is not an easy task, as the target users might have very different technological skills. More specifically, we consider that the process of simplifying routinely operations is the result of a long process that involves: the optimization of the service interface (e.g. graphical interface), the design of the hardware device (e.g. buttons, case, colors, etc.) and collecting and implementing feedbacks from the end-users.

The seamless Plug & Play requirement involves two other aspects that often are not considered during the design of a service, namely maintenance and updating. Next generation services are supposed to support the end-users with advanced operations requiring several levels of customization. To this purpose, a service should be maintained and updated remotely, by reducing as much as possible the intervention of an expert. Such an aspect is particularly important for specific categories of users that are skeptical in installing technologies in their private home.

Vocal and Gesture Control

The way a user interacts with a service installed at home determines the success or the failure of the service it-self. During the last 3 years, we observed the proliferation of the vocal assistants as the preferable way to access services available at home. More generally, the control interface of a service should be designed with natural interfaces, overcoming touch screens or mechanical keyboard inputs. We foresee not one single mode of interaction with a service, rather the introduction of multi-modal interfaces adapted to the needs of the target users. Among such modes, the vocal and the gesture recognition represent the most promising alternatives. Being able to control a service with the voice or with a simple gesture increases its popularity, its acceptance and the plethora of target users. However, such interaction modes require to be designed with high accuracy and low error rate. Accuracy determines the possibility of controlling an option with a fine-grained level and with responsiveness. As for example, to be able to control the loudspeaker with gestures of the left/right hand similarly to the rotation of the volume control switch. High levels of accuracy, allow the user to perceive a real control of a service, while low levels of accuracy reduce the engagement of the users in using the service. The error rate determines the frequency of failures to understand the user's inputs. This is the case of vocal assistants not able to understand vocal commands in noisy environments or far from the microphone.

Service Customization

We finally consider the possibility of customizing a service according to the end-user features. Such a level of customization represents one of the most challenging requirements for a new era of home services. The customization enables a service to specialize its behavior with an endless training process. The vocal assistant service previously mentioned, represents a meaningful example where customization and personalization determine the real added value of the service. In particular, the service can be trained to recognize the user's voice but, more importantly, to learn from the mistakes in order to improve the accuracy and reduce the error rate. As for example, a vocal assistant can refine its voice recognition engine when the user is far from the microphone, when the voice is altered by the environmental noises or altered by temporary respiratory diseases. The customization not only increases the sense of satisfaction of the end-user, but also it allows making a step forward to the current level of automation. More specifically, we consider the majority of the services for home environments available so far, are mainly designed to automate actions that could be achieved manually by a person. As for example, lighting scenarios control the heating system, control appliances, access to a streaming service etc. The next generation services are supposed to achieve goals not achievable by the end-user, hence services that embody prediction and reasoning principles.

3 Interoperable Technologies

Nowadays health related data ecosystem comprises a wide collection of complex heterogeneous data sources that must be handled on integrated and interoperable way.

Interoperability may be represented by (1) ability of one system component to exchange data with another in a manner that does not have to interpret the data it receives (2) semantic interoperability is the most complex form of exchanging data.

In current work a common ontology that defines a common vocabulary for researchers and engineers who need to share information in specific domain [*reference*] was developed and published. Are different reasons to develop ontology [16] our team manage next requirements with developed ontology (1) to share common understanding of the structure of information among team members and (2) to make domain assumptions explicit.

Ontologies are used to enable the interoperability among computer systems achieved by translating between different modelling methods, paradigms, languages and software tools [17] approach that was investigated withing current work.

UniversAAL [18] (uAAL) selected as best candidate for NESTORE and was extensively tested to understand (1) benefits of semantic interoperability at machine to machine data exchange (2) as well the technologies involved to support such approach. One result of the investigation is that functionality achieved by NESTORE with universAAL can be achieved with a lightweight and flexible technical stack. Using a semantic approach into technical implementation involve a large effort to learn and extend technical stack and it introduce a series of limitation in adoption most modern technologies.

To support the interoperability with uAAL a dedicated bridge NESTORE-uAAL was designed and teste to allow the communication and data exchange between the two systems NESTORE and Target System (Fig. 1).

Using the bridge is enabled integration with any other system that is based on the uAAL, can consider to a multi-deployment scenario in which components of different systems are installed on the same site or on different sites deployed on cloud. Each component sends context information to its own cloud, then information is elaborated in higher level context that is shared through uAAL context buses among the cloud-net. For example, the NESTORE-uAAL bridge would translate the semantic data written according to a uAAL ontology in the proper data format used by the NESTORE DSS to generate new advises for the Virtual Coach.

NESTORE Architecture

NESTORE adopted an evolutionary architecture approach [19] to support the interoperability of different ITC components and fulfil the requirement (1) Quality of technology (efficiency, effectiveness, usefulness, completeness and accuracy), (2) Reliability of the system (reliability, security, interoperability and ease of repair and maintenance), (3) Use of monitoring (frequency, modus operandi, user profile,

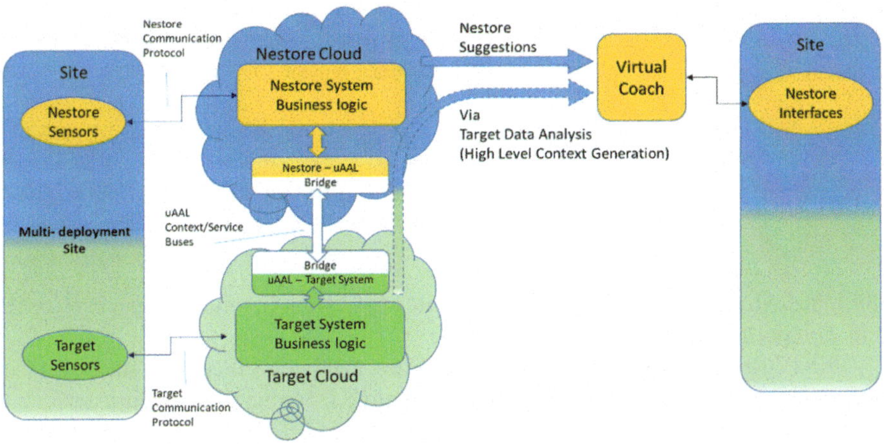

Fig. 1 NESTORE and uAAL multi-site deployment

context in the platform's use) and (4) Problem solving (useful alerts, false alarms, emergency calls, quality life improvement, etc.).

Architecture integrate the three interconnected and complementary components essential for the e-Coaching activity, which are the Monitoring System, the Decision support system (DSS) and the Virtual Coach (Fig. 2). These components always need strong solution relating integration, possibility to add easily Applications and all components must consider the cloud infrastructure requirements.

At one side, we find End User that will interact with the ecosystem on their environment/house using their smartphone or personal computers using mobile applications or web applications. Generated data by their associated devices (i.e. wearable, beacons, sleep monitoring device) are pushed to the NESTORE platform where are stored and different NESTORE components are pushing data back to End Users

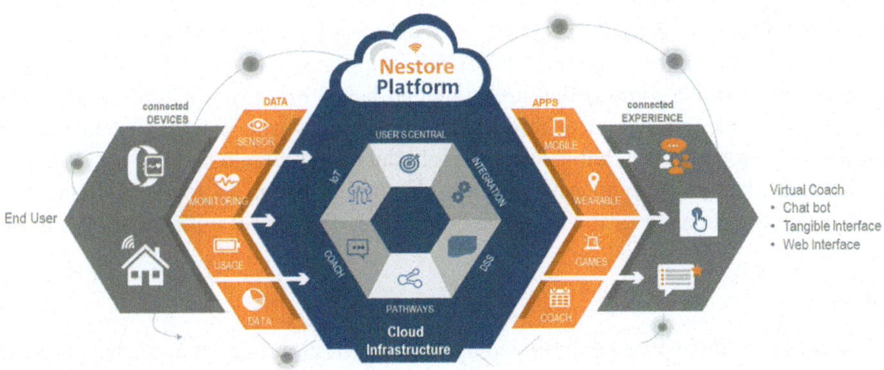

Fig. 2 High level NESTORE architecture

Table 1 NESTORE components an cloud deployment

NESTORE cloud	Provided services
Identity and access management	LogMeal API
Web applications	ZivaCare API
Decision support system	Robofuse IoT system
eCoach APIs	ZivaCare API
Communication bus	NESTORE API

through devices (i.e. wearable) as well mobile application (i.e. serious game, eCoach) and web portal (i.e. places, central portal).

NESTORE cloud infrastructure it hosts all the back-office part and oversees retrieving, elaborating and storing the data coming from the platform users.

To optimize the cloud infrastructure spending in different stages of NESTORE lifecycle a Hybrid cloud was adopted. Using an infrastructure as a service (IaaS) provider, NESTORE private cloud where created to accommodate most of the components providing best experience for managing security, maintenance and upgrades, minimizing the interoperability problems. Components provided by different partners on their own cloud system, and all of them are integrated within NESTORE using secure connections such industry standard protocol for authorization [20] and virtual private network (VPN) that certify a private communication channel, using encryption and other security mechanisms to ensure that only authorized users can access the network and that the data cannot be intercepted (Table 1).

Data exchange

For NESTORE inter-application communication/integration, the RESTFull API (Application Programming Interface) over HTTPS were selected as the preferred technology. An API is a set of functions and procedures that fulfil one or many tasks for being used by other software. It allows to implement the functions and procedures that conform to the API in another program without the need of programming them back. As RESTful systems usually communicate with the Hypertext Transfer Protocol (HTTP), a REST API is a library based completely on the HTTP(S) standard.

The communication between NESTORE components is made possible through representations of resources that are modelled based on developed ontologies. For NESTORE API, the format of those representations was selected to be JavaScript Object Notation (JSON) that is a lightweight data-interchange format.

Message bus provide an asynchronous communications protocol, meaning that the sender and receiver of the message do not need to interact with each other at the same time.

Message bus

Messaging is a key strategy employed by NESTORE cloud distributed environment. It enables NESTORE applications (i.e. ChatBot, LogIn/Register, etc.) and services (i.e. Decision Support System) to communicate and cooperate. It also sustains a scalable and resilient solution. Messaging supports asynchronous operations, enabling

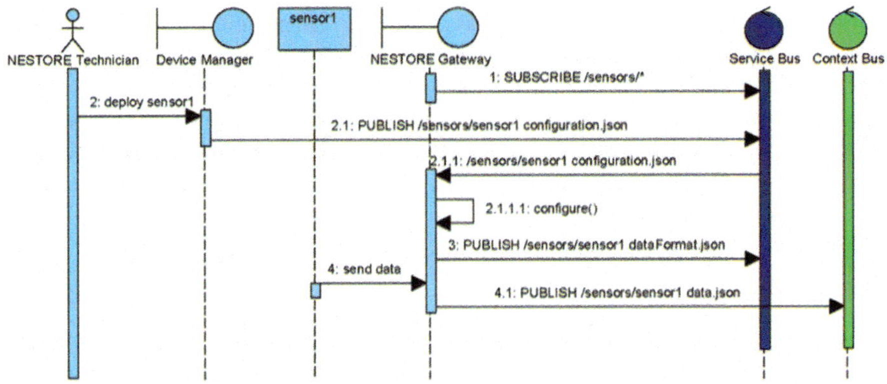

Fig. 3 Sequence diagram of the announce phase for discovering a newly deployed sensor

NESTORE to decouple a process that consumes a service from the process that implements the service. The NESTORE message bus enables a message to be posted to a queue via HTTP (always HTTPS) and this will ensure a simple and strong security model as well a universal accepted transport protocol represented by HTTP(S).

The modern message queue implementations (i.e. Apache MQ/Kafka, RabbitMQ) support having a single message be read by multiple endpoints. Messages become "invisible" to applications that have read them for some period of time before actually being removed. During this time, the message can still be read by other applications. This blurs the line between queues and buses, especially as it pertains to the 1:1 correspondence between queues and destination applications. Messages carry a payload as well as metadata, in the form of key-value pair properties, describing the payload and giving handling instructions to Service Bus and applications. In Fig. 3 is described the sequence diagram of the announce phase for discovering a newly deployed sensor. NESTORE allow application to send/receive messages encoded as MQTT for the IoT sub-system as well payloads encoded as JSON objects for the inter application communication.

Message queuing system

In a typical Big Data scenario, data flows coming from different sources continuously enter the system; the most used integration paradigm to handle data flows consists in setting up a proper message queue. A message queue is a middleware implementing a publisher/subscriber pattern to decouple producers and consumers by means of an asynchronous communications protocol. Message queues can be analyzed under several points of view, in particular policies regarding Durability, Security, Filtering, Purging, Routing and Acknowledgment, and message protocols (as AMQP, STOMP, MQTT) must be carefully considered.

Message queue systems are not a novelty and many proprietary as well as open source solutions have appeared on the market in the last years. Among the open source ones there is Apache Kafka [21]. A preliminary analysis seems to demonstrate that

Kafka is most widely used in big players' production environments as for instance by LinkedIn, Yahoo!, Twitter, Netflix, Spotify, Uber, Pinterest, PayPal, Cisco, Coursera among the others. Kafka is written in Java and originally developed at LinkedIn; it provides a distributed and persistent message passing system with a variety of policies. It relies on Apache Zookeeper [22] to maintain the state across the cluster. Kafka has been tested to provide close to 200 thousand messages/sec for writes and 3 million messages/sec for reads, that is an order of magnitude more that its alternatives.

Web of things

Web of Things [23, 24] component is used to support the data capture from different devices (i.e. things) and store in the NESTORE cloud using a gateway to communicate. RoboFuse [25] platform was selected as Web of Things component for NESTORE. A gateway can be a dedicated hardware device or software, under the NESTORE/RoboFuse platform is defined as Web of Things Agent (wotAgent) and it represents an essential component that enhance the interoperability.

Agents are software components that support communication with M2M (machine to machine) devices that are implementing different protocols (i.e. low-level serial links to IT protocols like web services) for communication and connectivity, a specific wotAgent where created for NESTORE platform referred as NESTORE Connect. Main functions of the wotAgent are (1) Translate the device specific interface protocol into a reference protocol. (2) Translate the specific domain model of the device into a reference domain model (3) Enable secure remote communication using various network architectures.

4 Challenges and Opportunities for a Seamless Integration

The challenge of gathering information

The idea of the NESTORE project was to build a virtual coach for the health of the user. There is no single information that can be gathered from the user to provide a meaningful assessment of the health and design a plan to maintain or improve it.

Knowing the health condition of the user is a huge challenge, it requires knowing many variables: they have to be gathered in a database and keep up to date in order for an automated system to take automated decisions and produce assessment on the user condition. To predict the future health condition even more information has to be gathered.

Many information can be simply asked to the user, like age or gender, height, weight; some need to be measured by a device, like the sleep cycles or heart rate while practicing a physical activity; some need to be derived, like playing a game to establish the cognitive state or through medically approved tests; finally some variable are hard to establish, like social interactions or nutrition habits.

There are many ways of gathering information, each with their advantages and drawbacks: the weight could be asked by an automated system every morning or be automatically uploaded into the system from a smart scale. Asking the user can be done through a Smartphone application or with conversational interface, voice or chat; in any way it is something the user has to do that was not in their habits. Using a scale every morning is also a procedure that might alter the user habits but it is less invasive and annoying.

Gathering information on how much the user sleeps requires a device with sensors installed on the bed of the user, such a device could require some manual operation of the user to synchronize it or could be smart enough to communicate automatically those information to a remote cloud. The latter is always preferable but is usually a more expensive solution. The setup and calibration of the device could also be technically challenging for the user and often requires assistance from tech savvy operators or familiar. The installation of the device itself could be subject to local conditions like the bed mattress type or bed configuration not allowing an easy installation.

A key factor to the success of a health monitoring system is finding a way to strike a balance between nagging the user with questions and procedures, introducing devices to use and learn and going on with life.

NESTORE Kit and user installation

A typical NESTORE installment for the pilot consisted of several devices and procedures to be added in the user life habits.

A trained NESTORE operator would assist the user with the installation and maintenance of the system during the duration of the pilot.

Some commercial devices where selected, a sleep monitoring system and a smart scale needs to be configured and then they send data to the cloud, NESTORE uses those commercial services APIs to periodically grab the data into the NESTORE platform.

A wearable wristband device prototype was developed for the NESTORE Pilot, equipped with heart rate, accelerometer and barometer sensors was mainly responsible for collecting physical data. A set of 10 beacons was also part of the NESTORE Kit, 5 to be placed around the house of the user to monitor movements and another 5 to be given to close family members and friends in order to monitor social interactions. It was also the wristband job to collect beacons signals as they were nearby. Finally, the wearable device implemented some active procedures to perform guided structured activities and some medical tests for the assessment of the physical condition of the user.

The choice to build a wearable device rather than using a commercially available one was driven by the specific needs established by the scientific committee. The wristband needed to collect nearby beacons and be able to guide the user through some specific tests and structured activity recording specific data. This alone took away the option of using most commercially available wristbands and left the NESTORE consortium with only two options: use a Smartwatch and develop the application to perform these operations or build a device from scratch. The NESTORE consortium chose the latter by exclusion: the smartwatch posed some technical challenges about battery consumption during the beacons scanning and would increase the cost of the system; it would also add another complex device to the ones the user needed to learn how to use.

A smart speaker prototype was also part of the kit, it was nicknamed tangible device. It is the voice interface of the NESTORE Coach allowing the user to communicate his state and ask questions. Devised before the spread of similar commercial devices like Google Assistant and Amazon Alexa.

Three smartphone apps, Android only for the pilot, were developed: NESTORE Coach and NESTORE Connect, NESTORE Game.

The NESTORE Coach app was the core of the Coach, containing a text chat similar to the voice interface, virtual games, user profile information and several other features to push the user into some good health habits or to collect information. One of the features of the NESTORE Coach allows the user to take a picture of food: it would then be identified by an AI system and added to the database as part of the information used to provide guidance.

The NESTORE Connect app was instead a companion of the wearable device, which did not have the capability to directly connect to the cloud to push the collected data. It would automatically synchronize the wearable data through Bluetooth and then with the cloud. It was also used to initially configure both the wearable and the smart speaker during the setup of the system.

The NESTORE Game was designed to be entertaining and at the same time stimulating the cognitive abilities.

Technical challenges of a seamless integration

For the Pilot there were many strict requirements, the user needed to have a modern Android Smartphone, an home WIFI, no prior health conditions and many others, but there was no requirement to be a tech enthusiast because part of the objective of the pilot was to obtain a fair assessment of the simplicity of the system and identify the pain points. This caused mixed feedback from users and some even dropped out.

The nature of the NESTORE platform is inherently technical, which, given the target, posed a barrier; the elderly are known to be, on average, less tech savvy than most of the population: the NESTORE consortium expected resistant in installing application on their personal devices, but in truth that wasn't a problem at all. They were more frightened by the many new technologies in their home and all the tasks to perform.

Many users had issues with the NESTORE wearable; due to time constraints, the wearable was not equipped with an operating system or a persistent memory on the configuration: once turned off it needed to be configured again. The NESTORE Connect App was initially designed to only be used interactively by the user with the assistance of a NESTORE operator on the initial setup and then to work without user intervention on synchronizing data from the wearable to the cloud but turned out to be used a lot by the user directly to restore the wearable device to its nominal usage.

The wearable device has a display that shows a clock with the current time and a step counters in nominal condition, and a fixed screen with a stylized smartphone if in need of configuration this made it one of the easiest parts to understand of the system: users focused a lot on this issue but for them following the setup and configure procedure on their own proved too challenging.

The wearable prototype battery, initially designed to last all day for about 6 months, double the duration of the pilot, had a reduced lifespan due to the delay in the start of the pilot caused by the Covid-19 pandemic and this contributed to the issue.

Due to a bug in the wearable performing the setup on the wearable could cause data loss, which meant the data had to be synchronized before setup. The synchronization could be a long (hours) process if a lot of data was to be synchronized. Being a prototype, the wearable could not be patched or updated remotely, but needed to be recalled to the factory, and this was not possible during the pilot. The lengthy recovery procedure, during which the clock would not be visualized, contributed to the perception of being a complex operation in the user.

Furthermore, many Android manufacturers implemented non-standard battery "optimizations" that directly violate the Android compliance requirements, in particular Huawei, Xiaomi and other Chinese devices: simply put, these devices force close apps and prevent automatic execution without user intervention; they implement this behavior against Android specifications in order for their device to have longer battery life at the expense of the correct functional behavior of applications installed. This is a known issue Google is trying to address for some years now and caused problems with the many Covid-19 pandemic tracking apps. Sometimes the user can circumvent these limitations by looking for battery optimization options in the smartphone and explicitly whitelist the NESTORE Connect App, but this is not an easy procedure and added to the confusion.

Another issue regarding the NESTORE Connect—Wearable communication was caused by a questionable requirement of Android: in order for an application to use Bluetooth it needs to request both the permission to have the user location and to turn on the GPS sensor on the device, regardless of the actual need of using the GPS. Many users kept GPS off on their device either due to privacy concerns or due to battery concerns and were not happy turning it on.

All of these issues summed up made the wearable device a major concern for users during the pilot and ultimately made the gathering of the related data difficult. It is also important to note that those problems with Bluetooth and background execution are not limited to Android; NESTORE would have similar challenges on iOS where background restrictions are even stricter.

From the preliminary data we obtained in the pilot we can see many users, with few exceptions, don't really use other features of the NESTORE system like the NESTORE Coach App, they don't take pictures of their food for the nutrition recognition system or use the chat either by text or voice.

On the other hand, data from the sleeping monitor was regular and perfectly gathered without big issues for the users. Probably because after the initial setup and calibration the user did not need to alter any habit. Sleeping in his or her bed was all he needed to do for the sleep monitor to collect the data and send it to the system.

Coaching

After an initial phase where the NESTORE Coach gathers information of the user to build a coaching plan to either improve or maintain the health of the user in the five different domains the system starts to give suggestions and hints to the user to add activity to his life or change habits. For example the user is invited through notifications inside the NESTORE Coach app to schedule and then perform structured physical activities: with structured it means the user has to follow a physical routine being guided by the wearable to increase or decrease the intensity at given intervals.

Most users did not schedule structured activities or they did not follow suggestions from the coach. It is hard to speculate on the reasons yet; the pilot is still running while we are writing this book. However, it is certain the complexity of the system plays a part in the role. Moreover, these lead to some preliminary conclusions.

It is the user fault, or is it not?

The NESTORE system is not free of issues but, technically, it works. Data for the five domains is collectable, complex systems interact with one another to derive data, perform assessment and construct an individual plan for the user through the decision system (DSS), the suggestions are then delivered to the user who is pushed to take action and decisions that changes life habits toward a better lifestyle that maintain or improve the health condition.

Yet many users did not use the system or were overwhelmed by it. It is clear that trying to use a virtual coach for every domain all at once was too much to take in for users.

Change is hard. The older you get, the harder it gets. The more you need to change the harder it is. The NESTORE Coach is ambitious! It wants to improve every aspect of the life of the person it's coaching. It wants to know everything and give advice and suggestions on every aspect of life. But users naturally resist change. Users often do not understand the whys and the whens they need to do one thing or another. Everything is new and complex and they do not see an immediate benefit in adding an annoying new task to their daily life.

In retrospect, it is easy to see, it would have been better to introduce changes in one domain at a time, taking more time for the user to metabolize changes and integrate them in their daily life.

There is also room for improvement in the technical aspects, it was clear from the sleep monitor that a system that can gather data without any direct user change in habit is perfect and there are possibly several aspects of the NESTORE system that could be improved in this regard. Some others could be simplified, even if it meant reducing the quantity or quality of information obtained: after all some information is better than no information.

5 Conclusions

There is much yet to explore, new creative and clever ways to obtain information minimizing the impact on the user's life.

Since when the NESTORE Project started many, new technologies were introduced in our life. Smart assistants with Google Assistant or Amazon Alexa are entering many houses nowadays, the concept of a smart assistant, revolutionary when NESTORE started, is now something we take for granted.

NESTORE has to become a modular system where each part of it can be added to the daily life of a person piece by piece and as seamlessly as possible. Technology needs to be transparent, easy, and intuitive. Change must be slow, gradual, and give time to the user to see the benefit before introducing more.

The future of machine learning and deep learning will revolutionize technology in the coming years; functions that seemed impossible just 5 years ago now are established and completely feasible. The reason is we have a new way of teaching a machine: we can teach by examples, the way humans and animals learn: they aren't yet good at it like we are, they need a lot of examples, thousands, but they can now understand things that were considered simply not possible before like picture content, spoken language, complex patterns.

References

1. Palumbo, F., Crivello, A., Furfari, F., Girolami, M., Mastropietro, A., Manferdelli, G., et al. (2020). "Hi This Is NESTORE, Your Personal Assistant": Design of an integrated IoT system for a personalized coach for healthy aging. *Frontiers in Digital Health, 2*, 20
2. Forkan, A., Khalil, I., & Tari, Z. (2014). CoCaMAAL: A cloud-oriented context-aware middleware in ambient assisted living. *Future Generation Computer Systems, 35*, 114–127.
3. Pereira, R., Barros, C., Pereira, S., Mendes, P. M., & Silva, C. A. (2014). A middleware for intelligent environments in ambient assisted living. In *2014 36th Annual International Conference of the IEEE Engineering in Medicine and Biology Society* (pp. 5924–5927).
4. Palumbo, F., Ullberg, J., Stimec, A., Furfari, F., Karlsson, L., & Coradeschi, S. (2014). Sensor network infrastructure for a home care monitoring system. *Sensors, 14*(3), 3833–3860.
5. Palumbo, F., La Rosa, D., & Chessa, S. (2014). GP-m: Mobile middleware infrastructure for ambient assisted living. In *2014 IEEE Symposium on Computers and Communications (ISCC)* (pp. 1–6).
6. Palumbo, F., La Rosa, D., Ferro, E., Bacciu, D., Gallicchio, C., Micheli, A., et al. (2017). Reliability and human factors in ambient assisted living. *Journal of Reliable Intelligent Environments, 3*(3), 139–157.
7. Ram, R., Furfari, F., Girolami, M., Ibanez-Sánchez, G., Lázaro-Ramos, J. P., Mayer, C., et al. (2013). universAAL: Provisioning platform for AAL services. In *Ambient Intelligence—Software and Applications* (pp. 105–112). Springer International Publishing.
8. Muhammad, G., Rahman, S. M. M., Alelaiwi, A., & Alamri, A. (2017). Smart health solution integrating IoT and cloud: A case study of voice pathology monitoring. *IEEE Communications Magazine, 55*(1), 69–73. https://doi.org/10.1109/MCOM.2017.1600425CM.
9. Guillén, S., Sala, P., Fico, G., Arredondo, M., Cano, A., Posada, J., et al. (2017). IoT European large-scale pilots–integration, experimentation and testing. *Cognitive Hyperconnected Digital Transformation: Internet of Things Intelligence Evolution.*

10. Guinard, D., Trifa, V., Pham, T., & Liechti, O. (2009). Towards physical mashups in the web of things. In *Proceedings of INSS*, Pittsburgh, PA (Vol. 9, pp. 17–19). https://doi.org/10.1109/INSS.2009.5409925.
11. Fielding, R. T., & Taylor, R. N. (2002). Principled design of the modern web architecture. *ACM Transactions on Internet Technology, 2,* 115–150. https://doi.org/10.1145/514183.514185.
12. Ruby, S. (2007). *RESTful Web Services*. Sebastopol, CA: O'Reilly.
13. Pautasso, C., & Wilde, E. (2009). Why is the web loosely coupled?: A multi-faceted metric for service design. In *Proceedings of the 18th International Conference on World Wide Web*. ACM, Madrid (pp. 911–920). https://doi.org/10.1145/1526709.1526832.
14. Ferro, E., Girolami, M., Salvi, D., Mayer, C., Gorman, J., Grguric, A., et al. (2015). The UniversAAL platform for AAL (Ambient Assisted Living). *Journal of Intelligent Systems, 24*(3), 301–319.
15. Furfati, F., Girolami, M., Lenzi, S., & Chessa, S. (2014). A service-oriented zigbee gateway for smart environments. *Journal of Ambient Intelligence and Smart Environments, 6*(6), 691–705.
16. Noy, N. F., & McGuinness, D. L. (2001). *Ontology development 101: A guide to creating your first ontology*. Stanford, CA: Stanford University.
17. Uschold, M. (1998). Knowledge level modelling: Concepts and terminology. *The Knowledge Engineering Review, 13*(1), 5–29.
18. https://github.com/universAAL/ontology
19. Evans, E. (2004). *Domain-driven design: Tackling complexity in the heart of software*. Addison-Wesley. ISBN 978-032-112521-7.
20. Internet Engineering Task Force. (2018). The OAuth 2.0 authorization framework: Bearer token usage. Retrieved from https://tools.ietf.org/html/rfc6750.
21. Kreps, J., Narkhede, N., & Rao, J. (2011). KAFKA: A distributed messaging system for log processing. In *Proceedings of NetDB* (pp. 1–7).
22. Hunt, P., Konar, M., Junqueira, F., & Reed, B. (2010). ZooKeeper: Wait-free coordination for internet-scale systems. In *Proceedings of the USENIX Annual Technical Conference—ATC 2010* (pp. 145–158).
23. Guinard, D., & Trifa, V. (2016). *Building the web of things: With examples in Node.js and Raspberry Pi*. Greenwich CT USA: Manning Publications Co. ISBN-13: 978-1617292682.
24. Atzori, L., Morabito, G., & Lera, A. (2017). Understanding the internet of things: Definition. *Ad Hoc Networks, 56,* 122–140.
25. RoboFuse. (2020). Retrieved from https://robofuse.com/.

Lifestyle Improvement and Virtual Coaching and ICT Services in the Human Domains Through Friendly Technology

Physical Activity Promotion and Coaching to Support Healthy Ageing

G. Manferdelli, A. Mastropietro, E. Denna, I. Kniestedt, M. Mauri, M. Civiello, S. Lukosch, G. Rizzo, and S. Porcelli

Abstract Physical activity plays a fundamental role in contrasting physiological deconditioning during ageing. Considering the complexity of the modifications that can occur in the physical activity domain, international guidelines recommend that older adults engage in a combination of aerobic, strength, flexibility, and balance training to promote active ageing and maintain adequate health status. For this reason, virtual coaches must be designed to prescribe appropriate physical activity plans in each of the specific target sub-domain. Technological solutions based on wearable devices and digital games are promising can be the key to a successful system. This chapter describes the physiological bases and the technological approaches implemented by the NESTORE system to evaluate users' functional abilities and to propose a comprehensive and individualised coaching plan in the physical activity domain according to the internationally recognised guidelines. The main technological NESTORE components, co-designed together with users to monitor their status and behaviour and coach them to perform effective physical activity, are (i) the NESTORE wristband that will assess the users' performances and monitor the main physiological parameters during aerobic activity and (ii) the NESTORE Pocket Odyssey mobile game that will engage the users during physical activities in the strength, flexibility and balance domains.

G. Manferdelli · A. Mastropietro (✉) · G. Rizzo · S. Porcelli
Institute of Biomedical Technologies, National Research Council, Via Fratelli Cervi 93, 20090 Segrate, Milan, Italy
e-mail: alfonso.mastropietro@itb.cnr.it

G. Manferdelli
Institute of Sport Sciences, University of Lausanne, Lausanne, Switzerland

E. Denna · M. Mauri · M. Civiello
Flextronics Design SRL, Milan, Italy

I. Kniestedt
Faculty of Technology, Policy and Management, Delft University of Technology, Delft, The Netherlands

S. Lukosch
HIT Lab NZ, University of Canterbury, Christchurch, New Zealand

G. Andreoni and C. Mambretti (eds.), *Digital Health Technology for Better Aging*, Research for Development, https://doi.org/10.1007/978-3-030-72663-8_9

1 Introduction

The benefits of regular physical exercise on health have been widely demonstrated in the scientific literature, whereas inadequate physical activity levels have been associated with about 10% of premature mortality [1–3], lower rates of all-cause mortality (e.g. coronary heart disease, high blood pressure, stroke, type 2 diabetes, cancer), as well as a higher level of cardiorespiratory and muscular fitness, healthier body mass and composition, and a biomarker profile that is more favourable for the prevention of cardiovascular disease, type 2 diabetes and the enhancement of bone health [4–6]. In addition, being physically active at ages over 65 has been associated with higher levels of functional health, a lower risk of falling, and better cognitive function, finally leading to a reduced risk of moderate and severe functional and role limitations in daily life activities [5].

Since deconditioning, low muscle tone, and/or low functional capacity contribute to poor health outcomes and low quality of life in older adults, the American College of Sports Medicine (ACSM) recommends that older adults engage in a combination of aerobic, resistance, flexibility, and balance training to promote and maintain health [7, 8]. The proposed physical activity guidelines suggest at least 150 min of moderate-intensity (increased breathing, able to talk) aerobic physical activity throughout the week or a minimum of 75 min of vigorous-intensity (breathing fast, difficulty talking) aerobic physical activity throughout the week or an equivalent combination of moderate- and vigorous-intensity exercise. These activities should be performed in bouts of at least 10 min of duration. Moreover, muscle-strengthening activities should be done involving major muscle groups, on 2 or more days a week. Older adults with poor mobility should also perform physical activity to enhance balance and prevent falls on 3 or more days per week [9]. In older adults, physical activity includes leisure-time physical activity, transportation (e.g. walking or cycling), occupational, household chores, play games, sports or planned exercise, in the context of daily, family and community activities [9].

In the last decades, the majority of the proposed strategies to match the current guidelines on physical activity and to promote a healthy lifestyle in older adults were resource-intensive, time-consuming and required costly interventions, especially in terms of human resources, factors that limited full participation and widespread dissemination [10]. It is therefore fundamental to develop effective and innovative solutions to spread a healthy culture among older adults.

2 Overview of NESTORE Coaching System in Physical Activity Domain

Modern society is flunked by technology which helps humans to perform several daily life activities. At these regards, wearable technologies can be innovative solutions for reducing sedentariness and, therefore, to increase adherence to current physical activity guidelines [11].

In this regard, NESTORE Coaching System wants to effectively and non-invasively act on the four main physical activity domains—aerobic, strength, flexibility and balance—by creating an individualized program based on continuous functional evaluations and user's needs. These four areas contribute to healthy ageing by maintaining functional capacity, strength, independence, and quality of life. In particular, the system is based on an initial evaluation of the users followed by an administration phase (see chapter "The Multi-domain Coaching Approach to Counteract Ageing Decline").

As part of the initial assessment, NESTORE Coaching System will ask the user to perform the modified-6-min Walking test (mod6MWT) and the modified-30-s Chair Rise test (mod30sCRT) to assess the user's aerobic fitness and lower limbs muscle strength, respectively. The mod6MWT is an adapted version of the clinical 6-min Walking test which is the simplest way to estimate the maximum oxygen consumption [12–14]. The mod6MWT measures the distance that the user can quickly walk on a flat, hard surface in 6 min. Subjects can choose their intensity of exercise and are allowed to stop and rest during the test. This test should be performed along a long, flat, straight, enclosed path with a hard surface that is seldom travelled [15, 16]. Based on the distance covered during the test, the user will be included in the "retain" group or the "improve" group. The mod30sCRT is administered using a folding chair without arms, with a standard height of about 43.2 cm, and which is placed against a wall to prevent it from moving. The participant is seated in the middle of the chair, back straight, feet approximately shoulder-width apart and placed on the floor at an angle slightly back from the knees. Arms are crossed at the wrists and held against the chest. The user should complete as many full stands as possible within 30 s and he is instructed to fully sit between each stand [17]. Depending on the number of stands completed the user will be assigned to the "retain" group or in the "improve" group. Thresholds for both tests are reported in Table 1.

As already highlighted in this book, the NESTORE coaching system wants to provide an individualized coach by meeting the user's needs. To optimize coaching prescription and avoid excessive engagement of the user, NESTORE will also take into account non-structured activities, defined as all the activities performed by the user which were not planned or included in the coaching programs. This comes from the need to create an active ageing model without being too intrusive in the user's life.

Table 1 Thresholds used in the mod6MWT and mod30sCRT. Accordingly, the user will be assigned to the "retain" group or the "improve" group

	Age	Man	Woman
mod6MWT	60–70	491 m	440 m
	70–80	400 m	350 m
mod30sCRT	65–69	12	12
	70–74	12	11
	75–79	11	10

3 Coaching Personalisation and Implementation Strategies

Exercise prescriptions designed for older adults should ideally include the four key components of exercise training (aerobic endurance training, strength/resistance training, flexibility, and balance) [18–21]. Although adjustments based on the user's goals and preferences are required, the focus remains on incorporating as many of the four components as possible into the exercise prescription. Many aerobic exercises, such as walking or running, can increase both endurance and strength to some degree. On the other hand, flexibility exercises require a separate prescription element: stretching exercises to enhance or maintain joint range of motion and to reduce pain. Finally, balance exercises challenge an older person's stability to improve his/her ability to avoid a fall when changing positions or negotiating uneven surfaces [22]. These four components of exercise training contribute to healthy ageing and the maintenance of functional capacity, strength, independence, and quality of life. Accordingly, coaching plans proposed by the NESTORE Coaching System covered these four intervention areas.

Cardiorespiratory function

Endurance training is crucial for improving the function of the heart, lungs, and vascular system, as well as for maintaining body weight and decreasing the risk for many chronic diseases [23]. In addition, older adults with increased cardiovascular fitness can perform more difficult physical tasks and exercise at higher intensities than those who do not undertake regular endurance activities.

NESTORE Virtual Coach will propose two alternative training pathways that will be identified accordingly to the status of the user previously assessed with the mod6MWT:

(a) Retain cardiorespiratory fitness. The coaching plans will be defined according to the general aerobic/endurance guidelines described above [4, 19].
(b) Improve cardiorespiratory fitness. The coaching plans will be based on the progressive increase of both duration and intensity, as tolerated by the subject, to achieve the exercise volume recommended by the guidelines [4, 19]. A typical example of a training program for a user in the improve group is shown in Fig. 1.

Interval conditioning will be the initial approach of choice because it is more flexible and produces rapid, specific aerobic endurance gains that positively influence the performance of daily activities. Moreover, interval training is timesaving compared to other types of programs.

After each training session NESTORE will ask the following parameters to the user:

- Recovery: using Total Quality of Recovery scale—12 h after the last session
- Fatigue: using Borg scale—following exercise cessation.

Moreover, the user will repeat the mod6MWT every 4 weeks to track changes in the user's cardiorespiratory fitness. Similarly, training adherence, fatigue and

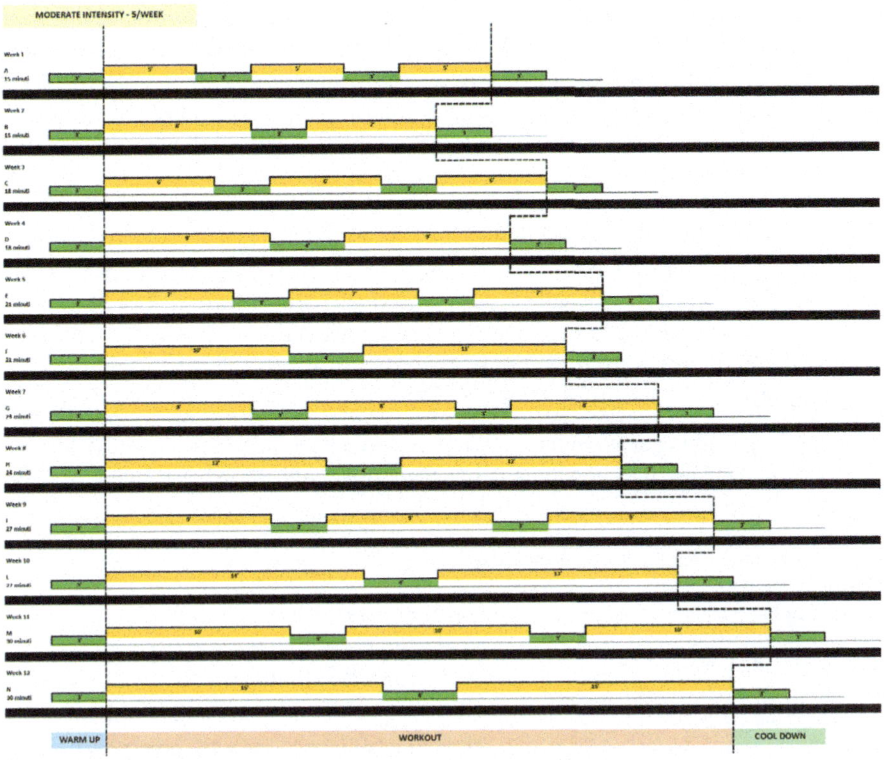

Fig. 1 A typical example of a coaching plan for a user who needs to improve his cardiorespiratory fitness. The intensity is light for the green bouts, while it is moderate for the orange bouts

recovery will be assessed too. Accordingly, the user will keep the same programme or he will be addressed to the other training pathways.

Strength

Older adults that regularly participate in a strength training program can improve muscle strength, function, bone density, and body composition as well as reduce their fall risk [24–26]. Strength training can also improve symptoms of many conditions: arthritis, osteoporosis, diabetes, and depression. ACSM recommends that older adults participate in strength training activities for at least 2 days per week [8], and the NESTORE system will follow these suggestions.

NESTORE Virtual Coach will propose two alternative target behaviours that will be identified accordingly to the status of the user assessed using the mod30sCRT:

(a) Retain muscle strength and power. The coaching plans for this target behaviour will be defined according to the general strength/resistance guidelines already reported previously in this chapter. In particular, the user will perform 3 sessions/week of moderate-intensity resistance exercises consisting of 3 sets each. Figure 2 shows a typical strength session for a user in the "retain" group.

(b) Improve muscle strength and power. The volume of exercise prescribed will begin at a low level and it will be increased as training continues. Moreover, as the load will be increased, so too should the length of the recovery period. The aim is to achieve the exercise volume as recommended by the guidelines. Progression may be individualized based on tolerance and preference in a conservative manner. In particular, each user included in this group will perform 3 sessions/week of light and moderate-intensity resistance exercises during the first 4 weeks and weeks 5–12, respectively. During weeks 1–4 of training, users will complete 5 sets for each exercise, while during weeks 5–12 they will complete 3 sets of 10 repetitions. Accordingly, repetitions and weights will be adjusted.

After each training session immediately following exercise cessation, NESTORE will ask the user his fatigue status using the Borg scale. Moreover, every 4 weeks

Session 1

- Chest press (1 set = 10 repetitions)
- Biceps curl (1 set = 10 repetitions)
- Chair squats (1 set = 10 repetitions)
- Seated leg extension (1 set = 10 repetitions)
- Abdominal crunch (1 set = 15 repetitions)
- Back extensions (1 set = 15 repetitions)

Session 2

- Overhead press (1 set = 10 repetitions)
- Push-ups (1 set = 10 repetitions)
- Standing hamstrings curl (1 set = 10 repetitions)
- Standing calf raises (1 set = 10 repetitions)
- Abdominal crunch (1 set = 15 repetitions)
- Back extensions (1 set = 15 repetitions)

Session 3

- Front shoulder raise (1 set = 10 repetitions)
- Standing triceps extension (1 set = 10 repetitions)
- Supine hip lifts (1 set = 15 repetitions)
- Side hip raise (1 set = 10 repetitions)
- Abdominal crunch (1 set = 15 repetitions)
- Back extensions (1 set = 15 repetitions)

Fig. 2 A typical example of a coaching plan for a user included in the "retain" group in the strength subdomain. The intensity is maintained moderate throughout the 12 weeks of intervention

NESTORE will ask the user to repeat the mod30sCRT to monitor changes in the user's lower extremity muscle strength. Based on the fatigue status in the last 7 days and on the values obtained in the test, the user will keep the same programme or he will be addressed to the other training pathways.

Flexibility and Balance

Flexibility training allows older adults to maintain or improve their ability to perform activities of daily living such as combing hair, reaching for objects on a shelf or the floor, getting dressed, or putting on shoes. Flexibility training especially exercises focusing on the hip extensors, has also been shown to improve several gait parameters—speed, stride length, and cadence—which may result in increased mobility and reduced fall risk. In addition, stretching helps to prevent injuries, such as muscle strain, as well as reduces pain in the knee, hip, lower back, and neck.

Similarly, loss of balance and stability problems can lead to an increased risk of falls, fractures, injuries, and functional loss. Moreover, improvement in balance will not only reduce the risk of falls and injuries but may also increase the older adults' confidence in their ability to perform activities of daily living. Balance training usually consists of positions or movements that challenge the individual to maintain posture and stability over a base of support.

It is therefore fundamental to train and maintain these functions in older people. For this reason, NESTORE will provide a unique training program for both flexibility and balance to all the users, which should be performed twice a week. The system will create a single session by randomly choosing 9 different exercises for flexibility (4 for upper limbs, 3 for lower limbs and 2 for lower back/abdominals) and 4 exercises for balance.

Flexibility exercises should be performed after an aerobic session or before a strength session, while balance exercises should be performed after a strength session. The user should perform each exercise 2 times in a row (keeping the position for about 20 s each) with 20 s of recovery between.

4 NESTORE Technological Solutions for the Physical Activity Domain

Two main reasons have highlighted the need to develop technology strategies to help older people to live independently as long as possible: the continuous ageing of our society and the subsequent increasing pressure on health and aged care services.

To date, several technologies have shown promise as effective, accessible, and inexpensive solutions to promote health and wellbeing in global populations. In this regard, wearable devices were reported to significantly increase daily physical activity levels [27]. Similarly, video games were shown to positively affects both physical activity levels and cognitive function [28, 29].

This chapter section focuses on digital interventions enclosed in the NESTORE Coaching System aimed to increase physical activity levels in the target population. Concerning the entire system, here we particularly focus on systems that monitor user physical activity behaviour and provide a visual guide to exercises, to improve the health-related goals through a virtual coach.

Wristband

The user activities data shall be collected by dedicated devices, these devices are deeply described in the monitoring system chapter, nevertheless, this paragraph will provide an overview of the wearable wristband that is the main sensor used for physical activity.

The wearable device is similar to a smartwatch (Fig. 3) and it has been designed and developed following user-oriented guidelines like simple usage, not invasiveness and fast wearability. Mechanical dimensions are similar to a common watch (see Fig. 4) with a practical magnetic bracelet easy to be opened-closed and adjusted. A

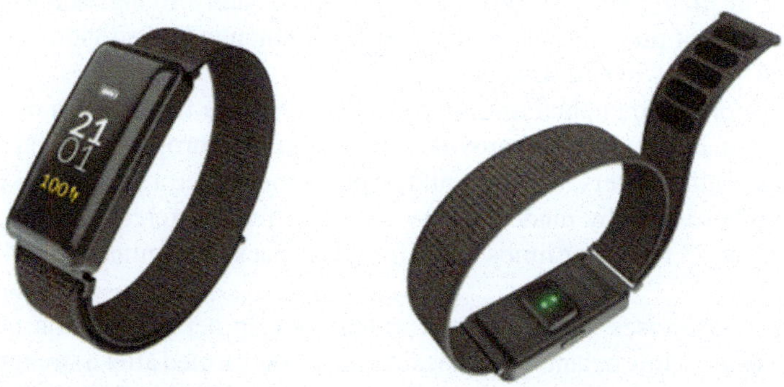

Fig. 3 Wearable wristband. It is visible the user interface composed of a color LCD and a multifunction button, while a heart rate sensor is present on the back of the device

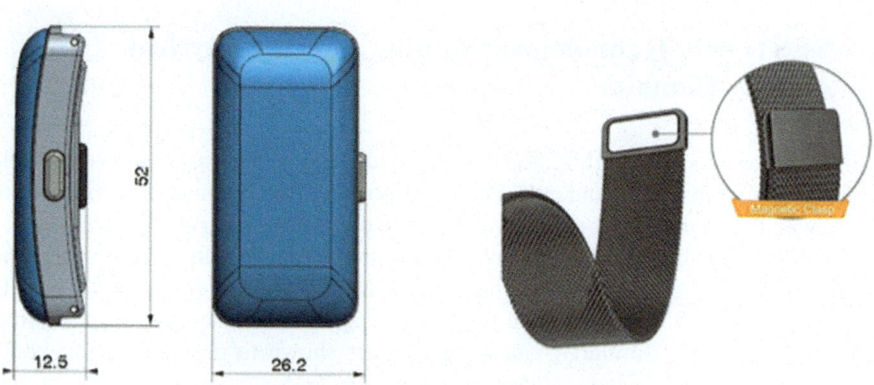

Fig. 4 Wearable wristband dimension and magnetic bracelet closure

color LCD display provides an easy user interface and a single multifunction button represents the main active user interface.

The wristband is equipped with sensors suitable to collect all the requested data about physical activities, in particular an accelerometer sensor that can detect walking base exercises and squats, while the combination with a barometer is used to refine the stairs count. The sensor present in the back of the wristband can measure also the heart rate of the user.

The purpose of the wristband is to collect data from the user and to transmit them to the cloud, passing to the app in the smartphone through a Bluetooth connection.

The physical structure involves different components like the smartphone app, the algorithm in the cloud that merges physical activities data with information coming from other sensors like the smart scale or nutrition, while a tangible interface is used for user feedback. In Fig. 5 the system architecture extract related to the wristband wearable is visible.

Once the user has connected the wristband to the app through a Bluetooth connection, the wristband starts to track standard activities performed by the user like walking steps, stairs and rest time that are analysed and processed by the algorithm to analyse sedentariness and daily activities of the user. In addition, upon app request, the wristband permits to start more a simplified/modified version of 30 s chair rise test and 6 min walking test, combining the measuring of the heart rate to the inertial sensors and transmitting the raw data to the app by Bluetooth, according to the synchronization protocol.

Even if the wristband is not designed to be a medical device, the sensors and the components used are based on the accuracy of the medical standard but the

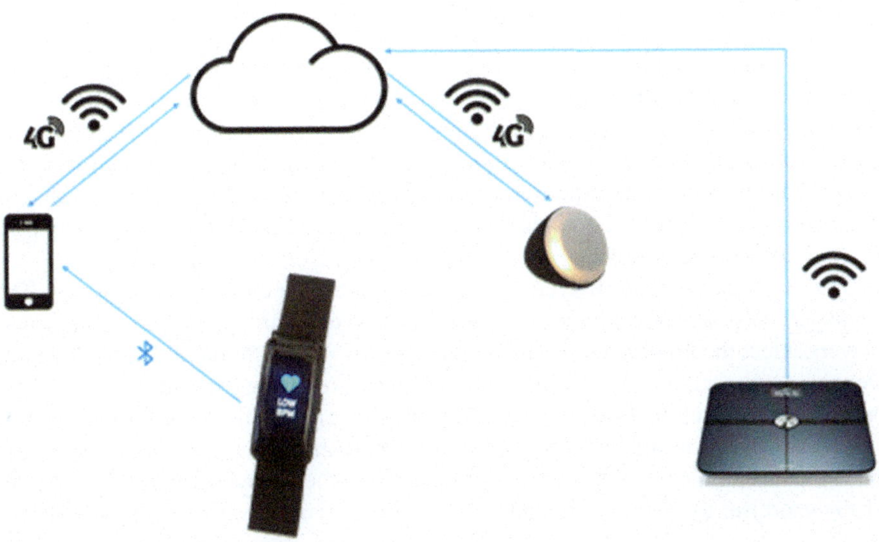

Fig. 5 Wearable architecture connection

measurements are comparable to common healthcare devices for fitness usage, hence the combination of data gathered both from heart rate measurement and inertial sensors provides a good indication of the physical activity profile of the user.

Games

'Exergaming' describes the use of digital games or game elements to encourage people to do physical exercise [30]. While the physiological effects of exergaming are not considered better than traditional fitness, with exergames providing light-to-moderate physical exertion [31], exergames have shown players to be more interested and engaged compared to general fitness. For this reason, they are considered to be effective in making physical activity more approachable to inactive people [32]. Digital games, however, are often not necessarily accessible to everyone. When developing games to support older people in maintaining their well-being, it is essential to develop them in such a way that they are easy to understand, do not rely on specialized hardware, and are aligned with the preferences and interests of the audience [33, 34]. For this reason, the NESTORE game was developed with the requirements and wishes of older audiences in mind [35]. To lower the barrier of entry, the game is developed for mobile phones as our user studies showed this was a type of technology used by most older adults. However, while phones are accessible to many users, they also come with limitations. Sensor input (and therefore the ability to monitor a user's performance) is limited. Hence, the design described below focuses instead on providing users feedback during their workout and light game mechanics to engage them over a longer period.

Pocket Odyssey, the game developed as part of the NESTORE system, consists of three components. The first is the 'Ship', which functions as the main 'hub' for the player and allows access to the other parts of the game. The other parts are the 'Gym' and the 'Submarine' mini-games. The Submarine game is designed for cognitive training and as such will not be discussed further. The Gym game is an interactive visualization of the exercise routines outlined earlier in this chapter. The first time a NESTORE user starts the game, they are welcomed by the character Nestor. He is the player's guide to the game. In the introduction, he informs the player that he requires their help in fixing up his ship. Once Nestor has established the premise of the game, he guides the player through a short tutorial that explains the basic functionality.

The Gym game helps players in following pre-defined exercise routines. The character Nestor performs these routines on-screen through timed animations. Players select the type of exercise they want to do—strength, flexibility, or balance. Depending on the choice, players then either start exercising (balance or flexibility), or they select which routine they would like to perform (strength). After making this choice, the player is shown a screen with an explanation for the upcoming exercise. The structure of these screens is always the same—they show the two key positions of the exercise, as well as a textual description of the movement to be performed (Fig. 6).

The Nestor character performs the exercise on-screen with the correct timing. Repetitions are counted in the top-right corner. Motivational text is provided at the

Fig. 6 Top: The initial ship (L) and customization options (R). Bottom: Example of an exercise explanation screen (L) and the Nestor character performing an exercise (R)

bottom to guide the player through the motions. If the player needs to perform the exercise on two sides (e.g., an exercise using a single arm), the game prompts the player to switch sides halfway through the repetitions. When the target amount of repetitions has been completed, the next exercise is explained. This process continues until the player has performed all exercises in the routine. At this point, the game checks whether the player has exercised enough for that day. If they have not, the player is prompted to continue with the next set. If they have, the game removes the option to continue and rewards the player. It is possible to finish a set, leave the game, and finish the required amount of sets later on. For flexibility and balance, there is no target to be reached. In these cases, routines only last for 1 set and provide a combination of movements.

Pocket Odyssey incorporates two types of reward, a feature adapted from existing mobile games such as Candy Crush Saga [36] or Homescapes [37]. The benefit of having multiple types of reward is the ability to pace the reward received by the player. The game aims to encourage players not just to play the game, but to play it the right amount (e.g., complete a physical exercise routine). A less valuable reward (coins) is used to reward basic interaction, while a rarer reward (stars) is used to reward commitment to achieving daily or weekly goals. These types of 'currency' can be used to fix up and decorate Nestor's ship to the user's taste. In doing so, the game provides an incentive to keep up with exercise regularly. While the content for the game is currently limited (i.e., users could 'finish' fixing up the ship), it could be expanded on to prolong engagement over a longer period.

5 Conclusions

This chapter summarized the physiological bases and technological approach utilized by the NESTORE Coaching System to evaluate older adults' functional abilities and to create individualized coaching plans in the physical activity domain according to internationally recognized guidelines.

The recent increase in sedentary behaviour, and therefore the prevalence of the associated disease, has pointed out the need to develop solutions aimed to increase physical activity levels in the general population. In particular, strategies are requested for specific age groups, such as older adults aged over 65, where it is fundamental to improve the quality of life associated with ageing. Among previous action programs, technological solutions have been proven to be effective in improving activity levels, also in the elderly. In this contest, NESTORE Coaching System wants to non-invasively and multidimensionally impact user's daily life physical habits by suggesting structured training sessions in the following subdomain: aerobic, strength, flexibility and balance. NESTORE final goal aims to bring the user to match the existing guidelines on physical activity by performing both daily non-structured tasks and structured activities.

References

1. Vidoni, E. D., Honea, R. A., Billinger, S. A., et al. (2012). Cardiorespiratory fitness is associated with atrophy in Alzheimer's and aging over 2 years. *Neurobiology of Aging*. https://doi.org/10.1016/j.neurobiolaging.2011.03.016.
2. Steell, L., Ho, F. K., Sillars, A., et al. (2019). Dose-response associations of cardiorespiratory fitness with all-cause mortality and incidence and mortality of cancer and cardiovascular and respiratory diseases: The UK Biobank cohort study. *British Journal of Sports Medicine*. https://doi.org/10.1136/bjsports-2018-099093.
3. Slemenda, C., Heilman, D. K., Brandt, K. D., et al. (1998). Reduced quadriceps strength relative to body weight: A risk factor for knee osteoarthritis in women? *Arthritis and Rheumatism*. https://doi.org/10.1002/1529-0131(199811)41:11%3c1951:AID-ART9%3e3.0.CO;2-9.
4. Physical Activity Guidelines Advisory Committee. (2008). *Physical activity guidelines advisory committee report*. Washington, DC US 67, 683. https://doi.org/10.1111/j.1753-4887.2008.00136.x.
5. Paterson, D. H., & Warburton, D. E. R. (2010). Physical activity and functional limitations in older adults: A systematic review related to Canada's physical activity guidelines. *International Journal of Behavioral Nutrition and Physical Activity*.
6. Paterson, D. H., Jones, G. R., & Rice, C. L. (2007). Ageing and physical activity: Evidence to develop exercise recommendations for older adults. *Applied Physiology, Nutrition, and Metabolism*.
7. Chodzko-Zajko, W. J., Proctor, D. N., Fiatarone Singh, M. A., et al. (2009). Exercise and physical activity for older adults. *Medicine & Science in Sports & Exercise*.
8. Pescatello, L., Arena, R., Riebe, D., & Thompson, P. (2014). *ACSM's Guidelines for exercise testing and prescription* (9th ed.).
9. WHO. (2010). Global recommendations on physical activity for health. *Geneva: World Health Organization, 60*. https://doi.org/10.1080/11026480410034349.

10. Coughlin, S. S., & Stewart, J. (2016). Use of consumer wearable devices to promote physical activity: A review of health intervention studies. *Journal of Environmental Health Science*. https://doi.org/10.15436/2378-6841.16.1123.
11. Stephenson, A., McDonough, S. M., Murphy, M. H., et al. (2017). Using computer, mobile and wearable technology enhanced interventions to reduce sedentary behaviour: A systematic review and meta-analysis. *International Journal of Behavioral Nutrition and Physical Activity*. https://doi.org/10.1186/s12966-017-0561-4.
12. Kervio, G., Carre, F., & Ville, N. S. (2003). Reliability and intensity of the six-minute walk test in healthy elderly subjects. *Medicine and Science in Sports and Exercise, 35,* 169–174. https://doi.org/10.1097/00005768-200301000-00025.
13. American College of Sports Medicine. (2014). *ACSM guidelines for exercise testing and prescription*.
14. Crapo, R. O., Casaburi, R., Coates, A. L., et al. (2002). ATS statement: Guidelines for the six-minute walk test. *American Journal of Respiratory and Critical Care Medicine*.
15. Enright, P. L. (2003). The six-minute walk test. In *Respiratory care*.
16. American Thoracic Society. (2002). Committee on proficiency standards for clinical pulmonary function laboratories. ATS statement: Guidelines for the six-minute walk test. *American Journal of Respiratory and Critical Care Medicine*. https://doi.org/10.1021/jo01342a038.
17. Alcazar, J., Losa-Reyna, J., Rodriguez-Lopez, C., et al. (2018). The sit-to-stand muscle power test: An easy, inexpensive and portable procedure to assess muscle power in older people. *Experimental Gerontology*. https://doi.org/10.1016/j.exger.2018.08.006.
18. Cress, M. E., Buchner, D. M., Prohaska T., et al. (2005). Best practices for physical activity programs and behavior counseling in older adult populations. *Journal of Aging and Physical Activity*.
19. Nelson, M. E., Rejeski, W. J., Blair, S. N., et al. (2007). Physical activity and public health in older adults: Recommendation from the American College of Sports Medicine and the American Heart Association. *Medicine and Science in Sports and Exercise, 39,* 1423–1434. https://doi.org/10.1249/mss.0b013e3180616aa2.
20. Fiatarone, M. A., O'neill, E. F., Ryan, N. D., et al. (1994). Exercise training and nutritional supplementation for physical frailty in very elderly people. *New England Journal of Medicine*. https://doi.org/10.1056/NEJM199406233302501.
21. U.S. Department of Health and Human Services. (2008). *2008 physical activity guidelines for Americans*. http://www.health.gov/PAGuidelines.
22. Sullivan, G. M., & Pomidor, A. K. (2015). *Exercise for aging adults: A guide for practitioners*. Springer.
23. Paterson, D. H., & Stathokostas, L. (2001). Physical activity, fitness, and gender in relation to morbidity, survival, quality of life, and independence in older age. *Gender, Physical Activity, and Aging*.
24. Hagerman, F. C., Walsh, S. J., Staron, R. S., et al. (2000). Effects of high-intensity resistance training on untrained older men. I. Strength, cardiovascular, and metabolic responses. *The Journals of Gerontology Series A Biological Sciences and Medical Sciences*. https://doi.org/10.1093/gerona/55.7.B336.
25. Hunter, G. R., McCarthy, J. P., & Bamman, M. M. (2004). Effects of resistance training on older adults. *Sports Medicine*.
26. Lemmer, J. T., Hurlbut, D. E., Martel, G. F., et al. (2000). Age and gender responses to strength training and detraining. *Medicine and Science in Sports and Exercise*. https://doi.org/10.1097/00005768-200008000-00021.
27. Bravata, D. M., Smith-Spangler, C., Sundaram, V., et al. (2007). Using pedometers to increase physical activity and improve health: A systematic review. *JAMA*.
28. Similä, H., Merilahti, J., Ylikauppila, M., et al. (2013). Comparing two coaching systems for improving physical activity of older adults. In *XIII Mediterranean Conference on Medical and Biological Engineering and Computing* (pp. 1197–1200). Springer, Cham.
29. Hanke, S., Meinedo, H., Portugal, D., et al. (2015). CogniWin—A virtual assistance system for older adults at work. In *International Conference on Human Aspects of IT for the Aged Population* (pp. 257–268). Springer, Cham.

30. Oh, Y., & Yang, S. (2010). Defining exergames & exergaming. *Proceedings of Meaningful Play*, 1–17.
31. Peng, W., Crouse, J. C., & Lin, J.-H. (2013). Using active video games for physical activity promotion: A systematic review of the current state of research. *Health Education & Behavior, 40*, 171–192.
32. Lee, S., Kim, W., Park, T., & Peng, W. (2017). The psychological effects of playing exergames: A systematic review. *Cyberpsychology, Behavior, and Social Networking, 20*, 513–532.
33. Marston, H. R. (2013). Design recommendations for digital game design within an ageing society. *Educational Gerontology, 39*, 103–118.
34. Nap, H. H., De Kort, Y. A. W., & IJsselsteijn, W. A. (2009). Senior gamers: Preferences, motivations and needs. *Gerontechnology, 8*, 247–262.
35. Kniestedt, I., Lukosch, S., & Brazier, F. (2018). User-centered design of an online mobile game suite to affect well-being of older adults. In: *International Conference on Entertainment Computing* (pp. 355–361).
36. King. (2012). *Candy crush saga*. https://king.com/it/game/candycrush.
37. Playrix. (2017). *Homescapes*. https://www.playrix.com/homescapes/.

Coaching Older Adults Towards a Healthier Lifestyle: Psychological and Technological Methods

Christina Röcke, Leonardo Angelini, Sabrina Guye, Mira El Kamali, Maurizio Caon, Omar Abou Khaled, and Elena Mugellini

Abstract This chapter discusses the theoretical behaviour change framework and its integration and implementation of behaviour change techniques that form the conceptual psychological basis for innovative but efficient coaching approach. We review the current state of e-coaching solutions for older adults that can be found in the literature and identify gaps. Finally, we review and discuss the technological implementation of behaviour change techniques applied in NESTORE to support healthy older adults to adopt a healthy lifestyle in all NESTORE well-being domains as reference case study.

1 Introduction

This chapter presents the insights collected during the NESTORE project for the definition of a multi-domain behaviour change model and its integration in a virtual coach for supporting the user's behaviour change.

From a theoretical point, selecting a specific health-behaviour change model (BCM) as underlying theoretical approach was important as many such models have been proposed in the literature. From the behaviour change techniques (BCTs) perspective, one needs to integrate the variables from the theoretical model with the more general (and digital) intervention strategies and BCTs and apply these to the intervention domains.

As an overarching theoretical framework to the NESTORE project, the lifespan theoretical model of selection with optimization and compensation (SOC) has been proposed. It is a lifespan theoretical model on developmental regulation, i.e., how individuals actively shape their own developmental trajectories in the context of all resources available to them and the changes in these resources with increasing age

C. Röcke (✉) · S. Guye
University of Zurich, University Research Priority Program "Dynamics of Healthy Aging, Andreasstrasse 15, Box 2, 8050 Zurich, Switzerland
e-mail: christina.roecke@uzh.ch

L. Angelini · M. El Kamali · M. Caon · O. A. Khaled · E. Mugellini
University of Applied Sciences of Western Switzerland (HES-SO), Fribourg, Switzerland

G. Andreoni and C. Mambretti (eds.), *Digital Health Technology for Better Aging*, Research for Development, https://doi.org/10.1007/978-3-030-72663-8_10

(i.e., gains and losses). Central tenets of the SOC model are that optimal lifespan development and successful aging are best represented by a positive balance between developmental gains and developmental losses through three strategies [5, 14]: selection of goals and preferences, optimization in terms of acquiring and improving means for goal attainment, and compensation as counteracting for losses in and blockage of goal-relevant means. The flexible implementation of the three proposed strategies is suggested to lead to the maintenance of one's functional capacity and well-being, and a wide range of empirical evidence supports the central tenets of the SOC model (e.g., [12–16]).

An important feature of NESTORE is that this coaching platform has been co-designed in participatory fashion, as a friend and companion that helps in assessing the current health status in key domains for aging and health, individuals' personal goals and aims to facilitate the monitoring and person-specific recommendations for health-related behaviour change. As such, it is important that NESTORE focuses on positive coaching strategies (e.g., educational information, highlighting benefits, planning for coping) rather than on negative ones (e.g., punishing, threats).

This chapter is structured as follows: after the introduction, we summarize in Sect. 2 theoretical BCMs from health psychology and outline why the NESTORE project primarily focuses on the Health Action Process Approach (HAPA) model. In Sect. 3, we provide an overview over commonly used BCTs and intervention strategies in the health (and aging) domains, including the specific strategies and techniques as they are applied to each of the NESTORE domains. Section 4 mainly summarizes the results of a literature on e-coaching conducted in the health domain, with a particular focus on whether and which health BCMs and BCTs are used across the NESTORE domains. In the fifth section, we describe how the NESTORE system can be implemented in terms of applying the conceptual HAPA framework in the planned e-coaching environment of NESTORE and illustrating the planned user journey of choosing well-being and health pathways and first illustrations of the planned interfaces. We close this chapter with a brief conclusion.

2 Theoretical Behaviour Change Models in Health Psychology

Given the wide range of changes observed in the general population of older adults, including health-related impairments, it is surprising that there is little research on health-behaviour changes in older adults [39]. However, the studies that exist and used theory-guided behaviour change have empirically shown to be effective (e.g., [33]). There are many different social-cognitive behaviour change models that provide a conceptual framework for describing and understanding how individuals can successfully adopt a change in behaviour in general, and some models also explicitly target health-related behaviours. These latter models aim to describe how individuals successfully replace health-compromising behaviours (e.g., sedentary behaviour, social reclusion) with health-enhancing behaviours (e.g., physical activity, social integration) through a process of adoption, initiation and maintenance of health behaviours [32]. The main goal of these (health) behaviour change theories is to understand how a set of psychological constructs can jointly explain how individual can be motivated to change an established behavioural pattern in the interest of improved or maintained overall long-term health. Many of these share a set of common variables that are listed in Table 1.

Table 1 Overview of key concepts in various behaviour change models

Key element	Definition	Strategies for behavior change
Threat	Event that is dangerous or harmful	Raise awareness that the threat exists, focusing on severity and susceptibility
Fear	Emotional experience in response to the perception of a personally relevant threat	Fear can powerfully influence behaviour and, if it is channelled in the appropriate way, can motivate people to seek information, but it can also cause people to deny they are at risk
Intentions	A person's conscious decision and plans to pursue a certain goal	Determine if intentions are genuine or proxies for actual behaviour
Self-efficacy	An individual's perception of or confidence in their ability to perform a recommended response	Raise individuals' confidence that they can perform response and help ensure they can avert the threat
Response efficacy	Perception that a recommended response will prevent the threat from happening	Provide evidence of examples that the recommended response will avert the threat
Barriers	Something that would prevent an individual from carrying out a recommended response	Be aware of physical or cultural barriers that might exist, attempt to remove barriers
Benefits	Positive consequences of performing recommended response	Communicate the benefits of performing the recommended response
Subjective Norms	What an individual thinks other people think they should do	Understand with whom individuals are likely to comply
Attitudes	An individual's evaluation or beliefs about a recommended response	Measure existing attitudes before attempting to change them
Cues to Action	External or internal factors that help individuals make decisions about a response	Provide communication that might trigger individuals to make decisions
Reactance	When an individual reacts against a recommended response	Ensure individuals do not feel they have been manipulated or are unable to avert the threat

Note Table adapted from World Bank [38]

Existing theoretical health-behaviour change models can be distinguished broadly into two types of models: (1) continuum models and (2) stage models. Continuum models (e.g., Theory of Reasoned Action [13], Theory of Planned Behaviour [2], Social-Cognitive Theory [6], Health Belief Model [28], Protection Motivation Theory [20]) describe the degree to which individuals are likely to act, and interventions based on such models focus on moving people closer to action. One characteristic of interventions rooted in continuum models is that they mainly target groups of people (instead of subgroups or individuals) and on changing all variables for all individuals, but no tailoring to particular subgroups occurs.

Stage models (e.g., Transtheoretical Model [26]), on the other hand, divide the behaviour change trajectory into qualitative and ordered stages, into which individuals can be classified. Within a stage, individuals are more similar than across stages. Thus, they provide a good framework for stage-matched treatments for subgroups of individuals. In the context of intervention research, stage models provide some advantages over continuum models because they are not overgeneralizing to the entire population. The HAPA, selected as the conceptual framework for the NESTORE coaching platform represents an integration between continuum and stage models of behaviour change [33] and additionally addresses the intention-behaviour gap that other models often neglect.

The HAPA [32] is one of the more recent models in the health-behaviour change literature. Its advantage over the earlier models is that it focuses on two distinct phases (i.e. the motivational phase and volitional phase) and on phase-specific psychological factors explaining or underlying behaviour change (or its failure) in each phase (see Fig. 1 for an overview). It thus allows a closer examination and understanding of those variables that underlie intention formation and it also addresses

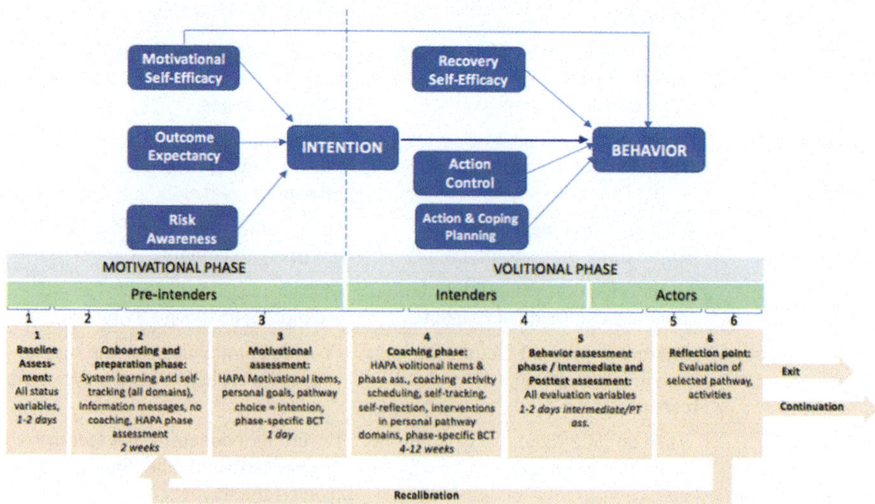

Fig. 1 The health action process approach model: mapping of study and system phases

the intention-behaviour gap by including variables (mainly from the self-regulation domain) that mediate the relation between intentions and the target behaviour. It is thus more comprehensive than other models, which often successfully predict intention itself, but then consider intentions to be the proximal predictor of behaviour, thus ignoring the often-found so-called intention-behaviour gap. In contrast, the HAPA model has identified distinct predictive factors for each of two phases, including post-intentional variables. As mentioned above, the HAPA model has both a continuum and a stage layer, addressing shortcoming of either model type. The inclusion of post-intentional variables as predictors of behaviour addresses criticism of traditional continuum models, which often fail to account for the lacking prediction of behaviour by intention alone. The distinction between two main phases, the motivational and the volitional phase, the HAPA also incorporates a stage-like layer.

According to the HAPA model, the motivational (pre-intentional) phase describes a number of variables thought to predict that individuals form the intention to improve their own health, often through a change in their usual behaviour in a particular domain. During this initial stage, individuals are considered as pre-intenders. Individuals who have made the decision to act and thus have formed an intention but have not yet started to act, are considered intenders in the model. The volitional (post-intentional) phase describes those variables that predict the success of setting the implementation into action. A person's perceived self-efficacy is emphasized in each phase as one of the key variables within the HAPA model [31]. Another important self-regulatory variable during the volitional phase is planning the when, where and how of behaviour, both in general and in the face of obstacles. Individuals in the action phase of the model are considered actors. The model has been applied to a wide range of samples/patient groups and targeting a variety of health behaviours [34].

Motivational phase: Three key variables to predict the intention to act [33]

- Risk awareness is thought to prepare the stage for a process of contemplation
- Positive outcome expectancies and self-efficacy jointly operate to form the intention.

Volitional phase: Three key variables predict the actual behaviour implementation

- Self-efficacy during the volitional phase is considered an important variable to overcome the intention-behaviour gap and a key asset of the HAPA model [32]; degree of confidence a person has about being able to get back on track after a relapse [31]
- Action planning (when, where and how the target behaviour will be performed): involves the prospective linkage of specific cues from the situational environment with concrete behaviours so that the intention is being put in place [29]. An additional self-regulatory strategy in the planning domain is coping planning, which describes how individuals will deal with problems or difficulties that arise in executing their plans [33]

- Action control: comprises sub-facets of general self-regulation [9], such as self-monitoring, awareness of standards, and self-regulatory effort, and has also been shown to be a reliable precursor of subsequent behaviour [35].

Much research on the basis of the HAPA considers interindividual differences, that is differences between individuals in a number of health domains (for overview, see [32]; see also D2.1). There is some initial evidence about the validity of HAPA assumptions on the within-person level (e.g., [8]).

One challenge within the NESTORE project is that NESTORE focuses on a multidimensional approach to health and aims to offer healthy older adults a variety of life domains to choose from and create one's own more holistic coaching intervention. The HAPA variables will have to be applied and assessed for the separate well-being and health domains in NESTORE in a way that allows a complete but yet economic and least burdensome data collection pipeline. There is some evidence in younger and middle-aged groups that multiple health behaviour change interventions (MHBC) versus single health behaviour change interventions (SHBC) can be effective and more efficient in terms of time and costs, but little is known about how these MHBC compare to the SHBC in older adults. Given that older adults often experience multiple health conditions and that even in relatively healthy older adults, changes in resources occur in several domains (e.g., physical, social, cognitive), it would be very useful to examine MHBC also in this age group (e.g., [17, 23]). One of the advantages of a focus on more than one domain that has been proposed is that mastery in one domain may foster self-efficacy for changing one's habits in a different domain. On the other hand, a drawback could be that individuals feel overwhelmed. A recent systematic review of six randomized trials that examined the comparative efficacy of two kinds of MHBC interventions suggests that both a sequential and a simultaneous approach can be equally effective, and that further research is needed to pinpoint whether one is indeed advantageous over the other and in which domain and for which population [17]. It is also noteworthy that much of this work targets classical health behaviours only (e.g., nutrition, physical activity, smoking), and even less is known through the lens of behaviour change models and interventions for domains such as cognitive and social well-being and health.

Figure 1 shows the HAPA phases and variables that each predict the intention first and the behaviour second. It also provides the general overview of system and general study components. Table 2 in addition indicates which BCT can be mapped onto the variables of the motivational and those of the intention formation and volitional phases. So far, the HAPA model has been used for single health domains and behaviours. Given the multi-domain approach within NESTORE, this strategy would need to be extended to include more than one domain. In order to allow for a clear evaluation of the predictive utility of the conceptual HAPA variables in each phase, in relation to the individually tailored interventions across domains, HAPA variables would need to be assessed for each NESTORE domain. Table 2 lists exemplar items for the physical activity domain, and these single items can both easily be implemented in the daily life monitoring and coaching phase and be assessed for all those domains a NESTORE user has chosen as part of her individual well-being pathway.

Table 2 Key variables from HAPA model distinguished by phase and including exemplary items and corresponding BCT

Variables proposed to predict the intention/the behaviour	Exemplary item for assessment (in daily life)	Corresponding behaviour change techniques (BCT)
Phase I: motivational phase		
Risk awareness	If I am not regularly physically active, the probability is high that I will have serious health problems	Educational messages/provide information about health consequences, self-monitoring/provide feedback, (social comparison?)
Positive outcome expectancy	There are more advantages than disadvantages in being physically active on a regular basis	Educational messages/provide information about health consequences, provide general encouragement, self-monitoring/provide feedback, praise
Motivational self-efficacy	I am confident that I will engage in regular physical activity in the next four weeks, even if it is difficult	Educational messages/provide information about health consequences, provide general encouragement, self-monitoring/radar according to recommendations?
Intention formation		
Behavioural Intention	In the next four weeks, I intend to be regularly physically active	Behavioural contract
Phase II: Volitional Phase		
Recovery self-efficacy	I am confident that I can be as physically active as I have planned during the next four weeks even as barriers arise	Provide general encouragement, prompt review of behavioural goals (plans for overcoming barriers and also regarding the personal goals), stress management
Action planning	I have made detailed plans for when and how I will be regularly physically active in the next four weeks	Calendar scheduling, set graded tasks, social support/social comparison for planning (ideas), time management
Coping planning	I have made a detailed plan regarding what to do if something interferes with my plans	Prompt barrier identification, problem solving

(continued)

Table 2 (continued)

Variables proposed to predict the intention/the behaviour	Exemplary item for assessment (in daily life)	Corresponding behaviour change techniques (BCT)
Action control: Awareness of standards Self-monitoring Self-regulatory effort	During the last 4 weeks, I was always aware of my intended training program During the last 4 weeks, I constantly monitored whether I was as physically active as I had planned During the last 4 weeks, I always tried to be as physically active as I had intended	Prompt review of behavioural goals, educational messages, self-tracking, model/demonstrate behaviour, instruction Self-monitoring, provide feedback Provide general encouragement, self-monitoring/review of performed activities, prompts/reminders (of plans to overcome problems and of goals)

BCT can then also be mapped onto the different motivational and volitional variables shown in Table 2 to personalize interventions not only with regard to a given target coaching domain and pathway but also with respect to the conceptual underpinnings of the HAPA framework.

In this context, the stage properties of the HAPA model are useful in following users along their health behaviour change process. As described in Schwarzer et al. [33], depending on a person's stage position (or mindset) as either pre-intender, intender or actor, different predictor variables are important for the intervention to be successful. For example, in the pre-intentional phase, prompting outcome expectancies and an appropriate level of risk information may be the intervention of choice, as well as highlighting the positive outcomes the new behaviour would have. In other subgroups, such as the actors, are thought to particularly benefit from supporting them in high-risk situations in which relapses are likely.

During the user journey of selecting a NESTORE well-being and health pathway, it is thus crucial to determine the mindset of a user both with regard to the person's overall willingness and plans to engage in (new) health behaviours, and also concerning the particular subdomains. One easy way of classifying individuals in terms of this mindset (in addition to determining the need for intervention based on the set of baseline status assessments and sensor inputs), one can ask users to self-classify their mindset using Likert Scale questionnaires.

3 Behaviour Change Techniques and General Coaching Strategies for Health and Well-Being

There is a large variety of intervention types that can be found in the behaviour change and coaching intervention literature: In a review of prominent health behaviour change researchers [1], 26 different general BCTs were identified (see left column of Table 3).

New intervention approaches specifically focus on a range of digital BCTs (see also [1, 27]). Several different types or delivery modes of digital interventions can be differentiated:

- Online workshop
- Emails
- Access to e-counsellor
- Website/mobile-enabled website
- Online portal
- Text messaging
- Mobile app
- Wearable and ambient sensors (e.g., Fitbit)
- Telephone counselling
- Social media (Facebook support group)
- Video conferencing (e.g., Skype).

Recently, a focus in the health-behaviour change literature has been on so-called digital BCTs [27], many of which are identical or can at least easily be mapped onto the more traditional (non-digital) BCTs (see right column of Table 3).

4 Health-Related e-Coaching and Digital Intervention Strategies

This section of the chapter focuses on digital interventions (i.e., e-coaching) for a healthy lifestyle in older adults. With respect to traditional eHealth interventions, here we particularly focus on systems that monitor user behaviour and provide personalized suggestions to improve health-related goals through a virtual coach. Such a coach can be simply embedded in smartphone devices (e.g., app), but can also have a more anthropomorphic and physical embodiment, for example in form of an Embodied Conversational Agents (ECA) or a robot. As defined by Banos and Nugent [7] in the introduction to a recent IEEE Computer special issue on E-coaching for Health, coaching a user means to "frequently, but not continuously, observe, listen to, question, understand, reason with, teach, and/or advise the users in order to change their behaviour and to improve their health". To this purpose, they continue, "intelligent systems are used to encourage progress toward specific health-related goals by providing tailored training and guidance". Warner [37] provides another definition

Table 3 Overview of general and equivalent digital behaviour change techniques

General Behaviour change techniques[a]	Digital Behaviour change techniques[b]
Provide general information	Pros and cons
Provide information on consequences	Provide information about health consequences
Provide information about others' approval	Social reward
Prompt intention formation	
Prompt barrier identification	Problem solving, behaviour substitution
Provide general encouragement	Verbal persuasion about capability
Set graded tasks	Graded tasks
Provide instruction	Instruction of how to perform a behaviour
Model or demonstrate behavior	Demonstration of the behaviour
Prompt specific goal setting	Goal setting (behaviour or goal)
Prompt review of behavioral goals	Review behavioural goals
Prompt self-monitoring of behavior	Self-monitoring of behaviour or goals or outcomes
Provide feedback on performance	Feedback on behaviour
Provide contingent rewards	
Teach to use prompts/cues	Prompts/cues
Agree on behavioral contract	
Prompt practice	
Use follow-up prompts	Prompts/cues
Provide opportunities for social comparison	
Plan social support/social change	Social support
Prompt model identification as role model	
Prompt self-talk	
Relapse prevention	
Stress management	Reduce negative emotions
Motivational interviewing	
Time management	
	Credible source
	Offering deals for healthy goods/services for completing self-monitoring (independent of behaviour reported)
	Framing/reframing
	Adding objects to the environment

Note [a]Abraham and Michie [1], [b]Roberts et al. [27]

of coaching. He says that "coaching is the ability for someone—or something—to ask thought-provoking questions that inspire the coachees to maximize their personal and professional potential by utilizing the tools, skills, and views the coachee already possesses." In this same paper, the goal of coaching is defined as "to help individuals develop internal and external structures that help them achieve success and to increase their potential by expanding their sense of what is possible." Although these two definitions differ to some extent, the core part remains the same namely the support activity of the coach to guide the user to exploit her full potential in order to achieve a target behaviour. As part of the above-mentioned special issue, Ochoa and Gutierrez [24] propose a loosely-coupled architecture for e-coaching system.

The key elements of the proposed architecture can be categorized in (1) data gathering, (2) data processing (which include sensor data analysis and decision making for adapting the intervention to the context) and (3) actuation of the intervention through the delivery of the coaching action to the user. Data analysis includes both the understanding of user variables (i.e., monitoring unit) and user actions (i.e., diagnosing unit). In particular, the intelligence of the system (i.e., learning unit) should be able to adapt the intervention according to different contexts: the state of users' variable, the user model (including users' preferences), the coaching plan and the progress throughout the coaching plan.

Kamphorst [18] propose a minimal set of features that each e-coaching system should implement. These can be considered as functional requirements that are complementary to the architectural requirement:

- **Social ability**: The coach should be able to engage in a conversation with the user.
- **Credibility**: The system has to be perceived as having expertise and being trustworthy.
- **Context-awareness**: The system needs to be aware of user context to propose ideas and actions that are relevant for the user.
- **Learning abilities**: The system needs the ability to ask questions, give feedback, and offer advice that is tailored to the individual user, building up and maintaining a personalized user model.
- **Data gathering**: The system will need to interface with different types of data streams (e.g., direct user input, but potentially also measurements of physical activities, mood self-reports, sleeping patterns), to provide individually tailored coaching.
- **Proactivity**: The system should initiate interactions with the aim of stimulating action.
- **Reflection**: The system should initiate interactions in a proactive manner, depending on user's sensed or predicted behaviour.
- **BCM integration**: The system needs to know how a behaviour change trajectory looks like in order to provide successful coaching.
- **Planning support**: In order to support users in setting themselves up for behaviour change success, the system should guide the user through the intention formation with appropriate planning strategies.

While Kamphorst [18] suggested important features that a e-coach system should have, Lentferink et al. [19] reviewed the key components that can significantly affect a variety of health outcomes, the adherence and the usability of an e-coaching intervention (based on 27 studies involving different age groups and coaching domains/health behaviours). **The following BCTs were found to positively affect both health outcomes and usability in the studies reviewed**:

- Setting short-term goals to eventually reach long-term goals
- Personalization of goals
- Praise messages
- Reminders to input self-tracking data into the technology
- Use of validity-tested devices
- Integration of self-tracking and persuasive e-Coaching
- Provision of face-to-face instructions during implementation, as key components for influencing both health outcomes and usability in a positive way.

Moreover, the following BCT was beneficial for both adherence and on usability:

- Provision of personalized content

It is important to note that in addition to the missing link between conceptual health BCMs and the literature on BCTs, as will be discussed in the following sections, few studies consider more than one behaviour/health domain and few include older adults in their samples or consider age-related differences and changes in the degree of effectiveness of select BCTs. So far, there is evidence for both age-related similarities and differences in some elements of behaviour change predicting variables (e.g., action and coping planning, [30]).

In addition, those reviews and meta-analyses that focus on older adults that can be found add an interesting perspective to the BCTs listed above. In a recent survey, 66 adults aged 65 and older rated several taxonomies of BCTs (including the one by Michie et al. [21] according to (1) how much they favoured each BCT in the context of a physical activity enhancing intervention. Further, one important aspect of (digital or traditional) interventions named by participants was *autonomy support*, meaning the importance of any BCT to help maintain rather than conflict with a person's own sense of autonomy and independence. As such, receiving professional support at the time of selecting the appropriate intervention based on credible information was regarded as highly desirable and useful. Planning activities such as diaries were, however, only helpful if they are not overly obtrusive into the flexibility of people to freely structure their daily life activities and adapting any intervention regime to the current (and possibly changing) day-to-day needs [4]. Another recent review on the effectiveness of both digital and non-digital interventions to enhance physical activity particularly in older adults also indicated that most interventions were tailored to the specific person and that self-tracking as a means of providing feedback to participants and as the basis for person- and time-specific interventions was related to reliable improvements in physical activity behaviour [22].

El Kamali et al. [11], recently reviewed the e-coaches for improving older adult well-being, highlighting that only few adopted a fully multi-domain approach and that there is a general lack of evidence on their effectiveness, as few controlled studies were carried out to assess e-coaches for older adults.

5 e-Coaching in NESTORE

In this section, we summarize the main intervention techniques and features implemented in NESTORE. In particular, in the following list we analyse the key components that could affect health outcomes, usability and adherence to the program [19]:

- *Reduction of activity options by setting short-term goals to eventually reach long-term goals*: goal setting is reduced from the high-level long-term intention making (pathway), to specific short-term multi-domain coaching activities, which in turn are composed of elementary training activities [3]
- *Personalization of goals*: users can not only choose pathways and coaching activities according to a predefined list provided by the system, but this list and the intermediate goal thresholds are adapted by the system according to user preferences and states ([36]; see also chapter "Perspective and Experiences of Decision Support System (DSS) and AI in Prevention and Care for Older Adults")
- *Praise messages*: praise messages are an integral part of the system and are provided on different interfaces (mobile apps and games, chatbot, tangible coach). In particular, motivational messages are always frased in a positive way.
- *Reminders to input self-tracking data into the technology*: as for praise messages, reminders are provided in different forms in each interface, e.g., through app notifications and through chatbot conversations. Both mechanisms allow bringing the user to the respective interfaces for inputting data in the system with an intuitive and immediate interaction.
- *Use of validity-tested devices*: Wearable sensors and beacons were developed according to user needs, while the other environmental sensors (smart scale and sleep monitor) used off-the shelves products. Each sensor was thoroughly tested (see also chapters "Monitoring in the Physical Domain to Support Active Ageing and Social Behaviour and Cognitive Monitoring in Healthy Ageing).
- *Integration of self-tracking and persuasive e-Coaching*: self-tracking is supported not only for those domains that need user input to enter data (e.g., nutrition (see chapter "Nutrition Monitoring as a Key Performance Indicators (KPI) in Prevention Services for Older Adults"), emotional experience (see chapter "Understanding Older Adults' Affect States in Daily Life for Promoting Self-reflection About Mental Well-Being") and personal goal attainment), but also for reviewing activities that are tracked by the system. At the same time the system leverages on the HAPA model to provide effective coaching according to the user motivation and mindset. A number of charts were integrated in the app to support self-tracking as well, contextual coaching was provided also in the charts to push users' to align to the coach recommendations.

- *Provision of face-to-face instructions* during implementation, as key components for influencing both health outcomes and usability in a positive way: although the NESTORE objective is to develop an intuitive system, leveraging on co-design and providing a gradual learning phase (e.g., through appropriate on-boarding via the chatbot), face-to-face instructions were provided at the beginning of each pilot test. Such instructions were complemented by step-by-step tutorials implemented inside the app.
- *Provision of personalized content*: all content was personalized by the different pilot sites, leveraging on co-design to conceive conversations and coaching activities that respect local traditions and facilities. A web interface was developed to facilitate the translation and adaption of the e-coach content [11]. Moreover, the system was tailored to individual levels according to user preferences: the user is able to choose among three different interfaces to access the coaching intervention frequency and timing of coaching activities (see Chap. 7).

The following list discusses how the NESTORE system implements the e-coaching system features described by Kamphorst [18]:

- *Social ability*: a conversational agent is an integral part of the e-coaching system supporting text based and voice-based conversations [12]. Moreover, to increase the user experience of such conversations, user's affect is assessed in order to adapt the conversation and build empathy with the user (see Chap. 11).
- *Credibility*: since the system is built according to the recommendation of experts in the different coaching domains it should have the needed credibility (see Chap. 2). In the onboarding phase, such scientific underpinning is highlighted by the chatbot. Moreover, informational messages are supported by scientific facts for people interested in the additional science behind the project. In general, information material on the scientific background of the project is provided in the NESTORE web site as additional source of reference for the users.
- *Context-awareness*: adapting and suggesting appropriated coaching activities is one of the main goals of the decision support system. Coaching activities are selected and adapted not only according to the user state and preferences but also according to context information such as proximity to local facilities.
- *Learning abilities*: a user dynamic model is built, storing users' system preferences but also preferences related to coaching activities. In particular, the selection of coaching activities among the provided list as well as the user rating at the end of the activity can be used by the Decision Support System to continuously improve user recommendations (see Chap. 7).
- *Data gathering*: the system will gather information from wearable and environmental sensors as well as from user self-reporting in the different interfaces [25], see also Chap. 4).
- *Proactivity*: the system initiates interactions by means of reminders and notifications, based on HAPA model integration in order to stimulate and motivate the user to commit with the chosen pathway. However, frequency of system prompts can be configured by the user in order to adapt to personal needs and time availability.

- *Reflection*: the user is stimulated to reflect on the impact of lifestyle choice thanks to educational messages. Self-reflection is also stimulated through self-monitoring and in particular through tangible ambient displays that reflect users' progress in the pathway.
- *Behaviour change model integration*: as the HAPA model is integrated in the system in order to deliver the different interventions in a time-appropriate manner (see Sect. 2 of this chapter).
- *Planning support*: In order to support users in setting themselves up for behaviour change success, the system guides the user through the intention formation as well as the volitional phase with appropriate planning [3].

6 Conclusion

Supporting individuals in their journey to maintained or better health requires a focus on changing unhealthy lifestyle habits or helping to continue adhering to healthy lifestyle choices and behavior. Several theoretical accounts about important antecedents and correlates of such health behavior change exist, as well as detailed inventories of (health) behavior change techniques (BCT). Leveraging novel technologies to support a healthy lifestyle is increasingly popular, but much of the work in aging falls short in adopting a clear integrative approach that is theory-based and combines evidence-based BCT employed through mobile technology and computing and capitalizes on an e-coaching format [10]. In NESTORE, we have designed an e-coaching platform that addresses these short-comings by adopting a theoretically informed definition of an e-coach and implementation thereof for the special use case of older adults who are community-dwelling and overall high functioning. This chapter outlines our approach and the results of a systematic review on ecoaching for health in late life, highlighting the need to collect methodologically sound information on the feasibility and impact of such approaches to maintain and improve late life well-being and health.

References

1. Abraham, C., & Michie, S. (2008). A taxonomy of behavior change techniques used in interventions. *Health Psychology, 27*, 379–387.
2. Ajzen, I. (1991). The theory of planned behavior. *Organizational Behavior and Human Decision Processes, 50*, 179–211.
3. Angelini, L., Mugellini, E., Khaled, O. A., Röcke, C., Guye, S., Porcelli, S., …, & Andreoni, G. (2019, June). The NESTORE e-coach: accompanying older adults through a personalized pathway to wellbeing. In *Proceedings of the 12th ACM International Conference on Pervasive Technologies Related to Assistive Environments* (pp. 620–628).
4. Arnautovska, U., O'Callaghan, F., & Hamilton, K. (2017). Behavior change techniques to facilitate physical activity in older adults: What and how. *Ageing & Society*, 1–27.

5. Baltes, P. B., & Baltes, M. M. (Eds.). (1990). *Successful ageing: Perspectives from the behavioral sciences* (Vol. 4). Cambridge University Press.
6. Bandura, A. (1997). The anatomy of stages of change. *American Journal of Health Promotion, 12*, 8–10.
7. Banos, O., & Nugent, C. (2018). E-coaching for health. *Computer, 51*, 12–15.
8. Bierbauer, W., Inauen, J., Schäfer, S., Kleemeyer, M. M., Lüscher, J., König, C., et al. (2017). Health behavior change in older adults: Testing the health action process approach at the interindividual and intraindividual level. *Applied Psychology: Health and Well-Being, 9*, 324–348.
9. Carver, C. S., & Scheier, M. F. (1998). *On the self-regulation of behavior*. Cambridge: Cambridge University Press.
10. El Kamali, M., Angelini, L., Caon, M., Carrino, F., Standoli, C. E., Perego, P., …, & Mugellini, E. (2021). Inclusion design and functionalities of a personalized virtual coach for wellbeing to facilitate a universal access for older adults. In *Proceedings of IEA 2021* (In Press).
11. El Kamali, M., Angelini, L., Caon, M., Carrino, F., Röcke, C., Guye, S., …, & Mugellini, E. (2020). Virtual coaches for older adults' wellbeing: A systematic review. *IEEE Access, 8*, 101884–101902.
12. El Kamali, M., Angelini, L., Caon, M., Khaled, O. A., Mugellini, E., Dulack, N., …, & Andreoni, G. (2020). NESTORE: Mobile chatbot and tangible vocal assistant to support older adults' wellbeing. In *Proceedings of the 2nd Conference on Conversational User Interfaces* (pp. 1–3).
13. Fishbein, M., & Ajzen, I. (1975). *Belief, attitude, intention, and behavior: An Introduction to theory and research.* Reading, MA: Addison-Wesley.
14. Freund, A. M. (2008). Successful ageing as management of resources: The role of selection, optimization, and compensation. *Research in Human Development, 5*(2), 94–106.
15. Freund, A. M., & Baltes, P. B. (1998). Selection, optimization, and compensation as strategies of life management: Correlations with subjective indicators of successful ageing. *Psychology and Aging, 13*(4), 531.
16. Freund, A. M., & Baltes, P. B. (2002). Life-management strategies of selection, optimization and compensation: Measurement by self-report and construct validity. *Journal of Personality and Social Psychology, 82*(4), 642.
17. James, E., et al. (2016). Comparative efficacy of simultaneous versus sequential multiple health behavior change interventions among adults: A systematic review of randomised trials. *Preventive Medicine, 89*, 211–223.
18. Kamphorst, B. A. (2017). E-coaching systems: What they are, and what they aren't. *Personal and Ubiquitous Computing, 21*(4), 625–632.
19. Lentferink, A. J., Oldenius, H. K. E., de Groot, M., Polstra, L., Velthuijsen, H., & van Gemert-Pijnen, J. (2017). Key components in ehealth interventions combining self-tracking and persuasive ecoaching to promote a healthier lifestyle: A scoping review. *Journal of Medical Internet Research, 19*(8),
20. Maddux, J. E., & Rogers, R. W. (1983). Protection motivation and self-efficacy: A revised theory of fear appeals and attitude change. *Journal of Experimental Social Psychology, 19*(5), 469–479.
21. Michie, S., Hyder, N., Walia, A., & West, R. (2011). Development of a taxonomy of behaviour change techniques used in individual behavioural support for smoking cessation. *Addictive Behaviors, 36*(4), 315–319.
22. Muellmann, S., Forberger, S., Möllers, T., Bröring, E., Zeeb, H., & Pischke, C. R. (2018). Effectiveness of ehealth interventions for the promotion of physical activity in older adults: A systematic review. *Preventive Medicine, 108*, 93–110.
23. Nigg, C., & Long, C. (2012). A systematic review of single health behavior change interventions vs. multiple health behavior change interventions among older adults. *Translational Behavioral Medicine, 2(2)*, 163–179.
24. Ochoa, S. F., & Gutierrez, F. J. (2018). Architecting e-coaching systems: A first step for dealing with their intrinsic design complexity. *Computer, 51*(3), 16–23.

25. Palumbo, F., Crivello, A., Furfari, F., Girolami, M., Mastropietro, A., Manferdelli, G., ..., & Rizzo, G. (2020). "Hi this is NESTORE, your personal assistant": Design of an integrated IoT system for a personalized coach for healthy aging. *Frontiers in Digital Health, 2*, 20.
26. Prochaska, J., Johnson, S., & Lee, P. (1998). The transtheoretical model of behavior change. In S. Schumaker, E. Schron, J. Ockene, & W. McBee (Eds.), *The handbook of health behavior change* (2nd ed.). New York, NY: Springer.
27. Roberts, A. L., Fisher, A., Smith, L., Heinrich, M., & Potts, H. W. W. (2017). *Journal of Cancer Survivorship, 11*, 704.
28. Rosenstock, I. M. (1974). Historical origins of the health belief model. *Health Education & Behavior, 2*(4), 328–335.
29. Scholz, U., Schüz, B., Ziegelmann, J. P., Lippke, S., & Schwarzer, R. (2008). Beyond behavioral intentions: Planning mediates between intentions and physical activity. *British Journal of Health Psychology, 13*, 479–494.
30. Scholz, U., Sniehotta, F. F., Burkert, S., & Schwarzer, R. (2007). Increasing physical exercise levels: Age-specific benefits of planning. *Journal of Aging and Health, 19*(5), 851–866.
31. Scholz, U., Sniehotta, F. F., & Schwarzer, R. (2005). Predicting physical exercise in cardiac rehabilitation: The role of phase-specific self-efficacy beliefs. *Journal of Sport and Exercise Psychology, 27*(2), 135–151.
32. Schwarzer, R. (2008). Modeling health behavior change: How to predict and modify the adoption and maintenance of health behaviors. *Applied Psychology, 57*(1), 1–29.
33. Schwarzer, R., Lippke, S., & Luszczynska, A. (2011). Mechanisms of health behavior change in persons with chronic illness or disability: the Health Action Process Approach (HAPA). *Rehabilitation Psychology, 56*(3), 161–170.
34. Schwarzer, R., Schüz, B., Ziegelmann, J. P., Lippke, S., Luszczynska, A., & Scholz, U. (2007). Adoption and maintenance of four health behaviors: Theory-guided longitudinal studies on dental flossing, seat belt use, dietary behavior, and physical activity. *Annals of Behavioral Medicine, 33*(2), 156–166.
35. Sniehotta, F. F., Scholz, U., & Schwarzer, R. (2005). Bridging the intention–behaviour gap: Planning, self-efficacy, and action control in the adoption and maintenance of physical exercise. *Psychology & Health, 20*(2), 143–160.
36. Subías-Beltrán, P., Orte, S., Vargiu, E., Palumbo, F., Angelini, L., Abou Khaled, O., ..., & Caon, M. (2019, June). A decision support system to propose coaching plans for seniors. In *2019 IEEE 32nd International Symposium on Computer-Based Medical Systems (CBMS)* (pp. 592–595). IEEE.
37. Warner, T. (2012). E-coaching systems: Convenient, anytime, anywhere, and nonhuman. *Performance Improvement, 51*(9), 22–28.
38. World Bank. (2010). Theories of behavior change. *Communication for Governance and Accountability Program (CommGAP)*. Washington, DC: World Bank. http://documents.worldbank.org/curated/en/456261468164982535/Theories-of-behavior-change.
39. Ziegelmann, J. P., & Knoll, N. (2015). Future directions in the study of health behavior among older adults. *Gerontology, 61*(5), 469–476.

Understanding Older Adults' Affect States in Daily Life for Promoting Self-reflection About Mental Wellbeing

M. Sykora, S. Elayan, L. Angelini, Christina Röcke, M. El Kamali, Elena Mugellini, and Sabrina Guye

Abstract In recent years, due to the rise in availability of unstructured big data and technological affordances, there has been a proverbial "explosion" of research within the field of sentiment analysis and affective computing, facilitating the study of in-situ communicated emotion and its accurate detection at an unprecedented scale. Increasingly the emotional dimension and its key important role is being recognized in e-coaching, with attempts at its integration within such systems. This chapter reviews the predominant extant models for representing affect, as well as emotion related states relevant to older persons' experiences, including the state-of-art for their automated detection and integration within e-coaching systems. Given the approaches available, we describe how the NESTORE system addresses emotion recognition, self-tracking and subsequent feedback intended to help older adults make sense of their affective experiences across their daily life, as well as the role it can play in holistic e-coaching systems. Finally, from the NESTORE experience, we draw recommendations about how future e-coaching system could be implemented in the future to include the emotional dimension.

1 Introduction

As has been outlined in previous chapters and throughout this book, a multidimensional approach is arguably needed to provide effective coaching towards older adult's wellbeing. Nevertheless, a limited number of e-coaching systems for seniors explored three dimensions or more [16]. NESTORE is centred around a more holistic

M. Sykora (✉) · S. Elayan
School of Business and Economics (SBE), Centre for Information Management (CIM), Loughborough University, BE.1.32 (Sir Richard Morris Building), Loughborough L11 3TU, UK
e-mail: m.d.sykora@lboro.ac.uk

L. Angelini · M. El Kamali · E. Mugellini
University of Applied Sciences of Western Switzerland (HES-SO), Fribourg, Switzerland

C. Röcke · S. Guye
URPP Dynamics of Healthy Aging, University of Zurich, Zurich, Switzerland

G. Andreoni and C. Mambretti (eds.), *Digital Health Technology for Better Aging*, Research for Development, https://doi.org/10.1007/978-3-030-72663-8_11

multi-domain approach to e-coaching than has normally been the case in most prior work. The focus of NESTORE is to reach beyond the usual physical aspects of ones' behaviour, and to also incorporate recommendations, plans and interventions in the nutritional, cognitive, and social domains of users' lives. An often overlooked dimension across e-coaching systems, is emotional wellbeing [16], although understanding a user's emotions is a key component for enabling emphatic interactions [10, 22, 28, 39].

To inspire future generations of emotion-aware e-coaches, in this chapter, we present the NESTORE *Emotional Wellbeing Engine*, based on a novel semantic model of emotions and affective states (encoded as an RDF/RDFs/OWL[1] linguistic ontology), and how this is integrated within the conversational agent of the NESTORE e-coach. The primary aim of this, is for the e-coach to automatically understand and track users' affective states communicated in spoken or written sentences, in the NESTORE tangible voice interface or text-based chatbot app. We address several gaps in e-coaching related literature [16], including: (i) the considered range of emotions and emotion related affective states (up to 24 discrete affect related states—e.g., disgust, sadness, motivation, awe, grief, hope, etc.), (ii) incorporating more than one popular emotion conceptualisation; and (iii) facilitating active social listening by providing users with an opportunity to correct and respond to automatically detected affective states. Moreover, our approach is primarily informed by the well-established stream of work from within the sentiment analysis field (e.g., [43]). While several conversational agents can be found among e-coaches for older persons, there is an overall lack of work leveraging approaches from sentiment analysis, where there seems to be a gap in literature around the emotional dimension within e-coaching systems. Specifically, there is a lack of integration efforts of existing emotions research and theory, where usually only one conceptualisation tends to be chosen. In NESTORE, the *Emotional Wellbeing Engine* enables the e-coach to provide users opportunity to reflect on how they feel, in order to help build a sense of emotional empathy and active listening [28] with the e-coach itself, and to subsequently allow users to monitor and reflect on their in-situ experienced affect over time, captured as unfolding in daily life (e.g., [4, 45]). Such close integration of emotion and broader affect monitoring, within the e-coach conversational interface, and the fine-grained range of affect and affect related states, presents a unique solution and a noteworthy step forward around the emotional dimension within extant e-coaching efforts for older persons [16].

In the next section we will first introduce considerations that are relevant to older persons' emotional experiences, followed by the various theoretical models for representing emotion related states. This is followed by a brief overview of where emotions fit in within the NESTORE e-coach system, and a section describing how we have semantically modelled these affective states to implement a broad emotion wellbeing recognition engine, including its implementation within the NESTORE e-coach.

---

[1]These are semantic modelling formalisms based on W3C standards, which allow to encode rich semantic information about a domain of interest in a machine readable format, see https://www.w3.org/TR/owl-features/.

Finally, recommendations, plans and interventions put forward by the conversational agent are supplied by the Decision Support System, (chapter "Perspective and Experiences of Decision Support Systems (DSS) and AI in Prevention and Care for Older Adults") this and the detailed design of the conversational aspects of the e-coach tangible and chatbot interface are discussed in earlier chapters of this collection. The focus of this chapter is on the sensing of emotions and affect for the overall understanding of emotional wellbeing within the NESTORE e-coach interface.

2 The Affective Dimension

There is a wide range of theoretical models to describe the affective space and the structure of emotions [8], and it is not necessarily obvious how these can be consolidated, and indeed there are open questions around how models of emotion can be meaningfully and effectively merged and interpreted. Establishing consensus amongst emotions researchers has been a challenge. Recent efforts, include a survey study undertaken by Ekman [14], in which just under 250 scientists from the emotions research community were surveyed on agreement across emotion labels, affective states, etc. (see, ibid., p. 32, for an overview) and found varying levels of agreement across emotional representations, especially beyond basic emotions. Consider the circumplex model, initially developed by Russell [44], in which valence (i.e., pleasure) and arousal (i.e., activation) are represented on a plane within an emotional circumplex of affect. On the model shown in Fig. 1, one can observe the valence running along the horizontal axis, and arousal along the vertical axes, with intermediate terms, such as excited–depressed and stressed–serene being the polar-opposites formed by intermediate states of valence and arousal. This model has been further refined across the years, for instance by Yik et al. [59]. Various lexical resources exist, which readily map onto the 2-dimensional valence and arousal circumplex model,

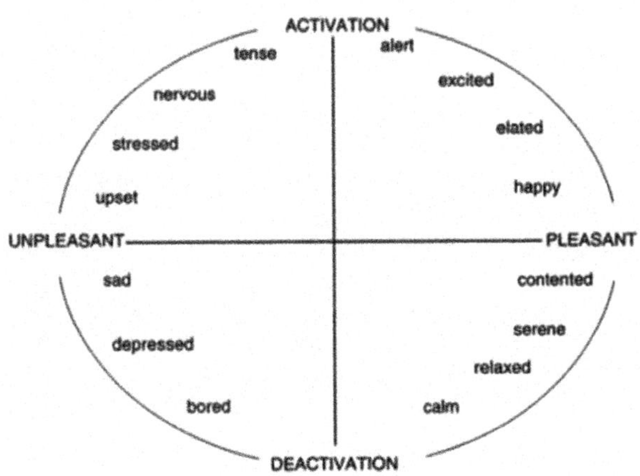

Fig. 1 Russell's circumplex model of affect [44]

such as the ANEW dictionary (see Table 1) or work by Choudhury and Counts [7] who used the circumplex model by extending various vocabularies, including the ANEW lexicon via crowdsourcing, and employed it for analysis of emotions on

Table 1 An overview of ten example lexicons/language resources for sentiment detection

Lexicon/Language resource	Description
ANEW—affective norms for English words [3]	A dictionary of 1,034 words rated for valence, arousal and dominance, and Spanish and Dutch ANEW versions also exist. Two separate (gender specific—annotated) lists are available
AFINN (Finn, 2011)	Contains 2,477 words, based on a number of existing lexicons and specific to Twitter, although its evaluation has been limited
Bing Liu's opinion lexicon (Liu, n.d.)	Dictionary of positive and negative words, 6,789 words in total. Also includes misspellings, morphological variants, slang, and basic social-media conventions
EmoLex [35]	Contains 14,182 words and their associations with eight emotions (anger, fear, anticipation, trust, surprise, sadness, joy, and disgust) and two sentiments (negative and positive)
EMOTIVE ontology [54]	Contains over 1,000 explicit emotional expressions (8 basic emotions) with various associated language elements (including a wide set of intensifiers, conjunctions, negators, interjections and linguistic analysis rules), represented in a formal semantic model, i.e. OWL ontology
LabMT [12]	Dictionary of happiness ranked and scored words 10,222
LIWC—linguistic inquiry and word counts [55]	A proprietary database of categorized regular expressions as entries, with over 80 linguistic (e.g., first-person singular pronouns, conjunctions), psychological (e.g., anger, achievement), and topical (e.g., leisure, financial) categories
MPQA—multi-perspective question answering subjectivity lexicon [58]	A dictionary containing 8,221 positive and negative words, strength of sentiment, POS and stem information
SentiStrength-2 vocabulary [56]	The dictionary, which comes with SentiStrength-2, contains 2,546 negative and positive scored words. Also includes intensifiers, negators and idioms
SentiWordNet [1]	Positive and negative real-valued sentiment scores associated to WordNet synsets. Includes POS information and a gloss—similar to WordNet synsets

social media (Twitter). Although arguably a state such as stress or more specifically anxiety would traditionally not be considered an emotion (e.g., as defined by Ekman 1992), still such states are related and closely linked to emotions, and the challenge is in interpreting what the various models allow us to represent in the context of a person's wellbeing.

A review of functional neuroimaging studies by Kragel and LaBar [30] suggests that empirical evidence probably aligns more closely with discrete models of emotion (e.g., Ekman's basic emotions) versus dimensional theories of emotion (e.g., Russell's circumplex), though some of the observations in ibid. are however open to interpretation and significant further research is needed to fully understand how various emotions are represented in the brain. It has been proposed that some sort of compromise and integration between discrete/categorical and dimensional emotion models may be the most meaningful approach to deal with representing affect [8]. Based on their empirical analysis of a large set of over 300,000 self-report judgements, Cowen and Keltner (ibid.) show that categorical labels may better capture reports of subjective experiences than commonly measured affective dimensions (e.g., valence and arousal). Nevertheless, the authors point out that the boundaries of emotional categories tend to be blurred, rather than discrete, and conclude that *"although categories are found to organise dimensional appraisals in a coherent and powerful fashion, many categories are linked by smooth gradients, contrary to discrete theories."* (ibid., p. E7900). Emotions research is however a vast interdisciplinary area of study, containing many competing, heterogeneous views, conceptualisations and theories with varying degrees of supporting empirical evidence. In the NESTORE Emotional Wellbeing model (described in Sect. 4), we have hence taken an approach that allows us to represent emotions and affect-related states as discrete categories, but also to have a mapping onto a simple dimensional valence and arousal affect space.

2.1 Beyond Basic Emotions: Love, Grief and Positive Affect

Ekman's basic emotions include happiness, sadness, fear, anger, surprise and disgust, although researchers such as Shaver et al. [49] and Sabini and Silver [46] argue that love, jealousy and other states need further consideration. Ekman [15], however, explains that some terms that are considered emotional are actually moods (which are conceptualised as a mixture of emotions). Moods, he argues, trigger different physiological responses than basic emotions. Ekman argues that states such as "love" or "hatred" involve more than one emotion and expand over an extended time period rather than being experienced in temporary bursts like the basic emotions. Notwithstanding, as these affective states bear strong emotional attributes, we have included love, hatred, and jealousy among other states in our semantic model (see Sect. 4). Ekman (ibid.) refers to states such as "love" and "hatred" as "emotional attitudes", and our ontology aligns with this labelling.

In their extensive review paper, Shiota et al. [50] point out the importance of "discrete" positive emotions, which have received fairly little attention by the broader research community to date. For instance, with respect to a discrete emotion model, Keltner and Haidt [26] propose to approach awe as a distinct discrete emotion in its own right, and are the first ones to critically argue and review its role, based around a prototypical definition (ibid, pp. 303–306) of perceived vastness and a need for accommodation. There is some initial evidence that *awe* in particular can have very positive health benefits, such as a reduced stress response or boosted creativity [34], as well as a range of other positive emotions (e.g., [53]). In fact, Shiota et al. [50] point out that despite trait positive emotionality and state positive-valence affect long having been the subject of intense study, differentiating among several "discrete" positive emotions, has only very recently started to receive more serious attention. Traditionally most work tends to provide a "bucket" category for positive emotions, and indeed even in Ekman's discrete emotion model, there is only one clearly positive emotion, *happiness*. Hence being able to detect and measure such additional fine-grained positive emotions, at least to some extent, including *awe, inspiration* and *hope* among others, is well within the scope and implemented in the NESTORE Emotional Wellbeing ontology.

Moreover, particular emotions (e.g., *anger, sadness*) are also commonly associated with psychological stress, while stress in itself is not an emotion [41], we have again incorporated it within the ontology (this time indirectly, as ontological properties), due to its inextricable effects on emotions and the immune system [40]. In Elayan et al. [17] a specialised system for automatically detecting and interpreting stressful expression from social media texts is proposed, and we direct the reader to (ibid.) for further details on the emotion and stress nexus. Research on religious coping conducted by Tix and Fraser [57] finds that spirituality or faith generate behavioural techniques that arise at times of stress. Jenkins and Pargament [24] also report that spirituality offers emotional comfort and hope in terminally ill individuals, giving the sense of purpose and meaning. *Hope* itself appears on Russell's circumflex model as positive with low activation, and Lazarus [32] argues that hope is a vital psychological resource, especially in aging since hope pushes individuals to seek improvement of one's state. Folkman [19] finds that hope and coping are inextricably linked—arguing that hope is vital in psychological wellbeing.

Given the above, we considered and incorporated affective characteristics most relevant to the NESTORE population (higher age demographic). More broadly, older adults have been known to demonstrate fairly good proficiency at emotion regulation [29], and most older people maintain high levels of day-to-day affective wellbeing [45], although many are increasing facing physical ailments, psychological stress, social losses, and growing dependency at the very end of life [31, 47]. Love and attachment to close family and friends becomes more important with age (ref, D.2.1). Being able to sense expressions of love or hatred would help inform and produce a more complete picture of the emotional wellbeing of a user over time. Moreover, some noteworthy factors in the wellbeing of potential users, that specifically came up during the NESTORE co-design workshops [9], included spirituality and faith (specifically their importance among an older sample of workshop participants), creativity, as well as inspiration, where workshop participants pointed out the aspect of legacy (i.e., *"the act of creating and making a mark that would live beyond"*), as well as specifically highlighting interests around creativity, such as art, writing and drawing, playing a role in creating a *"sense of balance"*. Also noteworthy was the explicit issue of sensing expressions that may indicate trust in the technology (e-coach system), in its reliability, as well as trust related to risk of user error. Co-design workshop participants also expressed concerns around anxiety and frustration with technology use, which is a noteworthy concern. Frustration in turn is conceptually represented on Russell's dimensional circumplex in the proximity of stress, and closely associated with Anger [36]. Many of these affective states are not trivial to model, such as for instance the fairly ephemeral state of inspiration [21], which does not directly fall under prior stream of sentiment analysis research (see Sect. 2.2).

2.2 Sentiment Analysis for Emotion Recognition

The understanding of emotions, moods, affect and attitudes is the focus of extensive emotions research, psychology and social psychology literature. Computer scientists have to often adopt simplified models of affective states in system implementations, where states are represented by discrete values along a small number of dimensions. Efforts in sentiment analysis literature, which is a well-established area of computational research centered around automatically measuring affect in human generated data, are most helpful, as these efforts generally represent more practical applications of emotions research.[2] As is evidenced in [37, 43] a large proportion of studies on sentiment analysis focus on the task of polarity classification (i.e. negative/positive sentiment valence), although this field currently represents a significant area of research that can be defined much more broadly with attempts at dimensional and discrete emotion recognition and a variety of evaluative language classification tasks. Pang and Lee [37] provide a useful overview of the various range of traditional problem tasks (e.g., sentiment polarity and degrees of positivity, detecting viewpoints and perspectives, non-factual information in text such as hate-speech, etc.). However, especially with the recent uptake of social media platforms there has been an increase in research intensity on affect detection, due primarily to easy access and availability of big data. With the rising popularity of smartphones and mobile sensors, there has also been a corresponding increase in research on affective computing through smartphones and mobile sensing technologies (e.g., accelerometers, GPS, etc.), and although affective sensing of acute stress and emotions from mobile sensors is out of scope for NESTORE, for a fairly comprehensive review on this stream of work, please see ([42], e.g., pp. 86–87).

[2] Although it should be noted, that a lot of sentiment analysis work also tends to trivialise and ignore significant work from traditional emotions research and social psychology, which we feel is often a missed opportunity.

In terms of sentiment analysis and affect detection methods, ([43], p. 16) identify three broad types of approaches to sentiment analysis, (i) Machine Learning based, (ii) Lexicon based and (iii) Hybrid approaches, which is essentially based on a combination of elements from (i) and (ii). In Thelwall et al. [56] review of prior work, the authors discuss three main types of approaches as well, (a) machine learning, (b) lexicon/linguistic analysis, and (c) polarity estimation from term co-occurrence. However, Ravi and Ravi [43] consider (c) polarity estimation to fall under the lexicon creation task, which although most often based on some type of term co-occurrence, often involve machine learning algorithms as well. Various other reviews, such as Canales and Martínez-Barco [6] or Cambria [5] also group approaches into these broad categories. Several authors (e.g., [5, 43, 54, 56]) have suggested that hybrid approaches that rely on a knowledge-base, that is either some lexicons or more expressive semantic models, and which leverage elements of statisticals/machine learning/NLP (Natural Language Processing) approaches, show the most promise. Ravi and Ravi [43] in particular point out the potential of Ontologies being used instead of lexicon based approaches, and their significance in achieving better performance in sentiment analysis, which is also echoed by a move within the AI community towards exploring formal semantic modelling in helping to deal with big data analysis and modelling (e.g., see paper by Janowicz et al. 2015—entitled "Why the Data Train Needs Semantic Rails").

In relation to lexicon approaches (ii), the language resources presented in Table 1 are an example selection of lexicons, some of which are used very widely within sentiment analysis, such as Bing Liu's Opinion Lexicon or LIWC [43]. Of-course there are many more lexicons than the ones shown in Table 1, some of which are highly domain specific. For example, the restaurant review or laptop review lexicons for analysing sentiment polarity in Yelp and Amazon reviews respectively, which were developed by Kiritchenko et al. [27] for the SemEval-2014 shared task (Task 4) on aspect-level sentiment analysis.

Some lexicons are more customised to online social media style slang (e.g., AFINN), than others (e.g., ANEW), although this can be beneficial when text-input that is likely to contain shorthand text or mistyped words, etc. is present in chatbot style interactions. It is important to point out that although most of the lexicon resources are dealing with fairly average language use from a variety of sources that cut across demographics, there are likely age-related biases across different sentiment analysis approaches, as was elaborated by Díaz et al. [13].

3 Emotions and the NESTORE e-Coach

The NESTORE e-coach interface is orchestrated and driven by the conversational agent, across both, the tangible and chatbot interfaces (as illustrated in Fig. 2. Conversations can be prompted both by the user and the Decision Support System and data is accessed and transmitted via different NESTORE APIs, and importantly, the affect-related state analysis is prompted by the conversational agent through the tangible

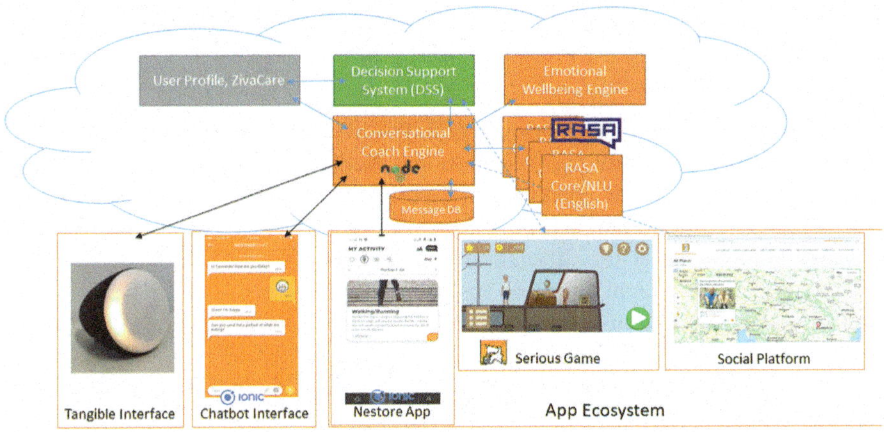

Fig. 2 Architecture of e-coach interfaces with a particular focus on the conversational agent and emotion engine

(voice based) coach interface. This interface asks the user to tell NESTORE how they feel today, and relies on the Emotional Wellbeing Engine.

The Emotional Wellbeing Engine implements an advanced sentiment analysis natural language processing pipeline, based on a formal semantic model, further detailed in Sect. 4. Although the engine undertakes text-based sentiment analysis, it is capable of processing affective expressions communicated through voice (tangible coach) and through text (via the chatbot), with the conversational agent managing the speech-to-text conversion. As part of an exchange with the tangible interface of the e-coach, the tangible will query the user at the end of the day to reflect upon how they feel, in order to elicit an affect rich response, which is then used by the *Emotional Wellbeing Engine* to record the user's emotional status. The e-coach can recognize the emotional status and update a specific chart in the app that shows the most frequent emotions in the last days, only when the user confirms that the recognized emotion is correct. This particular feature is directly related to experimental findings and recommendation by Klein et al. [28], in that empathy through "active listening" can be effectively facilitated by providing IT users an opportunity to correct and respond to automatically detected affective states. This not only allows the user for repair if the emotion is mis-detected, but also helps to make sure that the state of the user, especially if highly aroused, is conveyed accurately. Hence, the e-coach creates and helps to convey the sense for a user that their emotional state is valid, which as Klein (ibid.) proposes, can sometimes be as simple as naming what the individual is likely feeling and that feeling's validity.

4 Emotional Wellbeing Recognition in the NESTORE System

The semantic model of affect bearing expressions with a rich set of terms, phrases and phrase patterns, is at the core of the Emotional Wellbeing Engine. The model significantly expands and builds upon the prior work in EMOTIVE and Stresscapes (e.g., [17, 54]). Various important aspects were considered during its design, construction and population, such as the different conceptualisations and prominent models of affect, empirical results in emotions research, as well as work in the field of sentiment analysis, keeping in mind the feasibility and relevance to NESTORE virtual coach and characteristics of its user population, as presented in the earlier Sect. 2. The model facilitates the sensing and recognition of up to 24 emotion related affective states, listed below.

- Basic Emotion (6) → Anger, Disgust, Fear, Happiness, Sadness, Surprise.
- Emotion Related State (6) → Awe, Confusion, Frustration, Inspiration, Motivation, Shame.
- Emotional Attitude (8) → Empathy, Faith, Grief, Hate, Hope, Jealousy, Love, Trust.
- Associated Stress (4) → Acute Stress, Chronic Stress, Eustress, No Stress.

(these are represented as properties within the above states)

Basic emotions represent the more immediate and momentary emotional states, while *emotion related states* are affective states that are not considered basic nor have an autonomous physiological reaction, yet they do have a meaningful valence and arousal associated with them. *Emotional attitudes* on the other hand represent more longer lasting attitudes that tend to persist over time and have an affective dimension. Besides these 20 affective variables, each emotion, state and attitude is also mapped to a likely type of stress experience (e.g., eustress, acute stress, etc.), which is derived from work on dimensional emotion model of core-affect. The semantic *Emotional Wellbeing* model represents these affective types and links, as well as intensifiers, conjunctions, negators, perceived emotional magnitudes and valid parts-of-speech tags which are helpful in disambiguating non-affect bearing expressions.

The semantic model currently contains over 7000 statements, with over 1200 classes. It is based on semantic modelling formalisms, relying on W3C standards, specifically RDF/RDFs/OWL, using the semantic modelling tool Protégé.[3] This also means, thanks to standards adherence, that the developed models can potentially be augmented with semantic web based linked data ("Web of Data"). We have leveraged a number of lexical resources and databases in its' construction, including; ANEW [3], the Circumplex vocabulary by Choudhury and Counts [7], EmoLex [35], and the SentiStrength-2 Vocabulary [56], to name a few. A full list of consulted vocabularies is available in Table 1. We have also incorporated work by De-Silva et al. [11] from care online support groups, including emotion expressions found through a process that

[3]W3C's Protégé—https://www.w3.org/2001/sw/wiki/Protege.

was based on seed-words' similarities in a 200-dimensional word-embeddings space from a large corpus of online support groups posts text (4,795,428 posts). Being able to leverage this, meant the coverage/recall of the model would be improved. For some affect related states, such as "inspiration" we further drew on prior work by Gerrard et al. [21], and reviewed vocabularies in the semantic linguistic model FrameNet (see [2]) and ConceptNet (see [52]). The methodology required the need for approaches to rely on, and to leverage deep qualitative insights. Hence our methods primarily revolved around sociolinguistic discourse analysis, focusing on the semantics of particular expressions. Although this was predominantly a manual (human/expert-driven) analysis, focused on identifying the broadest range of commonly used explicit expressions indicative of emotional wellbeing states, the process was aided by use of computational semi-automated text analysis methods, specifically, concordances, collocation frequency statistics and topic modelling [25].

4.1 Implementation of the Emotion Engine

The NESTORE emotion engine itself is exposed through an authenticated and secured REST API service (over HTTPS/TLS encryption). The REST API provides automated sensing and recognition of the 24 emotion related affective states. As is detailed in the high-level architecture diagram in Fig. 3, multilanguage support is available through neural machine translation (NMT), specifically for Italian, Dutch, Spanish and Catalan.

The advantage of this approach means, that the tool can be readily extended to numerous languages supported by the available NMT models. The emotion recognition model is running a Python NLP and Ontology model based processing engine for efficient real-time affective language sensing. In order to make it possible for the NESTORE e-coach to provide feedback intended to help older adults make sense of their affective experiences across their daily life, the REST API also exposes several longer-term emotion analytics, such as inter/intra-person trends and distribution of

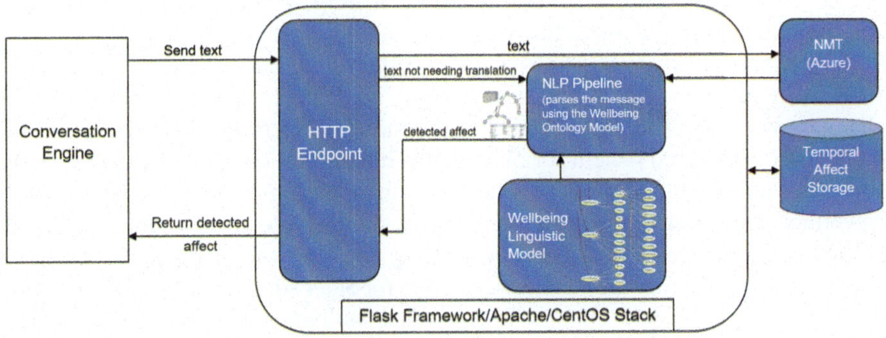

Fig. 3 Internal architecture of the emotion engine

affect for each of the 24 variables and variable groups. This allows the conversational engine to manage the self-tracking and to provide subsequent feedback intended to help older adults make sense of their affective experiences across the e-coach use in their daily life.

5 Discussion and Future Work

In this chapter we presented a novel semantic model and *Emotional Wellbeing Engine*, and how it is integrated into the conversational agent of the NESTORE e-coach. The NESTORE e-coach aims to achieve an emotional link between the users and the NESTORE platform, making them feel supported by the e-Coach, in an appropriate format and in a personalised manner. Variables from several prominent models are incorporated and adopted into the emotional wellbeing model, and a number of conceptualisations relevant to specific views of affect theory were considered in the design, construction and population of the semantic model. A current limitation is that as of the time of writing this chapter, the NESTORE pilot study is still underway, and hence a validation and more complete evaluation of the system across realistic use has not been possible yet. The ability to recognize a person's emotions is primarily intended for tracking their mental wellbeing and establishing an affective interaction between the user and the NESTORE e-coach. The emotional domain in NESTORE is monitored, with charts in the app and feedback provided in the tangible coach to support self-reflection, while it must be noted that no coaching is actually provided in this domain. This is primarily due to the complexity and inter-dependence across domains in relation to emotional wellbeing, but also some practical considerations, since NESTORE already includes a substantial number of interventions in the other domains. Moreover, most of the interventions in other domains also intend to help maintain or increase individuals' subjective wellbeing and sense of the quality of life given the improvement in the target domain (cognition, social behaviour, nutrition, physical activity), even without exclusively targeting wellbeing itself. Wellbeing interventions are mainly known from other age groups than those in later life and typically focus on approaches of expressive writing, gratitude, good actions and counting kindness, to name a few (e.g., [20, 38, 48, 51]). These kinds of interventions have been shown to be effective under certain conditions and particularly in the short run (e.g., Lyubomirsky and Layous [33]), while the long-term benefits for truly changing not only wellbeing states but the more stable status/disposition and the particular or sustained benefit for older adults remains an open question. Hence, the study and implementation of emotion-based interventions remain for future work. Nevertheless, the emotional understanding capabilities integrated within NESTORE to facilitate affective feedback and developing empathy with users, present a novel and substantial step forward within e-coaching for older adults. The ability for continuous monitoring to detect changes in emotional wellbeing may also be indicative of problems or challenges with regard to a persons' goal progress in the NESTORE domains. Data collected though the chatbot (e.g., affect questionnaires, nutritional information...), as well as data stemming from sensors monitoring, say physical activity or sleeping habits, within the NESTORE ecosystem, will be further corroborated in upcoming research papers. Since both the NESTORE conversational agent and the Emotional Wellbeing Engine have been built as modular components, they can be easily integrated in further projects to support emotion aware e-coaching.

References

1. Baccianella, S., Esuli, A., & Sebastiani, F. (2010). Sentiwordnet 3.0: An enhanced lexical resource for sentiment analysis and opinion mining. In *Proceedings of LREC* (Vol. 10, pp. 2200–2204).
2. Baker, C. F., Fillmore, C. J., & Cronin, B. (2003). The structure of the FrameNet database. *International Journal of Lexicography, 16*(3), 281–296.
3. Bradley, M. M., & Lang, P. J. (1999). *Affective norms for English words (ANEW): Instruction manual and affective ratings*. Technical Report—Center for the Study of Psychophysiology - Emotion and Attention, University of Florida.
4. Brose, A., Schmiedek, F., Gerstorf, D., & Voelkle, M. C. (2020). The measurement of within-person affect variation. *Emotion, 20*(4), 677–699.
5. Cambria, E. (2016). Affective computing and sentiment analysis. *IEEE Intelligent Systems, 31*(2), 102–107.
6. Canales, L., & Martínez-Barco, P. (2014). Emotion detection from text: A survey. In *Proceedings of the Workshop on Natural Language Processing in the 5th Information Systems Research Working Days (JISIC)* (pp. 37–43).
7. Choudhury, M., & Counts, S. (2012). *The nature of emotional expression in social media: Measurement, inference and utility*. Technical Report. Microsoft.
8. Cowen, A. S., & Keltner, D. (2017). Self-report captures 27 distinct categories of emotion bridged by continuous gradients. *Proceedings of the National Academy of Sciences, 114*(38), e7900–e7909.
9. Craig, C., Chamberlain, P., & Dulake, N. (2018). D7.1: Report on needs, values and suggestions to co-design. https://nestore-coach.eu/documents/20182/71466/NESTORE_D7.1.pdf/.
10. Danielescu, A., & Christian, G. (2018). A bot is not a polyglot: Designing personalities for multi-lingual conversational agents. In *Extended Abstracts of the 2018 CHI Conference on Human Factors in Computing Systems* (pp. 1–9).
11. De Silva, D., Ranasinghe, W., Bandaragoda, T., Adikari, A., Mills, N., Iddamalgoda, L., ... Gray, R. (2018). Machine learning to support social media empowered patients in cancer care and cancer treatment decisions. *PloS One, 13*(10), e0205855.
12. Dodds, P. S., Harris, K. D., Kloumann, I. M., Bliss, C. A., & Danforth, C. M. (2011). Temporal patterns of happiness and information in a global social network: Hedonometrics and Twitter. *PLoS ONE, 6*(12), e26752.
13. Díaz, M., Johnson, I., Lazar, A., Piper, A. M., & Gergle, D. (2018). Addressing age-related bias in sentiment analysis. In *Proceedings of the 2018 CHI Conference on Human Factors in Computing Systems* (pp. 1–14).
14. Ekman, P. (2016). What scientists who study emotion agree about. *Perspectives on Psychological Science, 11*(1), 31–34.
15. Ekman, P. (1994). Moods, emotions, and traits. *The nature of emotion: Fundamental questions* (pp. 56–58).
16. El Kamali, M., Angelini, L., Caon, M., Carrino, F., Röcke, C., Guye, S., Rizzo, G., Mastropietro, A., Sykora, M., Elayan, S., & Kniestedt, I. (2020). Virtual coaches for older adults' wellbeing: A systematic review. *IEEE Access, 8*(1), 101884–101902.

17. Elayan, S., Sykora, M., Shankardass, K., Robertson, C., Feick, R., Shaughnessy, K., et al. (2020). The STRESSCAPES ontology system: Detecting and measuring stress on social media. In *ECSM-2020—European Conference on Social Media*, Larnaca, Cyprus.
18. Finn, Å. N. (2011). ANEW: Evaluation of a Word List for Sentiment Analysis in Microblogs, Proceedings of the ESWC-2011 Workshop on Making Sense of Microposts: Big things come in small packages, Vol. 718 in CEUR Workshop Proceedings, pp. 93–98, Heraklion, Crete.
19. Folkman, S. (2010). Stress, coping, and hope. *Psycho-Oncology, 19*(9), 901–908.
20. Gander, F., Proyer, R. T., Ruch, W., & Wyss, T. (2013). Strength-based positive interventions: Further evidence for their potential in enhancing well-being and alleviating depression. *Journal of Happiness Studies, 14*(4), 1241–1259.
21. Gerrard D., Sykora, M., & Jackson, T. W. (2017). Social media analytics in museums: Extracting expressions of inspiration. *Journal of Museum Management and Curatorship, 32*(3). https://doi.org/10.1080/09647775.2017.1302815.
22. Hu, T., Xu, A., Liu, Z., You, Q., Guo, Y., Sinha, V., et al. (2018). Touch your heart: A tone-aware chatbot for customer care on social media. In *Proceedings of the 2018 CHI Conference on Human Factors in Computing Systems*, Montreal, Canada
23. Janowicz, K., van Harmelen, F., Hendler, J. A., & Hitzler, P. (2015). Why the Data Train Needs Semantic Rails, AI Magazine, Vol. 36, No. 1, pp. 5–14.
24. Jenkins, R. A., & Pargament, K. I. (1995). Religion and spirituality as resources for coping with cancer. *Journal of Psychosocial Oncology, 13*(1), 51–74.
25. Jurafsky, D., & Martin, J. H. (2014). *Speech and language processing* (Vol. 3). London: Pearson.
26. Keltner, D., & Haidt, J. (2003). Approaching awe, a moral, spiritual, and aesthetic emotion. *Cognition and Emotion, 17*(2), 297–314.
27. Kiritchenko, S., Zhu, X., Cherry, C., & Mohammad, S. (2014). NRC-Canada-2014: Detecting aspects and sentiment in customer reviews. In *Proceedings of the 8th International Workshop on Semantic Evaluation (SemEval 2014)* (pp. 437–442).
28. Klein, J., Moon, Y., & Picard, R. W. (2002). This computer responds to user frustration: Theory, design, and results. *Interacting with Computers, 14*(2), 119–140.
29. Kliegel, M., McDaniel, M. A., & Einstein, G. O. (Eds.). (2007). *Prospective memory: Cognitive, neuroscience, developmental, and applied perspectives.* Psychology Press.
30. Kragel, P. A., & LaBar, K. S. (2016). Decoding the nature of emotion in the brain. *Trends in Cognitive Sciences, 20*(6), 444–455.
31. Kryla-Lighthall, N., & Mather, M. (2009). The role of cognitive control in older adults' emotional wellbeing. In V. L. Bengston, D. Gans, N. M. Pulney, & M. Silverstein (Eds.), *Handbook of theories of ageing* (pp. 323–344). New York: Springer.
32. Lazarus, R. S. (1999). Hope: An emotion and a vital coping resource against despair. *Social Research*, 653–678.
33. Lyubomirsky, S., & Layous, K. (2013). How do simple positive activities increase well-being? *Current Directions in Psychological Science, 22*(1), 57–62.
34. Marchant, J. (2017). Awesome awe. *New Scientist, 235*(3136), 32–35.
35. Mohammad, S., & Turney, P. (2013). Crowdsourcing a word-emotion association lexicon. *Computational Intelligence, 29*(3), 436–465.
36. Oatley, K., & Duncan, E. (1994). The experience of emotions in everyday life. *Cognition & Emotion, 8*(4), 369–381.
37. Pang, B., & Lee, L. (2008). Opinion mining and sentiment analysis. *Foundation and Trends in Information Retrieval, 2*(1–2).
38. Pennebaker, J. W. (1997). Writing about emotional experiences as a therapeutic process. *Psychological Science, 8*(3), 162–166.
39. Picard, R. W. (1997). *Affective computing.* Cambridge, MA: MIT Press.
40. Plotnikoff, N. P., Murgo, A.J., & Faith, R. E. (1991). *Stress and immunity.* CRC Press.
41. Plutchik, R. (1991). *The emotions.* New York: University Press of America.
42. Politou, E., Alepis, E., & Patsakis, C. (2017). A survey on mobile affective computing. *Computer Science Review, 25*(1), 79–100.

43. Ravi, K., & Ravi, V. (2015). A survey on opinion mining and sentiment analysis: Tasks, approaches and applications. *Knowledge-Based Systems, 89*(1), 14–46.
44. Russell, J. A. (1980). A circumplex model of affect. *Journal of Personality and Social Psychology, 39*(6), 1161.
45. Röcke, C., Li, S. C., & Smith, J. (2009). Intraindividual variability in positive and negative affect over 45 days: Do older adults fluctuate less than young adults? *Psychology and Ageing, 24*(4), 863–878.
46. Sabini, J., & Silver, M. (2005). Ekman's basic emotions: Why not love and jealousy? *Cognition & Emotion, 19*(5), 693–712.
47. Scheibe, S., & Carstensen, L. L. (2010). Emotional ageing: Recent findings and future trends. *The Journals of Gerontology: Series B, 65*(2), 135–144.
48. Seligman, M. E., Steen, T. A., Park, N., & Peterson, C. (2005). Positive psychology progress: Empirical validation of interventions. *American Psychologist, 60*(5), 410.
49. Shaver, P. R., Morgan, H. J., & Shelley, Wu. (1996). Is love a "basic" emotion? *Personal Relationships, 3*(1), 81–96.
50. Shiota, M. N., Campos, B., Oveis, C., Hertenstein, M. J., Simon-Thomas, E., & Keltner, D. (2017). Beyond happiness: Building a science of discrete positive emotions. *American Psychologist, 72*(7), 617–643.
51. Smyth, J. M. (1998). Written emotional expression: Effect sizes, outcome types, and moderating variables. *Journal of Consulting and Clinical Psychology, 66*(1), 174.
52. Speer, R., Chin, J., & Havasi, C. (2017). ConceptNet 5.5: An open multilingual graph of general knowledge. In *Thirty-First AAAI Conference on Artificial Intelligence*, San Francisco, USA.
53. Stellar, J. E., John-Henderson, N., Anderson, C. L., Gordon, A. M., McNeil, G. D., & Keltner, D. (2015). Positive affect and markers of inflammation: Discrete positive emotions predict lower levels of inflammatory cytokines. *Emotion, 15*(2), 129.
54. Sykora, M., Jackson, T. W., O'Brien, A., & Elayan, S. (2013). Emotive ontology: Extracting fine-grained emotions from terse informal messages. *International Journal on Computer Science and Information Systems, 8*(2), 106–118.
55. Tausczik, Y. R., & Pennebaker, J. W. (2010). The psychological meaning of words: LIWC and computerized text analysis methods. *Journal of Language and Social Psychology, 29*(1), 24–54.
56. Thelwall, M., Buckley, K., & Paltoglou, G. (2012). Sentiment strength detection for the social web. *Journal of the American Society for Information Science and Technology, 63*(1), 163–173.
57. Tix, A. P., & Fraser, P. A. (1998). The use of religious coping during stressful life events: Main effects, moderation, and mediation. *Journal of Consulting and Clinical Psychology, 66*(1), 411–422.
58. Wiebe, J., Wilson, T., & Cardie, C. (2005). Annotating expressions of opinions and emotions in language. *Language Resources and Evaluation, 39*(2–3), 165–210.
59. Yik, M., Russell, J. A., & Steiger, J. H. (2011). A 12-point circumplex structure of core affect. *Emotion, 11*(4), 705–731.

Building Trust and Companionship in e-Coaching Through Embodiment

Mira El Kamali, Leonardo Angelini, Maurizio Caon, Giuseppe Andreoni, Nick Dulake, Paul Chamberlain, Omar Abou Khaled, and Elena Mugellini

Abstract E-coaches are promising tools for health interventions, being scalable and relatively low costs compared to human coaches. Nevertheless, they cannot compare to humans when it comes to trust and social companionship. Hence, many researches were held around the importance of tangible user interfaces in building trust and companionship during human-machine interaction. Co-design, in particular, is the act of creating with stakeholders within the design development process to ensure the results meet their needs and are usable. This chapter describes a design process method and the rationale for building an embodiment for a companion and a trustable e-coach. We also shed lights on the co-design process held in the NESTORE project, which was specifically conducted with older adults to build a vocal assistant that supports user's behavioral change, as well as to increase the social bonding with the NESTORE e-coach.

1 Introduction

At the beginning of the 21st century, researchers in Human-Computer Interaction started to theorize and implement interfaces that where bridging the physical and digital worlds, using representations and tools belonging the physical world to interact with the digital realm. Indeed, Tangible User Interfaces [1] aimed at establishing a direct coupling between digital information and physical objects, these

M. El Kamali (✉) · L. Angelini · M. Caon · O. A. Khaled · E. Mugellini
Humantech Institute, University of Applied Western Switzerland (HES-SO), 1700 Fribourg, Switzerland
e-mail: mira.elkamali@hes-so.ch

M. Caon
School of Management, Fribourg, Switzerland

G. Andreoni
Dip. di Design, University of Politecnico di Milano, Milan, Italy

N. Dulake · P. Chamberlain
Lab4Living, Sheffield Hallam University, Sheffield, UK

G. Andreoni and C. Mambretti (eds.), *Digital Health Technology for Better Aging*, Research for Development, https://doi.org/10.1007/978-3-030-72663-8_12

latter acting as both representation and control for information that was traditionally constrained behind a screen. Few examples of tangible interaction exist in commercial products, this is mainly due to the challenges related to production and maintenance of physical interfaces. As screen-based interfaces do not have physical parts that can break and can be easily updated at software level, they are generally preferred as main interfaces for connected objects [2]. However, some research studies demonstrated the benefits of tangible user interfaces for older adults, thanks to their intuitiveness and fast learning curve [3]. Bong et al. [4] found 21 studies using tangible user interfaces for supporting social interactions in older age. In particular, they highlighted that many studies lacked user involvement and of interdisciplinary collaborations during the design process. Moreover, authors reported that many studies did not test the prototypes presented in the article. In opposition, Co-design is a core method of approach adopted and embedded by the NESTORE consortium [5] in the research and development of the NESTORE system. We have developed co-design activity adopting co-design methods and tools. Through workshops, the experts in co-designing in this project have developed further tools to facilitate co-design within the workshops they have conducted with the Expert by experience group (UK), as well as to support non-design NESTORE project partners in the co-creation and development of NESTORE.

This chapter focuses on the design process to create a tangible interface, more specifically for creating an embodied conversational agent that able to build trust and companionship with the user. Section 2 presents a theoretical background of tangible embodiments conversational agents. Section 3 presents a design process method, whereas, Sect. 4 describes a use-case for the aforementioned co-design method: the NESTORE project case and its three design concepts derived from user requirements. Finally, Sect. 5 presents the final design of the NESTORE tangible coach.

2 Background on Tangible Conversational Agents in Increasing Trust and Companionship

Conversational agents might be presented to the user in different forms. In the last years, the most common forms of interaction modality with conversational agents are chats (i.e., chatbots available in messaging applications such as Facebook Messenger and Telegram) and vocal assistants (e.g., Apple Siri, Google Assistant, Microsoft Cortana). In both cases, the users have a limited understanding of the physical form of the agent. In the first case, this might be limited to the chatbot avatar, and in the second case only to the voice gender and pitch. Having a full embodied conversational agent might help the user to increase the trust on the agent and to build a stronger emotional bonding. At the same time, the conversational agent embodiment is important to set user expectations in terms of conversation abilities. While users would be happy to discuss and interact with human-like agents, the technology is very often not ready to meet these expectations. In this case, when the agent embodiment is too close to humans, but its behavior or form is not close enough to be perceived by the user as such, the user often develops a feeling of rejection, also known as the "Uncanny Valley" phenomenon [6]. El Kamali et al. [7] conducted a systematic literature review that aimed at individuating previous e-coaching interventions for promoting healthy lifestyles in older adults [ref.]. As part of it, they analyzed the different types of e-coach embodiments used so far and the insights found in previous studies, concerning different design choices. They found that not all e-coaches had a proper embodiment (in some cases only a simple digital intervention was implemented) and most embodiments were purely virtual representation of the e-coach, with no physical representation of the e-coach. In the next section, we delve more into the embodiments designed for the e-coaches for promoting healthy lifestyles in older adults.

3 Design Process Method

This section of the chapter focuses on a co-design process method. Co-design is the act of creating the design with users during the development. This will make sure that the results meet user's needs. The design process described by Chamberlain and Craig [8], grounds on an iterative co-design. Figure 1 resumes the different steps of the method described in [8] of the co-design process method. Workshops can be

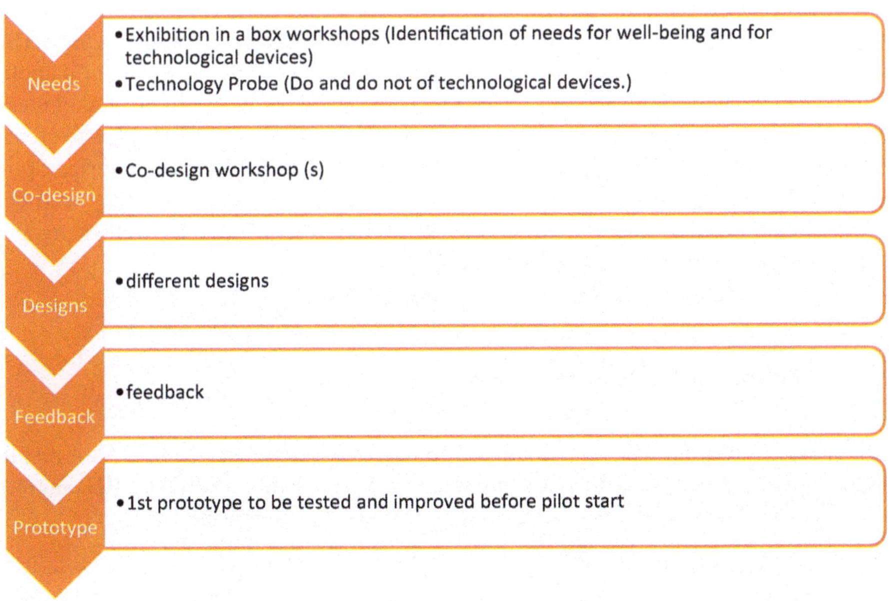

Fig. 1 Co-design process example

carried out with the "exhibition in the box" methodology which allows to determine general requirements for technological devices and most of them can be applied also to design the main product. Conducting the same type of workshop in different countries cab be helpful to derive specific requirements for the design from different sociocultural point of views. In particular, in the case of NESTORE tangible coach project, 4 countries were concerned: Italy, Spain, UK, The Netherlands. The workshop in UK focused on the co-design of the tangible coach, while interesting inputs and suggestions about the tangible coach appearance, personality and interaction modalities were discussed also in the other workshops (in Spain, The Netherlands and Italy).

As a next step, based on the requirements and the ideas produced by users during the workshops, different complementary designs are conceived, each answering different user needs. The different designs are then shown to the users in the next weeks to collect feedback about each solution, allowing them to build on the different design concepts and finally to propose new ideas, inspired by elements from each design. Finally, the analysis of such feedback can be used to understand the general user preferences and drives, to be integrated in the final design. The final design should be then prototyped and tested with the target users.

4 NESTORE Tangible Coach Co-design

NESTORE is a virtual coach that aims to help, improve and maintain the wellbeing of older adults. This virtual coach comes in different forms, distributed across different devices. One of the forms of the NESTORE coach is a conversational agent. The conversational interfaces are textual, through a chatbot embodied in a mobile application, and vocal through an embodiment in a physical device. The main goal of these type of interfaces is to have a natural conversation with the user. This helps to create a sense of companionship and bond through communication. Tangible interfaces, on the other hand, might be beneficial for supporting an emotional bonding with the e-coach embodiments and for stimulating self-reflection on personal well-being and for sustaining motivation towards the goal.

4.1 Preliminary Designs

We carried out a number of activities in order to identify user needs. As a result, below is a list of user requirements based on the results from the NESTORE tangible coach co-design workshops in Spain, Italy, UK and the Netherlands.

R1. Intelligible/controllable
R2. Robust
R4. Affordable

R5. Personalized
R6. Easy-to-use/learn
R7. Easy Authentication
R8. Accessible for all
R9. Transportable
R10. Appearance
R11. Context-Aware
R12. Unobtrusive
R13. Friendly.

Three different designs were derived then from user requirements and from previous findings found during the literature analysis.

4.1.1 Familiar Coach

The appearance of the familiar Coach resembles a knowledgeable bird and has design characteristics that are understated but recognisable (R10). The Familiar Coach is portable and can be moved around the house (R9). It has Nests setup in different rooms and can be easily moved from one Nest to another (R3). It is aware of its location and changes it coaching attitude to suit that location (R11), E.g. peaceful in the bedroom, reduced notifications (R12). The coaching attitude in locations can be personalised through the NESTORE App (R5). It uses Voice interaction (R6, R8) as its primary mode of communication supported by animated facial expressions on the exterior surfaces of the design as an indication of progress, notifications and a need that it would like to communicate with you. Areas of the Familiar Coach are touch sensitive, these areas are used to invoke communication, so you are in control (R1, R12). Users can have a conversation on a new coaching activity or to ask for progress/help on a current activity. If there is a lot of information to be passed on by the Familiar Coach, it will send useful tips and suggestions via text or email (Fig. 2).

4.1.2 Growing Coach

The Growing Coach would resemble a collection of elegant stems (R10). At the top of the stems are notification sails that unfurl to show progress and achievements throughout coaching activities (R12). The group of notification sails will show overall progress with slow movement and other sails will move quickly to show task achievement. The Growing Coach is designed to be in a fixed social space in the house (R3) and used as a touchpoint throughout the day (R7). It always shows progress notifications, but will wait for your presence to show achievements (R11). It will start by getting your attention using a soft sound before starting the notification sail movement. At the center of the notification sail there is a light source which illuminates the sail with different colors to indicate the NESTORE coaching activity. This can be personalized through the NESTORE APP to aid recognition (R5). With a touch

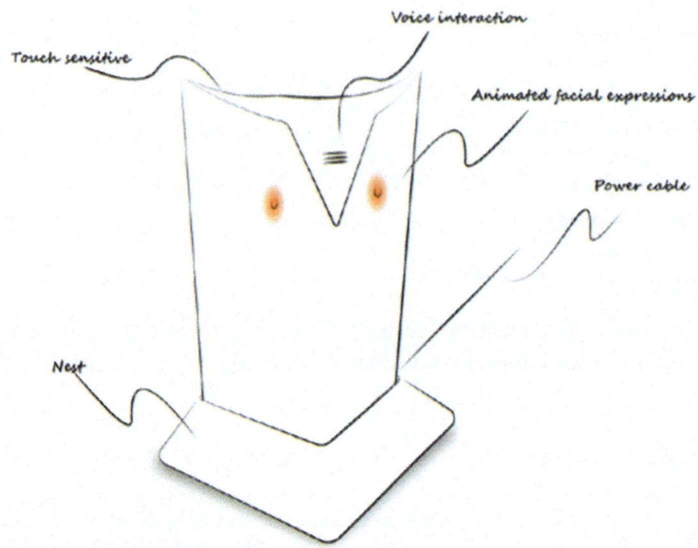

Fig. 2 Co-design concept of the familiar coach

gesture on the stem, the Growing Coach would repeat the last achievement notification (R6, R8). You can communicate with the Growing Coach via the NESTORE App and Chatbot (Fig. 3).

4.1.3 Compact Coach

The compact vocal coach is of stylish, solid geometric design that blends in with your environment (R10). Elements can be personalised (R5), such as the ability to the outer surface of the product and the wake word that you use to start a conversation can be changed (R8). It uses light communication to gain your attention when it wants to give you an update on your progress (R12). The compact vocal coach would have a light/group of lights at the front as a reference point, so that you know that you are speaking in the correct direction and that the coach is listening (R6). The attitude of the coach can be changed through tangible manipulation of the design and will give a visual reference on the outer surface of the compact coach to show the current coaching attitude (R1). Like a friend (r13), the compact vocal coach will send you a text from time to time, with some tips or suggestions that are relevant to your activities. This might be a link to a YouTube video on cooking. The Compact Vocal Coach contains a battery, which means (if needed) it could be moved around the house for periods of time (R9) without having to find a plug (R3) (Fig. 4).

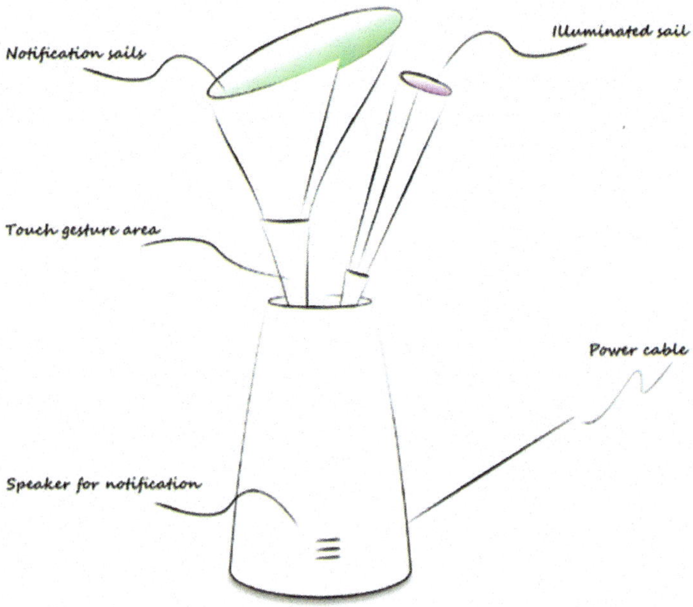

Fig. 3 Co-design concept of the growing coach

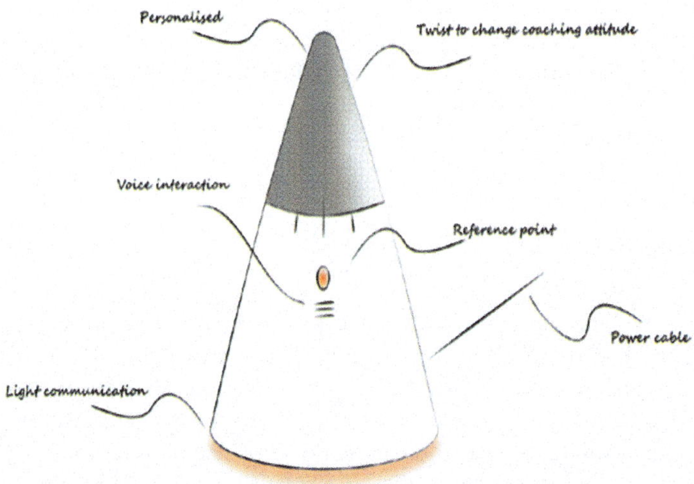

Fig. 4 Co-design concept of the compact coach

4.1.4 Survey and User Feedback

We sent a survey for 7 older people from the UK, 6 from Spain, 10 from the Netherlands and 10 participants from Italy, who preferred the Compact Coach design and voice interaction, visual cues, ease of charging(portability), appearance and ease of control were the most positively perceived.

4.1.5 Tangible Coach Final Prototype

The final design of the Tangible Coach is oval in shape, is white, and made of 3D printed plastic with a textile cover for a warm and emotional feel to the touch, meant to encourage tangible handling. The aim was to create a feeling of camaraderie. The tangible coach has its main face which is when the device is positioned on its side. This oval face is the main part of this body which looks like a human face. Users can communicate with it through its different lighting models. His human face expresses a specific act. Such acts are "Listening state" or "Thinking state" or "Speaking state" (Fig. 5). These acts are represented by LED patterns. The tangible coach has two main positions: Sleep state, where the tangible coach cannot hear or interact with the user, and the Awake state when the tangible coach is ready to communicate. Figure 2a and b shows respectively the sleep and awake position of the tangible coach. To switch between these two states, the user consists of touching the tangible coach and changing its position. The tangible coach aims to have a natural conversation with the user in four different languages (Italian, Spanish, Dutch, and English). The conversation can be two-sided: The user or the tangible coach can initiate the conversation (Fig. 5).

5 Conclusion

This chapter explains the co-design process method for building an embodied conversational agent. It also shows how this method was adopted in the NESTORE tangible coach project that aim to be a virtual coach for older adult' build a trustable e-coach and a companion for older adults. Vink et al. [9]. explicitly linked co-design to well-being and expanded the conversation about the influence of the co-design process on well-being. The final prototype of the NESTORE tangible coach can have natural conversation with the user and follow their wellbeing score and improvement. It is currently under pilot test with 60 users in the context of the NESTORE project.

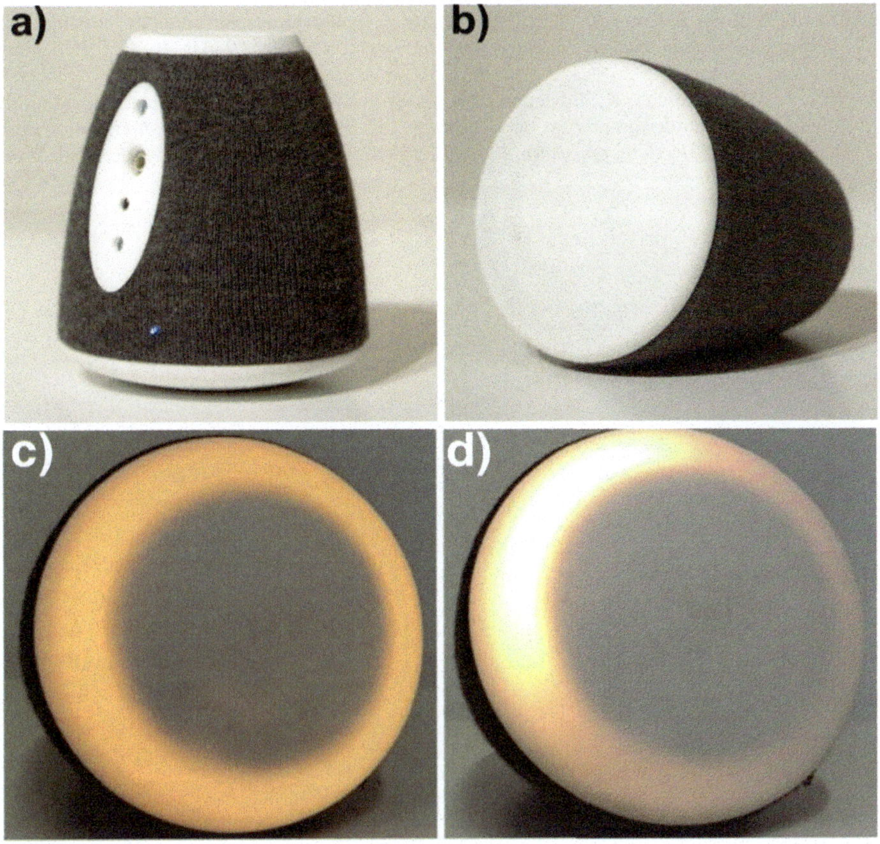

Fig. 5 NESTORE tangible coach final prototype

References

1. Ullmer, B., & Ishii, H. (2000). Emerging frameworks for tangible user interfaces. *IBM Systems Journal, 39*(3.4), 915–931.
2. Rowland, C., Goodman, E., Charlier, M., Light, A., & Lui, A. (2015). *Designing connected products: UX for the consumer internet of things*. O'Reilly Media, Inc.
3. Spreicer, W. (2011, June). Tangible interfaces as a chance for higher technology acceptance by the elderly. In *Proceedings of the 12th International Conference on Computer Systems and Technologies* (pp. 311–316). ACM.
4. Bong, W. K., Chen, W., & Bergland, A. (2018). Tangible user interface for social interactions for the elderly: A review of literature. In *Advances in Human-Computer Interaction*.
5. *NESTORE: A companion for better and healthier ageing—Shaping Europe's digital future—European Commission*. https://ec.europa.eu/digital-single-market/en/news/nestore-companion-better-and-healthier-ageing.
6. Mori, M. (1970). The uncanny valley. *Energy, 7*(4), 33–35.
7. El Kamali, M., Angelini, L., Caon, M., Carrino, F., Röcke, C., Guye, S., ..., & Mugellini, E. (2020). Virtual coaches for older adults' wellbeing: A systematic review. *IEEE Access, 8*, 101884–101902.

8. Chamberlain, P., & Craig, C. (2013). Engaging design–methods for collective creativity. In *International Conference on Human-Computer Interaction* (pp. 22–31). Berlin, Heidelberg: Springer.
9. Vink, J., Wetter-Edman, K., Edvardsson, B., & Tronvoll, B. (2016, May). Understanding the influence of the co-design process on well-being. In *Service Design Geographies. Proceedings of the ServDes. 2016 Conference* (No. 125, pp. 390–402). Linköping University Electronic Press.

Challenges, Limitations and Methodologies to Be Applied in the Development of an ICT-Based Intervention for Older People

L. Fernandez-Maldonado, N. Ferrero, T. Bakker, T. Mosheuvel, C. Ziylan, A. Hogendoorn, A. Attanasio, and A. Salvà

Abstract Recruiting older people as participants in research projects based in the use of new information and communication technologies (ICTs) is a challenge for health researchers, especially because persons with low IT skills self-perception are difficult to reach, but also when the eligibility criterion related to the technologies is sophisticated. This chapter presents a reflection in reference to the challenges, limitations and idiosyncrasies when researchers confront different recruiting situations and strategies to overcome the barriers to contact this audience during the NESTORE project fieldwork development.

Keywords Older people · Wellbeing · Health intervention · Technologies · Recruitment · Retention · Enhancers and barriers · Trust

1 Introduction

In any research study with human subjects the recruitment process is faced as a crucial crossroad when initial decisions have an important impact in the final results. Using the **metaphor of the road** from participants' recruitment to retention, this chapter aims to draw some of the steps that have been taken in the NESTORE project to plan, execute, monitor and evaluate the process of recruiting and retaining the participants and what lessons have been learned.

Recruiting older persons with diverse health status as participants in research projects is a challenge, particularly because persons with health impairments and in socially disadvantaged living conditions are difficult to reach [18]. 'Hard-to-reach' older people are likely to be implicitly and silently excluded from research if the

L. Fernandez-Maldonado (✉) · N. Ferrero · A. Salvà
Fundació Salut i Envelliment UAB, Barcelona, Spain
e-mail: Laura.fernandezm@uab.cat

T. Bakker · T. Mosheuvel · C. Ziylan · A. Hogendoorn
Preventie Collectief, Rotterdam, The Netherlands

A. Attanasio
La Meridiana, Monza, Italy

G. Andreoni and C. Mambretti (eds.), *Digital Health Technology for Better Aging*, Research for Development, https://doi.org/10.1007/978-3-030-72663-8_13

researchers do not explicitly and actively aim to involve them [18]. On the contrary, the idiosyncrasies of the NESTORE project required the election of subjects identified as "fit older people" (i.e. healthy, good physical performance and low risk of near-future disabilities) and to be Android smartphone owners. From its opening premise, the initiative was focused on the selection of the target population according to the approach of L. Fried and colleagues (see Fig. 1) that implied to exclude frailty or at risk to be frail population which couldn't apply recommendations to prevent decline. Frailty has been found to be a predictor of mortality, falls, worsening disability, hospitalisation, and care home admission in cohorts of elderly people [3, 15]. Various frailty classifications exist, but most widely cited is the frailty phenotype described by Fried and colleagues [13], which defines frailty as the presence of three or more out of five indicators: weakness (reduced grip strength), slowness (gait speed), weight loss, low physical activity, and exhaustion. People with one or two indicators are classified as pre-frail. This classification has been adapted for various epidemiological cohorts [2, 15, 25]. Fried and colleagues conceptualised frailty as a distinct clinical entity causing disability independently of clinical and subclinical disease, but frailty is widely seen as both a predictor and outcome of multimorbidity [13, 15, 23].

In theory, the NESTORE selected target group is the most suitable to achieve the required sample in opposition to the hard-to-reach population identified in the literature as vulnerable frail or at risk groups. However, the election of this target group undertakes two considerations. First, the result of the confrontation of researchers' views and participants' comprehension of what "good health" and "wellbeing" is. Secondly, the inherent difficulties associated with the strict but naturally excluding criterion of the study, as age range, to be the owner of updated technologies, enough adherence to IT use but also to be digitally skilled (digital literacy) and

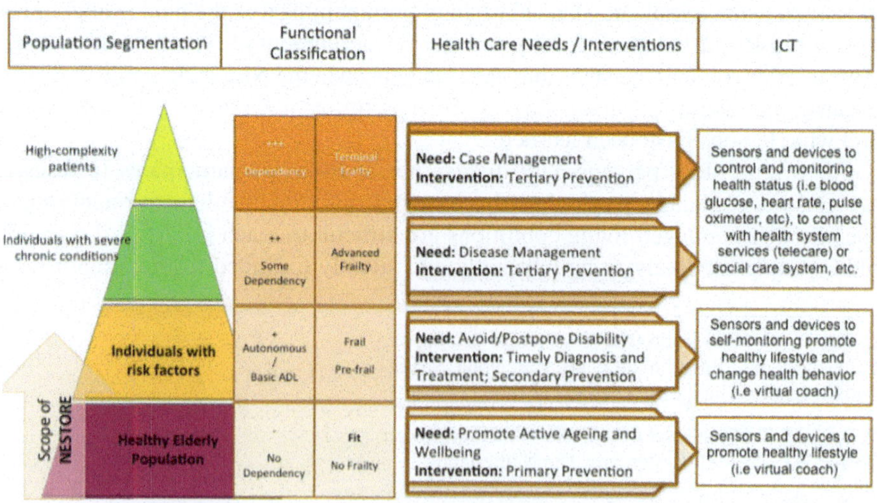

Fig. 1 Targeting older people model applied for NESTORE

the researchers' aspiration to achieve a gender balanced sample. The combination of all these aspects created the conditions to obtain a homogeneous sample, but also to experience barriers and limitations during the recruitment phase.

Any sample definition is determined by a process where study's primary and secondary aims and initial eligibility criteria considered have an important role in defining the size and sample characteristics. In the case of the prospective interventional study of the NESTORE project, the starting point was to settle the sample considering a convenient selection of cases in an early stage to document as many different experiences as possible. This study showed that the selected eligibility criteria created more difficulties to find suitable participants.

The study design based on mixed quantitative and qualitative methods contributed to generate a bonding-based process. Definitely, this was a core element in increasing participant engagement and involvement in the study. Other lessons learned were that despite the attractiveness of the project's purpose, some barriers pushed participants to decide not to continue with the screening process. Several participants were worried about the privacy of their personal data or developed a first impression of the complexity of the project that affected their final decision. This included aspects like the project's technological requirements, not only understood in required subjects' digital skills, but also in the highly demanding system tasks to foster their healthy aging and wellbeing in the intervention phase, as it was reflected in previous chapters.

In spite of each pilot site setting their own recruitment strategy according to their available channels, experience, suitability and country's pandemic situation, equivalences have been stated in the applied centered-person approach. By the end of the recruitment stage some similarities emerged in consonance with a theoretical approach known as TIBaR model of recruitment of 'hard-to-reach' groups (see Fig. 2). NESTORE recruitment and TIBaR model share the same philosophy concerning building up trust, offering and providing incentives, learning about and

Fig. 2 The TiBAR model

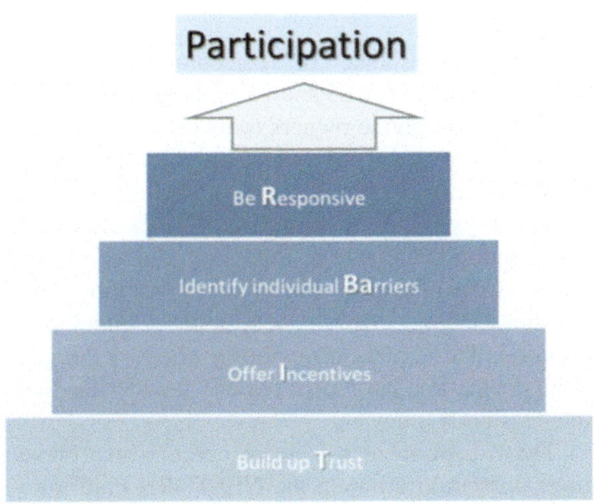

identifying specific individual situations and being responsive to overcome frequent barriers and help potential participants feel safe and comfortable [18]. During the study, the elements of TiBAR model helped the research team to focus on the final study goal as the road signs.

Recruitment success has to be evaluated not just regarding the inclusion and exclusion figures, but understanding it as a process in which other aspects such as the role of altruism, empathy and beliefs interact at the same time.

Evaluating what elements underlined the success or failure of recruitment, is required to understand the whole process of obtaining candidates not only as a mere mechanism of inclusion or exclusion of subjects, but also the whole process. The necessary mechanisms of trust, motivation and bonding to the study were generated. From the confluence of the exposed recruiters' values (coinciding with the TiBAR model) with those of the candidates, all of which interplayed in the project's subject retention results.

The Ethical committees in two of the pilot sites stated that direct monetary compensation could not be considered. On the opposite, the third pilot site could offer an economic incentive to participants due to the fact that their ethical committee encourages compensation in kind.

In spite of the fact that the pandemic seriously affected participants' final decision to join the study or continue with their participation when they balanced their contribution with the risk of COVID-19 infection, most of them decided to continue the pilot study. Nevertheless, the number of subjects dropped substantially since the outbreak of COVID-19′s first wave, although the pilot sites responded to the pandemic giving solutions, having continuous contacts and maximizing bonding activities with participants whenever it was possible.

2 Data and Methods

In this study, the subjects or "road companions" were defined as community dwelling older people between 65 and 75 years old (both included), living in their own homes, Android Smartphone owners (version 7.0 or greater) and with high-speed Internet connection at home. It was also an eligibility criterion to include those individuals who were cognitively, physically and mentally healthy enough to be able to use the technical system. At the same time, the system and its interventions were specifically addressed to healthy, high functioning older adults, without certain conditions that could require physician control and counselling. Thus, all the severe chronic diseases (cardiovascular, metabolic, neurologic or immunological) needed to be an exclusion criterion. This criterion obviously affected the generalization to the overall older adult population, but it is important to underline that generalization is not the aim in this feasibility study.

The exception to this were certain very prevalent controlled chronic conditions that could draw on the NESTORE Platform. This included individuals with controlled hypertension, hypercholesterolemia, hypertriglyceridemia and type 2 diabetes that could benefit from nutrition-based interventions, as well individuals with hypertension could benefit from aerobic exercises.

Otherwise, NESTORE's research project was developed as a person-centered design, which means that participants are involved from the beginning to the end in all the phases. This philosophy requires their active participation, for example in the preparation of informed consent. By using again, the road metaphor, this step can be understood not only as the road map but also the compass, because it gives crucial information about how the study will be and the direction that the research team will maintain to protect participants' rights during the study. The process of preparation included the active involvement of stakeholders (FAS members), a selected older people group (who improved the document highlighting the aspects that they were more concerned about). Several phases were used to review and improve the final document in terms of readability. One of the elements that participants valued positively was knowing that several universities were involved, and that the study was submitted to three ethical committees.

The sample size was not formally computed based on a statistical power analysis in relation to efficacy, but a convenience sample of 90 persons (30 per pilot site) was set. At each pilot site, 20 persons were allocated to the intervention arm and 10 persons to the control group, but this was considered adequate for the feasibility study and for other evaluation criteria and outcomes related to the validation of a novel technology at this stage of development.

2.1 Integration of the Recruitment Strategies

Even though pilot site institutions have different missions and aims, the recruitment strategies across the three pilot sites had similarities within the main TIBaR model axis. However, the recruitment sources were significantly different depending on the nature and activities of each institution. Each of the recruitment strategies have been documented by pilot sites, aiming for a certain comparability in recruitment strategies.

Fundació Salut i Envelliment UAB (FSiE) is an expert centre in the field of ageing and health in Barcelona (Spain). The Foundation performs research on all aspects of health and aging, both clinical and social, with a long history of research among others on dementia (including mild cognitive impairment and Alzheimer's disease), physical activity, falls, frailty, nutrition, disability assessment, as well as assistive technologies for the elderly. The **FSiE** has advised the Catalan government on issues related to the care of the elderly and especially those with chronic diseases. It also has frequent contact with patients, caregivers and older people associations, as well as nursing homes, long term care centres, etc. It has also experience in performing focus groups for qualitative and quantitative studies. **FSiE** has carried out several projects working together with the national and regional governments as well with other foundations and companies. The Foundation has also carried out numerous studies centred in patient's views in self-care and healthcare, patients' rights, as well as the active patient model or patients' information needs concerning health and management of illness and health literacy.

FSIE's strategy was based on institutional and individual contacts by phone or email (using a research volunteers' database) and collective presential or online dissemination activities. The first contacts were made through other entities and thanks to the collaboration of several gatekeepers working there. A total of 21 places were visited: senior's social centres (both day-care and leisure centres), cultural centres in different neighbourhoods, associations or foundations working for and with older adults and assisted- housing older people. But above all, in Barcelona, most of the interested people were particularly engaged through third age universities that offer language or general culture lessons for seniors.

The phone and email contacts were initially considered as an important moment where the content needed to be carefully selected. Because of this, a topic guide with the main aspects to be informed was prepared. Regarding the face-to-face dissemination activities, a power-point presentation and a leaflet were used to illustrate the basic statements of the project (background, aims, chronology and the inclusion and exclusion criteria concisely). The online campaign was based on the location of a banner in FSiE's website and social media profiles. A press release was also launched and other social channels such as Twitter and LinkedIn were used to do short communications.

In conclusion, from FSIE's experience, the most effective and operational way to recruit during this study was using the volunteers' research database and the face-to-face meetings mediated by the figure of NESTORE ambassadors (representatives and gatekeepers from different third age associations as the Associació de Temps Lliure, Seniors Españoles para la Cooperación Técnica (ASECOT) or Associació de Jubilats i Pensionistes de Ripollet,) who were committed to aid in the dissemination and the recruitment. This model was very effective, firstly, because it was based on the trust and knowledge construction, and secondly, because the meetings created the conditions to generate the adequate environment to facilitate candidates' questions and solve doubts, but also to let research volunteers to identify and know the research team before settling the first trust steps.

Preventie Collectief in Rotterdam is involved in the development of a community of seniors in Schiedam, near Rotterdam (The Netherlands). The **Preventie Collective** is formed by content-driven developers that want to contribute to effective prevention from intrinsic change-motivation. For the well-being of people, society and with lower social costs as a result.

The Nestore project's recruitment was done with the assistance of two senior organizations within Schiedam (a city next to Rotterdam): Seniorenwelzijn and Soos Blauwhuis. Seniorenwelzijn has multiple senior meeting centres in which recruitment took place. Soos Blauwhuis has one centre, which in the pilot study formed the heart of the recruitment and assessments. Seniors from these meeting centres already participated in the previous co-design sessions of NESTORE, which led to the development and design of the different components within the NESTORE Platform. Their main motivation to participate in these sessions was because of an interest in technology, but also their motivation to help us with developing technology that is suitable for (Dutch) older adults. The older adults visiting these centres are mainly healthy, independent community-dwelling older adults.

In the recruiting phase, face-to-face meetings with (groups of) seniors was proven to be the most effective strategy. During a period of half a year, many smaller and larger scale meetings were organized by the researchers, mostly linked to pre-existing gatherings. So the seniors were informed about NESTORE within their usual social group settings. Next to that, many local television and radio performances contributed to achieving more publicity and awareness regarding NESTORE, as did online (social) media and offline newspapers. In the end, nearly all participants who remained in the study were recruited by means of face-to-face contact from a social gathering in a meeting center of Seniorenwelzijn or Soos Blauwhuis. In addition, all of them were exposed repeatedly to the researchers' presence or informative meetings, which again underlines the importance of social bonding within a study with seniors.

These efforts combined led to many interested seniors, but because of the SARS-CoV-2 pandemic just before the actual start of the pilot study in the Netherlands, interests dropped substantially, leading to a lower number of included participants. Additionally, the initial plan was to increase engagement by regular social meetings at the senior center, and share and compare their experiences with each other, combining the social gathering of users with a form of competition. However, the COVID-19 outbreak obliged to modify this initiative.

Cooperativa Sociale La Meridiana, operating for forty years at Monza (Italy) engaged in the design and management of innovative facilities aimed at the older people and complex neurological patients. In the continuous search for a balance between the entrepreneurial aspect and the spirit of participation, mutuality and solidarity, **La Meridiana** builds concrete projects that combine the needs of the local community and those of public and private institutions. All this, always aiming to achieve high quality standards for the satisfaction of the customer and users, in full respect of the values that have always characterized its work. In addition to the care of the fragility of the cooperative activity it is oriented to the wellbeing of individuals and families and the professionals. Affections, emotions and desires are recognized and valued, as well as the right to live and express their beliefs.

La Meridiana's strategy was based on intensive use of social media, the organization of group meetings and phone calls. Through the contact with facilities users' relatives, they had the opportunity to generate a volunteers' pool to be asked to join the study.

Precisely, due to the current work of the three institutions it was developed a triple strategy for the recruitment: using their own institutions records (in the case of FSIE the volunteers' research database that provides candidates for the research projects was used), to perform an active search of new volunteers using alliances with seniors' organizations, centers, institutions and associations (as in the case of Rotterdam and Barcelona, but also FSIE contacted with cultural and senior's centers and NGO), and finally the use of social media to recruit people interested in technologies and with digital skills (as in the case of La Meridiana). This strategy was set in three steps as it will be explained in the results section. In each phase the provided information was mediated by the moment and the information that candidates needed. Depending on their previous experience in joining research studies the information corpus was adapted to their demands.

3 Results

A total of 236 people between the three sites were interviewed to be informed about the study, its requirements and to offer them the possibility to participate. 127 performed the screening phase, 78 of which met the inclusion criteria. The recruitment process required approximately 90–100 h per site within a 3–5 month period.

The final sample profile consisted of 30 women and 30 men, of medium-high socio-economic level, with studies, excellent health, very active people with high social activity. Additionally, in the case of the Spanish pilot site, 3 participants from Latin America enriched the ethnic and cultural background of the study. Regarding digital literacy, although the purpose of this study was not to evaluate in detail the participants' previous digital skills, the findings pointed that the knowledge of most of them was enough to use the Smartphone to attend calls, use WhatsApp or to install an application (even though some of them needed support). A short sample had quite an advanced level due to their professional background or personal interests.

After the recruitment, 6 candidates dropped-out before starting the intervention phase and 3 were replaced. In Monza 6 participants after installation were withdrawn because of the COVID-19 situation. Finally, in Barcelona, the initial objective of 30 participants was achieved, 12 in Rotterdam and 24 in Monza.

The remaining participants did not enter the study due to various motives. 102 of them didn't want or couldn't participate from the beginning because of different reasons: personal (i.e. lack of time or because their relatives' perception influenced their decision), technical issues (the very complex system to be installed and used, the feeling that the virtual system would be very intrusive), perception of their own digital skills (the feeling that they would not be able to carry it out due to lack of technological knowledge) or altruism profiles (participants were already engaged in other scientific studies related to healthy habits and cognitive wellbeing). On the other side, 49 of them were willing to take part, but could not because of health or technological impairments. Most of them had health issues, both physical or psychological, incompatible with the studies' eligibility criterion. It turned out to be extremely hard-to-reach people over 65 without comorbidities as thyroid disease, cardiovascular, respiratory or neurological conditions or cancer cured less than 5 years ago. Because of this, a short list of health conditions was re-focused in order to facilitate the inclusion of candidates with controlled thyroid disease, sleep apnea or acute disorders that didn't affect participants to perform the intervention, as long as the volunteers always had these health conditions controlled with a continued physician follow-up. In terms of technological requirements, many of the interested people were not able to participate because of not having an Android phone, not having an above 7.0 version or not having WiFi at home.

Turning now to the comparison of the recruitment process carried out by the pilot sites with the TIBaR model, many similarities have been found according to the previously announced steps involved:

1. Build up **T**rust
2. Offer **I**ncentives
3. Identify individual **Ba**rriers and
4. Be **R**esponsive.

3.1 Building Trust

The TiBAR model's philosophy is to build a positive relationship and trust with participants. Authors as Kammerer described two studies to illustrate this assertion: the population-based longitudinal study 'Operationalizing multimorbidity and autonomy for health services research in ageing populations' (OMAHA), was a joint study of Charité—Universitaetsmedizin Berlin and the Robert Koch Institute; and the study 'Maintaining autonomy after a fall in socially disadvantaged neighbourhoods' (NEIGHBOURHOOD) conducted jointly by IGF e. V. (Institute for Gerontological Research) and the public health research group at WZB (Social Science Research Centre) in Berlin, Germany. Both studies were based on various stimuli explicitly or implicitly offered to promote participation: the incentives. The studies were designed to learn more about a participant's personal situation to identify individual barriers. Ultimately, responsiveness was another important strategy to overcome barriers to participation [18].

Authors as McMurdo emphasized the need to maximize effective communication, involvement of carers, use of research networks, overcoming potential problems with access and transport to improve recruitment and retention [20]. This required getting to know candidates better to advance their needs and helping them to participate in the same conditions as the rest of volunteers.

Precisely, it is noteworthy to mention that in the NESTORE project there were several mechanisms and factors influenced by the same understanding of encouraging volunteering. This view helped in the recruiting process and enhanced participants' willingness and motivation during the fieldwork.

The creation of a multidisciplinary team in each pilot country was also important for the study. The different profiles contributed at every stage of the research with different skills. Authors reflected that non-material resources are essential, not only for their capacity for planning and organizing but also the recruitment of intensively qualified staff with soft skills such as language proficiency, flexibility and the ability to find the 'right tone' in communicating with participants from diverse socioeconomic milieus and strata [18].

In concordance to the TIBaR model, the crucial first step is to build up trust and confidence in communicating to gatekeepers and possible participants. This objective can be achieved via accessible informational materials (in easily comprehensive language), via trustworthy institutions, key agents and multipliers and also personal contact, based on transparent communication and careful data protection information [18]. This target was followed in the same way in the three pilot sites.

3.2 *Identify Individual Barriers*

Having defined what the important role of building trust is, another crucial enhancing factor was to organize the recruitment process in 3 stages to identify barriers. This step implied to dose and balance information depending on the moment and according to the management philosophy "just-in-time" versus "just-in-case": **first contact** (to inform in plain language what NESTORE was and the requisites to join), **in-depth interview** (to know better the volunteers' expectancies and their starting point to be volunteers), **recruitment visit** (to screen and to obtain more information about their needs and requirements). Finally, the process finalized with the **continuous retention activities** that were focused on making a special participants' follow-up trying to advance the barriers to facilitate their participation during the baseline assessment, intervention and post-assessment.

As it was previously mentioned, the aim of this **first contact** was to reach potential participants through people or entities of trust and to explain in general terms what the study consisted of. After this first action, any person showing interest was invited to come to the office to do an in-depth interview. During this interview the research team explained the study in more detail, solved all the possible doubts, tried to obtain a participant's profile of interests, needs, but also to identify barriers and manage their expectations. This step was essential, as it was the beginning of a bonding relationship of trust between the researchers and the participants.

During the **in-depth interview**, the three pilot sites obtained a first participants' profile to understand what motivated them to get involved in the study, their expectancies regarding their participation and if there existed any limitations or barriers that could affect their participation in order to be addressed at later stages.

In the in-depth interviews some limitations were verbalized in some cases to attend the visits because some participants had schedule problems to attend the visits or to travel long distances to reach the office. To overcome these obstacles, the research team always offered first the maximum flexibility in schedules but also the possibility of mobilising themselves depending on the type of the visit that required to be scheduled. When participants' presence was essential, the travel was organised (by taxi) and the cost paid. Every solution was always offered to help the participants' performance in the project. When the SARS-CoV-2 pandemic disrupted the fieldwork and participants' lives, the virtual assessments and phone-call visits were always prioritized.

Finally, during the **recruitment visit**, several measurements needed for the screening were taken. The length of this visit was of approximately an hour, where participants were adequately welcomed and guided in order to help volunteers to feel comfort and trust during their visit.

3.3 *Offer Incentives*

In terms of incentives, due to the already mentioned impossibility of material compensation in two intervention sites, this was mostly focused on immaterial rewards. This refers to the opportunity of the volunteers to express themselves, the chance of addressing personal concerns not directly related to the study's purpose (participatory incentive), to enjoy company (social incentive) and to be offered feedback on the results of the assessments (informational incentive) [18]. The volunteers in this project were also very interested in knowing the results of some of the performed tests.

Thus, the focus of the three pilot sites was based on the immaterial approach, because only the Rotterdam site was offering financial compensation to participants. The fact of contributing to something that volunteers knew that would be beneficial for others in the future, had a great influence in their recruitment and retention. The participants stated on several occasions that the main driving force behind their engagement was the knowledge that the results obtained with their participation would help to improve the NESTORE system, which, in turn, could help many people of their age in next years. This altruistic act gave them an individual resignification and also the incentive of social interaction. Not only with the research team, but also with the rest of the participants, taking part in the preparation meetings (in the case of the Barcelona pilot site) and/or with the family members and friends that would also take part in the study (because of the social beacons). Precisely, in the Barcelona site, the organisation of three participants' meetings before starting the field work turned out to be a good, helpful and a very valued practice for participants. Although these meetings were addressed to review and solve doubts about the informed consent, to explain in more detail the project chronogram, to solve questions and to display the devices on site, they had a positive output for this experience. These encounters worked as a merging experience that helped participants to feel part of a group and to share similar ideas. They met a space where to feel free to express their concerns about the project and expectations.

Finally, as mentioned before, there was an incentive for all participants that was to be informed about research results by the end of the study.

3.4 *Be Responsive*

Furthermore, during the NESTORE screenings, assessments and installations, it was common that participants emerged with personal issues and topics they could be worried about, whether or not related to the project. The research team was responsive and permeable to their interests and tried to be supportive, even though it was not related to the study's purpose. This could be considered a person-centered approach.

Given the conceptual and technical characteristics of the NESTORE project, it can be considered a complex initiative that requires to facilitate timely and adequate information for novel users. Since it works in several areas of wellbeing, it is composed of many devices, the vocabulary is sometimes very technical and the number of tests that the participants had to perform is high and some of them required a long time to be performed. It was considered important to provide participants with easily understandable information. In order to make the explanations easier to follow, the information was presented with visual aids (photos, graphics and the devices in place). In addition, new supporting materials were created to summarise the schedule of visits, to find the best moment to do the visits without disrupting their personal affairs and to reduce the risk of forgetting the scheduled appointments. The research team established a day-before reminder to facilitate the visits to participants. Additionally, a document with the research team's contact details (the office schedules and a phone number), was distributed to participants, to give them support in case of an emergency or if they need help using the system.

3.5 *Identified Barriers*

Despite the previously announced enhancer factors, several barriers also emerged. Thus, the main obstacle in our study, as mentioned before, was the difficulty of finding older people between 65 and 75 that could meet the criteria, not only the health requirements, but also all the technological criteria and to have enough free time to take part in it.

The NESTORE eligibility criteria are very specific, consequently it was very difficult to maintain the aim to detect the maximum of problems, when this capacity relies on: the number of subjects, the profiles diversity and the living situations and also the timespan of use. But also, to find participants with heterogeneous backgrounds that could lead to different views about the system or experienced diverse situations.

Having discussed the main barriers, this final section describes them and addresses ways of overcoming the difficulties for each of the categories.

3.5.1 Health Barriers

The percentage of Europeans aged over 65 is 20% [1, 6, 7]. Although this reality implies a huge pool for finding and recruiting subjects for aging studies, there are several circumstances that should be considered. Firstly, not only the increase of chronic diseases prevalence in European for this age range group. Furthermore, there are large differences in the burden of chronic conditions that also exist within EU Member States as well as among social-economic groups or regions [8–10]. The prevalence of diabetes, cardiovascular disease, COPD and depression is higher in people with lower levels of education as compared with people with a higher level of education. Although there are often socio-economic inequalities in cancer incidence and mortality, the pattern is not consistent [11]. Thus, the target of healthy older people could be hard-to-reach depending on the approach applied to understand the "good health" concept.

According to the results of the second wave of the European health interview survey (EHIS) there are health conditions with a high prevalence in population, for example in the EU-27, 53.3% of Europeans aged 75 years and over reported hypertensive diseases.

Hypercholesterolemia is a major cardiovascular risk factor that increases the incidence of atherosclerotic diseases in adults, although the association is less well established in the elderly. The relationship between cholesterol and atherosclerosis is primarily characterized by a rise in plasma concentration, although other mechanisms can also intervene [22]. Epidemiological studies conducted in different geographical areas have shown a high prevalence of hypercholesterolemia in later life. Western countries have the highest prevalence, consistent with the higher incidence of cardiovascular disease and death [12].

So far, this subsection has focused on health conditions, but there are social determinants that may affect some sample assumptions and need to be considered. Accordingly, if the NESTORE sample is compared with one of the most widely used models that attempt to illustrate the relationship between different determinants and health, the 'rainbow' model, developed by Dahlgren and Whitehead in 1991. This model maps the relationship between people, their environment and health. People are placed at the centre. Surrounding them in concentric half-circles are the various layers of influences on health: individual lifestyle factors; community influences; living and working conditions; and the more general social conditions (Dahlgren and Whitehead 1991 in [24]). The result will be that NESTORE participants are surrounded by the best conditions to avoid some of the determinant layers that affect the disadvantaged population strata, but this does not imply that this target was easily reached.

Secondly, according to Mody [21], major barriers for older adults' recruitment in aging research are related to their substantial health problems, social and cultural barriers, and potentially impaired capacity to provide informed consent. Additionally, institutionalized older adults offer another layer of complexity that requires cooperation from the institutions to participate in research activities that it is not the NESTORE pilot study's case. On the contrary, the NESTORE study revealed that the adopted health concept was one of the most important barriers for recruitment. From the confrontation between the formal understanding of the "good health" term (considered globally in the research by institutions and governments) with the accepted and assimilated "to be in good enough health" population's belief, it erupts discrepancy. This situation was not always easy to deal with because there appeared resistances or a hard disagreement with the cornerstone criteria for the seniors' recruitment. In fact, it was documented several times that there were participants who expressed dissatisfaction because they were rejected because they had a health condition not accepted in the study. On the other hand, several participants expressed their belief before and after their participation that those who could maximize the benefits of being engaged in this type of intervention are those who do not have a "good health" or "healthy habits". But, additional qualitative research is needed to offer more evidence of this users' perceptions.

3.5.2 Age Barrier

In the study an additional obstacle appeared related to the strict age range agreed at the beginning of the study. Research required to fix the age range to facilitate the sample characterisation and to be capable to compare results. But, in the case of this study, it is relevant the high rate of complaints in one of the pilot sites. Those volunteers were interested to join the study, but they were rejected because of their age. The rejection was in some cases interpreted as an intrinsic ageism or seniors' categorization as useless after a certain age or not having autonomy or good health. In any of the situations that researchers adopted the TiBAR model to justify why study requirements were settled and what limitations were dealing, but also the research team acquired the consciousness of the need to integrate all potential seniors' candidates in future studies, although they participate in different project research stages, as it was done in co-design phase.

3.5.3 Social-Economic and Cultural Barriers

As Mody [21] stated, there are social and cultural barriers that may impact the recruitment. In NESTORE project it was considered that age, gender and level of formal education also had a significant impact on the use of the Internet by individuals: differences revealed the existence of 'digital divide' across generations and educational attainment. 96% of individuals aged 16–24 were regular Internet users against 57% in the 55–74 age group. Individuals with a higher level of education were almost all regular Internet users (96%), while less than 60% of individuals with a lower level of education used the internet regularly. According to recent research into the Eurostat databases on Digital Economy and Society, there are gender gaps in basic ICT skills but, when it comes to complex skills, gaps become very pronounced and access is not sufficient to close them. In lower skills, gender gaps are larger in the older and more disadvantaged groups [4].

When researchers tried to diversify the cases targeted for recruitment, they found rejection or exceptions on the part of the gatekeepers working in several organisations located in neighbourhoods with social strata based on lower incomes. Several meetings were organized but it was stated that it was almost impossible to recruit candidates that could meet the criteria. Not only for the social determinants of health, but also for other important factors: mobility impairments, IT barriers, such as outdated phone models or not having WiFi at home.

As it was referred previously, one of the aims of NESTORE study was to have the maximum heterogeneity on the sample. This objective included to enrich the sample with the contributions from different ethnic populations. Authors as McMurdo stated that minority ethnic groups' profile is different from the Caucasian population and the representation of older people from an ethnic minority in clinical trials is poor. Thus, the choice of research topic should address and acknowledge the interest and diversity of the group [20].

The possibility of recruiting under-studied groups of older people was looked at, including those that are in third age apartments with services, but this choice required planning and expertise, especially regarding the possible security conditions in the building's Internet network.

3.5.4 Gender and Digital Divide Barriers

In one of the pilots sites it was documented that in the first recruitment stage it was easier to recruit women than men. Because of this, the recruitment strategy changed to try to obtain more men candidates and finally, a balanced gender sample was achieved. In fact, psychological research has found that women score higher on most measures of the traits, motivations, and values that predict helping others, and women are more likely to help family and friends. However, sex differences in the institutional helping behaviours of volunteering and charitable giving are small. This paper seeks to explain this apparent contradiction with the hypotheses that men have more resources and more social capital than women, which compensates for their lower level of motivation. The paper tests these hypotheses using data from the 1995 Midlife in the United States (MIDUS) survey. The data show partial support for these hypotheses, as men score higher on measures of income, education, trust, and secular social networks. However, women have broader social networks through religious participation [5].

3.5.5 Individual Barriers

In the context of identifying individual barriers in TIBaR model, authors establish that participation may be obstructed by individual and situational obstacles. In the studies previously announced, OMAHA and NEIGHBORHOOD, the major barriers found were mobility limitations of various kinds, language difficulties and responsibilities for the care of relatives. Also, the results of both studies pointed out that their participation was affected by their general workload, time constraints and critical and unexpected life events (the death or acute health problems of relatives). In the NESTORE three pilot sites it was a big awareness about the fact that these kinds of obstacles could arise, so participants were provided by support from the research team and as mentioned before, with an emergency telephone number.

The willingness to take part in the study also depended on the general workload (e.g., of civil engagement or caring for oneself and/or others) and time constraints that some older people experience (availability with regard to time) [18]. The difficulty of adjusting the evaluations to the participants' busy schedules.

As mentioned before, the participants' profile refers to very active people who performed different daily activities as: take care of relatives (i.e. grandchildren, spouse or other family members), participate in different cultural and leisure activities, travel, attend classes at the university and a few still go to work. But also, their profile was very altruistic, and they were involved in other research initiatives or social volunteering.

3.5.6 Length of the Assessments and Study Stages

Mody [21] states that, apart from travel cost and the need of assistance, feeling discomfort and fatigue also work as a challenging hidden barrier. Because of participants' busy profile, it was a challenge to align the study design with their daily activities' rhythm. The first informative interview took approximately one hour, half to explain the project in depth and another half to carry out the screening tests if interested. After this visit, the duration of the baseline assessments in the pilot sites was as follows: one hour to carry out the physical tests and characterisation of the sample (sociodemographic and health status), the cognitive and mental assessments including the 5 NESTORE App-based tests (three hours); and the nutritional evaluation (an hour). It was also necessary to schedule another day to carry out the installation at home (an average of between two hours to four) and in most cases several more contacts were needed by phone or in person both in the offices and in their homes, to check and fix failures in the system. After ending the two daily tracking weeks, users were committed to fulfil an online usability questionnaire and after this, they were asked to perform an intermediate assessment and finally, to complete the three additional final tests related to the Technology Acceptance Model (TAM). Participants needed to repeat all the tests mentioned previously in the final assessment by the end of the study.

As it follows, the evaluation took, on average, 10 h, and that is without including the needed hours to give the technical support or attend intervention group's doubts after the system installation. Reconciling all of these with the volunteers' lives was a big barrier, as well as managing their fatigue and frustration, for example when participants were performing some tests based on the use of the system or when some recurrent incidences emerged after the system installation. Pilot sites adopted strategies for this situation, as offering a coffee break and snacks to make the long evaluations more enjoyable or giving full support after the installation contributed to the fatigue reduction, but also participants could perceive a certain continuity in their follow-up during the intervention stage.

However, the fact that the evaluations were so numerous and long also had a very positive effect: the constant interaction between the researchers and the participants. After so many calls and meetings, the relationship between the two parties became one of trust and one of the reasons that helped and encouraged participants to continue in the project. Especially during the confinement, this relationship in most of the cases helped to maintain their interest in the project.

3.5.7 The Unexpected Barriers

Lastly, one of the biggest and unexpected barriers in the NESTORE project, and in the whole world, was to face the SARS-CoV-2 pandemic. In the research contest it is usual to develop a mitigation plan to establish the process to be applied to identify, record, manage and monitor risks and to define the steps for the contingency planning when an identified risk cannot be completely avoided or mitigated. But the circumstances occurred during the outbreak could not be expected neither contained, nor confronted in reference to what is described in a research study of these characteristics.

Considering that seniors are part of the highest risk group, all the research activities completely stopped for their safety. It continued a small scale by phone and email to facilitate online assessments or technological support. However, the participants' fear of getting involved or continuing in the project, understandable, affected the recruitment, assessment process and installations. Despite this, some good practices were applied to guarantee the participants and research team's safety as the "*Safety first decalogue*" document, where the main recommendations were compiled to be applied during the face-to-face assessments and installations when activities could be restarted. The document was based on official resources as the European Commission and the Center for Disease Control (CDC). Finally, when the field work continued, the research team prioritized measures that help to preserve their safety participation as the home visits with a strict safety protocol performance, organized and paid transport to the facilities and especially, online assessments for the tests that were able to be performed in a non-presential format. Even if these measures were extensively applied, the impact of the SARS-CoV-2 pandemic had an unforeseen impact with the increase of the abandonments during the intervention. Despite the critical situation, most of the participants agreed with performing the final assessment. This taken decision is indicative of their willingness grade with the aim of the project.

4 Conclusions

The main NESTORE project lesson learned was that the research road was based on trust and knowledge. Any taken direction needs to arrive at the same endpoint: to build a relationship based on respect, care and honesty but creating the correct conditions by means of a group of strategies addressed to enhance the recruitment and retain the participants. Promising strategies for building trust are suggested in the literature and can be summarized to involve stakeholders on different levels to play important roles in enabling access to targeted older persons [18].

Thus, four strategies are important for recruitment and retention pointed out by McHenry et al., namely: accessing an appropriate population, communicating and building trust, providing comfort and security, and expressing gratitude, giving valuable examples mainly for the retention of older people [19]. But also, Hughson et al. recognized barriers to the participation of culturally and linguistically diverse older people in clinical research: mistrust, communication barriers, cultural barriers, economic and time constraints, mobility and health issues as well as opportunity barriers [17].

As literature reflects, not every older person is hard-to-reach. Instead, healthy older people are often easier to access (because they are no longer working and their time is more flexible) and are more interested in taking part in research than younger, working people [14]. However, although the NESTORE sample design had a high potential to reach adequate candidates, the constrained eligibility criterion surfaced as a main barrier to obtain a representative and heterogeneous sample.

Because of this, it is mandatory to apply several good practices that could be applied for future studies based on practical approaches as authors as Mody highlighted: "when designing inclusion and exclusion criteria, one goal should be to align the criteria closely with the aims of the study and to assess whether the final enrolled population represents the target population. If the aim is to generalize results to older adults with complex health problems, then the criteria should allow their participation" [21]. Even the NESTORE project is not addressed to this target, engaging other seniors' profiles could enrich it when they contribute with their views about aging as it was done during the co-design phase of the project.

Our findings after the recruitment stage are in consonance with the TIBaR model for 'hard-to-reach' groups statements as: "the implementation of it requires a high degree of flexibility, increases the complexity of recruitment, and needs more extensive effort and resources [18]. On the other hand, if a middle-class bias can be reduced and the participation rates of socially disadvantaged people increase, so does the meaningfulness of the studies". Though the NESTORE pilot study had multidisciplinary teams and sufficient resources to achieve diversity in recruitment, the specificity of the eligibility criteria generated the sample homogeneity. Because of this, several strategies were applied to reduce this effect. As literature pointed out, it is a matter of pragmatism to identify these difficulties and modify the strategies for 'hard-to-reach' groups by making more and different efforts or including other authorities and/or trusted multipliers in the research process [18]. Authors pointed out that "even if the participants' trust is gained and they acknowledge the incentives, participation may still be hampered by individual and situational obstacles. It is important to be aware of such potential impediments in the course of the recruitment process. Possible means to do so are to retrieve literature about the difficulties of specific sub-groups or to organize preliminary interchanges with intermediaries and potential participants, as part of the telephone contacts or during the presentation of the aims of the study on meetings or events" [18]. In the case of the NESTORE project the three pilot sites had some contacts with intermediaries of several organizations to confront their realities before starting the recruitment in order to discuss the strategy and to adjust it. It is also a way to shift the view from possible complaints about 'hard-to-reach' groups to responsibility for high-quality research design. But, in the NESTORE project case although several alliances with different stakeholders were searched, finally it was impossible to arrive at other target populations because of the required technological requirements. In the future, if a hard-to-reach target population wants to be included, it will be mandatory to find feasible ways to sum material resources not only providing Smartphones to participants, but also access to Internet services from their homes and support to learn how to use these technologies in order to reduce the digital gap.

In reference to the type of the methodology selected that could contribute to participants' view, it could generate older people's motivation to participate especially in qualitative studies because of the multiple aspects, such as personal interest in the study objective and topic [16], altruism, the need for information or access to services and the wish for social contact and support or the hope for personal benefit [18]. In fact, the main values that make volunteering in research possible are altruism and empathy. These values require to be nurtured during the study stages. Veludo-de-Oliveira et al. concluded that volunteers fulfilled their agreement to take part in the projects independently of the motivation underlying their behavior, whether egoistic or altruistic. Volunteers do not differ in terms of altruism, empathy, and attitudinal and normative beliefs when compared by levels of committed volunteering behavior, but they do differ in terms of two control beliefs: lack of time and the hindrances to volunteering work [26]. To confront this reality, it is mandatory to apply enhancer strategies addressed to value constantly the individual effort of participants, to make a public acknowledgement of their contribution and to put their safety and rights above all are in consonance with socially responsible research that are aligned with TiBAR model. Therefore, practices as sharing and searching for potential participants' target and stakeholder's contribution when possible could contribute to creating not only more comprehensive and responsive documents, but also the correct climate to foster their participation. As in the case of the NESTORE project, that counted with the preparation of a key document as the informed consent before submitting it in the ethical committee. Consequently, any recruitment that pretends to be successful requires to start at the planning stage: piloting with a representative sample of older adults is essential to evaluate if the instructions, forms, questionnaires, measurement instruments are legible and appropriate for people, not only for those who may have visual or other sensory impairments, but also to have a particular attention to the time needed to complete different assessments allows appropriate breaks to be factored-in during assessment procedures [20]. Therefore, to seek a balance between obtaining the necessary measures and reducing the cognitive exhaustion of the participants could be a good measure to improve the participants' perception.

To maximize the participants' retention during the study is also important. Several practices could have good impact in the study as to prepare supporting easy-to-read materials for the prosecution of the planned activities to solve their doubts and guide them for the different stages of the study, to establish formal mechanisms to collect their views and contributions during all the fieldwork and to offer immaterial incentives when other incentives couldn't be considered.

By the end of the study, according to the responsible research principle, it is mandatory to share the main results or lessons learned of this experience with participants that desire to be informed.

Finally, in reference to being responsive, the TIBaR model states that flexibility and the use of appropriate resources are central to overcome the obstacles. The

NESTORE project potentiates this by developing an exhaustive mitigation plan being aware of the barriers and searching possible solutions even though unforeseen situations could happen at any moment, as produced by the SARS-CoV-2 pandemic.

References

1. Demographic profile of the older population. In: *World ageing 1950–2050*. United Nations (UN): United Nations, Department of Economic and Social Affairs, Population Division (2015). Retrieved December 15, 2020, from https://www.un.org/esa/population/publications/worldageing19502050/pdf/90chapteriv.pdf.
2. Bouillon, K., Kivimaki, M., Hamer, M., et al. (2013). Measures of frailty in population-based studies: An overview. *BMC Geriatrics, 13,* 64. https://doi.org/10.1186/1471-2318-13-64.
3. Clegg, A., et al. (2013). Frailty in elderly people. *The Lancet, 381*(9868), 752–762.
4. Davaki, K. (2018). The underlying causes of the digital gender gap and possible solutions for enhanced digital inclusion of women and girls. FEMM: Women's Rights and Gender Equality. Retrieved December 15, 2020, from https://www.europarl.europa.eu/RegData/etudes/STUD/2018/604940/IPOL_STU(2018)604940_EN.pdf.
5. Einolf, C. (2010). Gender differences in the correlates of volunteering and charitable giving. *Nonprofit and Voluntary Sector Quarterly, 40*(6). https://doi.org/10.1177/0899764010385949.
6. Eurostat. (2015a). *People in the EU: Who are we and how do we live?* Luxembourg: Eurostat. Retrieved December 15, 2020, from https://ec.europa.eu/eurostat/statistics-explained/index.php/People_in_the_EU_%E2%80%93_statistics_on_an_ageing_society#The_elderly_living_alone.
7. Eurostat. (2015b). Statistics on an aging society: The elderly living alone. *People in the EU: Who are we and how do we live?* Luxembourg: Eurostat. Retrieved December 15, 2020, from https://ec.europa.eu/eurostat/statistics-explained/index.php/People_in_the_EU_%E2%80%93_statistics_on_an_ageing_society#The_elderly_living_alone.
8. Eurostat's statistics on information and communication technologies (ICTs). Retrieved December 15, 2020, from https://ec.europa.eu/eurostat/web/information-society/overview.
9. Eurostat. (2020). European Health Interview Survey (EHIS). Retrieved December 27, 2020, from https://ec.europa.eu/eurostat/web/microdata/european-health-interview-survey.
10. European Parliamentary Research Service. (2014). Older people in Europe. Retrieved December 15, 2020, from: https://www.europarl.europa.eu/RegData/bibliotheque/briefing/2014/140811/LDM_BRI(2014)140811_REV1_EN.pdf.
11. Europeans of retirement age: Chronic diseases and economic activity. RIVM (2012). Retrieved December 15, 2020, from https://ec.europa.eu/health//sites/health/files/major_chronic_diseases/docs/rivm_report_retirement_en.pdf.
12. Félix-Redondo, F. J., Grau, M., & Fernández-Bergés, D. (2013). Cholesterol and cardiovascular disease in the elderly. Facts and gaps. *Aging and Disease, 4*(3), 154–169.
13. Fried, L. P., Tangen, C. M., Walston, J., Newman, A. B., Hirsch, C., Gottdiener, J., … McBurnie, M. A. (2001). Frailty in older adults: Evidence for a phenotype. *Journals of Gerontology - Series A Biological Sciences and Medical Sciences, 56*(3), 146–157. https://doi.org/10.1093/gerona/56.3.m146.
14. Golomb, B. A., Chan, V. T., Evans, M. A., Koperski, S., White, H. L., & Criqui, M. H. (2012). The older the better: Are elderly study participants more non-representative? A cross-sectional analysis of clinical trial and observational study samples. *British Medical Journal Open, 2*(6), e000833.
15. Hanlon, P., Nicholl, B. I., Jani, B.D., Lee, D., McQueenie, R., & Mair, F. S. (2018) Frailty and pre-frailty in middle-aged and older adults and its association with multimorbidity and mortality: A prospective analysis of 493 737 UK Biobank participants. *Lancet Public Health,*

3(7), e323-e332. https://doi.org/10.1016/S2468-2667(18)30091-4. Epub 2018 Jun 14. PMID: 29908859; PMCID: PMC6028743.
16. Herzog, A. R., & Kulka, R. A. (1989). Telephone and mail surveys with older populations: A methodological overview. In Lawton, M. P., & Herzog, R. A. (Eds.), *Special research methods for gerontology* (pp. 69–89). Amityville: Baywood Publishing.
17. Hughson, J. A., Woodward-Kron, R., Parker, A., et al. (2016). A review of approaches to improve participation of culturally and linguistically diverse populations in clinical trials. *Trials, 17*(1), 263.
18. Kammerer, K., Falk, K., Herzog, A., & Fuchs, J. (2019). How to reach 'hard-to-reach' older people for research: The TIBaR model of recruitment. *Survey Methods: Insights from the Field.* Retrieved from https://surveyinsights.org/?p=11822.
19. McHenry, J. C., Insel, K. C., Einstein, G. O., Vidrine, A. N., Koerner, K. M., & Morrow, D. G. (2015). Recruitment of older adults: Success may be in the details. *The Gerontologist, 55*(5), 845–853.
20. McMurdo, M. E., Roberts, H., Parker, S., Wyatt, N., May, H., Goodman, C., et al. (2011). Improving recruitment of older people to research through good practice. *Age and Ageing, 40*(6), 659–665. https://doi.org/10.1093/ageing/afr115.
21. Mody, L., Miller, D. K., McGloin, J. M., et al. (2008). Recruitment and retention of older adults in aging research. *Journal of the American Geriatrics Society, 56*(12), 2340–2348.
22. National Cholesterol Education Program (NCEP). (2002). Expert panel on detection, evaluation, and treatment of high blood cholesterol in adults (ATP III). Third report of the National Cholesterol Education Program (NCEP). Final Report. *Circulation, 106*, 3143–21.
23. Rockwood, K., Andrew, M., & Mitnitski, A. (2007). A comparison of two approaches to measuring frailty in elderly people. *Journals of Gerontology - Series a Biological Sciences and Medical Sciences, 62*(7), 738–743. https://doi.org/10.1093/gerona/62.7.738.
24. Scholz, N. (2020). Addressing health inequalities in the European Union: Addressing health inequalities in the European Union. https://www.europarl.europa.eu/RegData/etudes/IDAN/2020/646182/EPRS_IDA(2020)646182_EN.pdf.
25. Theou, O., Cann, L., Blodgett, J., Wallace, L. M., Brothers, T. D., & Rockwood, K. (2015). Modifications to the frailty phenotype criteria: Systematic review of the current literature and investigation of 262 frailty phenotypes in the Survey of Health, Ageing, and Retirement in Europe. *Ageing Research Review, 21*, 78–94. https://doi.org/10.1016/j.arr.2015.04.001. Epub 2015 Apr 4. PMID: 25846451.
26. Veludo-de-Oliveira, T. M., Pallister, J. G., & Foxall, G. R. (2015) Unselfish? Understanding the role of altruism, empathy, and beliefs in volunteering commitment. *Journal of Nonprofit & Public Sector Marketing, 27*(4), 373–396. https://doi.org/10.1080/10495142.2015.1080504.s

Innovation Impact Measured in Subjective (Usability and Experience), Social (Community Level) and Business (Companies and Institutions) Opportunities

Practicing the Test of New System-Services for Elderly Care: How to Introduce and Measure User Experience and Related Outcomes

Carlo Emilio Standoli, Maria Terraroli, Martina Scagnoli, Francesco Spelta, Roberto Sironi, Paolo Perego, and Giuseppe Andreoni

Abstract The implementation and, above all, the exploitation of e-health or m-health services come through the acceptance of the technology by users. If this could be assumed as implicit for the native digital people, indeed it is a very critical factor for current elderly population. For this reason, usability and its assessment are crucial not only to evaluate acceptance and its impact on efficacy of the intervention, but since the very beginning to retrieve dedicated requirements for system design and refinement. This chapter discusses the design process and user-experience development and test in new e-/m-health services for seniors.

1 Introduction

The Nestore project proposes a personalised e-coaching system for elderly users to improve their quality of life and health status. Through the use of interactive and technological tools, such as Smartphone Apps, Wearable and Environmental devices, and a Tangible interface, the user is monitored and in return receives information and suggestions that will help him or her to stay healthy and for active ageing in all human domains [1].

When designing such complex systems, involving interactions between the user and the range of different objects and interfaces, the active involvement of the user must be foreseen in all phases of the design process, from ideation to final design. This codesign participation makes possible to understand the real point of view of the users (and also that of the other stakeholders, if they are involved in the process), their knowledge and skills, their needs, expectations, both at a general level and related to the topic of the project, that is coaching for healthy lifestyles and active ageing. Especially when new technologies are introduced in our lives and/or the interaction between technological systems and the user—of any age, gender, cultural level, etc.—is novel, this codesign activity is at the basis of the possibility of success of the

C. E. Standoli (✉) · M. Terraroli · M. Scagnoli · F. Spelta · R. Sironi · P. Perego · G. Andreoni
Department of Design, Politecnico di Milano, Via Giovanni Durando, 20158 Milan, Italy
e-mail: carloemilio.standoli@polimi.it

G. Andreoni and C. Mambretti (eds.), *Digital Health Technology for Better Aging*, Research for Development, https://doi.org/10.1007/978-3-030-72663-8_14

product, system and service, tailoring them to people's abilities, needs, expectations, contexts and social determinants [2].

This chapter reports the activities carried out with users to develop and codesign the Nestore system, and it focuses on the definition of an integrated methodology and framework to evaluate its usability and acceptability, and the user experience while interacting with the Nestore system as a whole and with its components (i.e., the Tangible Object, the Wearable Device, the Nestore Coach App, and the Pocket Odyssey App).

The evaluation actions and activities are defined according to the International Standards [3–8], and reported by using evaluation tools already validated in the literature, such as the System Usability Scale (SUS) [9, 10], the Technology Acceptance Model (TAM) [11–13], the User Experience Questionnaire (UEQ) [14–16], the Companionship Scale [17, 18], and the Friendship Scale [19]. The use of all these methods and tools allows the team to measure the different domains of system functionality, usability and acceptance, and the user experience.

In addition, we have defined a set of activities and actions to be done by the users with the different components, to evaluate the effectiveness and efficiency of the system [4, 5]. These activities are identified to let the users familiarise with the system and to test if the Graphical User Interface (GUI) of the App, its logical flow and functioning, the data and feedback presented by the Tangible object and the Wearable, were clear, understandable, and in compliance with users' expectations.

This activity of testing and evaluation of the usability and acceptability, and the user experience is fundamental both for the iterative development and implementation of the system, and requires the users themselves in the codesign activity, with the final aim of having a functioning, usable system that proposes interactions and user experiences that persuade and motivate the person in changing their behaviours towards healthier actions, i.e. making choices, and doing activities that are positive for health and wellbeing [2, 20].

2 HCD Approach in Designing Interactive System-Services for Elderly

In designing a new product, service or system, especially in a market in which the options available to consumers are rapidly expanding, it is now well established that to meet users and consumers needs and demands, and provide returns for stakeholders, the designer has to develop new products, services and systems, and to create new interactions and experiences [20, 21]. To reach this goal, the designer has to actively involve users in the entire development and design process. Users must be involved not only as customers or consumers of products, services and systems, but also as experts who have knowledge, skills and experience of use that can enrich the design process in its many development stages [2, 22]. The designer and those involved in the design process (e.g., the project team, the company, the stakeholders etc.) must carry out this task in a responsible and humanitarian way [23], considering the needs of all the users connected in some way to the product, and the social, environmental and economic impact of its conception, production, use and disposal. In addition to the design of products, systems and services, the project team has the goal of defining interactions and user experiences, which allow the user to relate continuously—both in the short and long term—with these artefacts [20, 24]. In the healthcare and wellbeing field, this continuous interaction with products, services and systems has to be approached from different points of view, considering functional aspects (e.g., the accurate and continuous monitoring of physiological parameters), usability and acceptability aspects (e.g., related to the comprehension of the device and its use), and experiential and behavioural aspects. The latter relates to the ultimate aim of Design: through the product, service or system, the user can be directed, influenced and persuaded to behave in a way that has a positive impact on his or her physical, cognitive and social states, and therefore in a broader sense, can improve his or her health [20, 24–26]; designers should create artefacts that are meaningful for proposing interactions and experiences that lead to positive changes in people's life and behaviours, and in the case of Nestore, related to the domain of health and wellbeing. In this regard, the Interaction Design Association defines its discipline as: "*Interaction Design (IxD) defines the structure and behaviour of interactive systems. Interaction designers strive to create meaningful relationships between people and the products and services that they use, from computers to mobile devices, to appliances and beyond*" [27]. This definition is really clear about the role and importance of Interaction Design, and the role of creating a meaningful interaction that will positively affect the experience and, in a broader sense, the users' lifestyle. Besides, the last word "*beyond*" underlines the importance several dimensions in the development of any kind of artefact, current or future, physical or digital, tangible or intangible: the human dimension, the artifact dimension, and above all the dimensions of relationship and of interaction, and the related experience.

Regarding the human dimension, to proper develop a new product, service or system that answers, and fits users' needs and expectations, it's fundamental to identify the people who are relevant and meaningful to the use of products. There are different words that defines these people: *users, consumers, customers*, up to the most recent *prosumers*—a definition that is between the producer (who produces the good or service), and consumer (who uses the good or service) [28]. Adopting a Human-Centred approach, we acknowledge that it is necessary to define a target population of users, meaning all those who have an interest and a direct or indirect relationship with the product, in its different phases of ideation, production, use and consumption and disposal; according to this view, we have to consider all the stakeholders. Adopting Ergonomics and Human Factors methods, users must be characterised from a physical and cognitive point of view, as well as from a social and relational, cultural, contextual, etc. one [6, 8]. From this identification and analysis phase, the explicit, tacit and latent needs of the target population are gathered. In Nestore, we refer to a specific category of users, the elderly, who are changing (and often worsening) their physical and cognitive condition, affecting their health, social and relational spheres. Besides, Nestore proposes a coaching service that makes use of technological and interactive objects and systems, through innovative interaction channels (e.g., voice interaction), which these people have probably never used, and which they do not yet have the tools, language and experience to understand and use.

Regarding the artefact dimension, its requirements are defined both from the identification and analysis of the target users' needs, and from the opportunities given by the market and the technologies [29]. These artefacts must be responsive from the point of view of functionality, usability and acceptability, and ultimately from the interaction and experience they offer.

Regarding the interaction dimension, the world of artefacts is evolving on different levels. Firstly, the interaction channels between human and object are increasing, from tactile and haptic to vocal and gestural. This implies the creation of new languages, which have to be learnt, recognised and shared by both humans and machines. We can consider the voice interfaces, such as the one designed for the Tangible of Nestore or other commercial ones, such as the Amazon Alexa or Google Home Assistant. These products propose a spoken dialogue, based on a language that for humans is natural and ordinary, while for machines it is to be learnt and continuously adaptive. In this dialogue, this leads to basic misunderstandings, possible frustrations, or to the fact that the user adapts his/her language to what the machine can understand, thus losing the naturalness of this possible interaction. It should be emphasised that, although the verbal language is the main mode of dialogue between human and human, it is different for the interaction between human and machine: we have always related through other channels, mainly the tactile one (to provide input), the visual one or the auditory one (to collect feedback); the users' experience can therefore condition the acceptability of the interaction and the channel used by these objects.

A second level is the direction of the interaction. Again, users have a layered experience of an interaction that begins with humans (e.g., typing a command, touching an interface, etc.) and then the machine responses, through different channels and feedback. The direction of interaction is changing, and nowadays objects are becoming conversational, that means they actively interact with the user, sometimes starting the dialogue. We are surrounded by such kind of artefacts and interactions, such as Apps and their notification strategies, smart objects that acquire information about our habits and behaviours and offer us new customised services and experiences.

The pervasiveness of technological devices, the use of new channels of interaction between user and artefact, the interaction that becomes a conversation, are all aspects that must be designed and evaluated, so that the user has a positive experience [30]. The designer has to manage the complexity of these artefacts, always taking into account the characteristics, needs and requirements of the users who will use them. To do this, it is useful to involve users in the entire design process. This means the adoption of a Human-Centred approach to the design of these artefacts [8, 9]. This design process shows us four distinct phases or activities that must be carried out to arrive at the definition of a system, product or service that is satisfactory to the end-user. First, the understanding of the context of use, which derives from the analysis of the user (i.e., from the understanding and identification of his physical, demographic, social, cultural, environmental, contextual characteristics, etc.), of the activities he/she performs, and finally of the environment in which he/she is located (understood as the spatial, physical, social, cultural and organisational environment).

This phase is followed by the definition of user requirements, based on the identification of the user's needs, necessities, ambitions and expectations. These requirements are necessary to develop an artefact that will be adequate to the user's needs and expectations. Besides, these requirements are strictly linked to the entire product life cycle, covering the phases of conception, production, purchase, use, management and maintenance, and finally disposal.

The third phase is the conception and development of design solutions that meet user and product requirements. In this phase, prototypes and mock-ups are made, which become increasingly faithful to what the final product will be.

This implementation and modification of the prototypes are connected to the fourth phase of the design process, where they are tested and evaluated together with the users. This last phase, the testing phase, is very important especially in the case of a project like Nestore; in this project, interactive, persuasive and technological systems, are proposed to users who are unfamiliar with this type of object and interaction, have a low level of digital literacy, as well as altered physical and cognitive capacities (e.g., lowered vision, reduced hearing, reduced motor skills), due to ageing. This phase of testing, collecting and analysing results is fundamental to understanding and improving the artefacts, interactions and user experiences that have been designed. These four phases are iterative and necessary to each other to develop systems, products and services that are functional, usable and acceptable, and that provide positive and satisfying user experiences.

3 Nestore Experience of Use

The Nestore project proposes the improvement or maintenance of functional health (defined as the ability to carry out daily activities independently) and the well-being of the person, through personalised e-coaching service. The Nestore Coach manifests itself through a set of devices that acquire physiological, behavioural, nutritional, social and environmental data (see other chapters of this book, such as Chap. 4, for more details). Data are analysed, processed and returned through information and suggestions for the user on how to behave to maintain or improve their state of health. In Nestore, health and wellbeing are considered in physical, cognitive, nutritional, and social and relational dimensions. For this reason, the e-coaching system proposes pathways of interest, related to these specific dimensions of health, which are tailored to the user's abilities and needs, and which he/she can decide to follow voluntarily.

Both in its physical and tangible dimension and in its digital and non-tangible one, the Nestore system is pervasive in the life of the people who will use it. Its pervasiveness does not necessarily imply a negative reading or the intrusiveness of the system in people's lives; precisely to avoid this, the system was codesigned together with the users from the initial stages of the project.

As stated above, in Nestore the users were not only considered as the final users of the system; we have considered as users all those who enter into a direct or indirect relationship with the system, in all phases of the processes of conception, production, use and disposal of the product: they were actively involved in the entire design process. Through participatory observation and the use of interviews, the project team approached people's life and experiences, understanding and learning from their experiences and points of view. A collaborative design process was adopted, in which users were actively involved, sharing their knowledge and experience, and contributing to the design of innovative ideas and solutions. For the Nestore project team, this meant benefiting from the direct experience of the user to understand the context of use and the scope of the project. Codesign turns out to be a necessary methodology if we want to adopt a design approach that is Human Centred, namely that understands people's needs promptly, and responds through the creation of a physical or digital, tangible or intangible artefact that is functional, usable and offers a satisfactory user experience. In fact, through a series of focus groups, held in different European countries, the needs and requirements of the users themselves were identified and the requirements of the whole system were defined. For example, regarding the development of the Nestore Tangible and the Nestore Wearable device, several workshops and codesign sessions were organised to define the formal aspects of the two objects (e.g., the shape of the Tangible, or the presence or absence of the screen on the Wearable device), and the possible interactions with these two objects (e.g., designing and evaluating the vocal and visual interaction with the Tangible, and the haptic and visual interaction with the Wearable wristband). Moreover, the evolutions and developments of the system components were periodically presented to the users, to have direct feedback, useful for the implementation of the system itself. Finally, thanks to a Pilot Study, the system was tested by the first group of approximately 60 users (20 users from Italy, Spain and the Netherlands) for an extended period of 12 weeks. This period is necessary to test the system in a real context, with real users, to highlight possible criticalities related to functional aspects, usability, satisfaction and user experience.

In the following section, we present the integrated methodology and framework that was defined and used to evaluate the usability and acceptability of the systems. Besides, we have focused on the user experience and on the relationship that users have had while testing and interacting with the Nestore. We've adopted an integrated approach, using both qualitative and quantitative tools, to measure the entire experience of use.

4 Integrated Framework for the Evaluating Nestore Experience of Use

Usability, Acceptance and User Experience Evaluation has been designed for the Nestore System including also the perspective of the methodology and tools adopted to estimate if, how and how much the Nestore system and its single components (i.e.,

Tangible, Wearable, App, and the System as a whole) meet the users' expectations in terms of usability, ease of use, acceptance and engagement, and overall user experience.

To properly develop, evaluate and improve the components of the Nestore System, an iterative evaluation was designed and performed: at different stages of the pilot (e.g., at the installation, during the pilot and at the final stage), the users were asked to give feedbacks about their experience with Nestore. This evaluation was useful to understand the users' perception about the system and to iterative refine and implement the system accordingly to the users' needs and expectations [7]. During the pilot, this process means determining if the Nestore components and the whole system meets specific goals in terms of performance and users' satisfaction and to evaluate their long-term usability and acceptance level (summative evaluation process). The evaluation framework consists of a series of standardised, literature-validated tests used to assess usability, acceptability, and user experience; to these, some open-ended questions are included, allowing the user to give their feedback. Besides, some tasks were defined to evaluate the effectiveness and the efficiency of the communication and interaction with the different components (e.g., the use of LEDs lights in the Tangible, to give feedback about its status). These tasks were also used to let the users familiarise with the system.

It should be emphasised that the elements tested during the pilot were in a development stage or prototypes (items still in their iterative development and refinement phase); they were not products ready for the market. This means that the evaluation framework was fitted to every component's development stage in terms of software, hardware and integration within the system.

Usability was evaluated according to the International Standards and to the use of validated methods and tools, such as the SUS and the TAM surveys. According to the International Standard, usability can be defined as the "*extent to which a system, product or service can be used by specified users to achieve specific goals with effectiveness, efficiency and satisfaction in a specified context of use*" [7]. It deals with the interaction between a user (or a group of users) and an object of interest, that can be a product, a system or service.

According to Davis [10, 11], acceptance can be defined with two variables that influence products or systems use: perceived usefulness and perceived ease of use. Perceived usefulness can be defined as "*the degree to which a person believes that using a particular product or system would enhance his or her job performance*"; Perceived ease of use is defined as "*the degree to which a person believes that using a particular product or system would be free of effort*" [10, 11].

To measure Nestore components' usability, its effectiveness and efficacy, a set of standard daily activities and actions were defined. These activities were performed by the users at different stages of the pilot studies. These stages were: set-up and first use of the components/system, daily use, and extended use. The identification of these activities was linked to an overall understanding of the interface, the interactions, and the functionality of the single components and the system as a whole.

Concerning the tangible, how the object communicates was investigated, using both voice interface and visual feedback (i.e., the change in colour, intensity and pattern of LEDs, used to communicate whether the system is listening, thinking, charged or needs charging). Concerning the wearable, both aspects related to the interface (e.g., the comprehensibility of the chosen icons, the presentation of data on the achieved results) and the interaction modes (e.g., touching the screen or moving the wrist, to switch on the display) were investigated.

The comprehensibility and usability of the interfaces and the architecture of Coach App and Pocket Odyssey were investigated, through the definition of activities to be performed by the user. The functioning of these Apps was presented through a tutorial; one of the aspects investigated through this test was the visibility, recognisability and comprehension of icons and commands.

The results of these activities were deduced both from the system use data and from the answers provided by the users.

Regarding satisfaction and acceptance, a single joint survey has been adopted, integrating the SUS [9, 10] and the TAM [11–13] surveys. The SUS survey measures the satisfaction of users while interacting with products, services and systems; it is widespread because, on one hand, it can be customized and used for a wide range of products, services and systems, and, on the other hand, it is easy to manage, that means good reliability and validity measures, and solid benchmarks to aid in the interpretation of scores. On its base version, it is a 10-questions survey, to be filled in using a Likert scale approach or a Smiley scale. The scale measures the different degree of satisfaction, from strong disagreement to strong agreement.

The TAM survey theorizes that an individual's behavioural intention to accept and use a product, service or system is determined by two beliefs: perceived usefulness and perceived ease of use. To investigate and measure both these values, some questions can be defined, be filled in using a Likert scale approach or a Smiley Scale. Like the SUS survey, the scale measures a different degree of satisfaction.

To ease filling in the integrated questionnaire and make the response more immediate, a Smiley Scale was adopted.

Analysing both surveys and the questions proposed, we noticed a slight overlap; therefore, in order to avoid an overload of questions to the users, we decided to merge the two surveys, and to have a single one, consisting of 13 close-ended questions. These are shown in the Table 1. Regarding the results, we had multiple outputs, at different stages of the pilot (i.e., at the beginning of the pilot, after the user has familiarized with the system, and at the end of the pilot, when the user has expressed an overall evaluation of the system). In the survey described in Table 1, we can distinguish the satisfaction results from the acceptance results (9 questions for satisfaction and 4 for acceptance—the fourth question relates to both evaluations).

As mentioned earlier in this chapter, in a market oversaturated with supply such as the current one, users expect products, systems and services that go beyond the concepts of functionality and usability. These are two values that are indeed expected, but we also need to pay attention that they can fail in ensuring the success—especially in terms of adoption and use in the medium and long term—of these artifacts, even in the field of health and personal care, where the benefit of use should itself be a value perceived by the user [25, 30–32]. For this reason, designers are asked to introduce also the pleasantness of products, that allows to consider the new interactions and

Table 1 The survey defined for analysing the usability and acceptance of Nestore system, based on SUS and TAM surveys. In the protocol, the term system was replaced with Nestore Tangible, Wearable, Coach App, and Pocket Odyssey

SUS—TAM survey	
Satisfaction	I think that I would like to use *the system* frequently
	I found *the system* unnecessarily complex
	I thought *the system* was easy to use
	I think that I would need the support of a technical person to be able to use *the system*
	I found the various functions in *the system* were well-integrated
	I thought there was too much inconsistency in *the system*
	I would imagine that most people would learn to use *the system* very quickly
	I find *the system* very awkward to use
	I feel very confident using *the system*
Acceptance	I needed to learn a lot of things before I could get going with *the system*
	I find *the system* easy to use
	Using *the system* to help me maintain and improve my mental well-being is a good idea
	Using *the system* is beneficial to improve my overall wellbeing

user experiences [19, 25]. The International Standard defines user experience as "*person's perceptions and responses resulting from the use and/or anticipated use of a product, system or service*" [8]. The user experience is subjective and focuses on the act of use. In HCI, as technology becomes more pervasive and present in products, it is necessary to consider that they become not only more useful and usable, but that they embody factors that enhance aesthetic, hedonic, persuasive aspects, to design a user experience that involves all these different levels [18, 21]. Due to its subjective and contextual nature, it is very difficult to quantitatively measure the user experience arising from short, medium and long-term interaction with a product, service or system, especially for interactive ones. Usability and acceptance surveys (e.g., SUS and TAM) are not developed to provide detailed insights and feedbacks of some aspects that are fundamental to a person's overall impressions concerning the user experience, such as the product hedonic features. There are several surveys, validated in the literature, which make possible this transition from experiential and subjective data to more quantitative and objective data. For our evaluation, we used questionnaires specifically designed to measure the user experience, such as the UEQ [13–15]. To investigate the interaction with Nestore Coach—considering both the various channels (e.g., voice and visual), and the various objects (e.g., tangible, wearable, App)—some questionnaires concerning engagement and friendship were adapted. The results of these activities were deduced both from the system use data and from the answers provided by the users.

The UEQ served to get data from the overall user's perception, addressing both usability and hedonic dimensions. The UEQ survey consists of 6 domains:

- Attractiveness, that is related to the overall impression that users had about the product;
- Perspicuity, that is related to the ease of understanding and recalling the use of a product;
- Efficiency, that is related to the effort and consumption of resources (e.g., physical, cognitive, time-based, economic, etc.) spent in interacting with and using the product;
- Dependability, that is related to the extent to which the user is or perceives him/herself to be in control while interacting with the product;
- Stimulation, that is related to the excitement and motivation to use the product;
- Novelty, that is related to the degree of innovation and creativity of the product.

Attractiveness is a valence dimension (emotional reaction on acceptance/rejection dimension). Perspicuity, Efficiency, and Dependability are pragmatic quality aspects; Stimulation and Novelty are hedonic quality aspects. Table 2 reports the questions used to evaluate these 6 dimensions, using a 5-points Likert scale, from completely disagree to completely agree,

These six domains are investigated through a questionnaire consisting of twenty-six close-ended questions, namely a pair of terms with opposite meanings; users rate each item on a 7-point Likert scale. These 26 pair of terms are listed in the Table 3.

As mentioned, the Nestore coach is not a single product but manifests itself through different objects and makes use of different communication channels. The Nestore Coach introduces itself and interacts with the users as if it is a friend, a companion, a kind of gentle counsellor who proposes suggestions and activities to carry out to the users, to maintain their well-being in the different domains (physical, cognitive, social and nutritional). The novelty of the Nestore Coach is also in the way it interacts and relates with the elderly person. Both physical and digital interfaces have been designed: the Nestore Coach communicates to its user through

Table 2 The UEQ survey domains

UEQ dimensions	Question
Attractiveness	Nestore *Tangible/Wearable/Coach App/Pocket Odyssey* looks attractive, enjoyable, friendly and pleasant
Efficiency	I perform my tasks with Nestore *Tangible/Wearable/Coach App/Pocket Odyssey* fast, efficient and in a pragmatic way
Perspicuity	Nestore *Tangible/Wearable/Coach App/Pocket Odyssey* is easy to understand, clear, simple, and easy to learn
Dependability	The interaction with Nestore *Tangible/Wearable/Coach App/Pocket Odyssey* is predictable, secure and meets my expectations
Stimulation	Using Nestore *Tangible/Wearable/Coach App/Pocket Odyssey* is interesting, exciting and motivating
Novelty	Nestore *Tangible/Wearable/Coach App/Pocket Odyssey* is innovative, inventive and creatively designed

Table 3 The UEQ survey attributes. A 7-points Likert scale was used was used to define the closeness of the user experience to the meaning of the word, between two with opposite meanings

First attribute	Second attribute
Annoying	Enjoyable
Not understandable	Understandable
Creative	Dull
Easy to learn	Difficult to learn
Valuable	Inferior
Boring	Exciting
Not interesting	Interesting
Unpredictable	Predictable
Fast	Slow
Inventive	Conventional
Obstructive	Supportive
Good	Bad
Complicated	Easy
Unlikable	Pleasing
Usual	Leading edge
Unpleasant	Pleasant
Secure	Not secure
Motivating	Demotivating
Meets expectations	Does not meet expectations
Inefficient	Efficient
Clear	Confusing
Impractical	Practical
Organized	Cluttered
Attractive	Unattractive
Friendly	Unfriendly
Conservative	Innovative

visual and tactile, and vocal interfaces. The latter mode of interaction is the most recent and most interesting one: the aim is to simplify and make more natural the interaction with technological tools through voice dialogue. In the case of Nestore, the aim was to simplify the relationship between user and coach, and also to create a more engaging experience. Involvement and emotional loyalty are the basis of any relationship process that can continue over time. This is also valid in the relationship between humans and technological systems. As mentioned, this represents an innovative channel of relationship and interaction, still under development. It is not the natural human-to-human interaction, neither in terms of language quality, nor in terms of dialogue modalities (including all the visual, auditory, proxemic, affective aspects that this kind of interaction can offer). For this reason, two experimental surveys were used, created to evaluate the interaction between man and machine, when this

Table 4 The survey defined for analysing the Companionship scale

Companionship scale
My *Nestore Coach* provides me with companionship
Having my *Nestore Coach* gives me something to care for
My *Nestore Coach* provides me with pleasurable activity
My *Nestore Coach* is a source of constancy in my life
My *Nestore Coach* makes me feel needed
My *Nestore Coach* makes me play and laugh
Having a *Nestore Coach* gives me something to love
I get comfort from interacting my *Nestore Coach*
I enjoy watching my *Nestore Coach*
My *Nestore Coach* makes me feel loved

takes place through non-traditional channels, such as voice, and to evaluate the relational and affective experience that could be generated between the subjects of the interaction. To design and iteratively evaluate this process of interaction, relationship and emotional experience, questionnaires such as the Companionship Scale [14–16] and Friendship Scale [17–19] were selected and adapted.

The Companionship scale was defined based on other experiences in assessing the interaction between humans and digital artefacts, such as electronic and digital pets, and voice interfaces. Users had to answer 11 closed-ended questions, using a Likert scale to indicate their degree of agreement or disagreement with each one of the proposed sentences. The questions are presented in Table 4 and explore the affective and the relationship between the user and the Nestore Coach.

Since the Social domain is one of the areas of intervention of Nestore, at the end of the pilot, we proposed a test assessing social isolation and its opposite, social connection. Social isolation refers to living without companionship, social support or social connectedness. One of the Nestore aims is to strengthen the user's network of relatives and friends, since the social domain is really important in supporting active ageing. In our case, social isolation and connection are intended to measure the impact that Nestore has both in the relationship between the user and the Coach, and in the interaction with other users of the Nestore network. The questionnaire, presented in Table 5, is called Friendship scale, and proposes 6 close-ended questions, to define the degree of agreement or disagreement with the sentence. To answer, there is a 5-points Likert scale, related to time (1. Almost Always, 2. Most of the time, 3. About half the time, 4. Occasionally, 5. Not at all).

5 Conclusions

The evaluation of novel technologies has required an evolution of the evaluation methods and tools to be adopted for evaluating the user experience of complex

Table 5 The Friendship scale survey, to explore the Nestore Coach experience

Friendship scale (during the past weeks, ...)
It has been easy to relate to the *Nestore Coach*
I felt isolated from the *Nestore Coach*
I had the *Nestore Coach* to share my feelings with
I found it easy to get in touch with the *Nestore Coach* when I needed to
When with other people, I felt separate from the *Nestore Coach*
I felt alone and friendless without the *Nestore Coach*

multi-object and multimodal systems like the Nestore Coach. This integrated set of questionnaires and activities was defined to assess the usability, acceptability, interactions and user experience during the first testing phase of the Nestore system in a real, everyday environment and context.

The questionnaires based on SUS and TAM, and the UEQ survey, have been used for all the components of the Nestore system (i.e., Tangible, Wearable, Coach App, Social Platform, Pocket Odyssey, and the system as a whole), and users have been asked to answer in two stages: a few days after the beginning of the Pilot and at the end of it. In this way, it is also possible to compare the responses of individual users during time, to verify the possible changes in their evaluation of the components and of the overall system.

The Companion Scale and the Friendship scale are used only for the final evaluation, to understand the relationship that was created between the user and the Nestore Coach, given the type of innovative interaction proposed to the users.

This integrated approach of qualitative and quantitative methods, to measure the different dimensions of the interaction between the user and technological and digital devices and services, is essential to assess the overall user experience. The user experience cannot be subdivided into single domains (usability, acceptability, satisfaction, pleasantness, companionship), since each one influences the others. Especially in the case of users such as those involved in Nestore, while using innovative and complex systems, it is necessary to make this kind of assessment, mainly in the development and implementation phases of the system. This integrated approach, in addition to evaluating the system and its components, was useful to measure the impact of the project on people's daily life, in the different domains of the intervention of Nestore.

Due to the Covid-19 pandemic, all questionnaires were edited, delivered and answered in digital format.

References

1. Angelini, L., Mugellini, E., Khaled, O. A., Röcke, C., Guye, S., Porcelli, S., et al. (2019). The NESTORE e-coach: Accompanying older adults through a personalized pathway to wellbeing.

In *Proceedings of the 12th ACM International Conference on Pervasive Technologies Related to Assistive Environments* (pp. 620–628).
2. Ku, B., & Lupton, E. (2020). *Health design thinking: Creating products and services for better health.* MIT Press.
3. ISO. (2006). 20282-1:2006. *Ease of operation of everyday products. Design requirements for context of use and user characteristics.* International Organization for Standardization: Geneva, Switzerland.
4. ISO. (2013). 20282-2:2013. *Usability of consumer products and products for public use. Summative test method.* International Organization for Standardization: Geneva, Switzerland.
5. ISO. (2002). 16982:2002. *Ergonomics of human-system interaction. Usability methods supporting human-centred design.* International Organization for Standardization: Geneva, Switzerland.
6. ISO. (2011). 26800:2011: *Ergonomics—General approach, principles and concepts.* International Organization for Standardization: Geneva, Switzerland.
7. ISO. (2018). 9241–11:2018 *Ergonomics of human–system interaction. Part 11: Usability: Definitions and concepts.* International Organization for Standardization. Geneva, Switzerland.
8. ISO 9241–210:2019. *Ergonomics of human–system interaction. Part 210: Human–centred design for interactive systems.* International Organization for Standardization. Geneva, Switzerland.
9. Brooke, J. (1996). SUS: A "quick and dirty" usability scale. In P. W. Jordan, B. Thomas, B. A. Weerdmeester, & A. L. McClelland (Eds.), *Usability evaluation in industry.* London: Taylor and Francis.
10. Brooke, J. (2013). SUS: A retrospective. *Journal of Usability Studies, 8*(2), 29–40.
11. Davis, F. D. (1989). Perceived usefulness, perceived ease of use, and user acceptance of information technology. *MIS Quarterly*, 319–340.
12. Davis, F. D., Bagozzi, R. P., & Warshaw, P. R. (1989). User acceptance of computer technology: A comparison of two theoretical models. *Management Science, 35*(8), 982–1003.
13. Venkatesh, V., & Davis, F. D. (2000). A theoretical extension of the technology acceptance model: Four longitudinal field studies. *Management Science, 46*(2), 186–204.
14. Laugwitz, B., Held, T., & Schrepp, M. (2008, November). Construction and evaluation of a user experience questionnaire. In *Symposium of the Austrian HCI and Usability Engineering Group* (pp. 63–76). Berlin, Heidelberg: Springer.
15. Schrepp, M., Hinderks, A., & Thomaschewski, J. (2017). Design and evaluation of a short version of the user experience questionnaire (UEQ-S). *Ijimai, 4*(6), 103–108.
16. Schrepp, M., Hinderks, A., & Thomaschewski, J. (2017). Construction of a benchmark for the user experience questionnaire (UEQ). *IJIMAI, 4*(4), 40–44.
17. Lawson, S., & Chesney, T. (2007). *The impact of owner age on companionship with virtual pets.*
18. Luh, D. B., Li, E. C., & Gao, Y. R. (2010). The study on companionship scale of electronic pet. In *2010 IEEE 11th International Conference on Computer-Aided Industrial Design & Conceptual Design 1* (Vol. 1, pp. 533–538). IEEE.
19. Hawthorne, G. (2006). Measuring social isolation in older adults: Development and initial validation of the friendship scale. *Social Indicators Research, 77*(3), 521–548.
20. Hassenzahl, M. (2013). User experience and experience design. *The Encyclopedia of Human-Computer Interaction, 2.*
21. Newbery, P., & Farnham, K. (2013). *Experience design: A framework for integrating brand, experience, and value.* Wiley.
22. IDEO. (2015). *The field guide to human–centered design.*
23. Papanek, V., & Fuller, R. B. (1972). *Design for the real world*. London: Thames and Hudson.
24. Hassenzahl, M., Platz, A., Burmester, M., & Lehner, K. (2000). Hedonic and ergonomic quality aspects determine a software's appeal. In *Proceedings of the CHI 2000 Conference on Human Factors in Computer Systems.* New York, NY: ACM Press.
25. Norman, D. A. (2002). *The design of everyday things.* New York, NY: Basic Books.

26. Green, W. S., & Jordan, P. W. (Eds.). (2002). *Pleasure with products: Beyond usability*. CRC Press.
27. Soegaard, M., & Dam, R. F. (2012). The encyclopedia of human-computer interaction. *The encyclopedia of human-computer interaction.*
28. Pizzocaro, S. (2015). *Introduzione agli studi sull'utente. Conoscere gli utenti tra ricerca e design dei prodotti.* Edizioni Unicopli, Milano.
29. Pugh, S. (1990). *Integrated methods for successful product engineering*. Addison-Wesley.
30. Neely, S., et al. (2008). Evaluating pervasive and ubiquitous systems. *IEEE Pervasive Computing, 7,* 85–88.
31. Maslow, A. H. (1954). *Motivation and personality*. New York: Harper & Brothers.
32. Jordan, P. W. (1998). *An introduction to usability*. London, UK: Taylor & Francis.

SROI Methods for Impact Assessment in Economy of Wellbeing

E. Lettieri, C. Biasin, A. Selva, L. Isella, R. Onofrio, and P. Bertelè

Abstract Population ageing represents one of the major challenges that contemporary society is going to face in the coming years. This phenomenon is putting high pressure on the healthcare system and makes it necessary to identify specific instruments ensuring to live longer in healthy conditions, concept also referred to as healthy ageing. In this view, the European NESTORE H2020 project is a multi-dimensional and personalized virtual coaching technology for the enhancement of people's well-being and quality of life after their 65. However, the assessment of health promotion strategies like NESTORE is a thorny issue, being the benefits achieved in the long-term as a result of investments incurred for many years. Decision-makers need methodologies that show that what is invested today will pay back through the saving generated in the long-term. Traditionally, cost-benefit analysis (CBA) is employed: however, CBA has historically been under discussion. In recent times, social return on investment (SROI) methodology has been promoted as a more 'holistic' approach for demonstrating value-for-money of initiatives. Given the lack of evidence concerning SROI analysis of technologies, the authors developed and validated a model to perform a SROI analysis when evaluating innovative technologies promoting healthy ageing. To address the research question, an inductive approach has been employed, selecting as a starting point the real case of NESTORE, under the assumption of its future implementation in the Lombardy Region, in the autonomous community of Catalonia and in the province of South Holland. SROI for NESTORE has been defined involving as stakeholders the healthcare systems of the areas under consideration, beneficiaries (senior adults in health between 40 and 79 years) living in the three areas, the economic system and beneficiaries' familiar caregivers. In all the three areas analysed, the SROI ratios (calculated over a time horizon of 10 years) are higher than 1; therefore, the project results to be value-for-money. The result has been validated by NESTORE Consortium itself. This study contributes to the existing literature on the SROI, confirming that there is room for its application when dealing with healthcare technologies. In addition, it represents a useful aid for NESTORE decision-makers and distributors, supporting them in the definition of a suitable and detailed exploitation strategy for the initiative.

E. Lettieri (✉) · C. Biasin · A. Selva · L. Isella · R. Onofrio · P. Bertelè
Department. of Management, Politecnico di Milano, Piazza Leonardo da Vinci 32, Milan, Italy
e-mail: Emanuele.lettieri@polimi.it

G. Andreoni and C. Mambretti (eds.), *Digital Health Technology for Better Aging*, Research for Development, https://doi.org/10.1007/978-3-030-72663-8_15

Keywords Cost-benefit analysis · Social return on investment · Virtual coaching · Healthy ageing

1 Introduction

The increasingly urgent social phenomenon known as population ageing implies a reduction in the number of economically active people per pensioner, thereby putting more pressure on the healthcare system [21]. Therefore, for the coming decades, there is a societal goal to maximize the number of people who remain healthier and independent for longer [76]. This phenomenon is frequently referred to as "**healthy ageing**".

To face the challenge, we are assisting in a high-pace proposal for technologies aimed at promoting healthy ageing. Amongst them, **NESTORE**, a project funded by the European Union Horizon 2020 Research and Innovation Programme, is a multi-dimensional and personalized virtual coaching technology for the enhancement of people's well-being and quality of life after their 65.

Budget constraints require to identify **proper methods to support decision-makers in assessing the proposed technologies and selecting those to implement** [31]. Traditionally, value-for-money of technologies in healthcare has been assessed through cost-effectiveness, cost-utility and cost-benefit analyses.

Cost-Benefit Analysis (CBA), in detail, measures the ratio between the economic consequences of a project (benefits and losses) and the costs incurred to realize such project. However, CBA has been historically criticized: it evaluates costs and benefits from a **single perspective** (usually the one of the payer), neglecting comprehensive contributions from the complex network of actors that initiatives in healthcare typically involve [2, 59, 60].

In recent times, **Social Return On Investment (SROI)** approach has emerged: the underpinning idea is that investments should not only look at what pecuniary value they produce as direct shareholder value, but they should also include a wider range of benefits, from the view of multiple stakeholders, including the social and environmental dimensions besides the economic one [4, 27, 45].

Table 1 summarizes the main points emerged from the literature analysis on CBA and SROI in healthcare and offers a direct comparison of the two methods.

2 Methodology for the Calculation of SROI of Virtual Coaches Fostering Healthy Ageing

A standard and generally accepted framework to assess healthcare technologies through SROI does not exist. The authors adapted the framework proposed by Nicholls et al. [47] to calculate the SROI targeting virtual coaching technologies

Table 1 Comparison between CBA and SROI

Topic	CBA	SROI
Perspectives involved	Typically, point of view of **one single stakeholder** involved in the project: the healthcare system or patients	**Multiple stakeholders'** perspectives (beneficiaries, promoters and implementers, third parties)
Cost/input items involved	Different cost items are considered, according to the perspective adopted and the subjects assessed (cost items involved are only those related to the actor whose perspective is assumed)	The input items involved become more exhaustive as the analysis shifts from mere beneficiaries' involvement to promoter and implementers' and third parties' involvement
Benefit/outcome items involved	The considered outcomes are independent of the subject assessed. They are different according to perspective adopted (the benefit items involved are only those related to the actor whose perspective is assumed). The focus of CBA is mainly **on economic outcomes**	The outcome items involved become more exhaustive as the analysis shifts from mere beneficiaries' involvement to promoter and implementers' and third parties' involvement. Not only **economic outcomes** are considered, but also **social outcomes**
Benefit/outcome items monetization	Controversial. Authors **avoid monetizing outcomes not quantifiable as cost savings**	Easily enabled by proper **financial proxies**. (using also methods such as Willingness To Pay and Human Capital)

fostering healthy ageing and then applied it to the real case of NESTORE. The adapted framework is made up of five steps:

1. **Establishing scope and identifying key stakeholders**

Establishing the scope of analysis means defining the boundaries of analysis. The authors assumed that NESTORE is configured as a closed system (not integrated with other devices) and distributed and paid by the healthcare system as a medical device. The authors performed a prospective analysis under the hypothesis to distribute NESTORE among 40–79 individuals in health (not affected by chronic diseases), living in the Lombardy Region (Italy), in the autonomous community of Catalonia (Spain) and in the province of South Holland (the Netherlands) and willing to adopt a virtual coach. The next step is to identify the stakeholders, namely those people or organizations that affect or are affected by the initiative, either positively or negatively. The considered stakeholders are:

- **Beneficiaries**, namely the target of the virtual coach. They are the individuals in health between 40 and 79 years, living in the areas under consideration, and willing to adopt the virtual coach. More in detail, the adoption of a healthy ageing paths results in the reduced risk of morbidity of six morbidities: hypertension [36]; type 2 diabetes mellitus [36]; osteoporosis [35]; heart failure [35]; stroke [36]; alzheimer [58].

- **The Lombardian, Catalan, Southern-Dutch healthcare systems**, which benefit from the reduction in morbidity of beneficiaries thanks to the virtual coach, since the economic burden related to such morbidities is reduced. The healthcare system is the stakeholder in charge of distributing and paying for the virtual coach.
- **Beneficiaries' familiar caregivers** are those relatives of the beneficiaries that cover the role of caregivers. Therefore, the reduction in morbidity of beneficiaries prevents their relatives from becoming familiar caregivers and suffering from a deterioration of their own health state. This situation would allow them to get a job position since they are not totally devoted and absorbed by the caring activity. The authors considered only full-time familiar caregivers who are forced to leave their job for assisting their relatives: given the diseases on which healthy ageing practices can have a positive effect, stroke is the only morbidity requiring assistance from a full-time familiar caregiver [36].
- **Lombardian, Catalan, Southern-Dutch economic systems**, which include the companies where beneficiaries are employed as well as professional caregivers (professionals offering support, in exchange for a salary, to people that are not autonomous in their daily life). As for the companies, the reduction in beneficiaries' morbidity implies a diminished absence due to illness from the beneficiaries and avoidance of leaving job position from familiar caregivers. As for professional caregivers, the beneficiaries' morbidity reduction would result in their job destruction, negatively impacting the economy of caring services (also in this case stroke is considered the only disease among those selected requiring assistance from a full-time caregiver).

2. **Mapping outcomes**

Outcomes can be defined as positive and negative consequences of the project. In this step, it is necessary to identify the outcomes perceived by each stakeholder. Table 2 synthesizes the outcomes of virtual coaches for healthy ageing.

In this step it is also required to identify the inputs, that express what stakeholders are contributing in order to make the project possible. The healthcare systems of the three areas under consideration represent the only stakeholder in charge of providing NESTORE to the beneficiaries, paying for it: they will not go through any investment into fixed or intangible assets to provide NESTORE service. They will purchase all the elements needed to run the service (hardware, software, technical assistance, training courses) from external providers (identified by the consortium), on a monthly basis, simply paying for them to be provided to beneficiaries. In addition, the healthcare system will be in charge of paying a fee to GPs for each NESTORE prescription they realize.

Table 2 Outcomes per stakeholders

Stakeholder	Outcome	Rationale
Beneficiaries	**Reduced beneficiary's risk of diseases**	Morbidity reduction represents the major relevant outcome for senior adults in case of adoption of a virtual coach for healthy ageing
	Reduced beneficiaries' need for professional caregivers	Healthy ageing practices and the consequent reduction in beneficiaries' morbidity can lead to a reduced need for caregivers and, particularly, in a consistent fall in the number of employed professional caregivers. This would result in significant savings for the beneficiaries hiring them
Healthcare system	**Cost reduction due to reduced beneficiaries' morbidity**	Reduced beneficiaries' morbidity represents the major relevant outcome for the healthcare system in case of adoption of a virtual coach for healthy ageing, which leads to significant savings related to healthcare expenditures
	Cost reduction due to reduced familiar caregivers' morbidity	It is assumed that prevention technologies will also reduce the incidence of caregiving-related diseases resulting from lack of sleep, stress and heavy load handling, which leads to significant savings related to healthcare expenditures
Familiar caregivers	**Reduced beneficiaries' need for caring activity**	Healthy ageing practices and the consequent reduction in the morbidity can lead to a reduced need for caregivers. Therefore, virtual coaches prevent the relatives of beneficiaries from becoming familiar caregivers and from contracting caregiving-related diseases resulting from lack of sleep, stress and heavy load handling
Economic system	**Reduced beneficiaries' need for professional caregivers**	Healthy ageing practices and the consequent reduction in beneficiaries' morbidity can lead to a reduced need for caregivers and, particularly, in a consistent fall in the number of employed professional caregivers. This would result in a loss for the entire regional economic systems

(continued)

Table 2 (continued)

Stakeholder	Outcome	Rationale
	Reduced beneficiaries' work absence due to illness	The reduction in beneficiaries' morbidity implies reduced beneficiaries' work absence due to illness

3. **Evidencing outcomes (and inputs) and giving them a value**

Outcome indicators represent a preliminary step to monetize the identified outcomes: in fact, by multiplying each indicator value for its unitary monetary value, the monetary value for each corresponding outcome is obtained. To reach this purpose, financial proxies are used in SROI analysis to estimate the social value of non-traded goods. Sometimes monetization is a fairly straightforward process, other times monetization is harder. Table 3 synthesizes the indicators outlined for each outcome of NESTORE and the related value of the chosen financial proxies for each of the three areas under consideration. Given the prospective nature of the study, it was not possible to retrieve real data on field: therefore, indicators have been quantified by searching for quantitative studies on health and work consequences of healthy ageing paths for beneficiaries and familiar caregivers, as well as on costs for the healthcare system and enterprises.

Number of adults in health between 40 and 79 years old, willing to use the virtual coach: the indicator to measure such outcome corresponds to the number of beneficiaries, namely those people between 40 years and 79 years, who are in health and are interested in adopting the virtual coach in order to reduce the risk of contracting morbidities. In detail, data regarding 40–79 adults in health in the three areas were drafted from national databases [8, 29, 49–54]. The application of the Technology Acceptance Model to the case of a virtual coach for healthy ageing revealed an Intention To Use equal to 64.2% [67]. As a consequence, the authors applied a therapeutic adherence equal to 64.2% to compute the number of beneficiaries.

Reduction in the number of morbid beneficiaries: In order to calculate the reduction in the number of people contracting the considered morbidities thanks to the virtual coach, it was necessary to start from the epidemiology of such diseases in the areas under consideration. The epidemiology of the considered morbidities in Lombardy, Catalonia and South Holland has been calculated as the number of people currently affected by such diseases divided by the total number of inhabitants in the areas under consideration [28, 29, 39, 51–54, 61]. In order to estimate the probability for a healthy person to contract such morbidities during a year (without the adoption of virtual coah), to simplify the calculations, the age of 65 years old (the threshold between the two target groups included in the trial: 40–64 years and 65–79 years) has been considered as centroid age of analysis. In this way, it can be assumed that all beneficiaries are healthy people being 65 years old in the year $n = 0$ of analysis. In detail:

Table 3 Outcome indicators and values of the related financial proxies

Stakeholder	Outcome	Outcome indicator	Outcome financial proxy		Yearly value of outcome financial proxy		
					Lombardy	Catalonia	South Holland
Beneficiaries	Reduced beneficiary's risk of diseases	Number of adults in health between 40 and 79 years old, willing to use NESTORE	Willingness To Pay (estimated as the sum of annual cost of a gym membership and the annual cost of a nutritionist)		1,265 € [23]	1,061 € [11]	1,344 € [22, 68]
	Reduced beneficiaries' need for professional caregivers	Reduction in the number of employed professional caregivers	Cost saving equal to annual wage for a professional caregiver		17,940 € [5]	14,726 € [49]	18,808 € [40]
Healthcare system	Cost reduction due to reduced beneficiaries' morbidity	Reduction in the number of morbid beneficiaries	Cost saving equal to annual unitary disease cost for the healthcare system	Hypertension	864 € [12]	1,297 € [55]	234 € [67–74]
				Type 2 diabetes mellitus	1,300 € [12]	3,184 € [25]	1,349 € [67–74]
				Osteoporosis	900 € [12]	5,970 € [25]	235 € [67–74]

(continued)

Table 3 (continued)

Stakeholder	Outcome	Outcome indicator	Outcome financial proxy		Yearly value of outcome financial proxy		
					Lombardy	Catalonia	South Holland
	Cost reduction due to reduced familiar caregivers' morbidity	Reduction in the number of morbid familiar caregivers		Heart failure	1,500 € [12]	5,500 € [65]	3,370 € [67–74]
				Stroke	1,180 € [12]	4,351 € [25]	3,022 € [67–74]
				Alzheimer	4,269 € [12]	4,062 € [64]	33,704 € [67–74]
Familiar caregivers	Reduced beneficiaries' need for caring activity	Reduction in the number of needed familiar caregivers	Income increase equal to annual average wage	Women	32,255 € [20]	25,417 € [38]	33,792 € [10]
				Men		28,717 € [38]	
Economic system	(-) Reduced beneficiaries' need for professional caregivers	(-) Reduction in the number of employed professional caregivers	Economic loss equal to annual wage for a professional caregiver		−17,940 € [5]	−14,726 € [49]	−18,808 € [40]
	Reduced beneficiaries' work absence due to illness	Reduction in beneficiaries' annual work absence days	Cost saving equal to cost of a day of work absence (calculated as *annual average wage* * [(12 *months/year*)/(13 *paid months/year*)]/(220 *working days/year*)	Women	135 € [20]	107 € [38]	142 € [10]
				Men		120 € [38]	

- The probability to get morbidity between 65 and 79 years is obtained from the difference between the epidemiology of the morbidity at 80 + and the epidemiology of the morbidity at 40–64 years.
- The probability of morbidity between 65 and 79 years is assumed to be evenly distributed for each year of the 15 years of the range (from 65 to 79).

Therefore, the percentage of beneficiaries who get ill every year is computed as follows:

Probability of becoming affected by the morbidity during a certain year = Probability to get the morbidity between the 65 and 80 years old/15 years.

In order to quantify the risk reduction of contracting such morbidities thanks to the adoption of a virtual coach, the authors investigated the literature to outline how performing physical activity and having proper nutrition can reduce the risk of contracting each of the listed diseases respectively for women and men. The overall risk reduction was calculated as follows:

$Overall\ risk\ reduction = Risk_{\ Physical\ activity} + Risk_{\ Nutrition} - [Risk_{Physical\ activity} * Risk_{Nutrition}]$.

Table 4 shows the overall risk reduction thanks to the adoption of NESTORE for all the morbidities.

Afterwards, the probability of contracting each of the listed morbidities during a certain year with the adoption of the virtual coach is calculated as follows:

*Probability of contracting morbidities during a certain year with NESTORE = Probability of contracting morbidities during a certain year without virtual coach * (1 − overall risk reduction thanks to virtual coach).*

Table 4 Overall reduction in the risk of contracting morbidities thanks to te adoption of virtual coaches

	Risk reduction thanks to **physical activity**		Risk reduction thanks to proper **nutrition**		Overall risk reduction	
	Women (%)	Men (%)	Women (%)	Men (%)	Women (%)	Men (%)
Hypertension	15.0 [1]	14.0 [14]	18.0 [16]	18.0 [16]	30.3	29.5
Type 2 diabetes mellitus	30.0 [7]	11.0 [7]	40.0 [56]	16.0 [18]	58.0	25.2
Osteoporosis	36.0 [32]	12.0 [42]			36.0	12.0
Heart failure	25.0 [57]	25.0 [57]	24.0 [50]	24.0 [50]	43.0	43.0
Stroke	25.0 [36]	25.0 [36]	26.0 [24]	25.0 [24]	44.5	43.8
Alzheimer			36.0 [37]	36.0 [37]	36.0	36.0

Eventually, in order to calculate the actual reduction in the number people affected yearly by each of the selected morbidities thanks to the virtual coach, the following formula has been applied:

Reduction in the number of morbid beneficiaries = *Number of beneficiaries* * (*Probability of contracting morbidities during a certain year without virtual coah* – *Probability of contracting morbidities during a certain year with virtual coach*).

Reduction in the number of morbid familiar caregivers: as mentioned, among the selected morbidities, only stroke requires the presence of full-time assistance [36]. Firstly, the number of beneficiaries that each year requires a caregiver (without and with virtual coach) as a consequence of a stroke event is considered. Taking the aforementioned hypothesis that 100% of people that had a stroke event remains aid-dependent for the rest of their lives, the ratio morbid:caregiver is 1:1. In the case of NESTORE, the percentage of recourse to familiar caregivers by people affected by stroke, as well as the composition in age and gender of familiar caregivers in the three areas under consideration where retrieved by national databases and dedicated studies [8, 9, 29, 30, 61, 62].

The reduction in the number of familiar caregivers required every year by people suffering from stroke thanks to virtual coaches is calculated by multiplying the reduction in number of people affected by stroke and the percentage of recourse to familiar caregivers in the corresponding area. Literature reports the percentages of increase in morbidity as a consequence of being a caregiver (due to stress, lack of sleep or heavy load handling): 67% for the familiar caregivers of people affected by hypertension [26], 67% for type 2 diabetes mellitus [13], 26% for osteoporosis [66], 7% for heart failure [75], 24% for stroke [46], 34% for alzheimer [15]. Therefore, the probability for a caregiver to contract each of the considered morbidities is calculated as:

Probability for a caregiver to contract a morbidity = [(*Epidemiology women* 40–64 *years*) * (*% female caregivers* * *% caregivers between* 40–64 *years*) + (*Epidemiology women* 65–79 *years*) * (*% female caregivers* * *% caregivers between* 65–79 *years*) + (*Epidemiology men* 40–64 *years*) * (*% male caregivers* * *% caregivers between* 40–64 *years*) + (*Epidemiology men* 65–79 *years*) *(*% male caregivers* * *% caregivers between* 65–79 *years*)] * (1 + *Percentages of increase in morbidity as a consequence of being a caregiver*).

Eventually, the reduction in the number of morbid familiar caregivers is calculated by multiplying the reduction in the number of familiar caregivers and the probability for a caregiver to get each morbidity.

Reduction in the number of needed familiar caregivers: the calculation of the reduction in the number of familiar caregivers required yearly by people suffering from stroke thanks to NESTORE is the same reported for the outcome "reduction in the number of morbid familiar caregivers" of the healthcare system.

Reduction in the number of employed professional caregivers: as mentioned, it is assumed that 100% of the beneficiaries affected by stroke are in need of assistance from a full-time caregiver: those not resorting to familiar caregivers employ a professional caregiver. The percentage of recourse to professional caregivers is calculated as follows:

Percentage of recourse to professional caregivers = 1 − *Percentage of recourse to familiar caregivers.*

The reduction in the number of professional caregivers required every year by people suffering from stroke thanks to virtual coach is calculated by multiplying the reduction in number of people affected by stroke and the percentage of recourse to professional caregivers in the corresponding area.

Reduction in beneficiaries' annual work absence days: literature has been investigated to determine the average hospital length of stay that is usually required by each of the diseases impacted by virtual coaches: 6.9 days of work absences for those affected by hypertension, osteoporosis and Alzheimer [48], 7 days for type 2 diabetes mellitus [19], 7 days for heart failure [43] and 18.6 days for stroke [41]. Thanks to the adoption of virtual coaches, these absences may be avoided. The reduction in beneficiaries' annual work absence days is calculated by multiplying the reduction in the number of people affected yearly by each of the selected morbidities thanks to virtual coaches and the corresponding amount of days of work absence per year.

As for the input, the input indicator is represented by the number of beneficiaries, for each of whom the healthcare system incurs the costs of service and the fees to GPs. Such costs represent the financial proxy to monetize the input indicator. Since the NESTORE project is still in a development phase, the authors estimated the costs with NESTORE Consortium, considering an optimistic scenario where the yearly cost for implementing the project is equal to €600.

4. **Establishing impact**

This stage requires to account for how much of the outcomes would have happened anyway without the initiative and what proportion of the outcome can be isolated as being added by the analysed initiative. Therefore, four phenomena need to be quantified into percentages: *displacement* (how much of the outcome displaced other outcomes—e.g. reducing crime in one area may displace criminal activity to another area), *drop-off* (mitigation or decay of the outcomes over time), *deadweight* (amount of outcome that would have happened even if the initiative had not taken place), *attribution* (how much of the outcome was caused by the contribution of other organizations or people).

The authors assumed a value equal to **0% for displacement**: prevention paths for senior adults cannot result in worse health conditions for senior adults in adjacent regions or for those who are unwilling to join the NESTORE project. Analogously, **drop-off** value is assumed to be equal to **0%**: the authors assumed that the engagement encouraged by GPs results in an effective implementation of the project and resonance of its results along the whole selected time horizon. **Deadweight** is typically estimated through the creation of a control group. Therefore, the authors assumed a value equal to **0%**. However, the impossibility to estimate deadweight is involved as one of the limitations of the present research analysis. The authors considered an **attribution** equal to **95%** (5% outcome loss) for all outcomes (percentage of the outcome that is attributable to the NESTORE project itself). They assumed that only 5% of beneficiaries' morbidity reduction (and thus of all the outcomes it provokes) is caused by prevention interventions different from NESTORE. Such a low value is justified by the fact that beneficiaries involved in the analysis are individuals explicitly willing to adopt NESTORE.

5. **Calculating the SROI**

The Net Present Value (NPV) of the outcomes is calculated by adding up all the benefits and by subtracting any negative effect in different time periods through a discount rate. To calculate the actual impact of the initiative under analysis, it is necessary to deduct the four percentages previously calculated from the NPV of the outcomes. In the case of NESTORE, the NPV was computed on a time horizon of 10 years (i.e. the maximum time window allowing a complete overview of the benefits of NESTORE, without the risk of obsolescence of the technology) considering a cost of capital equal to 3.5% as HM Treasury [33] Green Book for public authorities recommends. Eventually, the SROI ratio is computed by dividing the NPV of the actual impact by the NPV of inputs.

3 Results

Table 5 synthesizes the calculation of the yearly value of the outcome indicators for each of the three areas under consideration. By multiplying the indicator values by the corresponding unitary financial proxies (Table 3), the monetization of each outcome item for a single year is obtained.

Eventually, Table 6 synthesizes the final value of each outcome, the total outcome, the impact, the input and the final computation of SROI.

4 Discussion

A first relevant conclusion is given by the fact that the SROI ratio assumes a final value higher than 1 in all the three areas under consideration: as a result, NESTORE is value-for-money.

Analysing the **contribution of stakeholders** to the total impact, it results that beneficiaries are the actors that benefit the most from the implementation of the project in each area under analysis (Table 7 and Fig. 1).

Moreover, exploring the contribution of each specific impact item (Fig. 2), it results that beneficiary's reduced morbidity (measured through Willingness to Pay) plays the most relevant role (Table 8).

Table 5 Yearly values of the outcome indicators of NESTORE in the areas under consideration

Stakeholder	Outcome	Outcome indicator		Yearly value of outcome indicator (*optimistic scenario of risk reduction*)		
				Lombardy	Catalonia	South Holland
Beneficiaries	Reduced beneficiary's risk of disease	**Number of adults in health between 40 and 79 years old, willing to use NESTORE**		1,713,672	2,357,268	651,080
	Reduced beneficiaries' need for professional caregivers	**Reduction in the number of employed professional caregivers**		32	420	575
Healthcare system	Cost reduction due to reduced beneficiaries' morbidity	**Reduction in the number of morbid beneficiaries suffering from**	**Hypertension**	6,208	17,820	5,906
			Type 2 diabetes mellitus	5,344	8,885	3,471
			Osteoporosis	11,956	3,843	1,778
			Heart failure	135	7,199	2,857
			Stroke	212	3,713	1,315
			Alzheimer	868	554	947
	Cost reduction due to reduced familiar caregivers' morbidity	**Reduction in the number of morbid familiar caregivers suffering from**	**Hypertension**	39	1,561	198
			Type 2 diabetes mellitus	13	495	82
			Osteoporosis	26	220	24
			Heart failure	1	165	7
			Stroke	1	60	10
			Alzheimer	1	5	2
Familiar caregivers	Reduced beneficiaries' need for caring activity	**Reduction in the number of needed familiar caregivers**	**Women**	81	1,696	331
			Men	99	1,597	409
Economic system	Reduced beneficiaries' need for professional caregivers	**(-) Reduction in the number of employed professional caregivers**		32	420	575
	Reduced beneficiaries' work absence due to illness	**Reduction in beneficiaries' annual work absence days**	**Women**	130,597	194,138	73,677
			Men	43,023	140,815	54,643

Table 6 Calculation of the SROI of NESTORE in the areas under consideration

			Lombardy	Catalonia	South Holland
N.P.V. of outcomes (time horizon 10 years)	Beneficiaries	Reduced beneficiary's risk of diseases	18,028,695,911.22 €	20,795,633,329.04 €	7,277,453,183.22 €
		Reduced beneficiaries' need for professional caregivers	24,740,579.56 €	268,615,466.54 €	469,557,836.51 €
	Healthcare System	Cost reduction due to reduced beneficiaries' morbidity	1,182,345,935.74 €	5,746,653,500.93 €	2,258,441,481.53 €
		Cost reduction due to reduced familiar caregivers' morbidity	829,212.53 €	67,854,708.09 €	2,929,943.16 €
	Familiar caregivers	Reduced beneficiaries' need for caring activity	252,064,765.74 €	3,859,563,883.23 €	1,084,676,483.82 €
	Enterprises	(-) Reduced beneficiaries' need for professional caregivers	−24,740,579.56 €	−268,615,466.54 €	−469,557,836.51 €
		Reduced beneficiaries' work absence due to illness	1,019,434,686.77 €	1,634,352,554.79 €	789,353,215.98 €
N.P.V. total outcome			20,483,370,511.99 €	32,104,057,976.08 €	11,412,854,307.71 €
N.P.V. total impact (attribution 95%)			**19,459,201,986.39 €**	**30,498,855,077.28 €**	**10,842,211,592.33 €**
N.P.V. total input			**8,551,160,115.99 €**	**11,762,679,585.79 €**	**3,248,863,028.23 €**
SROI (NPV impact/NPV input)			**2.28**	**2.59**	**3.34**

Table 7 Impact per stakeholder

	Lombardy	Catalonia	South Holland
Beneficiaries	€ 17,150,764,666	€ 20,011,036,356	€ 7359,660,469
Healthcare System	€ 1,124,016,391	€ 5,523,782,799	€ 2,148,302,853
Familiar caregivers	€ 239,461,527	€ 3,666,585,689	€ 1,030,442,660
Enterprises	€ 944,959,402	€ 1,297,450,234	€ 303,805,610

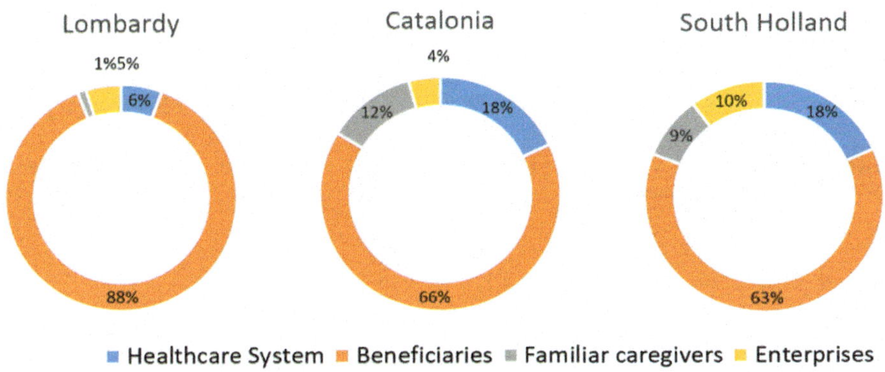

Fig. 1 Impact per stakeholder

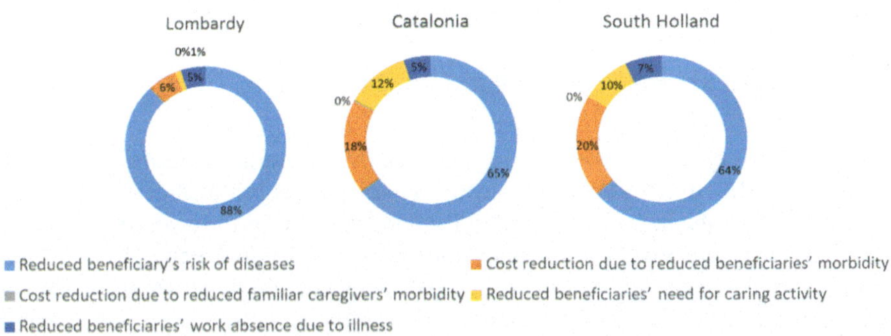

Fig. 2 Contribution of each impact item on the overall impact

This result is particularly relevant since it outlines the contribution that a SROI analysis can bring to the evaluation of a project, especially when compared to the traditional CBA method. In fact, CBA, performed involving only the outcomes and inputs related to the payer of the project's perspective, the healthcare system, would have neglected the role of beneficiaries, thus leading to the following results (Table 9).

The CBA on NESTORE provides a result that is lower than 1 in all the three areas considered. Differently from SROI, according to the CBA the NESTORE project is not value-for-money.

Table 8 Contribution of each impact item

Impact item	Contribution of each impact item		
	Lombardy	Catalonia	South Holland
Reduced beneficiary's risk of diseases	18,028,695,911.22 €	20,795,633,329.04 €	7,277,453,183.22 €
Cost reduction due to reduced beneficiaries' morbidity	1,182,345,935.74 €	5,746,653,500.93 €	2,258,441,481.53 €
Cost reduction due to reduced familiar caregivers' morbidity	829,212.53 €	67,854,708.09 €	2,929,943.16 €
Reduced beneficiaries' need for caring activity	252,064,765.74 €	3,859,563,883.23 €	1,084,676,483.82 €
Reduced beneficiaries' work absence due to illness	1,019,434,686.77 €	1,634,352,554.79 €	789,353,215.98 €

Table 9 Cost-benefit analysis of NESTORE

	Lombardy	Catalonia	South Holland
Benefits for the healthcare system	1,124,016,391 €	5,523,782,799 €	2,148,302,853 €
Costs incurred by the healthcare system	8,551,160,116 €	11,762,679,586 €	3,248,863,028 €
CBA ratio	**0.13**	**0.47**	**0.66**

5 Theoretical and Managerial Contribution

In terms of theory, the current study represents a **first attempt to create a replicable standard of the SROI model** to evaluate technologies in healthcare.

In fact, given the lack of a structured framework of SROI for assessing technologies, the developed model has defined a standard, easily replicable for the assessment of technologies fostering healthy ageing, for the evaluation of economic and social outcomes related to preventive initiatives and for the straightforward monetization of social outcomes thanks to the possibility to follow a step-by-step framework.

The creation of a standard framework has relevant managerial contributions, since it can be adopted by different decision-makers willing to assess the impact of technologies for healthy ageing in the area and society they represent. In particular, the model developed to assess the impact of NESTORE in the Lombardy Region, in the autonomous community of Catalonia and in the province of South Holland could be easily adopted to evaluate the same technology in the different areas where NESTORE promoters are willing to launch the initiative.

Moreover, promoters and developers of a general project have to guarantee three main points, when proposing such a solution [63]:

1. the **positive impact**, not only for the target but **for the whole society**;

2. the positive impact according to the **strategic objective** of the entity they represent;
3. the **economic sustainability of the initiative for the payer** (the SROI analysis has to guarantee that the entity in charge of the payment would return on the investment).

A SROI framework can play as a strategic tool to meet each of these points, thus providing the decision-makers with all the necessary information to make the most proper decisions, ensuring that the initiative they are promoting is managing the most economic and social implications and risks. As a matter of fact, in its complete and general form, the computation of SROI offers an overview on the general impact of an initiative, clearly stating which the **value generated for all the stakeholders** involved is.

6 Limitations and Further Development

The project limitations (and thus future developments) have been drafted retracing, step by step, the route followed by the authors to build the model.

1. **Establishing scope and identifying stakeholders**: as for the **scope**, the authors designed a model in which the National/Regional healthcare system plays the role of the payer and the virtual coach is presented as a medical device. Of course, as NESTORE case itself envisions, this is not the only viable alternative. The virtual coach could be conceived as a **"peace of mind" device** (not a medical device) and thus be distributed by health insurance companies, enterprises (as part of welfare programs) or paid directly by its target. As regards the stakeholders, the authors made the decision **not** to **involve** in the analysis **pharmaceutical and biomedical companies, family and friends and influencers**. The authors invite future researches to analyse and involve these alternatives and aspects in their analyses.
2. **Mapping Outcomes**: this step concerns identifying inputs, valuing inputs, clarifying outputs, describing outcomes. Looking at the **inputs** and their valuation, the authors envisioned a model in which the healthcare system oversees a monthly cost covering the whole service provision. However, when it comes to NESTORE case study, given its prospective nature, the quantification of this value **could not be precisely defined**. The authors invite future researchers, aware of the real cost for implementing the project, to correct the data and, if necessary, the whole consideration on the NESTORE initiative. Coming to the **outcomes** for a generic model, when dealing with the National/Regional healthcare system, the authors neglected some secondary aspects: **loss for those physicians and specialists** (especially nutritionists) that operate and work as private or public entities; **increased incomes for the service sector** coming from healthier adults (e.g. theatres, cinemas, restaurants, travel agencies, airline companies, hotels, etc.). Future analysis should quantify these implications and

define how they affect the overall SROI ratio for a virtual coach for healthy ageing.

3. **Evidencing outcomes and giving them a value**: given the **prospective nature** of the authors' analysis, the choice of indicators has been suggested by the literature, as well as the choice of financial proxies. Anyway, the impossibility to directly experience the outcomes provided by a virtual coach and to collect data regarding them represents the major limitation of the current study. Once NESTORE will be launched and used by citizens, future researchers will have the chance to conduct and ex-post evaluation of NESTORE, highlighting the main gaps between prospective and real evaluations. This consideration becomes particularly relevant when it comes to beneficiaries' **Willingness To Pay** for reduced morbidity enabled by the virtual coach, which builds up the majority of the overall impact in all the three areas analyzed. Another limitation of the current research is represented by the decision of the authors to involve the consequences and benefits resulting from **only two (physical activity and nutrition) out of the four domains** of healthy ageing covered by NESTORE (physical activity, nutrition, social sphere, and cognitive ability). Another critical aspect regards the **collection of the data**: epidemiological data about the population, costs incurred by the healthcare system to treat specific pathologies as well as the composition by gender, age and typology of caregivers. The sources to collect such data vary from country to country and, what is more, the same item may be quantified in a different way and considering different elements, depending on the source. Therefore, in order to insert the data in the model, it is required to make additional assumptions and adaptations on the data retrieved. In sum, the order of magnitude of the outcomes quantified may slightly vary from country to country, which makes the final results difficult to be compared.
4. **Establishing impact**: this step requires to define deadweight, displacement, attribution, and drop-off. As already evidenced by a literature review on the SROI, their estimation results to be really complex, above all when dealing with a prospective study. In detail, as it comes to deadweight, it requires the definition of comparison groups or benchmarks whose trends can be observed only in case of retrospective studies. Therefore, future researchers are invited to define control groups and to involve ex-post and proven-on-the-field values for deadweight.
5. **Calculating the SROI**: this step is mainly concerned with the choice of a proper time horizon and discount rate. For the time horizon, its selection is mainly related to the nature of the technology in place and its risk of obsolescence. This observation can be assumed as a major guideline for the model. However, when it comes to NESTORE case study, once again, it was possible to merely define an approximation of this value.
6. **Reporting, using and embedding**: an interesting aspect that rotates around mHealth solutions is that of using the data from users to improve the solution itself and to sell them to third parties. The authors decided to neglect this aspect in drafting a generic model for healthy ageing solutions because of its complex

technicalities and privacy implications; however, its involvement could reinforce the idea of SROI as a complete and holistic methodology. The last limitation to be underlined is the weak validation that the model has obtained so far. In fact, having shown the SROI model for NESTORE to the NESTORE Consortium represents just an initial approval step, without proving its definitive effectiveness. To overcome this limit, future researchers could try to adapt the SROI model developed by the authors to other contexts such as other technologies operating in the healthcare field, in order to verify its robustness and versatility.

References

1. Abramson, B. L., & Melvin, R. G. (2014). Cardiovascular risk in women: Focus on hypertension. *Canadian Journal of Cardiology, 30*(5), 553–559.
2. Ackerman, F. (2008). *Critique of cost-benefit analysis, and alternative approaches to decision-making*. Friends of the Earth England, Wales and Northern Ireland, London.
3. Ajuntament De Barcelona. (2018). Salut i qualitat de vida de les dones cuidadores de familiars. Resultats i valoració dels serveis municipals de suport a les cures. http://www.spora.ws/wp-content/uploads/2019/01/salutiqualitatdevidadonescuidadoresfamiliars_0.pdf.
4. Arvidson, M., Lyon, F., McKay, S., & Moro, D. (2013). Valuing the social? The nature and controversies of measuring social return on investment (SROI). *Voluntary Sector Review, 4*(1), 3–18.
5. Assistere.net. Quanto costa una badante. https://www.assistere.net/quanto-costa-una-badante/.
6. Banke-Thomas, A. O., Madaj, B., Charles, A., & van den Broek, N. (2015). Social Return on Investment (SROI) methodology to account for value for money of public health interventions: A systematic review. *BMC Public Health, 15*(1), 582.
7. Bassuk, S. S., & Manson, J. E. (2005). Epidemiological evidence for the role of physical activity in reducing risk of type 2 diabetes and cardiovascular disease. *Journal of Applied Physiology*.
8. CBS—Centraal Bureau voor de Statistiek. (2019). Gezondheid en zorggebruik; persoonskenmerken (Langdurige aandoeningen 1 of meer langdurige aandoeningen). https://opendata.cbs.nl/#/CBS/nl/dataset/83005NED/table?ts=1600760801848.
9. Catalunya Religiò. (2020). Les dones cuidadores dediquen 14 h al dia a la cura. https://www.catalunyareligio.cat/ca/dones-cuidadores-dediquen-14h-dia-cura.
10. Centraal Planbureau. (2018). Macro Economische Verkenning 2018 (sept 2017), raming voor 2017 en 2018.
11. Centro de Nutriciòn Jùlia Farre. (2020). Tarifas de nuestras dietas y servicios. https://www.centrojuliafarre.es/precios-dietas/.
12. Cerbino, N. (2019). Patologie croniche in costante aumento in Italia con incremento della spesa sanitaria. La cronicità non colpisce tutti allo stesso modo: si confermano le diseguaglianze di genere, territoriali, culturali e socio economiche. Osservatorio nazionale sulla salute nelle regioni italiane, Rapporto Osservasalute.
13. Chaput, J.-P., Després, J.-P., Bouchard, C., & Tremblay, A. (2007). Short sleep duration is associated with reduced leptin levels and increased adiposity: Results from the Quebec family study. *Obesity, 15*(1), 253–261.
14. Chase, N. L., Sui, X., Lee, D. C., & Blair, S. N. (2009). The association of cardiorespiratory fitness and physical activity with incidence of hypertension in men. *American Journal of Hypertension, 22*(4), 417–424.
15. Chen, J.-C., Espeland, M. A., Brunner, R. L., Lovato, L. C., Wallace, R. B., Leng, X., et al. (2016). Sleep duration, cognitive decline, and dementia risk in older women. *Alzheimer's & Dementia, 12*(1), 21–33.

16. Cook, N. R., Cutler, J. A., Obarzanek, E., Buring, J. E., Rexrode, K. M., Kumanyika, S. K., …, & Whelton, P. K. (2007). Long term effects of dietary sodium reduction on cardiovascular disease outcomes: Observational follow-up of the trials of hypertension prevention (TOHP). *Bmj, 334*(7599), 885.
17. Crowe, S., Cresswell, K., Robertson, A., Huby, G., Avery, A., & Sheikh, A. (2011). The case study approach. *BMC Medical Research Methodology, 11*(1), 100.
18. Van Dam, R. M., Willett, W. C., Rimm, E. B., Stampfer, M. J., & Hu, F. B. (2002). Dietary fat and meat intake in relation to risk of type 2 diabetes in men. *Diabetes Care, 25*(3), 417–424.
19. Donnan, P. T., Leese, G. P., Morris, A. D., & Audit, D. (2000). Hospitalizations for people with type 1 and type 2 diabetes compared with the nondiabetic population of Tayside, Scotland: A retrospective cohort study of resource use. *Diabetes Care, 23*(12), 1774–1779.
20. D'Andrea, A. M. (2019). Stipendi medi in Italia: differenze tra Nord e Sud, ecco chi guadagna di più. https://www.money.it/Stipendi-medi-in-Italia-1-570-euro-differenze-Nord-Sud.
21. European Commission & Economic Policy Committee. (2014). *The 2012 ageing report: Underlying assumptions and projection methodologies*. European Commission Directorate-General for Economic and Financial Affairs.
22. Expatistan. (2018). *1 month of gym membership in business district in Rotterdam*. https://www.expatistan.com/price/gym/rotterdam.
23. Federconsumatori. (2017). Sport: Indagine Federconsumatori sui costi delle palestre in Italia. https://www.federconsumatori.it/Showdoc.php?nid=20170907113855.
24. Fisher, M., Lees, K., & Spence, J. D. (2006). Nutrition and stroke prevention. *Stroke, 37*(9), 2430–2435.
25. Fundaciòn MAPFRE. (2017). El coste de la enfermedad potencialmente prevenible en España. https://www.grupoaseguranza.com/adjuntos/fichero_22844_20171114.pdf.
26. Gangwisch, J. E., Heymsfield, S. B., Boden-Albala, B., Buijs, R. M., Kreier, F., Pickering, T. G., …, & Malaspina, D. (2006). Short sleep duration as a risk factor for hypertension: Analyses of the first national health and nutrition examination survey. *Hypertension, 47*(5), 833–839.
27. Gargani, J. (2017). The leap from ROI to SROI: Farther than expected? *Evaluation and Program Planning, 64,* 116–126.
28. Gencat—Generalitat de Catalunya. (2018). Malaltia d'Alzheimer. Característiques i utilització de recursos sanitaris. Any 2016. https://govern.cat/govern/docs/2018/09/18/14/59/42eef2c8-832e-417b-ba81-aeb92fb93a7f.pdf.
29. Gencat—Generalitat de Catalunya, Departament de Salut. (2019). Resultats de l'enquesta de salut de Catalunya (ESCA). https://salutweb.gencat.cat/ca/el_departament/estadistiques_sanitaries/enquestes/esca/resultats_enquesta_salut_catalunya/; Estat de salut: AV42NC_1.- Pressió Alta Diagnosticada Per Un Metge O Metgessa; Estat de salut: AV42NC_15.- Ictus (embòlia/atac de feridura) diagnosticat per un metge o metgessa; Estat de salut: AV42NC_17.- Altres Malalties Del Cor (Angina De Pit, Etc.) Diagnosticades Per Un Metge O Metgessa; Estat de salut: AV42NC_3.- Diabetis (Sucre A La Sang) Diagnosticada Per Un Metge O Metgessa; Estat de salut: V37.- Estat De Salut Autopercebut; Sociodemografiques: Cuidador/a principal de les persones discapacitades de la llar.
30. Giuliani, G. (2018). Chi è il Caregiver: i Dati ISTAT. https://www.formazione-sanitaria.com/2018/01/23/caregiver-dati-istat-2018/.
31. Greenberg, D., Peterburg, Y., Vekstein, D., & Pliskin, J. S. (2005). Decisions to adopt new technologies at the hospital level: Insights from Israeli medical centers. *International Journal of Technology Assessment in Health Care, 21*(2), 219.
32. Gregg, E. W., Cauley, J. A., Seeley, D. G., Ensrud, K. E., & Bauer, D. C. (1998). Physical activity and osteoporotic fracture risk in older women. *Annals of Internal Medicine, 129*(2), 81–88.
33. HM Treasury. (2003). *The Green Book: Appraisal and evaluation in Central Government: London: HM treasury*. British Government.
34. Hamelmann, C., Turatto, F., Then, V., & Dyakova, M. (2017). *Social return on investment: Accounting for value in the context of implementing health 2020 and the 2030 agenda for sustainable development*. Copenhagen: WHO Regional Office for Europe.

35. Heath, J. M., & Stuart, M. R. (2002). Prescribing exercise for frail elders. *The Journal of the American Board of Family Practice, 15*(3), 218–228.
36. Howard, V. J., & McDonnell, M. N. (2015). Physical activity in primary stroke prevention: Just do it! *Stroke, 46*(6), 1735–1739.
37. Hu, N., Yu, J. T., Tan, L., Wang, Y. L., Sun, L., & Tan, L. (2013). *Nutrition and the risk of Alzheimer's disease*. BioMed Research International.
38. INE—Instituto Nacional de Esdatìstica. (2012). *Wages, income, social cohesion*. https://www.ine.es/jaxiT3/Tabla.htm?t=10882.
39. INE—Instituto Nacional de Esdatìstica. (2014). *European survey of health in Spain 2014. States of health: Relative figures (Table 2.16)*. https://www.ine.es/dynt3/inebase/en/index.htm?type=pcaxis&path=/t15/p420/a2014/p04/&file=pcaxis.
40. Job and Salary Abroad. (2017). *Caregiver for elderly Netherlands—Salary, How to find a job*. https://www.jobandsalaryabroad.com/en/netherlands/english-caregiveradults-netherlands.html.
41. Kim, S. M., Hwang, S. W., Oh, E. H., & Kang, J. K. (2013). Determinants of the length of stay in stroke patients. *Osong Public Health and Research Perspectives, 4*(6), 329–341.
42. Kujala, U. M., Kaprio, J., Kannus, P., Sarna, S., & Koskenvuo, M. (2000). Physical activity and osteoporotic hip fracture risk in men. *Archives of Internal Medicine, 160*(5), 705–708.
43. Maas, K., & Liket, K. (2011). Social impact measurement: Classification of methods. In *Environmental management accounting and supply chain management* (pp. 171–202). Dordrecht: Springer.
44. Mehra. (2014). Association of severe obstructive sleep apnea and elevated blood pressure despite antihypertensive medication use. *Journal of Clinical Sleep Medicine, 10*(8), 835–843.
45. Millar, R., & Hall, K. (2013). Social return on investment (SROI) and performance measurement: The opportunities and barriers for social enterprises in health and social care. *Public Management Review, 15*(6), 923–941.
46. Miller, G. E., Murphy, M. L., Cashman, R., Ma, R., Ma, J., Arevalo, J. M., … & Cole, S. W. (2014). Greater inflammatory activity and blunted glucocorticoid signaling in monocytes of chronically stressed caregivers. *Brain, Behavior, and Immunity, 41*, 191–199.
47. Nicholls, J., Lawlor, E., Neitzert, E., Goodspeed, T., & Cupitt, S. (2012). A guide to social return on investment: The SROI network. *Accounting for Value.*
48. OECD. (2017). *Health at a glance 2017: OECD indicators*. https://www.oecd.org/italy/Health-at-a-Glance-2017-Key-Findings-ITALY-in-English.pdf.
49. Oliva-Moreno, J., Aranda-Reneo, I., Vilaplana-Prieto, C., González-Domínguez, A., & Hidalgo-Vega, Á. (2013). Economic valuation of informal care in cerebrovascular accident survivors in Spain. *BMC Health Services Research, 13*(1), 508.
50. Pfister, R., Sharp, S. J., Luben, R., Wareham, N. J., & Khaw, K. T. (2011). Plasma vitamin C predicts incident heart failure in men and women in European prospective investigation into cancer and nutrition-Norfolk prospective study. *American Heart Journal, 162*(2), 246–253.
51. Regione Lombardia. (2017). *Alzheimer*. https://www.dati.lombardia.it/stories/s/muyn-z7dw.
52. Regione Lombardia. (2017). Diabete Mellito Tipo 2. https://www.dati.lombardia.it/stories/s/3bv3-9a78.
53. Regione Lombardia. (2017). Ipertensione arteriosa. https://www.dati.lombardia.it/stories/s/36mq-cwak.
54. Regione Lombardia. (2017). Scompenso cardiaco. https://www.dati.lombardia.it/stories/s/jy6d-bdcx.
55. Saez, M., & Barceló, M. A. (2012). Coste de la hipertensión arterial en España. *Hipertensión y riesgo vascular, 29*(4), 145–151.
56. Salmeron, J., Hu, F. B., Manson, J. E., Stampfer, M. J., Colditz, G. A., Rimm, E. B., et al. (2001). Dietary fat intake and risk of type 2 diabetes in women. *The American Journal of Clinical Nutrition, 73*(6), 1019–1026.
57. San Raffaele. (n.a.). L'attività fisica può prevenire il rischio di un infarto. http://www.sanraffaele.it/comunicazione/SRpedia/3127/l-attivita-fisica-puo-prevenire-il-rischio-di-un-infarto.

58. Scrafford, C. G., Bi, X., Multani, J. K., Murphy, M. M., Schmier, J. K., & Barraj, L. M. (2019). Health economic evaluation modeling shows potential health care cost savings with increased conformance with healthy dietary patterns among adults in the United States. *Journal of the Academy of Nutrition and Dietetics, 119*(4), 599–616.
59. Self, P et al. (2015) Econocrats & the policy process: The politics & philosophy of costbenefit analysis, Macmillan International Higher Education. (Cit. on pp. xiii, 7, 226).
60. Sen, A. (2000). The discipline of cost-benefit analysis. *The Journal of Legal Studies, 29*(S2), 931–952.
61. Sociaal en Cultureel Planbureau. (2017). Voor elkaar? Stand van de informele hulp in 2016. https://www.scp.nl/publicaties/publicaties/2017/12/19/voor-elkaar.
62. Sociaal en Cultureel Planbureau. (2017). Zorg en ondersteuning in Nederland: kerncijfers 2016. Ontvangen hulp bij het huishouden, persoonlijke verzorging, verpleging en begeleiding. https://www.wmoraad-sittardgeleen.nl/wp-content/uploads/2016/06/SCP-nov-17-Zorg-en-ondersteuning-Kerncijfers-2016.pdf.
63. Social Value UK. (2012). *A guide to social return on investment.*
64. The Economist Intelligence Unit. (2017). Impacto socioeconómico de la enfermedad de alzheimer y otras demencias (España). https://www.lilly.es/global/img/ES/PDF/Impacto-socioeconomico-de-la-enfermedad-de-Alzheimer_EIU.pdf.
65. Vela, E., Clèries, M., Vella, V. A., Adroher, C., & García-Altés, A. (2019). Análisis poblacional del gasto en servicios sanitarios en Cataluña (España):¿ qué y quién consume más recursos? *Gaceta Sanitaria, 33,* 24–31.
66. Verbeek, J., Mischke, C., Robinson, R., Ijaz, S., Kuijer, P., Kievit, A., …, & Neuvonen, K. (2017). Occupational exposure to knee loading and the risk of osteoarthritis of the knee: a systematic review and a dose-response meta-analysis. *Safety and Health at Work, 8*(2), 130–142.
67. Visconti, F., & Volani, E. (2018). *Engaging with a virtual coach for healthy ageing: An empirical investigation of the intention to use through a tam-extended framework.* Master of Science thesis at the university of Politecnico di Milano.
68. Voeding Plus Advies. (2020). Individueel voedingsadvies. https://www.voedingplusadvies.nl/tarieven-vergoedingen/.
69. Volksgezondheidenzorg.info. (2017). Zorguitgaven beroerte naar sector. https://www.volksgezondheidenzorg.info/onderwerp/beroerte/kosten/zorguitgaven.
70. Volksgezondheidenzorg.info. (2017). Zorguitgaven bloeddruk naar sector. https://www.volksgezondheidenzorg.info/onderwerp/bloeddruk/kosten/zorguitgaven.
71. Volksgezondheidenzorg.info. (2017). Zorguitgaven dementie naar sector. https://www.volksgezondheidenzorg.info/onderwerp/dementie/kosten/zorguitgaven.
72. Volksgezondheidenzorg.info. (2017). Zorguitgaven diabetes mellitus naar sector. https://www.volksgezondheidenzorg.info/onderwerp/diabetes-mellitus/kosten/zorguitgaven.
73. Volksgezondheidenzorg.info. (2017). Zorguitgaven hartfalen naar sector. https://www.volksgezondheidenzorg.info/onderwerp/hartfalen/kosten/zorguitgaven.
74. Volksgezondheidenzorg.info. (2017). Zorguitgaven osteoporose naar sector. https://www.volksgezondheidenzorg.info/onderwerp/osteoporose/kosten/zorguitgaven.
75. Walia, H. K., Li, H., Rueschman, M., Bhatt, D. L., Patel, S. R., Quan, S. F., et al. (2014). Association of severe obstructive sleep apnea and elevated blood pressure despite antihypertensive medication use. *Journal of Clinical Sleep Medicine, 10*(08), 835–843.
76. World Health Organization. (2015). *World report on ageing and health.* World Health Organization.

Building a Network Around Wellbeing Services that Empower Older Adults

I. Gheno

Abstract Comprehensive solutions require the involvement of a wide range of partners and stakeholders—first and foremost: the persons that the solutions are intended to. In societies where pervasive ageism still prevails, adopting a communication and dissemination strategy that is non-stigmatising and inclusive of the old age diversity is critical to ensure the success of the solutions' design and development. This chapter will aim at sharing insights about the target audiences of NESTORE as use case, and how they have been approached within the frame of the project.

1 Every Pathway to Ageing Counts

There is no such a "typical" older person. We all age since we were born, and the way we age depends from our genes, but mainly from our lifestyle, education and the environment we live in: "*only 20–25% of healthy life expectancy (HLE) is predetermined by genes; lifestyle and environment play a major role*" [1]. Through our experience of ageing, we encounter various challenges, which are differently coped by different subjects. Consequently, it becomes hard to conceive mainstreamed solutions that help ageing actively and healthy while ensuring tailored strategies, easily adaptable to each individual ageing path. This was exactly the challenge picked up by NESTORE.

This is important especially in Horizon2020 research projects, where the strong technological and infrastructural focus often tend to overlook the real needs, expectations, and capabilities of the final beneficiaries of those solutions. This is particularly relevant for some segments of the population, often excluded from the design of digital services (e.g., seniors, children, women, persons with lower digital literacy, vulnerable groups, people with migration background). Moreover, this tendency is exacerbated by the rapid digitalisation of public services that put large groups of the population at risk of exclusion. Even if it is slowly improving, access to Internet remains poor among people aged 65+. With only 51% of 65–74 years-old people

I. Gheno (✉)
AGE Platform Europe, Avenue de Tervueren/Tervurenlaan 168, box 2, 1150 Brussels, Belgium
e-mail: ilenia.gheno@age-platform.eus

G. Andreoni and C. Mambretti (eds.), *Digital Health Technology for Better Aging*, Research for Development, https://doi.org/10.1007/978-3-030-72663-8_16

having ever used the Internet [2], it is crucial to ensure that older adults are not left aside when developing ICT-based public services.

It is therefore crucial to set up a process allowing senior citizens to become active participants in the co-creation and service design of solutions that are meant to support them. Co-design and co-creation not only enable designers and developers to meet citizens' needs and expectations, but also to deliver cost-efficient solutions: less budget is lost on products and services which are not sufficiently well designed to ensure effective take-up. Only by tapping into the lived experience of becoming old that senior citizens can offer, we can jointly prepare for demographic change and an ageing society. Similarly, senior citizens can get involved in the definition, selection and development of tools and services that can be used by designers and developers to benchmark the age-friendliness of their work. This is based on an approach to co-creation that reflects the everyday life of senior citizens as situated and practice-based, meaning that the services to be co-created need to respond adequately to everyday practices (e.g. technology use, healthcare practices) of their future users.

There is a lack of knowledge on older citizens' needs and expectations, having often neither the resources nor the appropriate tools to understand such needs and expectations [3]. This is also linked to the widely spread assumption that policies targeting persons with disabilities answer older persons' needs as well. Such an assumption underestimates the heterogeneity among older persons and their experience of ageing, and results in applying only accessibility-related answers to demographic change. It is crucial to not only build solutions for senior citizens but also with them as they are the experts of technology-in-use.

2 The NESTORE Community

The project's methodological strengths are to be found in its co-design approach adopted throughout the project, in its thorough system validation with respect to usability, acceptability and effectiveness and in the development of a sustainable ecosystem involving citizens and stakeholders for the co-production of wellness. The foundation of such methodological architecture lays on the assumption that the final beneficiaries of every solution must be genuinely involved in conceiving, designing, and shaping each part of such solution.

NESTORE's departing point was the search for strategies and preferences people choose when willing to maintain mental and physical health. To detect these pieces of information, it was key to ask directly who may be concerned. Therefore, partners organised workshops with people aged 50 plus to refine the critical artefact methodology to be applied in NESTORE. Since its inception in 2007, Lab4Living/Sheffield Hallam University has engaged with and built an extensive network of community, hospital and patient groups who input into research. Thanks to this network, researchers engaged a minimum of 80 adults in the United Kingdom who fulfil the inclusion criteria for the study (aged 50 and over). Purposive sampling ensured that participants recruited include clear representation from different socio-economic groups and demographic data. An existing co-design methodology named 'exhibition in a box' [4] was selected as the basis of a series of workshops with participants (8 participants × 10 workshops). This methodology utilizes critical artefacts to elicit participant experiences and to scaffold conversation and has been tested in the context of tele-health and care research.

A follow-up step was the identification of ten people who took part in the workshops to contribute to a working group comprising of the research team and of a small group of the technologists within the NESTORE project. This group was involved in the analysis of the data from the workshops and in partnership with the design team and with technologists developed materials/objects/prompts/provocations that capture and articulate the priorities identified in the data. These materials formed the basis of another round of workshops to test the efficacy of the materials and to transfer the participants' perspectives to the technologists. These workshops additionally helped recruit participants to the pilot study groups. Data collected across the workshops was collated and supported the design and development of NESTORE.

Last, the NESTORE platform was tested in a sample of 60 older people for a minimum of three months. During pilot trial, participants used the system themselves, with due support from the pilot supervisors.

Such process helped building a first community aware of the challenge and the potential solutions address by the NESTORE system. Meanwhile an equally interested community saw the light: the Forum of Advisory Stakeholders (FAS).

Through the FAS, NESTORE benefitted from the implication of a pool of experts and stakeholders active at local and European level, adding value to the work and the multi-disciplinarity already guaranteed within the consortium. Being stakeholders' involvement key the project, and willing to ensure that NESTORE's direct beneficiaries (older people, formal and informal carers, family members) can effectively dialogue with technical and health professionals, the Forum of Advisory Stakeholder was set up at the beginning of the project to add an extra level of interaction, ensuring that stakeholders with different backgrounds, experiences and skills are able to follow up the project, to assist in the achievement of the key milestones and thus to help steering NESTORE via their direct advice. Such group gathered regularly, once per year, and convened at the project milestones to review the project results and provide recommendations. The composite configuration of the FAS, encompassing medical doctors, a representative of informal carers, an expert in technology and design, a journalist, and two advocate for public health, among others, allowed informative and informed exchanges among the group and with the consortium, and focused on accommodating the health and digital literacy level of the final beneficiaries of the NESTORE system. The FAS counted stakeholders active at pilot site level (in Barcelona, Milan and Rotterdam) and at European level (umbrella organisations active in the field of health and public health, working with their constituencies across the European Union and dialoguing directly with the European Institutions). Such composition has ensured to evaluate NESTORE along its path from different perspectives, thus enriching the conversation both at technology level and in terms of demand and supply, for what pertains the exploitation and communication strategies of the project.

3 Empowering Means also Avoiding Self-inducted Ageism

In an increasingly digitalised world, it is essential to find ways to secure that all citizens, regardless of their age, digital literacy and abilities, can continue to access information and participate in decision-making processes. Older adults can increase their use of digital solutions only if the proposed services are relevant, secure, useful, accessible and affordable. It is hence crucial to design appropriate, inclusive digital tools to support a wider participation of older citizens in the co-creation of solutions addressed to them.

However, to further reinforce the NESTORE community and allow the system to be broadly accepted and used, education and cultural shifts are also to be mentioned. The co-design and co-creation of solutions is essential but training older persons to use new devices is equally key. As the experience of the NESTORE pilots teaches, users can feel very powerless in front of technology if they are not correctly instructed to use it. It is necessary to convey educational and cultural elements to the users to sustain the growth of their abilities and motivation across the project, thus paving the way to an ever-lasting use of the proposed solutions beyond the project itself.

Following this approach, adopting a communication and dissemination strategy that is non-stigmatising and inclusive of the old age diversity is critical to ensure the success of the solutions' design and development. Research, education and communication, among others, need to deal with ageism if they want to achieve age-friendly tools and environments.

Within the term "ageism", the stereotypes, prejudices and discriminations based on people's chronological age are condensed. Whenever we feel "too old" or "too young", whenever age is the sole criteria for defining us and/or labelling our activities, ageism is right around the corner. The list of examples of ageism is very broad, as ageism is the most pervasive form of discrimination of our modern societies [5], very widespread, little condemned, and much accepted across the various populations in the world. "Ageism" itself is a word that has recently celebrated its 50th anniversary, as it was first coined by gerontologist Robert Butler in 1969 [6].

Ageism hits hard across the various levels of our societies. We are all experiencing ageist attitudes when we are exhorted to "fight ageing" with creams, make-ups, … when we are labelled as "slow as an old (wo)man". We ourselves interiorise prejudice and stereotypes around ageing, to the point this affects the way we age and the quality of our ageing. "*Who likes to think of his or her own older self? No one likes to think about ageing. Because when we do, most of us refer to negative stereotypes about older age. Is it because we do not want to be reminded about our own ageing that we tend to label older adults as belonging to a separate age group in a process of 'othering'?*" [7].

Self-inducted ageism or not, it is a very complex and multidimensional problem, that therefore needs various instruments and strategies to be tackled effectively. And especially, it needs everyone's attention and commitment, in order to be eradicated from our culture and our education systems. Part of the solution to cope with ageism is to set up a process allowing older persons to become active participants in the co-creation and service design of solutions that are meant to support them. Co-design and co-creation not only enable designers and developers to meet citizens' needs and expectations, but also to deliver cost-efficient solutions: less budget is lost on products and services which are not sufficiently well designed, acceptance and take-up is more likely and the risk of having ageist products and services in the market is minimised. Ageism in research is in fact very pervasive.

"*When it comes to technology, older adults are often stereotypically described as a homogeneous group that are lagging behind and associated with cognitive decline, frailty and needs. These stereotypes often affect designers in the design process of digital technologies. Though some studies have implied that the adoption of technology among older adults is on the rise and that older adults hold more positive views (than negative) about using technology, it is still the case that negative stereotypes and ageism might shape how digital technology for older adults is conceived and designed*" [8].

4 Conclusions

Many European projects make co-design and co-creation their essential engine in research. However, there is often the risk of using short-cuts, sometimes for budgetary reasons (engaging with users is costly and time-consuming), sometimes for time-related constraints, sometimes just for the fact that literature and statistics are not comprehensive enough to dive into the heterogeneity of the older population, which then falls out of picture. This results in research missing to deliver comprehensive solutions and in outcomes impacting only on a very limited range of the older population, and most of the times with stereotypical and not-useful solutions.

Considering the functional and cognitive abilities of each person, analysing the gender dimensions, exploring the professional, educational, social and cultural background matter. It is equally important to assess computer skills and experiences, alongside with health literacy. Also, working for ageing well means to encompass the views of the most marginalised groups, those whose voice is often unheard.

But it is not only about co-designing and co-creating with users. It is also about how this is done. To avoid becoming a mere tick-box exercise, attention must be given to all details, starting from the language used: jargon and ageist expressions are so widespread in the research world and in our societies that is hard to get rid of them and can be found since the first invitation letter or the presentation of the project itself (e.g. starting an interview by saying "it is known that older people have memory issues"). The setting in which the sessions and study take place also matter (e.g. inaccessible venues, inaccessible timeslots, difficulty with virtual meetings), alongside non-verbal communication also play an important role on the outcome.

Only by tapping into the lived experience of becoming old, we can jointly prepare for demographic change and an ageing society. Similarly, older people can get involved in the definition, selection and development of tools and services that can be used by designers and developers to benchmark the age-friendliness of their work. This is based on an approach to co-creation that reflects the everyday life of older persons as situated and practice-based, meaning that the services to be co-created need to respond adequately to everyday practices (e.g. technology use, healthcare practices) of their future users [9].

It is crucial to not only build solutions for older people but also with them as they are the experts of technology-in-use. Because, as stated by the World Health Organization, "*older people are the ultimate experts of their own lives*" [10].

References

1. Policy Brief No. 5, MOPACT project, Biogerontology: A novel tool to stay healthy in old age. https://mopact.group.shef.ac.uk/wp-content/uploads/2013/10/MoPAct-Policy-Brief-5-Biogerontology-a-novel-tool-to-stay-healthy-in-old-age.pdf.
2. https://ec.europa.eu/eurostat/statistics-explained/index.php/Internet_use_statistics_-_individuals#Internet_activity_by_age_group.
3. Based on a survey undertaken by AGE Platform Europe and the Council of European Municipalities and Regions in 2012 on the occasion of the European Year 2012 on Active ageing and solidarity between generations. Further based on Donder et al.: Developing Evidence-Based Age-Friendly Policies: A Participatory Research Project, 2014, 05-12, chapter in SAGE Research Methods Cases.
4. https://nestore-coach.eu/documents/20182/71466/NESTORE_D7.1.pdf/bb442d8a-02f2-436f-857f-957b7f13468e.
5. https://www.who.int/ageing/ageism/en/.
6. https://ageismhurts.org/what-is-ageism.
7. https://www.equaltimes.org/ageism-the-most-acceptable-form-of#.X4RfE5MzZyw.
8. Mannheim, I., et al. (2019). Inclusion of older adults in the research and design of digital technology. https://www.mdpi.com/1660-4601/16/19/3718.
9. https://juliane.jarke.info/?cat=25.
10. WHO. (2007). Global age-friendly cities: A guide. https://www.who.int/ageing/age_friendly_cities_guide/en/.

Exploitation, Dissemination, and Communication: An Integrated Framework in EU Research

E. Lettieri, L. Marone, N. Spezia, and I. Gheno

Abstract Europe's ageing demographics gave rise to the gold rush by entrepreneurs and innovators who started to investigate the market of solutions for older adults. Now joined by big players from the Information and Technology sector, the Silver Economy is a lion's den where EU-funded research and innovation projects sometimes struggle to find a place. This chapter presents the dissemination, exploitation, and communication strategy developed for a virtual coach for healthy ageing designed within the "Horizon 2020" EU research and innovation programme, taking account of the latest macroeconomic forces at stake and aiming at the successful adoption and diffusion of this innovation in the healthcare market.

1 Introduction

In the last decades, the healthcare systems of the most developed countries have been facing a number of challenges that required great flexibility and the ability to adapt to fast changes. These include: ageing population, growth of chronic diseases, shrinking of the gross domestic product (GDP), increased pace of technological innovation, consumerization, and digital transformation [13]. Furthermore, the ongoing COVID-19 emergency has brought out new urgent issues -usually destined to the least developed countries [20]—such as epidemic preparedness, infectious disease prevention, hospitals' capacity saturation, and health care sanitation. Struggling with this combination of challenges and adversities, the resilience of healthcare systems has been dramatically put at risk. In such tough conditions, the innovation brought by new products, services, and business models can provide vital solutions [5].

However, innovation development is a complex process composed of different critical phases and interactions with a large group of usually very diversified actors.

E. Lettieri (✉) · L. Marone · N. Spezia
Department of Management, Economics, and Industrial Engineering, Politecnico di Milano, Via Lambruschini, 4/B, Milan, Italy
e-mail: Emanuele.lettieri@polimi.it

I. Gheno
AGE Platform Europe, Avenue de Tervueren 168/2 1150, Brussels, Belgium

G. Andreoni and C. Mambretti (eds.), *Digital Health Technology for Better Aging*, Research for Development, https://doi.org/10.1007/978-3-030-72663-8_17

Moreover, to be successful, innovation must be adopted by several organizations, requiring to be largely diffused in the field of application [16]. Therefore, all the activities, processes, and strategies necessary to effectively make the innovation spread in the market and across organizations assume a role of paramount importance. In such context, innovators must pay great attention to strengthen communication and knowledge sharing through the value chain, nurture long-term relationships with the most relevant stakeholders, and manage and monitor the interdependent decision-making processes [11, 15, 18, 21].

Healthcare is one of the most complex and diversified sectors, it includes patients and patients' associations, clinicians, hospitals, pharmacies, pharmaceutical and medical technology companies, agencies, authorities, and policymakers at different institutional levels (national, regional, and local) and insurance companies, as well as scientific associations, universities and research centers, intermediaries, and employees in the health system. In this ecosystem, different players might take the role of innovator. Funding several projects around the continent, the European Commission (EC) can be considered an innovation booster for several sectors, healthcare included. Within its latest research and innovation programme, "Horizon 2020" (H2020), almost €8 billion of funding were made available for health-related research [6]. This latter aims at tackling issues such as population ageing, increasing burden of non-communicable diseases, expensive innovative healthcare and medicinal products, and slow pace of digitalization uptake by leveraging on solutions mainly based on personalized, digital, and preventive care [7]. The funding is usually assigned to public-private collaborations -the so-called Consortia—in which partners from different countries, industries, and academia come together to develop a common project. EC-funded projects are typically characterized by high innovation potential, partnership centrality, transnationality, organizational variety and diversity, long length duration, no structured decision-making hierarchy, and high degree of risk uptake. These specific features create a context of unique complexity. Hampered by this complexity, many EC-funded projects risk to leave no significant impact, failing to exploit their innovation potential [19]. For this reason, the EC identified the necessity to design and implement more effective Dissemination and Exploitation (D&E) strategies for every EC-funded project. Dissemination means sharing research results of the project with potential users—peers in the research field, industry, other commercial players, and policymakers, whereas exploitation is the use of results for commercial purposes [8]. An effective D&E strategy leads to outcomes such as: launching of the innovative products or services to market, transfer of results and best practices to different and broader contexts, potential tailoring to the needs of others, continuation after the funding period has finished, influences on policy and practice, as well as serving the public good [17]. Therefore, an effective D&E strategy is crucial for the successful adoption and diffusion of innovation, and ultimately to "bring innovation into action" in EU-funded research. Furthermore, the provision of a detailed and thorough D&E plan is also a mandatory condition required to access the research funding [9].

While the necessity and importance of these issues have been highlighted, little has been said by past contributions about how to operatively design and develop a D&E

strategy. Current and future EC-funded projects could greatly benefit from evidence-based guidelines and frameworks to support the dissemination and exploitation of project results. For this reason, the authors decided to report in this chapter their experience matured within the ground-breaking EC-funded project named NESTORE—Novel Empowering Solutions and Technologies for Older people to Retain Everyday life activity. This H2020 project aims at developing and bringing to the market a personalized and artificial intelligence-enabled virtual coach for the wellbeing and care of European senior citizens (65 and older). Using the NESTORE experience, this study furthers both theory and practice by illustrating how dissemination and exploitation activities can be organized within an EC-funded project to lead to the successful adoption and diffusion of innovation in the healthcare sector.

2 The Empirical Context and Research Design

NESTORE is a 36-month pan-European H2020 research project, which objective is to develop an integrated portfolio of innovations for the healthy ageing of European citizens aged 65 or older. The efforts of the project led to the development of a multi-dimensional and personalized virtual coaching technology. A virtual coach proposes activities, feedback, and motivation according to its user's personality, punctual needs, preferences and moods, while monitoring several parameters from different sources [2, 10]. Virtual coaches have a strong potential to maximize users' adherence to the program resulting in a higher probability of reaching the goal of health promotion [12].

As a virtual coach, NESTORE supports healthy ageing on five different levers: physical activity, nutrition, social, cognitive, and psychological health. The technology of NESTORE operates through tangible objects and sensors, software and apps, and artificial intelligence. Specifically, the system works on 3 levels: Sensing, Reasoning, and Coaching. The first is a multi-parameter and multi-domain physical sensing layer able to gather the user's key parameters (in the five well-being dimensions). It includes a wearable smart bracelet, a set of beacons for environmental monitoring and social interaction assessment, a smart scale, and a sleep monitoring device. The second level encompasses the intelligent Decision Support System able to analyze the seniors' behavior and suggest personalized "pathways of interest" following the Health Action Process Approach (HAPA). The third level includes the multi-function tangible objects, which can assume different configurations to communicate and engage the users with personalized coaching activities. NESTORE strategy is to differentiate itself from other eHealth solutions; the effectiveness of its feedback is ensured by the scientifically validated multi-disciplinary knowledge provided by experts in the different health domains involved.

The NESTORE Consortium is a collaborative and complex network composed of 15 partners from 8 European countries, including 7 universities and two research institutions, while the industry is represented by three SMEs and one large corporation (Table 1). Furthermore, NESTORE also benefits from the direct involvement of

Table 1 NESTORE consortium

Partner	Country	Type
AGE PLATFORM EUROPE	Belgium	Societal
CONSIGLIO NAZIONALE DELLE RICERCHE	Italy	Research
FLEXTRONICS DESIGN SRL	Italy	Industrial
FUNDACIO EURECAT	Spain	Industrial
FUNDACIO SALUT I ENVELLIMENT	Spain	Research
HAUTE ECOLE SPECIALISEE DE SUISSE OCCIDENTALE	Switzerland	Research
LA MERIDIANA DUE—SOCIETA' COOPERATIVA SOCIALE	Italy	Societal
LOUGHBOROUGH UNIVERSITY	United Kingdom	Research
NEOSPERIENCE SPA	Italy	Industrial
PREVENTIVE COLLECTIEF	Netherlands	Societal
ROPARDO SRL	Romania	Industrial
SHEFFIELD HALLAM UNIVERSITY	United Kingdom	Research
TECHNISCHE UNIVERSITEIT DELFT	Netherlands	Research
UNIVERSITAT DE BARCELONA	Spain	Research
UNIVERSITAT ZURICH	Switzerland	Research

a pool of external experts and stakeholders, with different backgrounds, experiences, and skills that follow the project. Such group has been named as Forum of Advisory Stakeholders (FAS) and gathers regularly once per year to review the project results and provide recommendations.

3 An Integrated Conceptual Framework for Setting an Effective Exploitation and Dissemination Strategy

The H2020 programme focuses on research to develop innovations for a smart, sustainable, and inclusive growth of the EU. These innovations target some of the most compelling challenges for the European society, as well as the worldwide community. To meet these objectives, it is crucial to successfully transfer innovations from the laboratory to the market. Following this paradigm, the activities of dissemination and exploitation of project results have taken a primary role. This is in line with the latest literature that highlights the setting of an effective strategy able to enclose communication [11], and business networking on the basis of standardized guidelines [21], as a decisive element influencing the market acceptance and diffusion of an innovation.

To support this, the NESTORE consortium has formalized five steps that might be followed to set an effective dissemination and exploitation strategy for EC funded projects in the health and social care context.

These steps were collected in an original framework named the Exploitation and Dissemination Canvas that was discussed by the whole Consortium and then approved by the three EC reviewers. The whole process was carefully managed by the Core Exploitation Team (CET), a board established to support and supervise the exploitation activities ensuring the alignment among Dissemination and Exploitation. The CET is composed of: the Scientific Coordinator of the project, the Project Manager, the Exploitation Leader, and the Communication and Dissemination Leader.

The Exploitation and Dissemination Canvas displays all the necessary pieces of information, their interdependence, and temporal sequence. It targets exploitation and dissemination objectives with an integrated approach and it is designed to be replicable in other EC-funded projects (especially related to the healthcare sector).

Step I: External Analysis

The first step deals with an in-depth analysis of the external landscape. This first step requires a mixed-method approach to get information about both the "demand" and the "supply" sides, allowing the combination of evidence gathered from various sources of data.

The demand side

The NESTORE Consortium agreed that good exploitation should be driven by the users' needs and requirements. To meet this expectation, two different paths were followed. First, the Consortium started collecting data made available by institutional reports and other secondary data sources about final users' characteristics (e.g. demography, health status, and prevalence of the chronic disease, IT literacy). This desk analysis was performed on a panel of 11 European Countries focusing on the targeted health domains: nutrition, physical, social, cognitive, and psychological. Table 2 reports data for the 3 pilot-site Countries (Italy, Spain, The Netherlands) as an example.

Second, the "voice of potential users" was also considered. For this purpose, a survey was designed and administered to the target users from two NESTORE pilot countries (Italy and Spain) applying a theoretical framework based on two very popular theories: the Technologies Acceptance Model (TAM) [3] and the Theory of Planned Behaviour (TBD) [1]. The most significant insights from the survey are shown in Fig. 1. First, the intrinsic motivation supported by the perception of the utility and expected benefit—Perceived Usefulness according to the TAM model—resulted to be the most significant determinant of the users' intention to use a virtual coaching system similar to NESTORE. Moreover, the impact of Perceived Ease of Use was also relevant, suggesting the importance to develop a system simple to use. Besides the Perceived Usefulness and the Perceived Ease of Use, the analysis shows that social pressure (the Subjective Norm) has an indirect effect on the intention to use a digital solution for healthy ageing. It indeed affects the perception of usefulness (in both countries) and the perception of usefulness (only in Italy); these are both exposed to the moral persuasion exerted by groups of people that are important for the user. This finding confirms the need for the NESTORE Consortium to engage

Table 2 Desk analysis on European countries (focus to pilot-site Countries)

	Italy					Spain				
Physical	Total population	Close to NESTORE target (55–64)		NESTORE target (65–74)		Total population	Close to NESTORE target (55–64)		NESTORE target (65–74)	
		Males	Females	Males	Females		Males	Females	Males	Females
BMI (%)										
Underweight	3.7	0.6	3.3	0.8	1.9	2.6	0.4	0.8	0.6	2.1
Normal	52.5	34.4	51	33.4	44	46.4	26	42.7	23.2	31.7
Overweight	43.8	65.1	45.7	65.8	54.1	51	73.6	56.5	76.3	66.2
Obese	10.5	16.7	14.7	15.1	16.7	16.2	24.3	21.3	22.5	26.9
Work-related physical activity (%)										
Heavy	6.8	9.8	4.9	3.1	1.7	3.2	3	1.3	0.7	0.4
Moderate	28.1	29.5	33.9	23.9	31	16.7	19.9	16.1	17.3	11.7
None or light	65.1	60.7	61.2	73	67.3	80.2	77.1	82.6	81.9	87.9
	Total population	Close to NESTORE target (50–64)	NESTORE target (65+)	Males	Females	Total population	Close to NESTORE target (50–64)	NESTORE target (65+)	Males	Females
Taking part in **sports/physical exercise** (>once a week) (%)	32	28	14	35	29	35	29	28	39	32
Nutrition	Total population	Close to NESTORE target (55–64)		NESTORE target (65–74)		Total population	Close to NESTORE target (55–64)		NESTORE target (65–74)	
		Males	Females	Males	Females		Males	Females	Males	Females
0 portions	23	19.7	14.8	14.8	12.2	25	20.4	11.9	14.7	11.2

(continued)

Table 2 (continued)

	Italy					Spain				
Physical	Total population	Close to NESTORE target (55–64)		NESTORE target (65–74)		Total population	Close to NESTORE target (55–64)		NESTORE target (65–74)	
		Males	Females	Males	Females		Males	Females	Males	Females
1-4 portions	65.1	69.1	68.1	68.1	68.5	62.6	64.5	69.7	70.2	69.3
5 portions or more	11.8	11.2	17.1	17.1	19.4	12.4	15.1	18.4	15.2	19.5
Frequency of fruit (%)										
At least once a day		74	80.3	80.6	85.3	66.7	72.6	81	80.2	84.2
1–3 times a week	11.1	10.8	7.4	7	4.9	16.3	13.8	8.9	7.4	6.7
4–6 times a week	12.7	11.6	10.1	10.3	8	12.6	10.5	7.7	10.7	7.8
Never/occasionally	5.3	3.6	2.1	2.1	1.8	4.4	3.1	2.3	1.7	1.3
Alcohol consumption (%)										
Every day	14.1	28.1	10.3	38.3	16.6	15.3	41.7	13.2	44.7	13.2
Every week	24.4	29.9	17.2	24.1	11.4	22.3	20.9	18.4	16.1	9.6
Every month	20	18.5	17.6	14.3	12.2	18.8	12.5	15.2	10.1	11
Never or not in the last 12 months	32.8	16.3	44.2	17.1	50.2	31.3	18.5	40.4	21.1	52.1
Social	Total population	Close to NESTORE target (50–64)	NESTORE target (65+)	Males	Females	Total population	Close to NESTORE target (50–64)	NESTORE target (65+)	Males	Females

(continued)

Table 2 (continued)

	Italy					Spain				
Physical	Total population	Close to NESTORE target (55–64)		NESTORE target (65–74)		Total population	Close to NESTORE target (55–64)		NESTORE target (65–74)	
		Males	Females	Males	Females		Males	Females	Males	Females
Face-to face contact with **family members** or **relatives** (>once a week)	84	86	86	81	87	77	77	82	75	79
Face-to face contact with **friends** or **neighbours** (>once a week)	87	85	87	86	88	90	88	93	91	90
Phone/internet contact with **family members** or **relatives** (>once a week)	81	80	80	77	85	85	82	86	80	90
Phone/internet contact with **friends** or **neighbours** (>once a week)	76	65	76	74	77	75	72	53	77	73
	Total population (16 +)	Close to NESTORE target (55–64)		NESTORE target (65+)		Total population (16 +)	Close to NESTORE target (55–64)		NESTORE target (65+)	

(continued)

Table 2 (continued)

	Italy					Spain				
Physical	Total population	Close to NESTORE target (55–64)		NESTORE target (65–74)		Total population	Close to NESTORE target (55–64)		NESTORE target (65–74)	
		Males	Females	Males	Females		Males	Females	Males	Females
		Males	Females	Males	Females		Males	Females	Males	Females
Cinema/Live performances/cultural sites/attending living sports (people with no activity limitation) (%)										
Cinema (1–3 times)	25.3	19.5	16.7	10.5	7.4	12.6	11.3	12.9	3.5	5
Cinema (+12 times)	5.1	2.6	2.5	1.7	1.4	3.4	1.2	1.9	0.4	0.9
Theatre and concerts (1–3 times)	22.2	16.6	19.1	10.8	11.2	14.5	14.7	12.5	6.5	8
Theatre and concerts (+12 times)	1.3	1.2	1.1	0.8	0.8	1.3	1.1	1.8	0.5	0.8
Cognitive	Total population	Close to NESTORE target (≤64)		NESTORE target (≥65)		Total population	Close to NESTORE target (≤64)		NESTORE target (≥65)	
		Males	Females	Males	Females		Males	Females	Males	Females
Prevalence of **dementia** (%)	2.09	0.04	0.05	0.64	1.36	1,75	0,04	0,05	0.56	1.11
Psychological	Total population	Close to NESTORE target (50–64)	NESTORE target (65+)	Males	Females	Total population	Close to NESTORE target (50–64)	NESTORE target (65+)	Males	Females
Satisfaction with life (1–10)	6.6	6.6	6.4	6.6	6.6	7	6.6	7	6.9	7

(continued)

Table 2 (continued)

	Italy					Spain				
Physical	Total population	Close to NESTORE target (55–64)		NESTORE target (65–74)		Total population	Close to NESTORE target (55–64)		NESTORE target (65–74)	
		Males	Females	Males	Females		Males	Females	Males	Females
Happiness (1–10)	6.8	6.9	6.4	6.8	6.8	7.3	6.9	7.2	7.3	7.3
Perceived health status as good or very good (%)	81.6	67	33	71	65	73	63	48	79	68
Have felt **lonely** (%)	7.2	6	13	6	8	6	11	5	5	7
WHO-5 mental **well-being scale** (%)	59.4	60	52	61	58	68	63	63	70	65

	The Netherlands				
Physical	Total population	Close to NESTORE target (55–64)		NESTORE target (65–74)	
		Males	Females	Males	Females
BMI (%)					
Underweight	2.3	0.2	1.1	0	0.9
Normal	50	33	45.5	32.3	43.1
Overweight	47.7	66.8	53.4	67.7	56
Obese	12.9	16.2	17.6	14.6	20.8
Work-related physical activity (%)					

(continued)

Table 2 (continued)

	The Netherlands				
Physical	Total population	Close to NESTORE target (55–64)		NESTORE target (65–74)	
		Males	Females	Males	Females
Heavy	NA	NA	NA	NA	NA
Moderate	NA	NA	NA	NA	NA
None or light	NA	NA	NA	NA	NA
	Total population	Close to NESTORE target (50–64)	NESTORE target (65+)	Males	Females
Taking part in **sports/physical exercise** (>once a week) (%)	70	75	59	71	69
Nutrition	Total population	Close to NESTORE target (55–64)		NESTORE target (65–74)	
		Males	Females	Males	Females
0 portions	45.9	48.8	33.8	36.1	24.2
1–4 portions	29	28.1	36.5	33.7	38.1
5 portions or more	25	23.2	29.8	30.1	37.7
Frequency of fruit (%)					
At least once a day	41	38.9	54.8	53.4	65.1
1–3 times a week	20.9	20.2	15	15.6	11.3
4–6 times a week	27.6	28.6	22.6	21.4	16.7
Never/occasionally	10.4	12.3	7.6	9.6	6.8

(continued)

Table 2 (continued)

	The Netherlands				
Physical	Total population	Close to NESTORE target (55–64)		NESTORE target (65–74)	
		Males	Females	Males	Females
Alcohol consumption (%)					
Every day	NA	NA	NA	NA	NA
Every week	NA	NA	NA	NA	NA
Every month	NA	NA	NA	NA	NA
Never or not in the last 12 months	NA	NA	NA	NA	NA
Social	Total population	Close to NESTORE target (50–64)	NESTORE target (65+)	MALES	FEMALES
Face-to face contact with **family members** or **relatives** (>once a week)	75	75	79	73	76
Face-to face contact with **friends** or **neighbours** (>once a week)	87	84	87	87	88
Phone/internet contact with **family members** or **relatives** (>once a week)	85	84	82	81	90
Phone/internet contact with **friends** or **neighbours** (>once a week)	73	66	57	70	76
	Total population (16+)	Close to NESTORE target (55–64)		NESTORE target (65+)	
		Males	Females	Males	Females
Cinema/Live performances/cultural sites/attending living sports (people with no activity limitation) (%)					
Cinema (1–3 times)	28.7	19.5	20.2	11.5	10.9

(continued)

Table 2 (continued)

	The Netherlands				
Physical	Total population	Close to NESTORE target (55–64)		NESTORE target (65–74)	
		Males	Females	Males	Females
Cinema (+12 times)	4	1.7	0.9	0.9	0.5
Theatre and concerts (1–3 times)	36	30.9	30.5	23.8	19.9
Theatre and concerts (+12 times)	2.6	4	3.5	1.4	2.2
Cognitive	Total population	Close to NESTORE target (≤64)		NESTORE target (≥65)	
		Males	Females	Males	Females
Prevalence of **dementia** (%)	1.47	0.04	0.05	0.46	0.92
Psychological	Total population	Close to NESTORE target (50–64)	NESTORE target (65+)	Males	FEMALES
Satisfaction with life (1–10)	7.7	7.7	7.7	7.7	7.7
Happiness (1–10)	7.8	7.9	7.7	7.8	7.8
Perceived health status as good or very good (%)	73	69	64	76	70
Have felt **lonely** (%)	3	2	6	2	4
WHO-5 mental **well-being scale** (%)	65	67	70	68	63

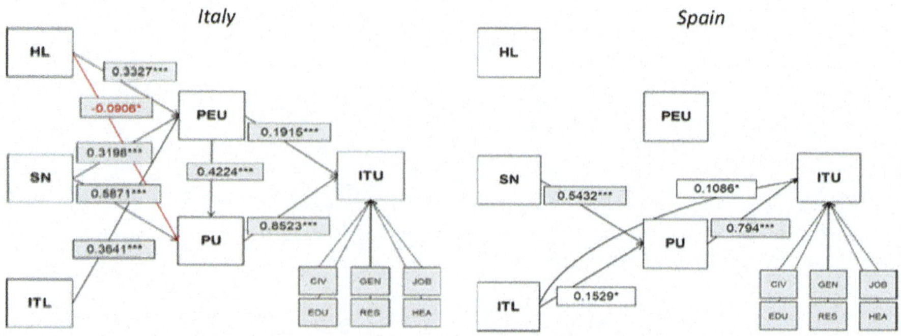

Fig. 1 Statistical results from the survey administered in Italy and Spain

in a conversation with this group of stakeholders. Concerning IT Literacy, the two countries show different results. In Italy, IT literacy, as well as Health literacy, affects mainly the Perception of ease of use, while in Spain IT literacy positively affects the intention to use, mirroring its effect on the perception of usefulness. Finally, all the control variables (the socio-demographic variables) do not affect the intention to use confirming the selected reference target.

From the involvement of the FAS in this step, it was suggested how some users may like to use NESTORE just when needed, i.e. not on a continuous basis, while some others may need to be motivated on a punctual basis through an on-going "nudging" process. Therefore, NESTORE should be flexible enough to accommodate these different preferences. Furthermore, the FAS suggested that NESTORE's approach against loneliness should change according to the cultural and social-economic statute of its users, which may vary significantly from person to person. Such dimension was not comprehensively embraced by the project before then.

The supply-side

The supply-side should investigate the competitor landscape of the reference market.

Within the NESTORE project, the reference market—the "wellbeing" market—is wide, and includes different solutions, from generic pieces of advice in magazines to free-of-charge mobile APPs able to monitor the physical activity or other behaviors, to fitness wearable devices, and telemedicine services. Therefore, the supply side was investigated by clustering the potential competition along with different perspectives including (i) products and/or service similar to NESTORE; (ii) Apps specialized in health prevention and in engaging potential user into a healthier lifestyle; (iii) Start-Ups developing products or services for the wellbeing and healthy lifestyle market by leveraging on digital technologies.

Information on products or services already in the market were collected systematically through a dedicated template interrogating different online databases. For the Health App segment, a different strategy was followed. The number of Health App available on the two-leading platform (Google Play Store and Apple App Store) indeed is around 325,000 health apps, with an estimated 78,000 new Health Apps entering the market every year. Considering the impressive size of the market, the developing rate, and the complex quality assessment, a systematic analysis of the whole app published in the databases resulted particularly challenging and ineffective to the project's purpose. The Consortium addressed this issue by defining some App archetypes on the base of five main polar characteristics: (i) Free – Paid; (ii) Medical – Health and Fitness (H&F); (iii) No/basic coaching – Advanced coaching; (iv) Mono-dimensional – Multi-dimensional; (v) Integrated with devices – Standalone. Table 3 offers a synoptic overview.

For the Start-ups analysis, a sample of 1,580 Start-up (founded between 2015 and 2019) was extracted from Crunchbase, the most qualified source of data about Start-Ups. The dataset has been created filtering Start-up categories with the following terms: "healthcare, mHealth, personal health, home healthcare". It contains information about the organization (name, foundation date, headquarters location), and the funding received (total funding amount, last funding date, last funding amount). Subsequently, the Start-Ups have been classified according to 15 macro-categories. Figure 2 shows the domains that have been more challenged in the last years and confirms that there is an interest for the areas covered by NESTORE: Intelligent tools to suggest diagnosis and/or disease management, Information on prevention and lifestyle, and Lifestyle monitoring with respectively 178, 98, and 30 Start-Ups identified. Regarding the funding amount, the median value per category (Fig. 3) was calculated to have comparable and reliable results. Results show that in the considered period, The Macro-category Intelligent tools to suggest diagnosis and/or disease management collected a median value of funds around $2,560,000, the Information on Prevention and Lifestyle collected a median value of funds around $1,340,000, and Lifestyle monitoring around $1,335,000. Considering that NESTORE covers mainly these three Macro-categories, the median value that has been jointly collected by them is aligned to the budget the EC Commission allocated for the NESTORE project. The advantage of NESTORE is that these areas will be integrated into a coherent innovative, multi-domain, cross-disciplinary, and personalized coaching system to support healthy older adults to sustain their wellbeing and capacity to live independently.

Once collected all the information needed, the overall competition has been analyzed along two main dimensions: digitalization (i.e. use of digital technologies) and personalization (i.e. tailoring coaching activities). This two-level matrix refers to the existing ways in which senior adults can get information, advice, motivation, or incentive regarding the five NESTORE dimensions. According to the two characteristics, coaches have been classified in:

Passive inputs: solutions characterized by no/basic personalization (it means that people receive information but no feedback from the instructor/author/speaker) and no digitalization. This category includes newspapers, magazines, public events, advertising, informative brochures.

Quantified self: no personalization but digitalization is supported by the use of mobile devices, apps, and wearable technologies. (e.g. Basic Mobile apps, app + devices for self-measurement; common wearables including fitness trackers, smartwatches).

Table 3 Health App polar type classification – relevant examples are displayed

App's name and logo	Payment	Category	Coaching	Dimensions	Equipment	
	LUMOSITY	Free	H&F	Basic	Mono	Stand alone
	MIND GAMES	Free	H&F	Basic	Mono	Stand alone
	ENDOMONDO	Free	H&F	Advanced	Multi	Stand alone
	HRV4 Training	Paying	H&F	Advanced	Mono	Integrated with devices
	Calorie Counter	Free	H&F	Advanced	Mono	Stand alone
	Lose It!	Free	H&F Medical	Basic	Mono	Stand alone
	WYSA	Free	H&F	Advanced	Mono	Stand alone
	Headspace	Free	H&F	Basic	Multi	Stand alone
	HealthLab Diabetes	Free	H&F Medical	Basic	Multi	Stand alone
	ETERLY	Free	H&F	Advanced	Multi	Stand-alone OR integrated with devices
	Fitbit	Paying	H&F	Advanced	Multi	Integrated with devices
	Lark	Free	H&F	Advanced	Multi	Stand-alone OR integrated with devices

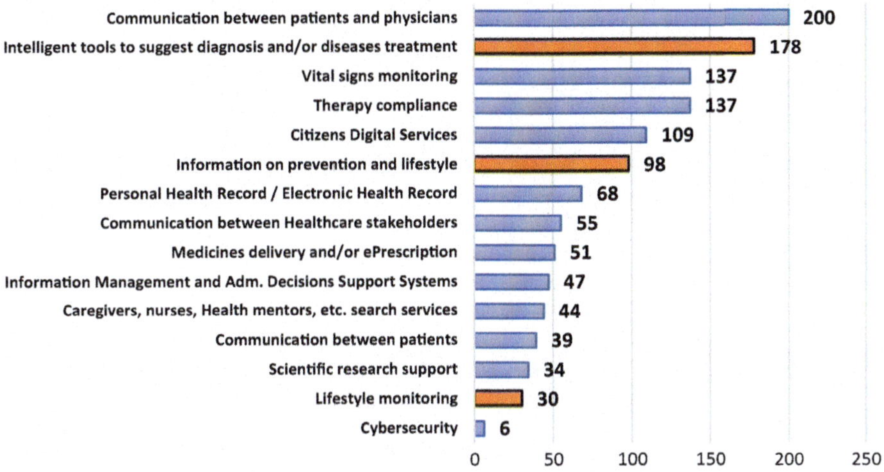

Fig. 2 Distribution of start-ups against the macro-categories

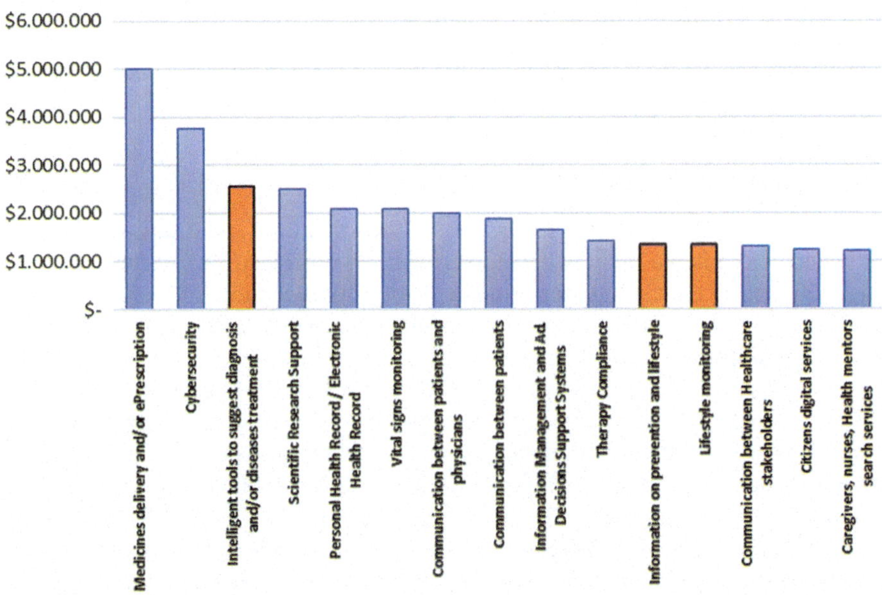

Fig. 3 Median value of gathered funds for each macro-category

Coach next door: advanced personalization but no digitalization. The coach knows the trainee and provides a customized service but the digitalization is not supported. Examples are personal trainers, integrated training Centers, nutrition and wellness Centers, and gyms.

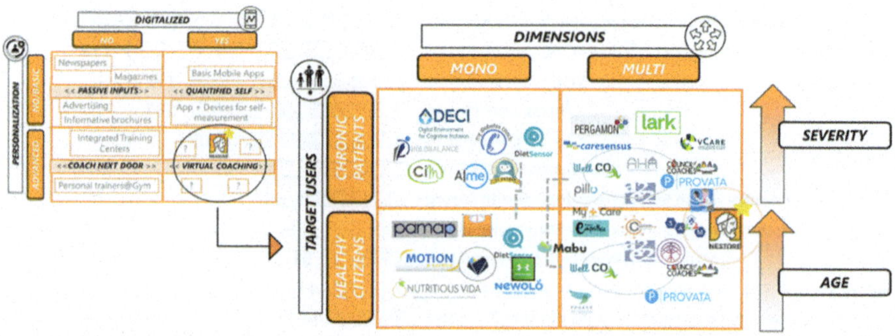

Fig. 4 NESTORE benchmarking matrix

Virtual coaching: users receive information, motivation, and feedback from the instructor that provides a customized service reinforced by the use of mobile devices, apps, and wearable technologies that can track activities (e.g. NESTORE).

Being the healthy ageing and prevention market a relevant but overcrowded market, the benchmark focused on the solutions that are most similar to the NESTORE. Therefore, the Virtual coaching category has been deeply analyzed considering the Target Users (healthy citizens and chronic patients) and the Dimensions covered (targeting the five NESTORE dimensions). The main results of the positioning are shown in Fig. 4.

Step II: Internal Analysis

The internal analysis should focus on the identification and study of the most promising exploitable outputs developed within the project. Despite the reference angle for setting the exploitation strategy is the entire solution, EC-funded projects are often the result of a portfolio of innovations that might enter into the market as standalone solutions. According to the latest in-scope literature [4], on average nearly two new or substantially improved products or services can be outlined within each ICT European project. In this view, the Internal analysis should help to discover the 2/3 most innovative exploitable outputs from the project and subsequently to design the most appropriate exploitation strategy, thus maximizing their commercial potential.

Within the NESTORE Project, the so-called exploitable outputs were collected through one-to-one interactions with the Consortium partners based on a structured questionnaire grounded on the Innovation Radar (IR) method: a method endorsed by the European Commission and by the reviewers to collect important insights about innovation and innovators. Being designed as a reporting tool, the Innovation Radar questionnaire was adapted to the specific NESTORE case. Besides the original IR questions, the questionnaire was integrated with others investigating the Technology Readiness Level (TRL), the main competitors, and the partners' strategy.

Table 4 NESTORE exploitable outputs classified by typology

Products	
Ex.O. 3 Sheffield	Design prototype
Ex.O. 1 TUD	Mobile digital game
Ex.O. 2 Zurich	Serious game for cognition
Ex.O. 2 FSIE	Gender checklist
Ex.O. 1 LU-CIM	Use habits recognition module
Ex.O. 2 LU-CIM	NESTORE EMOTIVE wellbeing engine
Ex.O. 1 NEOS	Sensor patient monitoring architecture
Ex.O. 3 HES-SO	Tangible coach
Ex.O. 1 Flex	Wearable device—smart bracelet
Ex.O. 2 Flex	Charging station
Services	
Ex.O. 2 EURECAT	Decision support system
Ex.O. 1 HES-SO	Conversational agent
Processes	
Ex.O. 1 Sheffield	Co-design methods
Ex.O. 1 HES-SO	Design guidelines
Know-how	
Ex.O. 3 Flex	Algorithm
Ex.O. 1 CNR	Descriptive models for healthy ageing
Ex.O. 2 CNR	Coaching plans
Ex.O. 3 CNR	The NESTORE specific ontology
Ex.O. 1 Zurich	Evidence-based intervention program
Ex.O. 1 FSIE	Steps for interaction system-individual
Ex.O. 2 HES-SO	Implementation of behaviour change

Table 4 shows the heterogeneity of the 21 innovative outputs that might emerge from the NESTORE project. Among them, 10 outputs have been classified as products (48%), 2 outputs as services (9.5%), 2 outputs as processes (9.5%), and 7 outputs as know-how (33%). This stratification is promising and in line with the methodology since products or services (unlike processes and know-how that are low ranked) are the preferred exploitable outputs being their potential more easily accessible.

For the analysis, the NESTORE Consortium adopted consolidated guidelines [4] to assess the score associated with the IR questionnaire. The IR has two main dimensions of analysis: the "Innovation Potential" and the "Innovator Ability". The NESTORE Consortium argued that at the stage of the project, the first dimension is more relevant than the second. In this view, the analysis of the scores associated with the Innovation Potential Indicator helps to select the 2/3 more promising classifying the outputs based on their "potential" by clustering them in Low, Medium, and High-Potential Innovations.

Step III: Scenario crystallization

The cornerstone of the Canvas is the crystallization of the exploitation scenarios: the most suitable business cases to bring the EC-funded project results to the market and generate the expected impact. The identification of the exploitation scenarios should be informed by both internal and external analysis and should be crafted according to two main directions: commercialization and further research. The first refers to Go-To-Market scenarios where the project results are commercialized on the market, the second refers to the need for collecting additional funding to progress further what will be developed and tested within the project. This is especially relevant, for example, when the strategy is to engage a conversion with payers that might be interested in gathering evidence from larger-size pilots, not frequently committed to EU-funded projects. For example, despite the opportunity for commercial exploitation of the NESTORE solution as a whole (or of single components) remains the preferred objective, the Consortium partners' claims that the search for additional funds to progress the results achieved within the project should be strongly considered. The main reason beyond is the fact that NESTORE is running small-size pilots to test the feasibility and performance of the NESTORE solution, but engaging a business conversation with health authorities and agencies requires a higher level of evidence. The Partners are aware that reaching this level of evidence and insights requires more research effort, eventually through a large scale pilot.

Reflecting on the experience of the NESTORE project, we suggest that the exploitation scenarios should be grounded on two or more exploitation hypotheses. The NESTORE Consortium, for example, started the process by identifying two dimensions: on one hand the level of integration along the value chain and on the other the revenue stream. The first is mainly related to the "openness" towards external players and suppliers of physical products/services, defining the possibility to transform NESTORE into an interoperable platform able to collect and digest data from different devices and services. The Consortium has argued that having a close system would make the communication and data sharing among the different parts of the solution easier, ensuring also the reliability of the retrieved data. On the contrary, an open system could offer users a complete and more flexible experience, allowing also the use of other smart devices not developed by NESTORE. However, this would also result in a higher complexity in the management of users' data, and poorer interaction quality. Concerning the revenue stream, the Consortium has envisaged two different possibilities: (i) freemium for the citizens (or with small co-payment) with a third party that pays for the service—it may be the case of public health care authorities or agencies that intend to offer the service to their citizens—or for the data (e.g. companies that are interested in aggregated data on lifestyle behaviors for both research and commercial purposes) or (ii) out-of-pocket paid by citizens.

Step IV: Exploitation and dissemination alignment: the stakeholder involvement

The fourth step is the involvement of the most relevant stakeholder in the scenario selection and validation.

We argue that a successful exploitation strategy for the EC-funded project is strongly dependent on the capacity of the Consortium partners to engage a conversation with those groups of stakeholders that more than others might positively affect the results of the exploitation strategy. A robust approach to identify and select the most relevant stakeholders was developed.

Nine main types of stakeholders, that concur in parallel for the creation, implementation, and diffusion of NESTORE, were identified by the CET board. Each category, together with examples of the possible actors to be involved, is listed below:

- **Standard makers**: Such as scientific communities, health authorities, technology privacy, or ethics standard makers who are involved in formulating policies, especially in matters of health and health technologies.
- **Payers**: They are the actors potentially in charge of the payment and distribution of the NESTORE solution. Al already stated, the NESTORE solution has a high potential either as a B2B (Business to Business) or B2C (Business to Consumer) business model. Thus, the Board has included in the ecosystem different payer options for who NESTORE could be of interest for generating value. For example, NESTORE could be provided by Health Care Institutions to support the delivery of new health prevention services or by Health Insurance companies for improving their portfolio of services. NESTORE could also be of strong interest to Large Corporations interested in aggregated data on lifestyle behaviors for research and commercial purpose. Moreover, the Consortium has also decided to include citizens as a payer option, however high regard to the European project requirements of affordability and economical accessibility from the users has been observed.
- **Investors/funders**: Engaging in a conversation with investors and funders such as the European Commission, Institutional funds, Private funds, and Business angels is considered of paramount importance to the project because of the development phase of the NESTORE system. These actors, indeed, could provide the consortium of financial resources for proper, consistent, and legal development of the solution behind the end of the project.
- **Providers of physical products/services and Manufacturers of hardware and software for connected care**: The Board decided to include this stakeholder group starting from the assumption that the NESTORE solution could operate as an open solution.
- **Channels**: They represent the pathways through which the NESTORE target segment could be reached out. To design the ecosystem, the Board has considered different channel options clustering them into physical channels, such as pharmacies and drug stores, tech retails, gyms and fitness centers, and virtual channels such as e-commerce.
- **Influencers**: Influencers could create a network effect around the solution. For NESTORE, these include mass media, physicians and specialists, and third age advocacy groups.

Step V: Scenario refinement and business plan

The last step to effectively set an exploitation strategy is the designing and fine-tuning of the exploitation scenarios based on the insight gathered from the stakeholders involved. This step should not be considered as a one-way street, but rather as a continuous circular journey. The identified Exploitation scenarios should be continuously refined and fine-tuned by constantly including insights resulting from the monitoring of the external and internal context. Moreover, several activities to support the building of the envisioned ecosystem should be put in place to gather more feedback and ideas from the several stakeholders identified in Step IV. Furthermore, a Business Model Canvas should be developed for each exploitation scenario, offering a holistic view on how the project results could create, deliver, and capture value. The Business Model Canvas should be complemented with the Financials for the different exploitation scenarios, supporting the choice of the most promising exploitation direction.

Finally, the FAS suggested that an economical study on the return of investment would also help this process. Within NESTORE project, a systematic literature review on Social Return on Investment (SROI) and cost-benefit analysis were performed. However, little evidence on quantified metrics to depict the social return of investment was found. This topic is further analyzed in the chapter "SROI Methods for Impact Assessment in Economy of Wellbeing".

4 Discussion and Conclusions

This study aims at contributing to the ongoing debate over the innovation difficulties of Europe -that is the failing of several EC-funded projects in bringing innovation to market, despite the growing efforts from the EC both in terms of funding and political message [19]—with a focus on the peculiar context of the healthcare sector. A novel framework to align dissemination and exploitation activities within EC-funded research projects has been proposed. This methodology is composed of five sequential steps.

The first step covers the analysis of the external landscape encompassing both the demand and the supply side. The demand side includes the study of the specificities and priorities of the different countries involved (desk analysis) and the analysis of the potential users to understand their intention to adopt the project solutions. The supply side should consider (i) comparable or substitute products or services, (ii) innovative start-ups in the referred market, and (iii) other projects targeting the same needs or developing similar solutions that may enter the market in the future. This first step allows a comprehensive understanding of users' and stakeholders' characteristics and the potential market that the project solutions might leverage. The second step analyses the internal context identifying the exploitable outputs of the project. This step refers to a framework that sees an innovative project as a portfolio of possible outputs, each with different characteristics and expected potential [14]. The third step is about the crystallization of the exploitation scenarios, the most suitable business case to bring the EC-funded project results to the market and generate impact. The identification of the exploitation scenarios should be informed by both internal and external analysis and should be crafted according to two main directions: commercialization and further research. The fourth step considers the alignment between exploitation and dissemination, with this approach the most relevant project stakeholders are involved in defining and validating the exploitation options. Nine different types of stakeholders have been proposed, this classification can be suitable and generalized also for other projects involving a similar ecosystem. In the fifth step, the exploitation scenarios design is finalized together with the development of the business models, which support the choice of the most promising scenarios for future development.

This framework has been proposed to address some of the root causes and barriers to innovation capitalization in EC-funded projects. These include the lack of defined schemes, skills, and knowledge on dissemination and exploitation activities. Many Consortia seem to consider dissemination and exploitation as abstract activities, only marginally linked to the "real work" of the project and with no added value [8]. Therefore, the real potential of an effective dissemination and exploitation strategy results to be underestimated. This study aims at reversing these beliefs, providing a well-structured and evidence-based model. Furthermore, the proposed framework can be useful to address other elements of the complexity characterizing these projects such as great organizational variety, lack of a decision-making hierarchy, and very long project duration. For all these reasons, the described model could be adapted and replicated in other EC-funded projects maximizing the impact of research, as well as promoted by EC officers leveraging on NESTORE experience and results to highlight the crucial role of dissemination and exploitation activities. In any case, these efforts should also be complemented by a set of structured and comprehensive European policies aiming at furthering the integration of the European capital, labor, product, and services markets, easing the interaction between different actors in the innovation landscape and, at the same time, ensuring healthy competition, external financing, and private risk funding [19].

The framework and the findings presented are subjected to some limitations. First, even if involving a portfolio of heterogeneous innovations, the study is based on a single case using an inductive approach. The proposed model should be replicated on different research projects to better discuss the generalization of our results. Second, the innovations developed within the NESTORE project have not been launched on the market yet. Therefore, a longitudinal study to evaluate the results on the market of these innovations (i.e. their adoption and diffusion over time) should be considered for future research. This latter will allow further validation and improvement of our method designed to bring EC-funded project innovation into action in the healthcare context.

References

1. Ajzen, I. (1991). The theory of planned behavior. *Organizational Behavior and Human Decision Processes, 50*(2), 179–211. https://doi.org/10.1016/0749-5978(91)90020-T.
2. Brandenburgh, A., van Breda, W., van der Ham, W., Klein, M., Moeskops, L., & Roelofsma, P. (2014). Increasing physical and social activity through virtual coaching in an ambient environment. In Lecture Notes in Computer Science (including subseries Lecture Notes in Artificial Intelligence and Lecture Notes in Bioinformatics). LNCS (Vol. 8610). https://doi.org/10.1007/978-3-319-09912-5_28.
3. Davis, F. D. (1989). Perceived usefulness, perceived ease of use, and user acceptance of information technology. *MIS Quarterly: Management Information Systems, 13*(3), 319–339. https://doi.org/10.2307/249008.
4. De Prato, G., Nepelski, D., & Piroli, G. (2015). Innovation radar: Identifying innovations and innovators with high potential in ICT FP7, CIP & H2020 projects. JRC Scientific and Policy Reports—EUR 27314 EN. https://doi.org/10.2791/61591
5. Elton, J., & O'Riordan, A. (2016). Healthcare disrupted: Next generation business models and strategies. Wiley.
6. European Commission. (2014). HORIZON 2020 in brief. In Directorate-General for Research and Innovation. https://doi.org/10.2777/3719.
7. European Commission. (2019). Health. https://ec.europa.eu/info/sites/info/files/research_and_innovation/knowledge_publications_tools_and_data/documents/ec_rtd_factsheet-health_2019.pdf.
8. European IPR HelpDesk. (2016). Fact sheet plan for the exploitation and dissemination of results in Horizon 2020. European IPR Helpdesk, 1–11.
9. European Parliament. (2014). Participation rules Horizon 2020. *Official Journal of the European Union, 1290*, 81–103.
10. Fasola, J., & Mataric, M. (2013). A socially assistive robot exercise coach for the elderly. *Journal of Human-Robot Interaction, 2*(2), 3–32. https://doi.org/10.5898/jhri.2.2.fasola.
11. Makkonen, H. S., & Johnston, W. J. (2014). Innovation adoption and diffusion in business-to-business marketing. *Journal of Business and Industrial Marketing, 29*(4), 324–331. https://doi.org/10.1108/JBIM-08-2013-0163.
12. Mastropietro, A., Roecke, C., Porcelli, S., del Bas, J., Boquè, N., Maldonado, L. F., & Rizzo, G. (2018). *Multi-domain model of healthy ageing: The experience of the H2020 NESTORE project*. Italian Forum of Ambient Assisted Living (Ed.). (pp. 13–21). Springer.
13. McKinsey & Company. (2019). Fit for the future: The common challenges facing healthcare systems—And how to meet them. https://www.mckinsey.com/industries/healthcare-systems-and-services/our-insights/fit-for-the-future-the-common-challenges-facing-healthcare-systems-and-how-to-meet-them.
14. Nogeste, K., & Walker, D. H. T. (2005). Project outcomes and outputs: Making the intangible tangible. *Measuring Business Excellence, 9*(4), 55–68. https://doi.org/10.1108/13683040510634844.
15. Payne, A. F., Storbacka, K., & Frow, P. (2008). Managing the co-creation of value. *Journal of the Academy of Marketing Science, 36*(1), 83–96. https://doi.org/10.1007/s11747-007-0070-0.
16. Rogers, E. M., & Everett, M. (2003). *Diffusion of third edition*. https://doi.org/82-70998.
17. Siakas, K., Messnarz, R., Georgiadou, E., & Naaranoja, M. (2012). Launching innovation in the market requires competences in dissemination and exploitation. *Communications in Computer and Information Science, 301*. https://doi.org/10.1016/j.csi.2013.08.001.
18. Storbacka, K., & Nenonen, S. (2015). Learning with the market: Facilitating market innovation. *Industrial Marketing Management, 44*, 73–82. https://doi.org/10.1016/j.indmarman.2014.10.009.
19. Veugelers, R., Cincera, M., Frietsch, R., Rammer, C., Schubert, T., Pelle, A., et al. (2015). The impact of Horizon 2020 on innovation in Europe. *Intereconomics, 50*(1), 4–30. https://doi.org/10.1007/s10272-015-0521-7.

20. WHO. (2020). Urgent health challenges for the next decade. https://www.who.int/news-room/photo-story/photo-story-detail/urgent-health-challenges-for-the-next-decade.
21. Woodside, A. G., & Biemans, W. G. (2005). Modeling innovation, manufacturing, diffusion and adoption/rejection processes. *Journal of Business and Industrial Marketing, 20*(7), 380–393. https://doi.org/10.1108/08858620510628614.

Aspects of Ethics and Data Management in Healthy Ageing Digital Services

Data Treatment in Complex Research Studies in Light of the GDPR Rules. A Critical Analysis

V. Del Core, L. Guzzetti, and Giuseppe Andreoni

Abstract The introduction of the new GDPR regulation had strong impact on clinical research and also in EU funded international research program involving several partners. This chapter is presenting the practice designed and implemented in the NESTORE project (as relevant case study which is used to build procedures and documentation to be exploited in the following research projects) in relation to privacy, data management issues including data sharing, sharing this perspective as good practice for next actions in the same framework. This was the first case study to develop a proper GDPR compliant approach and DPIA so that it was adopted ad best practice among all projects in this Politecnico di Milano university and shared among other consortia. This chapter discusses regulation, obligations, adopted measures and procedures for properly implementing the GDPR.

1 Introduction

General Data Protection Regulation (GDPR) directive [1] entered into force in Europe on 15th of May 2018 and have established a common framework for data treatment in respect of the privacy obligations. This is important for any activity including research so that this aspect have to be adequately considered in any research activity including human subjects, both healthy volunteers and patients.

In principle, Article 5 par. 1 letter b. and art. 89 par. 1 of the EU regulation defines the rules for the use of personal data for scientific purposes, that still has a favorable discipline given the public relevance. However, this particular data treatment requires a correct balance between the protection of the person and the research purpose, providing for appropriate precautions, in order to prevent, as far as possible, a prejudice to the rights and freedoms of the interested party.

V. Del Core · L. Guzzetti · G. Andreoni (✉)
Department of Design, Politecnico di Milano, Milan, Italy
e-mail: giuseppe.andreoni@polimi.it

G. Andreoni
Institute of Bioimaging and Molecular Physiology, National Research Council, Segrate, Milan, Italy

G. Andreoni and C. Mambretti (eds.), *Digital Health Technology for Better Aging*, Research for Development, https://doi.org/10.1007/978-3-030-72663-8_18

From this point of view, in order to understand the level of protection of the rights and freedoms of the interested parties and on what risks can materialize with the treatment specifically developed for the research activity. Assessment of the privacy risks associated with the interested parties participating in any research project, it is preferrable to adopt a privacy impact assessment. Today, on this point, even the ethical committees start to ask for this written preliminary evaluation and opinion from the scientific proposers even during the research study preparation.

In relation to H2020 funded research programs, the NESTORE initiative represented and excellent occasion to apply the GDPR and to develop the adequate documental and assessment framework of projects in relation to GDPR itself. NESTORE is representative of a wide category of projects concerning human health and lifestyle in the prevention framework. NESTORE developed an "intelligent system" in the form of an integrated companion to help the user to maintain health and wellness, leveraging upon the 5 domains of the human nature: Cognitive capabilities, Physiological status and physical activity, Mental and psychological wellbeing, Social interaction, Nutrition. Therefore, a complex set of data, including user's lifestyle and health related parameters, and environmental data, were collected, stored and managed during the project lifecycle.

The general data flow that is implemented in the NESTORE project is described in the following Fig. 1.

Data that will be collected are classified into two main categories: (a) general Personal Information or Private data, (b) Lifestyle Data and Health Data or Sensitive Data.

General personal information, also called common personal data, includes anagraphical data and all those data that are released directly by the users based on agreement on the management conditions. These data are mainly collected under informed consent agreement and are taken also in form of questionnaires, questions and answers, including dialogue with chatbot, preferences and other personalization tool.

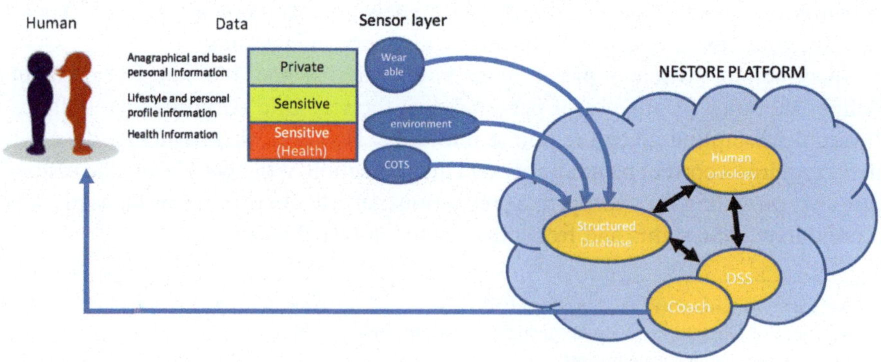

Fig. 1 Data flow in the NESTORE project

Lifestyle and Health Data are acquired from sensors, both environmental and wearable. Lifestyle Data includes environmental data acquired using sensors, smartphone (e.g. meal pictures), tangible interface (sensors on the tangible interface), environmental devices, or other sources (e.g. weather forecast web pages etc.…). These data allow for the reconstruction of the user lifestyle including environmental conditions and social activities. These data are classified as personal data under the privacy regulation.

Sensitive Data includes all the health data acquired through wearable or other devices, including certified medical devices. Sensitive data relates to physical status, mainly collected by wearable, and psychological and cognitive status, collected in serious games and social interaction. Being sensitive and specific data with health relevance, in the NESTORE project, all measures (as technical as organizational) have been implemented and verified in order to guarantee security and data minimization in accordance with recital no. 156 of GDPR.

The collected data are stored into the NESTORE cloud platform as a source to be managed by the Decision Support System (DSS) which generates inputs for the coaching guidelines. Data are managed and stored through a structured database that is implementing the requested level of anonymization and cryptography through an Interface between common personal data and sensitive data, as well as a closed binary and proprietary data format to prevent from the risk of use by other persons or parties out of NESTORE (Fig. 2).

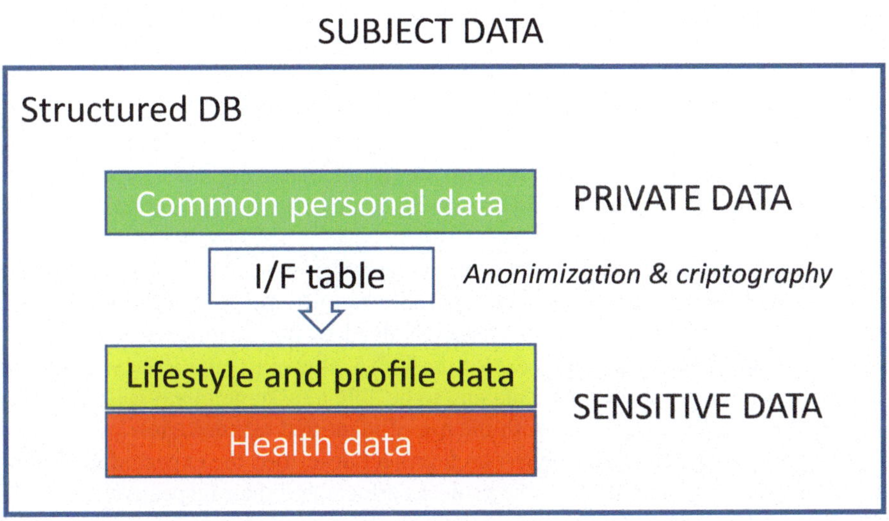

Fig. 2 Data structure and layers in the NESTORE project

2 The Data Protection Impact Assessment (DPIA)

The NESTORE project for its contents and for the use of personal data required an overall assessment for the purposes of the protection of personal data of the processing activities. The choice to carry out a privacy impact assessment as required by art. 35 of the GDPR, responds to the general hypothesis in which the data controller deems it appropriate to carry out a self-assessment with respect to the treatments he/she intends to place. The general hypothesis concerns treatments which, providing in particular the use of new technologies that can present a high risk for the rights and freedoms of individuals, considering in particular the nature, object, context and purpose of the treatment. The regulation clarifies the use of a new technology, defined "in accordance with the degree of technological knowledge achieved" (see no. 91), may lead to the obligation to conduct a DPIA, as the use of a technology can generate consequences on the individual and social or somewhat unknown in certain situations. Therefore, the DPIA allows the owner/controller to understand what risks may arise from the holder and manage these risks.

The DPIA referring to the research project allows to satisfy the concept of accountability which in art. 5 par. 2 of the regulation states that the data controller is in charge of complying with the principles established for the processing of personal data. These are the principles listed in letters (a) to (f) of paragraph 1 of art.5, i.e. principles of lawfulness, correctness, transparency; the principle of minimization, the principle of purpose limitation, the principle of conservation limitation, the principle of data accuracy, and finally the principle of integrity and confidentiality. The DPIA must be able to prove this compliance ("accountability"). Responsibility is also referred to by art. 24 of the regulation, according to which the Data Controller, within the scope of application, of the context and purposes of the processing, as well as of the risks having different probability and severity for the rights and freedoms of persons, implements and demonstrates all the technical and organizational measures adequate to guarantee, and that the processing is carried out in accordance with the regulation.

Therefore, the impact assessment is particularly useful on a research project where particular personal data are collected, as it allows to frame the current state of the level of risk to which the personal data involved in the treatments object of the research would be exposed. The use of the DPIA allows to take a decision on the overall management of personal data and to be able to assume in a responsible way the treatment that is carried out with the use of identified technologies.

The impact assessment in the research project described the expected treatment, qualifying the responsibilities of the project partners and their respective roles. The DPIA has identified potential risks to data and the rights and freedoms of data subjects. In addition to the above, the DPIA has specified the controls that are necessary to ensure a treatment that guarantees the rights and freedoms of individuals, qualifying the technical and organizational measures intended to satisfy the protection of personal data.

The DPIA adopted for NESTORE has been periodically updated to take into account the evolution of the research project and to keep track of any changes, the type and flows of the data processed as well as the level of risk of the treatments or other events that may occur in the life cycle of the research project. This recursive approach following system design also allows us to prove compliance with the principles of privacy by design and by default. This is a good practice and suggested approach.

In order to verify the adequacy and appropriateness of measures to manage and treat data, several tools have been developed and made available. Regarding this aspect, one of the most interesting and freely accessible tools is that one provided by the French Data Protection Authority (CNIL) which allows for an overall evaluation of the processing of personal data. The CNIL has made available a software to help the owners with a view to carry out the impact assessment on data protection [2]. Although it was conceived as a methodology for small and medium enterprises, nevertheless this tool allows to focus on the main elements to be analysed for an impact assessment procedure on data protection [3]. Therefore, the methodology proposed by CNIL was considered a useful support for the orientation and execution of a DPIA, even if it should not be understood as a pre-built scheme for each impact assessment that must be integrated according to the types of treatment examined.

In this sense, for the NESTORE research project it was however a methodology to be considered valid as it allowed researchers to analyze in detail the topic of personal data protection. For this reason, it was adopted by NESTORE management team dedicated to privacy issues.

In short, the CNIL methodology allows for the:

1. *Definition of the purpose of the treatment* by qualifying the research areas and what objectives the researchers set themselves.
2. *Analysis of the legal basis of the processing*: it is the identification of the legal context that makes the processing lawful and therefore according to art. 6 and art. 9 allows to carry out the processing. The analysis of the legal framework underlying an assessment of the lawfulness of the processing involves in many cases the assessment of individual EU national legislations: in fact, as pursuant to art. 89, there is a delegation to individual national legislations for the exercise of exceptions to the rights of interested parties in the field of research. Therefore, the evaluation of a research project may involve an analysis that is often not simple even by national legislation.
3. *Analysis of compliance with the processing principles*: the purpose limitation, the data minimization (evaluation that the data are proportional and necessary for processing), and the storage limitation (definition of processing and use times) are the elements that have to be considered and analyzed.
4. *Analysis of the rights of the interested parties*: this step consists in the evaluation of whether the interested parties can exercise their rights according to what methods and procedures to be adopted for this. In the field of research, this area becomes particularly delicate precisely in consideration of the aforementioned art. 89.

5. *Analysis of the roles of the treatment*: it intends to identify the position of the owners and of any managers who exercise the treatment. Therefore, in a context such as research projects, the definition of roles and respective responsibilities also becomes essential for the regulatory aspects of relationships among partners. In particular, it is necessary to analyze the ways in which the partners have defined the purposes and means of the processing. If these are shared, a joint ownership will be defined. Also, in the processing of data in research projects it will be necessary to indicate the role of subjects who support the project from an infrastructural point of view, qualifying the external data processors pursuant to art. 28 of the GDPR.
6. *Analysis of organizational measures*: the organizational measures are the operating methods that the processing requires. In this point it is necessary to define the responsibilities, the organizational roles of the participants in the research team, and the capabilities, such as data access privileges and training that such people have obtained.
7. *Analysis of technical measures*: this step is dedicated to the verification of the design and implementation of the technological and organizational platform that implements the technical measures ensure the confidentiality, availability and integrity of personal data. The measure could be related to the implementation of data anonymization, pseudo-anonymization, cryptography and other security related technical measures [4].
8. *Verification of the menaces and threats for data protection.* According to the system design in relation to the technical measures aforementioned, a detailed risk analysis should be carried out in order to verify risks sources and relevance of the corresponding impact in the eventuality of their occurrence. Protection, countermeasures and minimization of probability and impact should be carefully analyzed to design the proper and adequate safety procedures and techniques.
9. *Assessment of the adequacy of the risk mitigation measures.* Finally, the DPIA evaluates the appropriateness of the contingency plan mitigating the occurrence of threat and menaces to data breach. If also this last point is matched the DPIA is completed.

The final step is the final assessment provided by the Data Protection Officer of the leading institution of the research consortium, who has the responsibility to approve the DPIA.

3 The Data Sharing Agreement (DSA)

The DPIA has demonstrated the the overall compliance of the NESTORE project with the regulations for data protection and has highlighted the risks of the processing in relation to freedom and dignity of the person. Again, by the analysis carried out through the DPIA, it was then necessary to qualify by an agreement the methods for sharing information among the partners of the project with respect to the research aims.

In particular, a Data Sharing Agreement is necessary to establish and define how the data will be shared and divided in each phase of the life cycle of the same, i.e. from collection, to their use for research purposes up to their cancellation or anonymization. The DSA allows not only to define the sharing standards but also the roles that are assigned among the project partners for the processing operations that are necessary. The agreement allows to define how the data transfer will be carried out since the data generation (i.e. when the subject provide them for the first time) up to storage or publication at the end of the project, through what methodology and in which form, in order to ensure compliance with the principle of transparency, proportionality and reasonableness in the use of data in the research project.

The definition of such procedures allows to comply with the accountability principle as required by art. 5 par 2 of the GDPR, by demonstrating the responsibility with respect to compliance with the norms and rules regulating the data protection.

Therefore, the DSA allows defining among all project partners several issues.

1. *The role of the partners in each phase of the treatment.* The agreement shall identify all the organizations participating in the data exchange, indicating their respective contact points, their Data Protection Officer (DPO), or other employee. In addition, a specific procedure must be provided in the event that the sharing of data or participation in the project activity should engage new and additional institutions. In the case of NESTORE it was expressly provided that the entry of new organizations to the treatment would require the written consent of all partners. The choice to regulate the transfer also makes it possible to identify who among the partners has a joint ownership role based on the fact that means and purposes are shared with respect to subjects who may have a different role of data controller. This means that the DSA allows for a very easily processing the provisions of art. 26 regulating in an optimal and transparent way the mutual responsibilities regarding the observance of the obligations deriving from the GDPR, with particular regard to the exercise of the rights of the interested party. Different roles other from the owners, may also be identified: for example, it can be foreseen the presence or the appointment to data processors pursuant to art. 28 or the identification of people with specific roles and authorized for processing pursuant to art. 29 of the GDPR.
2. *The purpose of data sharing.* The objective of the DSA shall cover all steps of data and outcomes from their processing. It is necessary to design the complete dataflow and describe what is needed to happen to data at each stage for their safe management and treatment. In summary, the agreement must

   - identify the objectives to be achieved through the treatment,
   - explain why data sharing is necessary to achieve these goals,
   - describe in general the benefits that are intended to be obtained by individuals or by companies.

3. *The set of data to be shared.* It is necessary to specify what data are subject to sharing and processing. This is a point made explicit and described in detail in the annexes of the DSA, by specifying with respect to the institutions (and its employee) what kind of access is allowed. In some cases it could be appropriate to share only some pieces of information related to the person, omitting other material or anonymizing it as for the purposes of the research it may not be necessary to know the identity of the individual. In some cases, it may be appropriate to define the levels of permission for accessing to certain data structures, so that only specific members of individual institutions with specific roles in the framework of scientific research can access them; for example, personnel who have received adequate training to carry out research. From this point of view, the agreement allows for the compliance with the data limitation principle and avoids the disclosure of irrelevant or excessive information. The types of particular data are also documented by identifying the relevant conditions for their processing. This was important in NESTORE when processing health data that could produce incidental findings, i.e. possible health risks for the subject derived from the collected data and assessed by medical experts, so that it is needed to inform the subject (in accordance with ethical rules and the procedures agreed with the subject when signing the Informed Consent to the Research).
4. *Definition of the procedures for governing the agreement.* There are 3 points that are of particular importance:
   (a) The definition of data breach countermeasures, their procedures and the related management also in relation to notifications to the Guarantor or interested parties;
   (b) The method of managing the rights of the interested parties, establishing the procedures to manage requests for access, complaints or questions from the public;
   (c) to establish and have common rules for the storage and deletion of shared data, based on their nature and content, and what procedures are needed to process the data for carrying out the research.
5. *Definition of the standards* that will be observed for the transfer and reception of data among the partners.
6. *Qualification of the technical and organizational measures* that will be adopted by the partners.
7. *Identification of the legal basis for sharing data since the beginning of the processing.* This is a minimum requirement. In the case of NESTORE, the legal basis refers to the consent of the interested parties for their treatment and for their sharing among the partners. Both the legal basis identified through the privacy policy communicated to the interested parties and the form adopted for consent are contained as an attachment in the agreement.
8. *Qualification of the technological infrastructure* that will be adopted for the transfer of data between partners, allowing compliance with the principles set

out in art. 32 regarding the adoption of the organizational and technical measures necessary to ensure the security of the processing of personal data.
9. *Definition of the rules of the processing also with respect to the transfer of data outside the EU.* This is important when data are shared with partners outside EU. In this case special procedures shall apply, specifically if differences in GDPR rules are present. For example, the Brexit introduced this special need, i.e. to take into account this point.

The DSA has the advantage of helping the project partners to justify the sharing of data, demonstrating the awareness of the treatment and its traceability as all the legal and technical elements for the management of the treatment have been taken into consideration.

Therefore, the DSA provides a structure intended to demonstrate the commitment that the project partners have had to ensure the requirements required by the principles on the protection of personal data.

It should be clarified that there is no predefined format for the data sharing agreement. The form in which the text can be drawn up can have a variety of forms which depend on the size of the processing and the complexity of data sharing. In the case of NESTORE, a text has been conceived and written to provide for a minimum set of common rules that qualify the context of the processing that tends to bind all the organizations involved. From this point of view, the agreement must be drafted in clear, concise and easy to understand language as the processing and transfer of data involves institutions operating in different fields and contexts for the execution of the project.

The text of the agreement is accompanied by a series of annexes that are drawn up to ensure a clear and complete description of the technical and organizational measures taken for the processing. Qualification rules for technical and organizational measures and also the common agreement about the roles that the partners assume in the execution of the project must be clearly stated.

All the legal information relating to how the data will be collected and the privacy policy form that will be adopted for the research project are also indicated in the attachments.

The adoption of an agreement that qualifies the context, defines the rules among the partners and describes their roles in the management of the treatment, in the event of a violation of the law, allows to prove the commitment that the project partners have adopted to ensure compliance with the personal data protection regulations.

4 The Informed Consent

Informed consent is the process aiming at obtaining from a subject his/her permission for conducting some form of research on a person, or for disclosing a person's information. This permission is mandatory to be received before conducting any data collection or intervention on a person. The informed consent form consists of two parts: the information sheet and the consent certificate.

Once defined the data to be collected, their processing and treatment techniques and the owners and processors, in accordance with the purpose of the processing, the owner must provide the data subjects, before processing, with the information required by the rules (Article 12 of the GDPR). This is done through the information sheet. It is a document explaining in detail all the treatments, processing methods, management and traceability of data through which the subject can understand and decide in full freedom and awareness if he/she is giving his/her consent to personal data collection and treatment, and also pursuing the right for the individual to be informed.

Specifically, the information sheet is a communication addressed to the interested party that has the purpose of informing the citizen, even before he/she becomes interested (i.e. before the treatment begins), on the purposes and methods of the treatments carried out by the data controller, It is a duty of the data controller to ensure the transparency and correctness of the treatments from the design stage of the treatments themselves on, and to be able to prove it at any time (principle of accountability).

The information sheet is also intended to allow the interested party to provide valid consent, if required as the legal basis of the processing. In this case, the information is not only due on the basis of the principle of transparency and correctness, but it is also a condition of legitimacy of the consent. For this reason, the informed consent form must be written in language easily understood by the subjects, it must minimise the possibility of coercion or undue influence, and the subject must be given sufficient time to consider participation [5]. Furthermore, the informed consent has to include also the explanation about the procedures for data anonymization (not reversible) and pseudo-anonymization in light of provisions set by art. 89, paragraphs 1 and 2, of GDPR, so that the data treatment is legal and respectful of the principle of transparency.

5 Conclusions

This chapter describes the data treatment in complex research studies in light of the GDPR rules. Any multi-partner, international and scientific research study involving humans shall comply with the regulation concerning data protection and privacy measures. For this purpose, a structured protocol is suggested to be properly design and adopted. A general flow of procedures, deriving from the experience of coordinating and managing a European project dedicated to the design and test of solutions for Active and Healthy Ageing, led us to design the following step-by step analysis and assessment.

1. Analysis

    1.1. Context analysis.

   1.2. Mapping of processes related to the processing of personal data by each partner, definition of roles and responsibilities (process workflow).
      1.2.1. Mapping of data flow.
      1.2.2. Organizational analysis.
      1.2.3. Technical analysis.
      1.2.4. Role of partners.
      1.2.5. Process flow design.
      1.2.6. Analysis of the lawfulness of the processing.
   1.3. Assessment of the privacy risks connected to the interested parties participating in the project, use of the DPIA according to the CNIL methodology.

2. Design of the system (technical measures and procedures) for data protection.

   2.1. The definition of the organizational and technical measures implemented in the research project among all the partners to guarantee the protection of personal data.
   2.2. Processing of a privacy notice to those interested in the project and related informed consent.

3. Definition of a legal framework (data sharing agreement) among the partners of the project.

   3.1. The roles of qualified partners as joint controllers or data processors depending on the data management condition and their role in project management.
   3.2. The need to transfer data in the context of Brexit or to partners outside EU for the purposes of scientific research.

4. Preparation of the informed consent for subjects participating to the research study and inclusion in the experimental protocol.

From all the above, this chapter highlights the importance of systematizing the organizational and technical measures adopted for project management to document the privacy by design and by default of the project.

This is the lesson learnt from our case study, the NESTORE project, and that have been proposed as general and reference framework for other research studies. This procedure is currently adopted in our scientific institution as good practice.

References

1. https://eur-lex.europa.eu/eli/reg/2016/679/oj.
2. https://www.cnil.fr/en/open-source-pia-software-helps-carry-out-data-protection-impact-assesment.
3. ENISA. (2017, December). *Handbook on security of personal data processing*. ISBN 978-92-9204-251-6. https://doi.org/10.2824/569768.

4. ENISA. (2021, January). *Data pseudonymisation: Advanced techniques and use cases*. ISBN 978-92-9204-465-7. https://doi.org/10.2824/860099.
5. Manti, S., & Licari, A. (2018). How to obtain informed consent for research. *Breathe (Sheff), 14*(2), 145–152. https://doi.org/10.1183/20734735.001918.

Ethical, Legal and Societal Issues of Research and Innovation in NESTORE

Itziar De Lecuona

Abstract Ageing population is growing faster in the European Union. Information and Communication Technologies can provide solutions for Active Ageing. NESTORE will develop an innovative, multi-dimensional, personalized coaching system to support healthy ageing by generating and sustaining motivation to take care of health and by suggesting healthy nutrition and personalized physical and mental coach, as well as social interaction, to prevent decline and preserve wellbeing. The chapter analyses the ethical, legal and societal issues (ELSi) of the research and innovation processes in NESTORE project. First, the work will study some of the prominent ethical issues posed by NESTORE and how to assure autonomy and informed consent. Second the work focuses on the personal data treatments and how to assure privacy and confidentiality according to the General Data Protection Regulation. Finally, it includes the Responsible Research and Innovation approach for this particular project. The main goal is to provide practical information on how to implement the NESTORE ELSi that could be useful for future projects based on the convergence of technologies and decisions data driven oriented to foster research and innovation in ageing and wellbeing.

1 Introduction

One of the most important challenges that western societies must tackle is ageing. The increase in life expectancy results in the rise of a population with physical and psychological dependencies and with multiple ailments. In our society, which idolizes consumption and youth, there's a lack of awareness about the situation of elderly people and frequently it seems to be a taboo subject. NESTORE is a multidisciplinary, European Union funded consortium aiming to develop an innovative, multi-dimensional, personalized coaching system to support healthy ageing by generating and sustaining motivation to take care of one's own health; and suggesting

I. De Lecuona (✉)
Department of Medicine – Bioethics and Law Observatory, UNESCO Chair in Bioethics at the University of Barcelona, Barcelona, Spain
e-mail: itziardelecuona@ub.edu

G. Andreoni and C. Mambretti (eds.), *Digital Health Technology for Better Aging*, Research for Development, https://doi.org/10.1007/978-3-030-72663-8_19

personalized nutritional and physical advice in the form of a digital coach, as well as boosting social interaction, preventing decline and preserving wellbeing.

This project is designed to use personal data to improve decision-making in real-life settings. Personal data are the gold of our time, and health, biometric and socio-demographic data are special categories of data [1] that require the highest protection because they say everything about us; and because they could be used for unwanted purposes and give rise to covert discrimination, with profound implications for people's freedom and that of future generations. The possession of personal datasets by third parties, whether private or public initiatives, could affect our rights depending on the uses, giving these third parties extraordinary power over us. The decisions taken in the field of health research and innovation and in highly digitized contexts will mark the lives of people, groups and societies.

Since the beginning of this century, Europe has been committed to a data-driven society. It is a political and economic decision, which also includes knowledge creation and transfer processes. The goal is a single and competitive digital market, capable of guaranteeing the protection of people's rights and freedoms and promoting research and innovation based on the intensive exploitation of datasets, including personal data [2]. In the field of healthcare this commitment results in more personalized medicine, more efficient health care systems, the prediction of the adverse effects of drugs with a smaller number of people exposed to risk, active ageing and well-being; and pandemic prediction and management systems. All these areas, in which many substantial public and private research and innovation consortia are funded, based on the said technologies and on the development of mHealth, are underlain by the exploitation of datasets, including personal data, and for which the participation of third parties traditionally outside the field of biomedicine and healthcare is necessary. These third parties, who may be either private companies or even public authorities, are interested in accessing different personal datasets, for what they may say about their owners and for what they could predict, an interest that may be different from, and even contrary to, that of the research project leaders [3].

In the digital society we have ceased to be anonymous and have become re-identifiable. Our gender, postcode and date of birth identify us with a very high percentage of success [4]. Due to the development of technology and the huge amount of personal information amassed in different databases, and to the data we disclose, it is possible to create patterns of behaviour, predict conducts and, therefore, improve decision-making. For that it is necessary to programme algorithms that are fed by datasets including personal data. These personal data, as the main raw material, are the property of their owners, who in turn will be the final targets of the results of the research and innovation processes with the special situation of health data.

The current review model—born and raised in the second half of the twentieth century—for analysing research projects in which humans take part and/or their data personal is used, is outdated and ineffective, due to the technical, ethical and legal challenges posed by personal data processing in the twenty-first century. Nowadays the analysis of the ethical, social and legal issues must focus on protecting people by safeguarding their personal data and ensuring their owners' privacy and confidentiality. The exercise of autonomy to make free and informed decisions must be promoted and guaranteed to avoid discrimination (specifically when it is covert) with fairness and transparency. There has to be a balance between maximizing the benefits and minimizing the risks also includes processing personal data properly. We are facing a new paradigm in research and innovation based on data driven interventions where providers of data are final users and participants of research. This new digital approach were data and datasets are fuelling almost all activities of our lives, pose challenging situations and questions that should be solved, and it is an evolving situation full of grey areas in data protection in research.

The main objective of this chapter is to integrate the ethical, legal and societal issues of the NESTORE project, including international guidelines such as the General Data Protection Regulation and Responsible Research and Innovation aspects. The aim of this analysis, and of the project at large, is to ensure that the rights and freedoms of the subjects involved are guaranteed, including the protection of personal data—and those involving what are considered special categories-, and additionally, to ensure freedom of research. NESTORE aspires to use its results to improve the quality of life of the elderly and promote active ageing and well-being with the help of the best technology possible, while respecting and promoting freedoms and human rights of the subjects involved.

2 Autonomy, Information and Informed Consent

One of the key innovation elements in NESTORE is the design of "pathways of interest" able to provide hints and services according to the user's preferences, while ensuring that the overall wellbeing and health status is maximised. NESTORE leverages on the following novel Information and Communication Technologies:

(1) multi-domain unobtrusive monitoring system, including wearable and environmental sensors and tangible objects
(2) an intelligent Decision Support System, to analyse the participants behaviour and provide personalized targets toward wellbeing
(3) active coaching, developed as a conversational agent, embodied in a physical companion that assumes different forms, able to establish affective communication through multimodal communication channels and to engage older people with personalized coaching activities in a single or multiple domain [5].

These interventions pose challenges to the participants and responsibles of the study regarding autonomy, privacy and ethical issues that must be analysed.

Any potential research participants must understand that their participation in any given study does not always imply a direct benefit to their health or specific condition. Furthermore, they should be aware that their contribution could be for improving scientific knowledge only. The process of informing research participants should begin with a general description that should be very brief, with relevant information expressed in clear and understandable terms according to the potential participants.

Information provided to participants should inform about the purpose of the project to be an innovative, multi-dimensional, cross-disciplinary and personalized coaching system. In our case with the NESTORE project, it should be ensured that research participants would receive adequate information and the proper explanations to understand that the NESTORE system is like a virtual friend, a companion and a coach. Importantly, in case of incidental findings, participants should first know what these are and that they are will be immediately informed if researchers detect any sign during the evaluations or system use period that could indicate a potential health problem that requires a medical follow-up. Participants will receive an alert to seek the proper care and attention from the appropriate healthcare services.

Participants of any research project should be informed about the type of data, including personal data of special categories of nature, and receive a clear explanation regarding its use, implications for privacy and other rights implied and the specific purpose of the treatments proposed. A key issue of the information process and informed consent procedure is to inform subjects about data protection measures to assure respect for privacy and confidentiality and any kind of potential or real discrimination of the research subject by misuses of data.

Regarding economic compensations, research participants should be informed that their participation in the study will not cause any economic burden for them and should be aware of the conditions established for travel expenses, dietary expenses or reimbursements. It is important to note that any economic compensations should not be established to a limit that would affect or modify the free will of participants to the extent of coercion or undue influence to participate. While research should always avoid conflict of interest, if any does exist, researchers should declare it clearly and transparently and participants should be aware. Participants and members of society should understand that there are different types of conflict of interests, not only economic, but also of a personal natural, hierarchical, etc. At any time, researchers should check and avoid misconceptions of participants regarding the specific intervention proposed.

The verbal and written process of information should be accompanied by an informed consent template covering all these aspects to be signed by research participants, where they can decide whether to comply with the proposed research. The specific template should include again, general information about the project (title, reference, funding, principal investigator, etc.) and the name and surnames of the potential participant. As a general guide, this informed consent template should clearly state that participants:

(1) have read the information template given to them about the research study after being informed of the abovementioned issues;
(2) can ask questions about the study;
(3) have received enough information about the study;
(4) have spoken with the researchers involved in the project;

(5) understood that their participation is voluntary and that they can withdraw from the study at any time and without giving any explanation and without this having an impact on their situation (medical care, etc.).

In order to promote autonomy and according to the general rules and requirements information and informed consent procedures, all research interventions, including those like NESTORE, should provide the following information:

- title of the study;
- clear information regarding who is in charge of the research and funding (adding references if necessary) and the identification of the main researchers.
- This information should be followed by a brief introduction in order to inform participants about the proposed research to decide whether participate.
- In the same process of information and informed consent templates, participants should be aware that the research has been approved and reviewed by the entitled research ethics committee of the research centre involved.
- Specific information should be provided about the ethical and legal framework applicable, integrating international, European, national and local guidelines and regulations depending on the type of research and paths to follow.
- Give potential participants names, phone numbers and contact addresses of the main researchers to contact them at any time and to make them understand that they can ask any questions.
- Likewise, they are free to be part or to revoke consent at any time without any explanations and with no negative consequences i.e., In receiving treatments, if this is the case, etc.).

The final goal is to provide to potential participants with all elements they may need to make a rational decision and assure that their consent is free and voluntary. Information on informed consent is part of a process that includes verbal communication and written information and that obliges those responsible for research to provide any information that the participants should need at any time.

3 Personal Data Protection in Digital Environments

In May of 2018, The General Data Protection Regulation [6] introduced new requirements to assure that privacy and confidentiality will be protected through data treatments. The General Data Protection Regulation has established specific principles, rights, obligations, guarantees and institutions such as the Data Protection Officer as an independent advisor on data protection. The key point is to assure that data owners have the control over their personal information and how it is treated by controllers and processors.

For treatments in research of personal data of special categories, i.e., health care data, which is the case in the NESTORE project, the General Data Protection Regulation establishes not only specific guarantees, but also specific security measures that the NESTORE project has carefully analysed and followed.

The main questions to be answered for European Research Projects such as NESTORE regarding data treatments including personal data and partners involved are:

(1) Is the information and informed consent process of participants developed according to the General Data Protection Regulation?
(2) Will the data be anonymised, codified or pseudonymised in the framework of the research process?
(3) Where are the data (main researcher´s institution, format, database, etc.)?
(4) Will the data to be sent or shared between partners?
(5) Will cloud services be deployed to store data and conditions?
(6) Will the project require the services of third parties for data treatments and what will be the possible implications of this for participants/data owners?
(7) Will the data to be sent/transferred outside of the European Union?

To give a practical example, the following steps will be taken to assure data protection in the NESTORE project, which is based on datasets that include personal data and special categories of data:

(1) All partners involved should be clearly identified and those responsible for data treatments should be determined too, due to co-responsibility (art. 26 General Data Protection Regulation). As stated before, the principle of minimisation of data, is an obligation of the NESTORE team to determine if the data that are going to be treated are adequate, pertinent and proportionate to the purpose determined.
(2) All procedures for personal data collection should be identified and this information will then be crucial to build the information and informed consent process accordingly (interviews, records, tracking, monitoring, etc.), as described above. At this point all technological solutions for storage should be analysed (cloud, servers, networks, etc.) and the measures to guarantee data protection that should be deployed should be determined.
(3) Consequently, transfers of data, if any, should be identified. If there will be third parties in charge of data treatments, the contracts should be built and reviewed accordingly. International data transfers, if any, should be determined too. For this reason, it should be checked if there is a specific informed consent of the entitled person for the transfer process; the Privacy Shield or the Authorisation of Data Protection Authorities (art. 45 to 49 General Data Protection Regulation).
(4) In the case of the NESTORE project, due to the results of the previous analysis and because of the potential high-level impact of the NESTORE interventions in the rights and freedoms of potential participants, the next step is to undergo a Data Protection Impact Assessment (DIPA).

All participants in research, and members of projects such as NESTORE, should understand the meaning of personal data in the digital society. As defined in the General Data Protection Regulation, Personal data means information relating to an identified or identifiable natural person. An identifiable natural person is one who can be identified, directly or indirectly, in particular by reference to an identifier such as a name, an identification number, location data, an online identifier or to one or more factors specific to the physical, physiological, genetic, mental, economic, cultural or social identity of that natural person (art. 2(a) General Data Protection Regulation).

The General Data Protection Regulation establishes the obligation to carry out a Data Protection Impact Assessment (DPIA) in research projects based on personal data treatments, in particular when using special categories of data with the aim of analysing in depth and minimizing the human rights and liberties risks of individuals involved. A DPIA must: describe the nature, scope and purposes of the processing; assess necessity, proportionality and compliance measures; identify and assess risks to individuals and identify any additional measures to mitigate those risks. From the DPIA an action plan will result that must be carried out to mitigate the risks detected and which will have to be reviewed periodically and updated in the event of possible changes in data processing. It is important that this review not be thought of as a mere formality, but as a living process that may be subject to change and which makes it possible to properly monitor the project and the guarantees to be applied for personal data protection. The Data Protection Officer (DPO) is the independent figure advising on these procedures.

The goal of adequate data protection protocols is to prevent participants from being identified, understanding that the main researchers and those granted specific permission and access would, if necessary and justified, connect personal data of participants with i.e., medical records. Only the entitled authorities (i.e., healthcare), and Research Ethics Committees involved and staff involved in the study, will have access, for the purpose of making sure data and procedures of the research, this is compatible with protecting confidentiality at all times. Transfers of participant´s personal data between partners and third parties should be determined and explained to those affected from the beginning of the project and data transfer agreements must be signed. This should only involve encrypted data, which in no case will contain information that can identify the participant directly (such as name and surnames, initials, address, social security number, etc.). It must be said that any staff in contact with personal data should apply the highest standards of protection of privacy stated in deontological, ethical and legal regulations.

Additionally, participants should be informed that according to the General Data Protection Regulation they can also limit the processing of incorrect data, request a copy or transfer of the data provided to the study to a third party (portability). To exercise these rights, or if participants would like to know more about confidentiality, they can contact the principal investigator of the study and the entitled Data Protection Officer (DPO) through the specific email assigned (each institution should add a specific address). Furthermore, participants should be informed that if they decide to leave the study, no new data will be collected, but data generated for research purposes until that time cannot be destroyed. Participants should be informed about the obligations of the responsible of the treatments to keep the data collected for the study and indicate for how long after its completion.

4 Ethics and Research Integrity

For all activities funded by the European Union, ethics is an integral part of research from beginning to end, and ethical compliance is seen as pivotal to achieve real research excellence [7]. Research, including its outcomes and the way it is conducted, should be morally grounded and acceptable to society [8]. Honesty, accountability, fairness and good stewardship should be core principles of research and innovation. Scientific integrity is a core issue for the NESTORE project. It applies to the public and the private initiative that should be working together to become a digital, data driven society where research and innovation are core elements [9].

There is not a scientific integrity definition shared by the scientific community. Censurable behaviours can be found in all research areas: in supervision, statistics data uses, or in publishing and plagiarism. The causes of censurable behaviours are separated into individual, organizational—among which there is the lack of institutional policies that are ethically solid and fair—and structural ones, like the pressure to get good results and funds to support researches or appearance of new areas with an undeniable therapeutically potential that create economic, social and media interest, for which there is available finance, more competitiveness.

Considering the great cultural, social and economic differences it can be difficult to draw up one set of guidelines that will apply to every country. Therefore, The Declaration of Helsinki [10] of the World medical Association or the Council for International Organizations of Medical Sciences International ethical guidelines for health-related research involving humans [11] have long been held as a reference standard of ethical practice guidelines for the scientific community.

These international codes of conduct can act as templates to be followed by each country to draft their own code of conduct, with rules and policies specific to their national structure and systems, that will identify with both their workforce and citizens. In the European context, the All European Academies, a consortium of 50 academies from almost all EU member states, has done this with their European Code of Conduct for Research Integrity [12]. It serves as a framework of self-regulation for the European research community. The Code states four core principles of good research practice: reliability, honesty, respect and accountability, and gives recommendations on how to respond adequately to violations of these principles.

The Singapore Statement on Research Integrity [13] states that it is "intended to challenge governments, organizations and researchers to develop more comprehensive standards, codes and policies to promote research integrity both locally and on a global basis". Like the previous code, the Singapore Statement also lays out four basic principles for research integrity: Honesty, accountability, professional courtesy and fairness and good stewardship. While the two documents differ slightly in their chosen principles, the overall idea is the same: responsible research, with a solid foundation of integrity and ethical principles, is vital to all disciplines, worldwide, and will increase the validity of results and the public trust.

5 Responsible Research and Innovation

Responsible Research and Innovation is a dynamic, iterative process in which all stakeholders become mutually responsive and share responsibility for both the process and its outcomes. In this framework, scientific inquiry is a process not limited to the perspective of the researchers. Societal actors such as citizens, policymakers, business or third sector organizations can and should be involved during the whole research and innovation process. The objective of RRI is to create high-quality science aligned with the values, needs, and expectations of society [14]. Implementing Responsible Research and Innovation leads to a more engaged public, responsible actors, and responsible institutions. It also has benefits for research and innovation, as Responsible Research and Innovation strives for making science and technology more ethical, sustainable and socially beneficial.

Ethics, public engagement, gender equality, open access and scientific education are the transversal agendas of Responsible Research and Innovation in HORIZON2020 European Research Program and an essential part of NESTORE from the inception of the project and throughout its lifecycle. Societal expectations of the elderly are crucial to move the project forward and should be aligned with research and innovation processes. That means considering gender equality goals, to promote with the NESTORE coach ageing and wellbeing responding to the needs of women too. In this sense it is a fact that women live longer and are capable of being more independent. In particular, the NESTORE project has specific goals regarding dissemination activities, and up to now has been very active in delivering information through its website [15] related to ethical, legal, societal and even technical issues on ageing and wellbeing in this digital society.

NESTORE is a multidisciplinary project that has been deployed and developed following the principles and human rights of the UNESCO Declaration on Bioethics and Human Rights (2005) [16], The Council of Europe Convention on Biomedicine and Human Rights (1997) [17] and in particular will consider all legal and ethical requirements at European, international and national level and global approach. For all activities funded by the European Union, ethics is an integral part of research from beginning to end, and ethical compliance is seen as pivotal to achieve real research excellence. Research, including its outcomes and the way it is conducted, should be morally grounded and acceptable to society [18]. Honesty, accountability, fairness and good stewardship should be core principles of research and innovation.

Ethics in Responsible Research and Innovation relates to three main areas, ethical research, research integrity, and societal acceptability. Ethical research conduct implies the application of fundamental ethical principles and legislation to scientific research in all possible domains of research. Research integrity means that research methods, activities, and processes are guided by standards, guidelines, and protocols; open to external scrutiny (for example, ethical bodies extended to societal stakeholders); and open to internal reflexivity (nurtured by a culture of open deliberative integrity). Social acceptability includes the consideration of the short-term and long-term implications of the research, and this should respond to actual social needs and reflect the basic values of society.

Data Management issues and in particular the principles "Findable, Accessible, Interoperable and Reusable" and are in close relation with the open access agenda and above all, scientific education—including digital literacy—is one of main goal. The objective is to empower the elderly and those individuals related to them (caregivers) in the use of new devices and technology. Likewise, the aim is to help them to have a better quality of life and reduce the burden of the health care system. Members of the NESTORE project have been proactive in coordinating and participating in activities of dissemination and knowledge transfer to promote public engagement. NESTORE research project should promote equal opportunities between men and women and aiming, to the extent possible, for a gender balance at all levels of personnel assigned to the action, including at supervisory and managerial level. NESTORE partners from Fundació Salut i Envelliment have developed a checklist to assess gender view to the experts and technologists. This checklist could be used before or after the development of material, recommendations or feedback addressed to end-users. The goal of this tool was to help to achieve a gender perspective in NESTORE project to be more aligned with H2020 program and their gender perspective.

The NESTORE partners also reflect this attention to gender equality, by encouraging and supervising measures for the promotion of gender equality within the consortium Age-related and gender-related physiological differences among individuals were also considered on the definition of the parameters required to characterize the functional status of healthy elderly people and to follow their variations over time. At the Co-Design process, the gender dimension was considered during the design of the NESTORE solution and its components, in order to meet their needs through a participatory approach. The recruitment focused on a good gender balance and diverse ethnic representation.

Responsible Research and Innovation implies that the stakeholders in collaborative research projects such as NESTORE (staff members, researchers, data processers, research participants, charities, etc.), work together to ensure that the outcomes of the research are relevant to and align with, the needs of society. Public engagement as one of the key agendas of RRI is especially present in the NESTORE project. To provide an example from the very beginning of the research project, the first research intervention of the project was based on a series of workshops that took place at Sheffield Hallam University (March 2018), where up to 80 people aged 50–70 participated. A specific methodology was applied, and participants were recruited and observed, recording their interventions in audio tapes.

To begin, participants were informed about the overall aim of the research. Secondly, participants were informed that the co-design research intervention is to build understanding of attitudes and factors of health in community-living older people between 55 and 70 years old to technology, which can play a key role in supporting the needs of the ageing population.

The workshops included the following elements, which can act as a general guide to other similar EU projects:

- A description of the research project and the aims of the workshop and how this relates to the wider research programme in which it is positioned, if applicable.
- A description of the activities that will be used within the workshops and individuals were invited to give written consent to take part.

The goal was to answer the following questions: What do you understand by the term technology?; Can you describe particular technological products that you find helpful/unhelpful; What are the factors that help/hinder your engagement/use of technology?; Are there particular design features that you find helpful?

Regarding the benefits, risks and expected outcomes, participants were informed that the workshops will enable people to share their expertise, think and talk about what makes life meaningful. Researchers should aim to create a safe environment where the participants feel comfortable to talk openly. Through activities and discussions, participants will generate ideas about how future technologies could act as a coach to offer advice to help them to engage in meaningful activities. This can be a very valuable opportunity for the participants to feel included and heard, and for the researchers also, as they may not have considered some of the points raised by the participants. As this is a co-design process, the participants are acknowledged throughout the research and will have the opportunity to continue to engage, contribute and feedback to the project as active 'team members' throughout.

References

1. Personal data are any information relative to a living, identified or identifiable individual. The separate information, which complied could lead to the identification of a particular person, is also classed as personal data. Examples of personal data: name and surname, address, email address of the kind name.surname@company.com, national identity number, location data (such as a mobile telephone's data location function), Internet Protocol (IP) address, a cookie identifier, the telephone's advertising identifier, the data in the possession of a hospital or doctor, which could be a symbol to uniquely identify a person. See European Union "What are Personal Data?" https://ec.europa.eu/info/law/law-topic/data-protection/reform/what-personal-data_es.
2. European Digital Single Market. https://ec.europa.eu/digital-single-market/en/news/digitalyou-digital-trust.
3. De Lecuona, I. (Coord.) .(2020). Guidelines for reviewing health research and innovation projects that use emergent technologies and personal data, UB editions, Barcelona.
4. Sweeney, L. (2000). Simple demographics often identify people uniquely. Carneggie Mellon University, Data, Privacy Working Paper 3. Pittsburgh. https://dataprivacylab.org/projects/identifiability/paper1.pdf.
5. Cordis NESTORE. https://cordis.europa.eu/project/id/769643/it.
6. Regulation (UE) 2016/679 of the European Parliament and the Council, of 27 April 2016, relative to the protection of individuals with regard to the processing of personal data and the free circulation of these data, repealing Directive 95/46/EC (General Data Protection Regulation) (Text relevant for the purposes of the EEE). https://eur-lex.europa.eu/legal-content/ES/TXT/?uri=CELEX:32016R0679.

7. COM. (2001). European Governance—A White Paper. Brussels.
8. Engage2020. (2015). In E. Andersson, S. Bussu, & H. Davis (Eds.), *Science, society and engagement—An e-anthology*.
9. Casado, M., et al. (2016). Declaration on scientific integrity in responsible research and innovation. Universitat de Barcelona Editions. https://www.publicacions.ub.edu/refs/observatoriBioEticaDret/documents/08489.pdf.
10. WMA. Declaration of Helsinki. https://www.wma.net/es/que-hacemos/etica-medica/declaracion-de-helsinki/.
11. CIOMS. *Guidelines for health-related research involving humans*. https://cioms.ch/wp-content/uploads/2017/01/WEB-CIOMS-EthicalGuidelines.pdf.
12. ALLEA. All European Academies. *The European code of conduct for research integrity*, Berlin. https://allea.org/wp-content/uploads/2017/05/ALLEA-European-Code-of-Conduct-for-Research-Integrity-2017.pdf.
13. Resnik, D. B., & Shamoo, A. E. (2011). The Singapore statement on research integrity. *Accountability in Research, 18*(2), 71–75. https://doi.org/10.1080/08989621.2011.557296.
14. Gerber, A., Forsberg, E. M., Shelley-Egan, C., Arias, R., Daimer, S., Dalton, G., & Steinhaus, N. (2020). Joint declaration on mainstreaming RRI across Horizon Europe. *Journal of Responsible Innovation. Routledge*. https://doi.org/10.1080/23299460.2020.1764837.
15. https://nestore-coach.eu/ethics.
16. Universal Declaration on Bioethics and Human Rights, UNESCO. (2005).
17. Council of Europe. (1997). Convention for the Protection of Human Rights and Dignity of the Human Being with regard to the Application of Biology and Medicine: Convention on Human Rights and Biomedicine.
18. Charter of Fundamental Rights of the European Union. (2000).

From Research to Action: What's Next?

Other Advanced Research Initiatives in Elderly Care and Fragility Prevention

Giuseppe Andreoni, E. Konstantinidis, D. Petsani, P. Bamidis, D. Gatsios, D. I. Fotiadis, Harm op den Akker, M. Inés Torres, J. Tenorio-Laranga, G. Cordasco, E. González-Fraile, A. Esposito, M. S. Kornes, G. Chollet, B. Fernández-Ruanova, V. Veleva, M. Žnidaršič, B. Ženko, A. Osojnik, R. Wheeler, K. Gand, H. Schlieter, S. Kyriazakos, M. Caprino, L. Nicolas, J. Kropf, I. Luengo, P. Jimeno, and Cinzia Mambretti

Abstract Based on the lessons learnt from the co-design, development and integration processes, the research findings and the outputs from the engagement with a network of stakeholders over the course of the EU funded initiatives, this chapter will aim to help sketching the future policies and research funding programmes for ageing well in Europe. The chapter presents the visions and the perspectives of the running projects in the frame of the H2020 Personalized Medicine-15 call.

---

[1]This paragraph has been authored by Giuseppe Andreoni and Cinzia Mambretti on behalf of NESTORE consortium.

G. Andreoni (✉)
Department of Design, Politecnico di Milano, Via G. Durando 10, 20158 Milan, Italy
e-mail: giuseppe.andreoni@polimi.it

E. Konstantinidis · D. Petsani · P. Bamidis
Lab of Medical Physics, School of Medicine, Aristotle University of Thessaloniki, Thessaloniki, Greece

E. Konstantinidis
WITA S.R.L, Trento, Italy

D. Gatsios · D. I. Fotiadis
Department of Materials Science, Unit of Medical Technology and Intelligent Information System, University of Ioannina, Ioannina, Greece

H. op den Akker
Innovation Sprint, Brussels, Belgium

M. I. Torres
Universidad del País Vasco UPV/EHU, Leioa, Spain

J. Tenorio-Laranga · E. González-Fraile · B. Fernández-Ruanova
Osatek/Osakidetza, Bilbao, Spain

G. Cordasco · A. Esposito
Università degli Studi della Campania "Luigi Vanvitelli", Caserta, Italy

M. S. Kornes
Department of Old Age Psychiatry, Oslo University Hospital, Oslo, Norway

G. Chollet
Intelligent Voice, London, UK

G. Andreoni and C. Mambretti (eds.), *Digital Health Technology for Better Aging*, Research for Development, https://doi.org/10.1007/978-3-030-72663-8_20

1 Introduction[1]

The Active Healthy Ageing is one of the main focus of European research among the recent calls in the Horizon 2020 Framework Programme, in the frame of the pillar Societal Challenge and its dedicated topic "Health, demographic change and well-being", a specific action was dedicated to Personalized Medicine for people as they age. The overall strategic orientation for the 'Health, Demographic Change and Well-being' Work Programme 2016–2017 is 'promoting healthy ageing and personalised healthcare'. Some insights about this demographic situation, the context, beeds and challenges to be tackled by coming research initiatives are offered also in the next paragraphs by the single contributions.

This call (namely Personalised coaching for well-being and care of people as they age, TOPIC ID: SC1-PM-15-2017) supported a panel of project implementing new solutions for a personalised "virtual coach", for empowering and motivating people in need of guidance and care due to age related conditions, in cooperation with their carers where relevant, and to help them improve and maintain their independence, functional capacity, health status as well as preserving their physical, cognitive, mental and social well-being.

The solutions have to be firstly designed and implemented by considering usability and ease of user interaction as essential design elements of the "coach". This aspect has been integrated by intelligent ICT environments, access to relevant physiological and behavioural data, new forms of accessible interaction based on tangible user interaction concepts, open platforms and emotional computing.

The "virtual coach" should provide personalised advice, guidance and follow-up for key age-related issues in daily life which impact the person's ability to remain active and independent, for example diet, physical activity, risk avoidance, preventive measures, lifestyle and activity management, leisure, social participation and overall

---

V. Veleva · M. Žnidaršič · B. Ženko · A. Osojnik
Institut Jožef Stefan, Ljubljana, Slovenia

R. Wheeler
Balkan Institute for Labour and Social Policy, Sofia, Bulgaria

K. Gand · H. Schlieter
Faculty of Business and Economics, Technische Universität Dresden, Dresden, Germany

S. Kyriazakos
Department of Business Development and Technology, Aarhus University, Aarhus, Denmark

M. Caprino
Department of Neurorehabilitation Sciences, Casa di Cura del Policlinico, Milan, Italy

L. Nicolas
European Health Telematics Association, Brussels, Belgium

J. Kropf
Center for Health & Bioresources, AIT Austrian Institute of Technology, Seibersdorf, Austria

wellness. The goal should be to preserve physical, cognitive, mental and social well-being for as long as possible and to facilitate interaction with carers (where relevant).

The call funded the following proposals that, at the time of writing this chapter, are carrying out pilot studies to validate their approaches and solutions (Table 1).

If NESTORE project has been extensively discussed along the book a short summary of each project is here provided.

CAPTAIN aims to develop and validate useful and easy to use ICT tools for empowering and motivating people in need of guidance and care. It proposes a technology designed to turn the home of an older adult into a ubiquitous assistant introducing home augmented reality using interactive and tangible interfaces. CAPTAIN proposes a "transparent" technology designed to turn the home of the older adult into a ubiquitous assistant specifically designed to compensate for their physical and memory impairments during their daily living. To do so, it leverages on a few state of the art technologies, as follows: "Projected augmented reality" to project, through use of micro-projectors, contextualised (directly on walls, floor, tables, etc.) information and instructions on top of the real environment. To achieve this, CAPTAIN fosters a user-centered co-design methodology which is based on

Table 1 The projects funded under the H2020 PM-15 call

Project title	Project acronym	Grant agreement no.
Coach Assistant via Projected and Tangible Interface	CAPTAIN	769830
Council of Coaches	COUCH	769553
Empathic, Expressive, Advanced Virtual Coach to Improve Independent Healthy-Life-Years of the Elderly	EMPATHIC	769872
HOLOgrams for personalised virtual coaching and motivation in an ageing population with BALANCE disorders	HOLOBALANCE	769574
Novel Empowering Solutions and Technologies for Older people to Retain Everyday life activities	NESTORE	769643
Supporting Active Ageing through Multimodal coaching	SAAM	769661
Virtual Coaching Activities for Rehabilitation in Elderly	vCare	769807
Wellbeing and Health Virtual Coach	WellCO	769765

I. Luengo · P. Jimeno
HI-Iberia Ingenieria y Proyectos SL, Madrid, Spain

C. Mambretti
Fondazione Politecnico di Milano, Milan, Italy

constant involvement of older adults (the Captain Stakeholders' Community) in the design, development and testing stages. Older adults will benefit from the creation of effective contextualised assistance in their home environment forming a virtual coach who is stimulating and enhancing elderly capabilities. This coach will act as a constant, vigilant and pleasant companion, ubiquitously present, that provides contextualised advice to help preserving elderly mental and physical, cognitive and social well-being. The participatory design process adopted in Captain harnesses the expertise of all levels of the stakeholder ecosystem in order to deliver an effective tool for people in need of guidance and care due to age related conditions.

COUCH introduces a radically new virtual coaching concept based on multiple autonomous, embodied virtual coaches. Together, they are a personal council that fulfills the needs of older adults in an integrated way. Each Coach has his own expertise, personality, and style of coaching; they might not always agree with each other, but they all share a single goal: to support the elderly across every aspect of well-being, including physical, social, cognitive and mental support. The Council members listen to the user, inform the user, help the user to set personal goals and inspire the user to take control of her/his health. Novel spoken dialogue interaction technologies will be provided as embodied conversational agents that will join in conversations with the user. The platform will not be confined to a constrained number of Coaches—rather it will enable developers and innovators to introduce new Coaches that provide additional know-how and services. Hence, COUCH will enable a new virtual coaching ecosystem, bringing together healthcare services providers with innovators to implement novel ideas.

EMPATHIC is based on a conceptual and ethical framework focused on the people rights and responsibilities, which is based on principles established by the United Nations: (a) Dignity, including privacy, obtrusiveness and equal access; (b) Autonomy, which requires respect for self-determination of people, recognition of the heterogeneity of people and respect to their preferences; (c) Participation. According to these principles EMPATHIC has designed a virtual coach to engage the healthy-senior user to enhance wellbeing through awareness of personal physical status, by improving diet and nutritional habits, by developing more physical exercise and by social activity. The developed methodology and tools are provided in open-source access in the software engineering process of implementing socially-centred ICT products.

Seniors will benefit from EMPATHIC-VC toward physical and mental health improvements: independent seniors are less likely to be socially excluded, show reduced risk factors for depression thus maintain their sense of value and importance to the society to which they contribute. Distinct needs and preferences of females are taken into consideration when designing and developing the coach, thus assuring a higher impact in elder women due to their longer life expectancy.

HOLOBALANCE focuses on balance disorders due to age related progressive loss of functioning of sensory information and the inability to control body movements because currently there is a total lack of personalized coaching solutions for people with balance disorders to participate in balance and gait physiotherapy and activity promotion.

The overall objective of HOLOBALANCE is to develop and validate a new personalized hologram coach platform for virtual coaching, motivation and empowerment of the ageing population with balance disorders through augmented reality games, along with easy-to-use sensors that can be customized to implement and coach the user with specific, individualized exercises, offering new forms of accessible user interaction. HOLOBALANCE will engage the experts related to the management of people suffering from balance disorders, towards developing a multi-stakeholder user centered coaching ecosystem.

SAAM is specifically addressing the needs of elderly above the age of 60 in economically under-developed regions with low technological proficiencies, who are most vulnerable in terms of access to support services, economic deprivation and social isolation. Eight assessment and coaching domains, four being part of the basic system (Activity, Mobility, Sleep and Social Activity) and four as advanced system (Cardio-vascular health, Cognitive decline, Nutrition, and Language based emotional state) were selected. The project's progress beyond the state of the art is exemplified by three core innovations: an unobtrusive and fully ambient data collection mode that does not require user interaction, the use of cheap common hardware for sensing and coaching so as to allow widespread adoption of the system, and the use of primary user's social circles as part of a multi-modal coaching system. The user-side of the SAAM system consists of a set of affordable off-the-shelf devices connected together with the edge gateway that further connects them to the cloud-based part of the SAAM system. These devices include stationary components such as smart power meter, UWB localization sensors and an integrated ambient sensor that enable completely unobtrusive user activity monitoring. Activity monitoring can be further enhanced with optional wearable sensors or smartphones. Based on the sensing data the cloud-based part of the system performs coaching in four main domains of the user's life: mobility (ability to move), daily activity, sleep quality and social activity. The main innovation of the system is that the coaching actions are not rendered only directly to the user, but primarily through his or her social circle, thus positively affecting social interactions.

vCARE develops and investigates a Virtual Coaching solution encapsulating a set of coaching services for empowering and motivating people, helping them to proceed with a personalized rehabilitation by means of a virtual avatar. For this, vCare monitors the patients' daily activities, conditions, and habits to provide personalised feedback to recover the Quality of Life thanks to coaching programmes initialised by specialists in a well-elaborated clinical pathway as a tailored rehabilitation plan. According to this plan, vCare enables the personalization of the intensity and way of interaction and will trigger suitable exercises (serious games, cognitive training programs, etc.), suggestions and feedback driven by smart-home sensors (replacing the eyes of a human caregiver) or sensors for vital data, the avatar itself (replacing the caregiver's face and interaction possibility) or the machine learning and reasoning (replacing the human's assessment abilities) but also based on patient preferences. The project mission is to utilize the virtual coach in terms of the virtual avatar as communication mean for the patient.

WellCo provides a virtual coach supporting people to adopt healthier behaviour choices in physical activity, nutrition, mental status or social wellbeing. The solution proposed leverages data from sensors worn by the users, validated questionnaires and other information about users' daily life, preferences and context to provide recommendations that ensure the adoption of healthier behaviour choices by users. According to the behaviour change wheel model, the personalization of recommendations assesses the capability and opportunity of the user to perform the change and determines the best way to provide it in order to motive the user in its follow-up through the WellCo Senior App. Other two applications will be available for WellCo: Informal Caregiver App, and the Expert Web App. WellCo incorporates a deep learning classifier aimed at catching the facial features indicating the emotion of the user. Through the affective module, the virtual coach is able to generate the most suitable dialogue and expressions in order to set emotional connection with the user. Then, the WellCo: Behaviour Change Recommender merges this data with those coming from sensors, Life Plan and validated questionnaires into four recommenders: wellbeing recommender (provides recommendations based on users' status and wellbeing expectations), emotion (recommendations to change the mood of the user), social (recommendations to foster social interaction) and general recommender (tips for wellbeing) that are automatically adapted to users' preferences. Personalization enables to provide recommendations adapted to the capabilities and opportunities of the user, favouring the motivation and adoption of them by the user.

In the following paragraphs, the visions and the experiences of these projects funded under the same call are shared and integrated so to contribute in building a common vision in this framework. All projects were stimulated in a wide reflection about challenges and opportunities by answering to the following questions:

- What are the challenges on Aging and Healthcare for Europe in 2030?
- What is the Vision of your project about Aging and Healthcare to tackle these challenges and transform them into opportunities?
- What are the main concepts of the project, the methodology, the developed tools, the outcomes?
- What is the expected impact of your project?
- Please describe the exploitation models and/or channels and/or opportunities.

2 Technology for Aging in Place: The CAPTAIN Solution as an Answer to Existing Challenges[2]

2.1 Challenges on Technology Supported Active and Healthy Ageing in Place

Technological advancements have provided the answers to most of the humanity challenges over the last years, including the support of older people to stay healthy, independent and active, able to remain at their home environment for as long as possible [1–3]. Although the benefits are nowadays well documented [4, 5], researchers and inventors are still struggling to create technologies that are easily adopted by older people with poor results in adherence and user experience [6]. Cho [7] argues that improved perceived ease of use becomes even more important for older adults, as they may have lower levels of digital competences and commonly they find difficulties in maneuver the navigation structure of apps and other software [8]. However, older adults are shown to be willing and interested to use new methods to manage their health and also value their privacy and control over their data [9, 10]. The issue is even more noticeable when technology usage requires more time and effort to solve a problem than before. Technology still fails to become a daily, trusted companion that supports ongoing activities, avoiding stealing time and being inappropriately intrusive. It becomes apparent that the challenge we have to overcome is to create technology that serves older people respecting their needs and habits and not the other way around, which is to convince them to adopt technology.

2.2 The CAPTAIN Vision and Solution

CAPTAIN's [11] vision is to bring improved well-being, safe and flexile independent life into the own homes of people in need. To achieve this, it tries to turn the homes of older adults into a gentle coach within an empowering space, providing intuitive interaction, guidance and help for independent living, whenever and wherever it is needed, leading to physical, cognitive, mental and social well-being.

CAPTAIN, aiming to win user's trust and avoid consuming too much of the user's time, is built on top of two main pillars:

- Spontaneous and organic interaction, eliminating the common interaction patterns where the user either has to launch a smartphone application or tap on a notification on her/his smartphone,

---

[2]This paragraph has been authored by Evdokimos Konstantinidis, Despoina Petsani, Panagiotis Bamidis, Maria Nikolaidou, Michalis Timoleon, Nikos Athanasopoulos, Andoni Beristain, Roberto Álvarez Sánchez, Giuseppe Conti, Francesco Verrini, Valentina Conotter, Kiko Núñez, Unai Diaz-Orueta, Louise Hopper, Joanne Carroll, Maxim Kostin, Rosa Almeida, Raquel Losada, Wolfgang Kniejski, Angela Ivanova, Francesco Tessarolo from CAPTAIN project.

- The "right" moment and the "right" time of interaction, based on information from the user's behavior and movement inside the house

To do so, CAPTAIN delivers "transparent", state-of-the-art technology such as real-time 3D sensing technologies, speech analysis, non-invasive physiological and emotional data analysis, and intelligent comprehension of user's behaviour and actions for the creation of an environment, which allows the coaching of adults towards leading a healthy and fulfilling lifestyle. CAPTAIN UI blends content with the environment by using micro-projectors, a camera for recognizing and monitoring the user as well as a microphone for voice interaction. In order to empower the users, the system is based on the I-Change model [12] that guides users to: (1) set goals, (2) achieve their goals, (3) get feedback for the process. This functionality is based on the creation of SMART goals from experts in the domain of health and wellbeing [13]. Following a plugin based architecture, any specialized organization can create an additional SMART goal that could be delivered by the system. The plugin describes the SMART goal that it is achieved and the schedule of interventions a user has to perform to achieve the goal.

CAPTAIN aims to address a broad range of older users and tries to achieve behavior change with brief interventions throughout the day. The technology blends in their home environment leaving it untouched when it is not needed.

2.3 Design and Development Methodology

To avoid the commonly made mistake of mismatch between the user needs and preferences and the ways that they are tackled by products [10, 14], CAPTAIN deployed an innovative, user-centered methodology. The design of the system was done following the Design Thinking, Lean Startup and Agile process [15]. During the first Design Thinking session, end-users were asked to consider the most important parts in which they need support in their everyday lives. The discussion was done based on personas representing the end-users to assist participants empathize and start talking about their experiences without revealing personal information [16]. 53 older adults and 38 informal and formal caregivers participated in the session across 5 European countries (Greece, Italy, Spain, Ireland and Cyprus). After the analysis of the qualitative data collected, the team noticed a strong will of the participants to be motivated and change their attitude towards a healthier life rather than strictly guide or patronize them. That validated the initial hypothesis that the system should be a coach rather than an assistant. Furthermore, CAPTAIN employed User interaction through voice and gestures as they are considered a more "natural" way of interacting with a system and requested by most of the participants in the Design thinking session.

During the Lean Startup and Agile process, three Minimum Viable Products (MVPs) were created. The initial MVP was a power point presentation using an ordinary projector. The presentation was controlled by a facilitator in order to create the perception that the system is interacting with the user. This prototype was tested by

75 older adults and 44 informal and formal caregivers. The most important feedback was about the simplicity of the UI appearance and the interaction flows. The second MVP was a computer-based application that detected the user and initiated a simple interaction flow of presenting some information after it gets some confirmation from the user. The goal was to receive feedback about the voice and gesture interaction and the automate generation of content using projections. The basic outcome was about when the system is initiated as the users would like to have some control on that and the approval of gesture and movement-based interaction.

The third CAPTAIN MVP is based on a new hardware device and an initial casing design. Furthermore, the device was tested in a real house by an end-user in order to investigate any problems with the size, the cables and the projection brightness and quality. The device was tested by an older adult with the presence of a facilitator. An informal discussion followed in order to get the appropriate feedback. Currently, CAPTAIN is in the stage of installation in real homes in order to assess the user acceptance and usability.

2.4 *Envisaged Impact*

The envisaged impact of CAPTAIN project is summarized in the following pillars:

- Serve the needs of older adults in an unobtrusive, non-invasive way in order to achieve improved quality of life and empowerment of setting goals;
- Improve effectiveness of the care processes through more effective coaching processes involving older adults in care homes or home scenarios;
- Enhance home care prevention, in order to delay cognitive and physical impairment of older adults; and
- Support more independent living and improve quality of life and dignity of cognitively impaired aging users by helping them be more independent and for longer time.

2.5 *Towards Business Exploitation of CAPTAIN*

This coaching technology is essential for significant commercial use based on different use cases, related business schemes and scenarios. CAPTAIN consortium strongly believes in the impact of CAPTAIN in the community and the establishment of a CAPTAIN spin-off company is a milestone for the project. This spin-off will allow heavily building upon CAPTAIN success stories and leveraging the business models implemented in the project pilots as use cases into international markets. It will also maintain the CAPTAIN vision and commercialize the CAPTAIN project results.

3 Council of Coaches promotes elderly health[3]

3.1 Engagement with Supporting Technologies Is the Challenge for Healthy Ageing e-Coaches

From the perspective of Council of Coaches, we see many great technology solutions being developed to tackle the problem of aging and healthcare. However, we fear that too many people that are not used to or not interested in using these technologies will not be able to benefit from the support that is available through such technologies. There are many important societal and healthcare challenges to be tackled as mentioned by our fellow projects: independent living, loneliness, risk of falling, and safe home environments to name a few. But the main challenge for us is how to make the many technological solutions to these problems inclusive for older adults. How do we keep older adults, but also younger audiences (when it comes to preventative services) engaged with the technologies, so they can benefit from the smart coaching and support they provide?

3.2 A Vision of Collaborative Coaches

Council of Coaches aims to tackle the challenge of how to keep older adults engaged with a coaching solution that focuses on the broader domain of health and wellbeing in various domains. We introduce a radically new concept of virtual coaching, called the "Council of Coaches". The council consists of a number of virtual characters—each specialized in their own domain—that interact with each other and with the user to inform, motivate and discuss about health and well-being related issues (e.g., physical, cognitive, mental and social well-being). The individual coaches will listen to the user, ask questions, inform users, discuss between themselves, jointly set personal goals and inspire the user to take control of his health. Any combination of specialized council members collaboratively covers a wide spectrum of lifestyle interventions, with a substantial likelihood of positive impact on outcomes related to chronic disease or prevention. By introducing the concept of a group of virtual coaches, many opportunities arise for creating fun and engaging interactions around the topic of the user's health. Users that are not immediately willing to engage with the application (the coaches) can sit back and listen to the virtual coaches as they discuss between themselves what lifestyle advice would work for them [17].

[3]This paragraph has been authored by Harm op den Akker on behalf of COUCH consortium.

3.3 The COUCH Web Application Design

In Council of Coaches, a total of four iterations of technical- and functional demonstrators have been developed, based on user input, and evaluated with end-users. Early in the project, a vision on Responsible Research and Innovation (RRI) was established in how the Council of Coaches project handles ethical issues and how to develop a coaching application within ethical, legal and societal boundaries. The main outcomes of the project are its two core demonstrators—one "Functional Demonstrator", that served to demonstrate the proof of concept of the Council of Coaches concept, and a second "Technical Demonstrator" that served to push the boundaries of state-of-the-art embodied conversational agent systems.

The Functional Demonstrator (Fig. 1) is a stable, highly scalable web application. This application underwent several design cycles, in which the focus was on aesthetics, user interface, content and robustness (speed and reliability). The end-result is an easy-to-use application that runs on any device with a web-browser, in which the core ideas of a Council of virtual coaches were demonstrated with 92 end-users for a period of 5-9 weeks.

The second main outcome is the project's "Technical Demonstrator", a software platform in which various state of the art components are integrated, allowing content creators to develop their own applications that employ multiple embodied conversational agents. Various end-user studies have been performed using the technical demonstrator, gathering evidence on e.g. user-interaction paradigms, and fundamental questions of vicarious persuasion. Released as a fully open-source platform

Fig. 1 Screenshots of the Council of Coaches "Functional Demonstrator", used to demonstrate the core concept of having multiple virtual coaches for lifestyle support

under the name "Agents United", the platform is fully available to the public on GitHub.[4]

3.4 The Envisaged Impact of COUCH Solution

From the onset, we believed strongly that the simple idea of putting multiple virtual coaches in the room would create great opportunities for engaging users, not only in the healthcare domain, but in any situation that calls for a fun, and personalized way of providing information to users (e.g., eLearning). Primarily, the project has demonstrated, through a series of studies, that the core concepts indeed work. For example, does vicarious persuasion indeed work better than direct persuasion? A study by Kantharaju et al. [18] suggests that it does. As the project's results are finding its way in scientific journals and proceedings, we hope to have set a solid foundation for further research in this topic.

The desire to spin off future research in this area, and to entice people to start exploring opportunities using multiple embodied conversational agents to promote health, or for any other application domain has always been the main driver for the project. As such, there has been a great focus on developing open-source tools and to create communities of developers and innovators around those tools. The Agents United platform mentioned earlier is an example of an open-source platform that resulted from the Council of Coaches project, which allows developers to create state-of-the-art 3D embodied conversational agent systems that include high levels of automation in terms of verbal and non-verbal behaviours. But for those professionals and companies that need a lower barrier for entry in the virtual coaching domain, the project has also released the WOOL Platform: a fully open-source platform that is designed to allow domain experts with little technical skills to author engaging, personalized dialogue. The platform, released under the MIT license, provides the tools and software libraries to easily embed those dialogues into web- or mobile applications.[5]

3.5 Exploitation Strategies for COUCH

Council of Coaches identified two distinct exploitable outcomes that are currently being pursued. The first is the "Council of Coaches as a Product", and it is tied directly to the functional demonstrator that is depicted in Fig. 1. The demonstrator is a highly scalable, robust solution that contains many hours of coaching content on various domains. This demonstrator forms the basis for efforts to develop digital

[4]For more information see: www.agents-united.org.
[5]For more information see: www.woolplatform.eu.

therapeutics services between two of the consortium's SMEs (Roessingh Research and Development, and Innovation Sprint).

The second exploitation pathway has been touched upon before, and relates to the two open-source platforms that were released as outcomes of the project: The Agents United platform and the WOOL Platform. By providing these platforms to the community, the project's partners hope to create traction and be in the forefront of innovation on virtual coaching in the exciting years to come.

4 The Empathic Promotion of a Satisfying and Independent Lifestyle[6]

4.1 Social Challenges and Innovation Opportunities to Support Elderly Independency and Wellbeing

Population ageing is one of the social challenges of the 21st century that directly concerns Europe as well as other developed communities. The decline of the fertility rates along with the increase in life duration result in a fast raise of the percentage of the population above 65. In Europe, this percentage is expected to growth from 16% in 2010 to 29% in 2060 [19]. Moreover, this population segment expected to be predominantly female and includes a growing number of elder persons above 80. In this context, social challenges to be addressed are, among others:

- A high demand of infrastructures and services targeting the elderly needs and wishes. In particular, the extended preference of ageing at home has to be fulfilled while taking into consideration specific cultural facts as well as the diversity of societies.
- A cross-cutting approach covering different sectors such as health, housing, low-income persons and adequate living conditions in cities and rural areas.
- Support healthy older people to remain productive and have an independent life in their community as long as possible. To this end, a wide range products and services need to be conceived to assist a certain standard of living and wellbeing as people age. Furthermore, technology is in the core of most of nowadays innovative products and services.

Currently there is a huge demand for autonomous systems able to assist people on several needs in their aging. Provisions of support have been made either through the monitoring and detection of changes in the physical, and/or cognitive, and/or social daily functional activities, as well as in offering therapeutic interventions [20]. These

[6]This paragraph has been authored by M. Inés Torres, J. Tenorio, G. Cordasco, E. González-Fraile, A. Esposito, M. S. Kornes, G. Chollet, B. Fernández-Ruinova.

systems have targeted vulnerable elder people who face complex and stressed interactional exchanges. In this context, strong emotional behaviors arouse, having as consequences discomforts, loss of control, anxiety, stress, depression, misplaced conducts. These behaviors are furtherly affected by several factors including personality, individual traits, social and cultural information [21–23]. Having an EMPATHIC coach for facing such daily facets would be desired. To do so there is a need to develop "experimental and theoretical models of behaviors for implementing computational paradigms that should produce ICT interfaces equipped with a human level of automaton intelligence" [22, p. 48]. Their design has to take into account the user involvement and interests. Users must judge the developed technology acceptable and useful in their context of use. Text, voices, or nonverbal communication must be appropriately exploited to generate feedback messages but also capture user's acceptance and trustworthiness.

4.2 Vision of the EMPATHIC Project

As a consequence of the previous context, there is a need to follow a novel user centered approach focused on making the interaction personalized to the prospective users, accounting of their age, gender, culture, preferences, personality, role, occupation, and responses to the system's strategies. The interactions and feedback messages must be tailored to the knowledge the system has about that specific user at that specific interactional instant, with system's reactions attuned by the knowledge gained during previous interactional turns, and the whole history of users-device interactions.

The EMPATHIC Research and Innovation project researches, innovates and validates new paradigms, laying the foundation for future generations of Personalised Virtual Coaches to help elderly people to live independently. The wellness coaching advice promotes healthy habits and behaviors, by challenging each user to transform their personal goals and needs into actions. The EMPATHIC Virtual Coach engages the healthy-senior user to take care of potential chronic diseases, maintain a healthy diet, have adequate physical activity as well as encourage social engagement, thus contributing to the older adults' ability to maintain a satisfying and independent lifestyle. The EMPATHIC Agent motivates the user through a friendly virtual coach to reach pre-set benefits, whose achievement are measured through project-defined metrics. Our ambition was to create a personal, friendly and familiar environment for the users, avoiding the threatening effects of unfamiliar new gadgets or an excessive focus on medical supervision. The project looks beyond the basic medical and physical needs of a person, to the link between body and emotional well-being. The EMPATHIC Agent is designed to be capable of perceiving the emotional and social state of a person, in the learned context of the senior users' expectations and requirements, and their personal history, and responds adaptively to his/her needs.

4.3 Main Concepts and Outcomes of EMPATHIC Project

The EMPATHIC project implements the concept of coaching through a virtual conversation agent. Nevertheless, the aspiration is not to conceive and put into practice a coach who provides personalized nutritional advice or recommendations for physical and social activities adapted to the particular conditions of the user. In contrast, the project proposes coaching strategies aimed to get behavioral changes on the user. Coaching dialogs are logical structures based on question-answer model with the objective to understand needs, restrictions and goals of the user [24, 25]. The goals need to be accepted by the user. Therefore, coaching dialogs will promote the user's self-awareness and guide the user through realistic and healthy goals. Each dialog follows a sequential structure based on the GROW (Goal, Reality, Options and will of action plan) which was proposed by professionals of health coaching.

In this framework, EMPATHIC project (a) Provides automatic personalised advice guidance (through the coach) having a direct impact in empowering elder users into a wide of advanced ICT keeping improving their quality of life and level their independent independency living status of the people as the age [26]; (b) Identifies non-intrusive technologies to detect the individual's emotional and health status of the person through non-intrusive technologies [27]; (c) Implements health-coach goals and actions through an intelligent computational system, intelligent coach and spoken dialogue system [28] adapted to users' intentions [29], emotions and context (d) Provide the virtual coach with a natural, empathic, personalised and expressive communication model [24, 29, 30].

In addition the main technological goals carried out are: (a) the development of a simulated virtual coach allowing to develop coaching conversations between professionals and end-users, which enables the project to acquire a corpus of dialogues as well as engage the end-users on the design decisions as well as evaluate the progress (b) the integration a proof-of-concept of the technology running on different devices and (c) the validation through field trials performed in three different countries (Spain, Norway and France) with three distinct languages and cultures (plus English for research and development) of the proposed methods, approaches and solutions.

4.4 Expected Impact of EMPATHIC Project

Nowadays, at the beginning of the 21st century, most elderly people may experience barriers to access to some philological or coaching-based interventions. Those barriers are related to mobility, accessibility, economical or even lack of awareness. Those type of interventions may be especially relevant for those suffering a decrease of their well-being (e.g. suffering social isolation, sadness, depression or anxiety).

The use of information and communication technologies (ICTs) is becoming a cost-effective way to overcome those barriers mentioned above. Moreover, ICTs enable in an accessible and scalable way the promotion of health, prevention, active aging and even early diagnose. Thus, ICT based therapies can reach thousands or millions of people simultaneously.

Speaking about ICT based therapies and important concept raises. Low intensity interventions refer to brief therapies, group treatments, self-help approaches, such as bibliotherapy and computerized treatments. Low intensity interventions represent a new paradigm in evidence-based practice and the delivery of health and well-being services to promote healthy habits and to increase access (availability, utilization and equity) to them. In that sense, EMPATHIC project, is a clear example of low intensity intervention promising and providing impact as described below:

- New model of psychological/health care that limits specialist time or used this time in a highly cost-effective manner.
- The development of new services which can be more efficient as well as effective.
- Key element in a stepped and collaborative care model. The low intensity intervention represents and initial step before refereeing to a human professional.
- New ways of working and new workforces that provide more rapid and flexible access to early intervention and preventive programs. People can access to short weekly sessions of about 10–20 min, depending on persons time availability.
- New ways of training new and skills.
- New ways of assessment, monitoring and evaluation of variables and key elements related with well-being and health.
- New ways of increase adherence and engagement to e-coach through more attractive, relevant and interesting.
- New communication tool with our target population to deliver coaching.
- New ways to disseminate services in a massive scale to sparse populations located in remote communities, e.g. providing recommendations based on personal desires, needs or interest.
- Intervening in a way that the patients' choices are respected (anonymity, time slots….)
- Tailored intervention with best matching between program contents and idiosyncratic patient's needs.

In conclusion, low intensity can be a great solution to a stepped support service model where the intensity of the coaching can be adjusted depending on the situation. The elderly population is highly heterogeneous, and they may need from different types of solutions, e.g. professional support, activities recommendations, awareness of the local offer etc.

4.5 *Exploitation of the Results and Concluding Remarks*

We are living in a longevity revolution. The numbers are clear, the 20% of the population in western countries is over 65 years and this percentage is growing. However, the old age does not depend on the age but with the dependency. Even though, senior population is highly heterogeneous, there is a main profile of active person, consumer and committed with the community. We are speaking about retired people with a lot of active years to enjoy. People that expect quality of life, contribute to the community and postpone the old age.

Considering this reality, there is a need to accommodate current products and services to this new demography [31]. In other words, adapt the current market to the senior qualities (not necessarily create new offer). Therefore, there are a lot of efforts, from different entities, to centralize and "silverize" the current offer. Regarding active aging, especially relevant the offer related to culture, leisure, physical activity and healthy nutrition. This offer can be (and will be soon) centralized and adapted through different platforms age friendly. Most probably, through public-private collaborations. Those initiatives will open new spaces for virtual advisors and coaches.

This type of solutions is a very suitable environment to integrate and exploit a virtual coach such EMPATHIC. We are speaking about a virtual coach capable to understand (in an automatized way) the needs of each user (as a unique individual). In that sense, EMPATHIC is trained to understand needs related 4 main areas: Leisure and culture, social relations, physical activity and nutrition. Those areas are key for a suitable active aging. Moreover, EMPATHIC is engaging and motivating the users to take actions.

Therefore, connecting EMPATHIC with the local offer, especially the silver offer, provides a huge potential for both public and private entities. First, it can provide a real sensor of the senior needs and desires from a specific area. Second, connects the local offer with the seniors' interests. The local offer can be public or private, but the strengths rely on the personal suggestions linked with the local offer. Imagine somebody that feels a bit blue and through EMPATHIC ends up buying a ticket for the local theatre.

On that scenario, the exploitation model relies on both the public and the private sector. The public contribution would help the implementation and an initial maintenance. The expected source would be local entities which aim to both provide response to the demographic challenge and stimulate the local economy. After the implementation and the market penetration, the maintenance would come from the private offer, as a percentage of the sales coming from an EMPATHIC recommendation.

5 The Solutions of HOLOBALANCE to Manage Equilibrium Disorders[7]

5.1 Challenges in Active and Healthy Ageing

One of the challenges the older Europeans face is falls. Function and flexibility deteriorate as people age and along with dizziness which can be caused from several

[7]This paragraph has been authored by Dimitrios Gatsios and Dimitrios I. Fotiadis on behalf of the HOLOBALANCE consortium.

inner-ear, vestibular nerve and central nervous system diseases, lead to balance disorders and, sooner or later, to falls. Hospitalizations due to fractures caused by falls and the resulting limited functionality when olders return at home are associated with high healthcare costs and caregiving burden that affect the society more widely.

Current guidelines lack information on specific balance components to be included in falls interventions and more specific evidence-based guidelines are required. Current falls interventions provide some benefit, but due to lack of training, insufficient number of clinicians and cost many older adults receive no or sub-optimal falls interventions.

5.2 The HOLOBALANCE Vision in Ageing and Healthcare

HOLOBALANCE aims to become a state-of-the-art system providing an evidence-based, gradually progressive, multifactorial, individualized falls intervention, through cutting-edge technology and improving clinical practice. HOLOBALANCE essentially aims to provide balance rehabilitation at patients' home, remotely supervised by expert physiotherapists.

5.3 The Proposed Solution for AHA by HOLOBALANCE

For people without dizziness problems, exercises such as bending over and head movements, aiming to stimulate and retrain the vestibular system and eventually stabilize gaze, improve gait etc. Personalized balance rehabilitation programs are considered more effective than non-specific exercises in improving symptoms.

The long-term maintenance of the effects of the developed home-based program, requires the lasting adoption of a healthier and more active lifestyle from community-dwelling older adults. To promote such behavioral change HOLOBALANCE has adopted the COM-B ('capability', 'opportunity', 'motivation' and 'behaviour') model and the whole interaction with the older adults is designed accordingly.

HOLOBALANCE includes three types of coaching:

1. Balance rehabilitation exercises provided by the holographic coach which interacts with the patients or in the form of Augmented reality exergames, and Internet of Things devices that capture and evaluate the performance of the exercises and enable the interactions. Two holographic interfaces have been developed: a projector-based which requires a $2 \times 2 \times 2$ box and a head mounted device equipped with a smartphone.
2. Cognitive Training provided with Augmented Reality Games designed and developed to stimulate cognitive skills (attention, memory, psychomotor abilities). Cognitive training is combined with auditory tasks that aim to improve speech in noise perception and auditory memory.

3. Multilevel motivation and physical activity promotion with a dedicated mobile app enabling activity planning and monitoring with an activity tracker, as well as offering networking and competition functionalities.

5.4 The Expected Impact for HOLOBALANCE Project

In the short term, HOLOBALANCE will provide a platform facilitating multi-directional sharing of information between HOLOBALANCE actors and stakeholders. In the mid-term, HOLOBALANCE will transform healthcare for patients at risk of falling by: providing individualized input with a strong motivational component to improve adherence and services accessible to a wider population; requiring low-level expertise to administer the intervention; supporting self-management and promoting sustainable behavior change; reducing reliance on the health care system. In the long term, HOLOBALANCE will create value for: service providers by pinpointing intervention strategies and enhancing outcomes; the scientific community with the evidence produced; policy makers by determining health service provision priorities.

5.5 The Proposed Exploitation Model for HOLOBALANCE Solutions

HOLOBALANCE can be exploited as a Service offered by balance physiotherapists with the support of a company constituted by the members of the consortium involved in the design and development of the platform. The supervised training can be implemented in the healthcare facility with the projector-based box or at patients' home with the head mounted device. Currently both are being pilot tested and evaluated in a proof-of-concept study aiming to recruit up to 80 patients in the HOLOBALANCE intervention and 80 controls.

6 The Multimodal Coaching of SAAM Project[8]

6.1 What Are the Challenges on Aging and Healthcare for Europe in 2030?

Europe faces an on-going crisis in caring for its ageing population. The ageing process creates many daily difficulties increasing over time: financial, social, and physical insecurity, loneliness, medical problems, management issues, and many

[8]This paragraph has been authored by Vera Veleva, Martin Žnidaršič, Bernard Ženko, Aljaž Osojnik and Richard Wheeler on behalf of SAAM Consortium.

others. Social care and assisted living services struggle as the population ages, and older citizens are under increasing pressure to live at home, often alone, for as long as possible. This is further complicated by the increased mobility of younger generations that contributes to increasing levels of isolation. On the other hand, access to health and social services for the elderly is often limited in lower-income countries or in resource-poor settings around the world. Thus, there is a clear need for formulating more sustainable models for health and care delivery, especially considering the ageing population.

6.2 What Is the Vision of Your Project About Aging and Healthcare to Tackle These Challenges and Transform Them into Opportunities?

SAAM is focused on a single goal: *providing new methods supporting Europe's ageing population to remain active and live independently for as long as possible.* SAAM does this by employing a holistic approach, contributing to physical, mental and social well-being, in particular by focusing on continuing participation in social, economic, cultural, spiritual and civic affairs, and not just the ability to be physically active or to participate in the labour force.

SAAM is flexible enough to provide assistance to most seniors but focuses on one of the most under-served segments of the population—those above the age of 60 in economically under-developed regions with very low technological proficiencies. These are also more likely to live in an area with poorly developed social housing and support services, and more likely to suffer from economic deprivation and social isolation later in life.

To tackle these challenges, we need to have in mind that ageing takes place within the context of friends, neighbours, family members, community, and support and care services. We see these as important supporting and enabling elements of active ageing, and SAAM system is designed to provide feedback to and involve these social circles of ageing users, and to support them in helping the elderly to live independently.

6.3 What Are the Main Concepts of the Project, the Methodology, the Developed Tools, the Outcomes?

The core concept of SAAM is based on a seamless and highly autonomous modular active ageing coaching system that supports seniors to continue living independently and increase their overall well-being. SAAM uses technology-enabled approaches with a novel and practical emphasis on ambient sensing and learning user needs and preferences, and effective coaching by leveraging the user's social support networks.

User-centred design is a priority for SAAM, and it is grounded on experience of four care organisations acting as project partners. Technical development is supported by two extensive user surveys conducted during the project—one at the beginning of the project, eliciting user needs and requirements, and one towards the end of the project involving pilot testing with end users from Austria, Slovenia and Bulgaria. Care organisations were also actively involved in development of situation assessment, coaching and rendering models.

SAAM system aims at supporting seniors in maintaining themselves in personal homeostasis with respect to wellbeing by balancing between available individual resources and challenges [32]. The basic assumption is that supporting the homeostasis (resources—challenges balance) of the senior in single domain-specific situations contributes to supporting their overall wellbeing.

SAAM core intervention domains are sleep, mobility, activity, and social activity and they are pilot tested with real end-users. SAAM is also developing advanced system components for intervention in other domains, but these are tested primarily in laboratory settings.

As an ICT system SAAM consists of fixed and wearable sensors, edge computing and communication devices, cloud infrastructure, all linked together with custom software. Users interact with the system through a multimodal interface as well as more standard mobile and web application.

SAAM system is devised in a way that takes into account and adapts to users' personal needs, preferences, living environment, and their social connections. Adaptive coaching of this kind is done in SAAM by a series of hardware and software components that are dedicated to various coaching domains and are denoted as coaching pipelines. A coaching pipeline consists of sensor data processing components, reasoning models for selection of a suitable coaching action and components for personalization of outputs that are communicated to the users (Fig. 2 Coaching pipeline architecture).

Sensing is performed by the hardware components, while actuation refers to rendering coaching actions to the user through various interfaces. The steps in between are completely invisible to the users. Sensing is done as unobtrusively as possible.

SAAM is designed to keep the users active primarily by enhancing interactions with their social circles. It introduces specific user roles: primary user (PU), secondary user (SU), coach and caregiver. Coaching rendering is done via text or light + audio messages, while the actuation uses several persuasive strategies (suggestion, self-monitoring and commitment bias) and is tailored to PU's preferences. The timing for coaching actions from different pipelines is combined not to overwhelm the users. For PUs unwilling or incapable of using the SAAM system rendering is done through

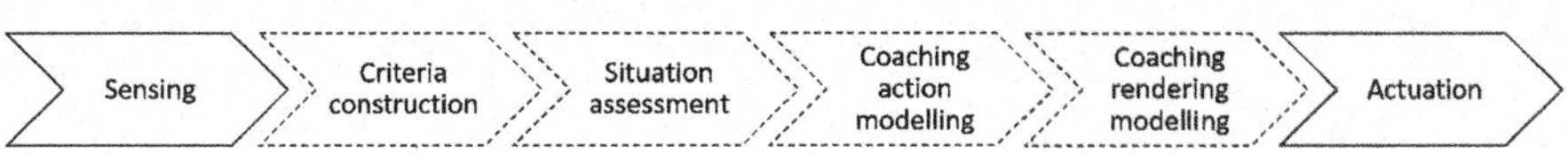

Fig. 2 Coaching pipeline architecture in SAAM project

SUs—a countermeasure to boredom and technology rejection by PUs. In this way, PUs who are not technologically apt can also benefit from SAAM coaching through their SUs. Thus, coaching is as unobtrusive as possible.

6.4 What Is the Expected Impact of Your Project?

One of the expected project impacts is creating a low-cost, extensible and inclusive coaching system providing support for users of varying language, physical, and technological capabilities. SAAM is a scalable coach providing for flexible user interactions, including ambient data collection and an "invisible helper". For users unable or unwilling to interact with technologies, the system's novel "social circles" capability engages the user's social networks to act as coaches to support healthy independent living.

Diversity of data streams and decision support methods sensitive to the needs and preferences of individual users provides a more useful and practical system, offering better and less intrusive, personalised coaching recommendations.

6.5 Please Describe the Exploitation Models and/or Channels and/or Opportunities

The final product development for low-end markets such as Bulgaria focuses on the low cost components: core system with a smart power meter, Wi-Fi router, and (optionally) an inexpensive mobile phone. In this configuration that we call "basic SAAM", we likely have the strongest product with the most benefit for local authorities. Also in this case, it is important to provide maximum impact with minimum user interaction in line with the latest research and developments in the field. This approach allows for machine learning for user behavioural nudging that is context independent. This concept is worth considering as the SAAM basic product, as it is coherent with the abilities of our original elderly user cohort (low ICT familiarity, likely unable to use a mobile phone, unlikely to welcome gadgets, likely to have a strong emotional attachment to their home). In this way "SAAM makes your (smart) home caring".

A promising concept in the long run is to partner with external smart meter companies producing smart home kit infrastructure that is then offered as a package to electricity companies' end-users to "enable a smart home and smart energy usage infrastructure". In this configuration, SAAM product would include back-end software, intelligence, and workflow architectures for their hardware to turn a "smart home" into a "caring home".

7 Virtual Coaching for Telerehabilitation: Insight to the European vCare-Project[9]

7.1 Project Context Introduction

The vCare project designs a Virtual Coach (VC) that supports the rehabilitation phase after the occurrence the particular Non-communicable diseases (NCDs) stroke, PD, and heart failures/ischemic heart disease. Such pathologies represent a major public health challenge globally in the 21st century diminishing quality of life (QoL) [33]. The efficient implementation of the secondary prevention measures through adequate rehabilitation is essential in this regard. However, given that the institutionalized rehabilitation programs usually last only for a definite period the continuity of care is often interrupted after the transition from the institutionalized rehabilitation to the home self-rehabilitation environment. Within vCare, the patients' home rehabilitation is amended by advice for a healthy behavior and monitoring and motivating the execution of distinct (physical) exercises such as serious games. This way, also the VC tries to compensate the absence of a human caregiver and enrich the traditional care schemata of more or less defined check-ups by doctors and therapists. The VC motivates patients to perform therapy and prevention measures and personalize its recommendation to the behavior, preferences and habits of the patient.

In particular, by utilizing the VC in the vCare-project, we aim to enhance the QoL of patients by helping them to adhere to the care plan that consisted of personalized healthy recommendations for daily activities. The permanent coaching shall lead to a continuous reduction of risk factors that are related to the probability of a relapse of the disease, the manifestation of disabilities, or the decline of (mental) health (see Fig. 3).

7.2 Principle Project Approach and Methodology

The vCare project focuses on building a VC solution for the rehabilitation in the home environment that integrates existing technical solutions in order to provide a holistic user experience, that works on defined care pathways which are personalized continuously, and that provides a verifiable clinical evaluation in terms of patient's engagement, medical recovery and QoL (TRL 7). Therefore, vCare is deploying a twofold joint medical and technical implementation and testing phase for the validation studies in order to assess the VC system's appropriateness gradually concerning the project progress (see Fig. 4). This allows to collect real-time feedback from the user perspective (patients, therapists, and physicians). The project evaluation should demonstrate in particular how the specific challenge of empowering and motivating

[9]This paragraph has been authored by Kai Gand, Hannes Schlieter, Sofoklis Kyriazakos, Massimo Caprino, Luc Nicolas, and Johannes Kropf on behalf of the vCare consortium.

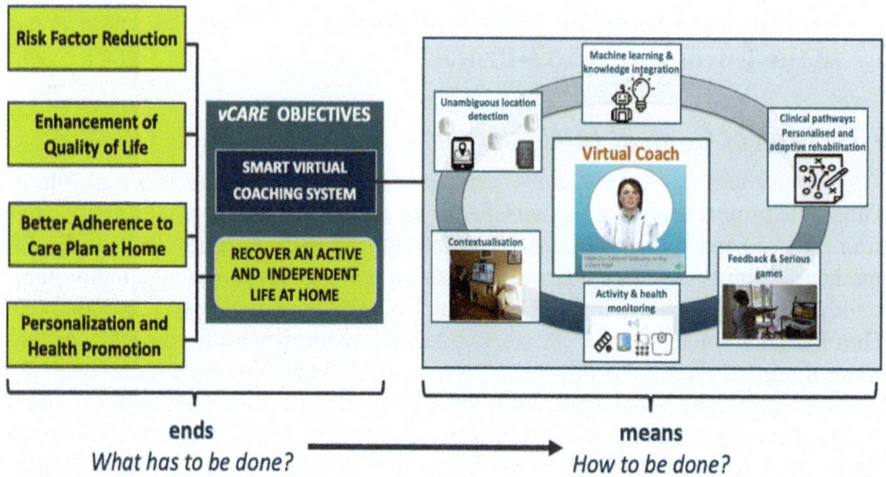

Fig. 3 Overview of vCare's objectives (What has to be done?) and implementation measures (How to be done?)

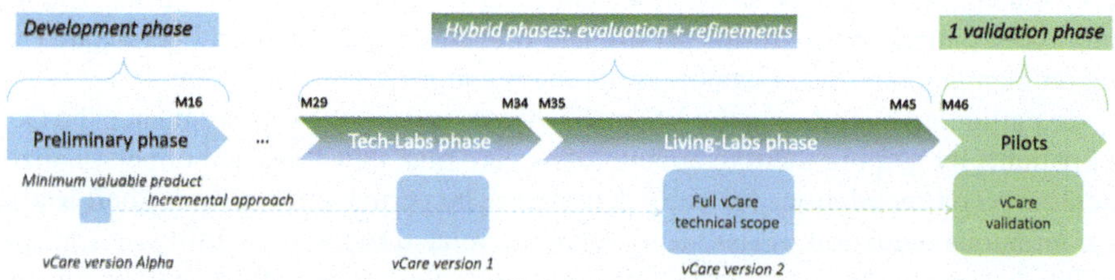

Fig. 4 Overall implementation plan

via a VC works in a clinical setting. For building the VC the clinical expertise is used, on the one hand, to derive the basic rehabilitation needs as well as the necessary clinical pathways. On the other hand, the technicians ensure that the VC solution properly works and is adapted to the patients' needs and pathways. To in turn ensure this overall ambition, an iterative, tripartite testing strategy is in place: First, within the TechLab phase the sole functioning of the technical components and their interplay have been tested having the therapists substituting the patient behaviors. Second, the Living Lab simulates the homes by research apartments providing a protected environment and support for the patients trying out the VC solution. Third, within the Pilot phase the patients use the solution in their real home setting.

The overall aim of the pilot study is to refine and test the use of the vCare coaching system to find out if it is useful in motivating and empowering patients with various functional impairments and comorbidities to engage actively in performing personalized rehabilitation activities in order to be independent and to improve their QoL.

The continuous technological progress is changing the impact of the user on the approach to a VC as health professional. A good interaction between the user and the VC can ensure a trusty relationship. Thus, looking at secondary prevention of chronic diseases, vCare might particularly impact medication adherence and extend existing rehabilitation programmes, providing a great opportunity to guarantee the continuity of care between hospital and home. vCare will show that is possible to deal with complex clinical situations.

7.3 The vCare Project's Perspective on the Future of Ageing

The vCare system is a persuasive and non-obtrusive technology that helps people change their habits and improve their home-based rehabilitation. Therefore, they can become healthier and gain more healthy time of living. In general, when broadly looking on the VC literature an increased diffusion of technologies with strong interaction with human beings in the world of health and medicine can be confirmed [34]. In the future, this relationship might even be strengthened in the medical sector fostering patients' engagement toward a process of self-awareness and self-confidence in health management. According to the lessons learned from the vCare project [35] and the current trends in the scene, we predict the following directions for the future of aging combined with the use of VC:

Ubiquity of the VC: Advanced modes of presence will lead to ubiquity of the VC in daily life and allow further interaction modes. Broadened augmentation in terms of a further integration of VC into the reality might in turn broaden its abilities to guide the user and therefore increase the literacy of the suggested actions.

Advanced sensory capabilities: Advanced sensing and acting levels will allow seamless adaptation in relation to the people's conditions.

Multiple Coaches: Multiple linked coaches and other assistant systems could allow an even monitoring and guidance of the user.

AI grounded treatment knowledge: Advanced AI may also infer novel treatment and well-being strategies grounded on common health data ecosystem. It is very likely that such changes could improve the management of increasingly complex clinical situations, especially for cases of chronic diseases and disabilities (as one needs to expect a further increase of case counts here).

Converging Wellbeing and Health Care enhancing Quality of Life: In the future, both healthy as well as frail or sick, younger and ageing people could be supported by VC. Results from the primary prevention or even well-being could be more easily transferred to the more complicated and specific one of secondary prevention. When assuming also a broader evidence of the (perceived) usefulness and advantageousness it might become possible to transfer the VC's support modes to a broad range of use cases for preserving physical, cognitive, mental, and social well-being for as long as possible. More specifically, the VC will educate and finally empower patients to increase their adherence to drug therapy and to pursue physical and cognitive rehabilitation programs to regain independence with a healthier lifestyle and a better quality of life.

Desired commercialization path and formalities: In order to reach the directions listed above, it is important to address the challenges of the regulatory framework to operate eHealth or Digital Therapeutic (DTx) solutions. The vCare project has identified this challenge and is already investigating pathways to address potential barriers. Already today, elements of vCare are classified as Medical Devices with CE mark and the project is further developing a commercialization strategy for the post-project period.

8 WellCO Recommends Healthier Behaviour Change[10]

8.1 Ageing Challenges for 2030: The WellCo Perspective

Important challenges arise in Europe with regards to healthcare and ageing due to it will be up to all of us to ensure that social welfare and healthcare systems are made more resilient for the next generation [36].

On the one hand, it is expected that people remain working till older ages in the next decades. The reason is that this is one of the more realistic solutions to ensure the sustainability of resources to finance the higher healthcare costs associated with population ageing.

On the other hand, the digitalization of the healthcare sector and the advances in artificial intelligence and big data offer an opportunity to reduce the gap between the demand and the quantity and quality of the supply of healthcare. In this sense, the COVID-19 pandemic seems to have accelerated the adoption of digital solutions, especially the use of telehealth, with virtual consultations and remote patient monitoring [37].

Finally, a sustainable, efficient and cost-effective future for health also requires a population health management approach with special attention to prevention policies. This culture will permeate all areas of society, so it is expected that in the near future: unhealthy behaviours are taxed, companies award to those employees that have healthier habits (e.g. paying if cycling instead of using the car [38]) and that the demand of digital applications for healthcare experiences a tremendous growth in the coming years.

---

[10]This paragraph has been authored by Inmaculada Luengo and Paloma Jimeno on behalf of the WellCO consortium.

8.2 WellCo Supports Elderly Empowerment

WellCo vision is to empower elderly people and general population on the importance of the prevention through the acquisition of healthier behaviours. It is crucial for an ageing population to reduce the risk of developing preventable chronic conditions which are accounted mainly from unhealthy behaviour like physical inactivity, smoking, poor diet, etc. Although currently just after developing any disease the population pay attention and try to change their behaviour, it is important to raise awareness about this disease prevention and how the ICT could help us on an easy and comfortable way with a solution like WellCo, a personalised wellbeing coach (Fig. 5).

In the current pandemic times, ICT solutions has raised a special importance, due to the limitations on presence attendance and follow up by the health professionals. Also, it seems that people incrementally are raising awareness on the importance of being healthy and improving their wellbeing habits.

Thanks to the holistic approach of WellCo, it is possible to guide people on the different key age-related issues like diet, physical activity, risk avoidance, preventive measures, lifestyle, activity management, leisure, social participation and overall wellness. So, the possibilities and opportunities allow WellCo to act as a holistic coach or as domain specific one just focalizing the monitoring and recommendations in that domain.

Leveraging state-of-the-art artificial intelligent technologies, WellCo implements algorithms capable of reasoning, extracting knowledge and adapt to personal needs, emotional and behavioural patterns with the purpose of getting enough information about the environment surrounding the user. The access to this information enables the system to have information about the areas of wellbeing where the user requires

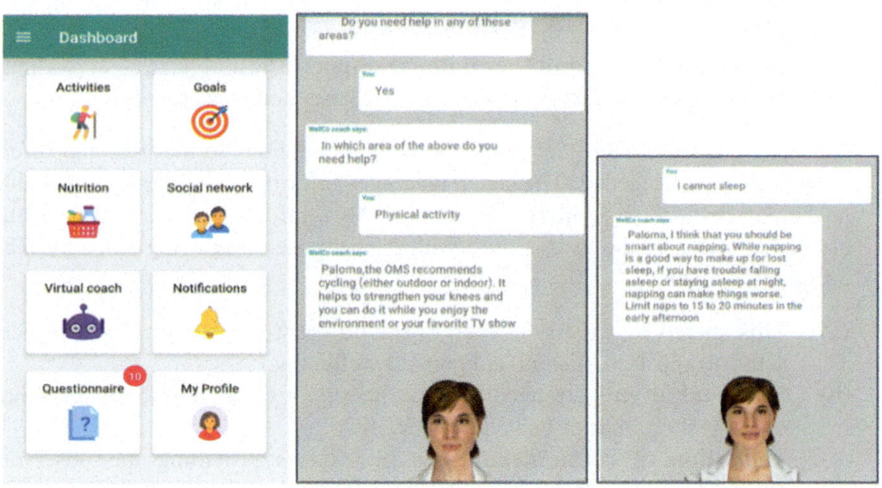

Fig. 5 Dashboard and Affective-Aware Coach in WellCo system

to improve. This information together with the capabilities and opportunities of the user are utilized to offer the user motivational recommendations to change his/her habits and ensure that healthier behaviours are adopted and maintained in the long term.

8.3 The WellCO Approach

The WellCo concept is developed from the Behavioural Change Wheel [39], a new method that characterises and designs behaviour change actions through three essential conditions: capability, opportunity and motivation to perform the change action ("COM-B" system). Taking this as baseline and considering that behaviour change interventions focused on fear and warning are not enough, the methodology that WellCo adopts to deal with behaviour change is as follows:

- WellCo leverages **wearable sensors and AI-based algorithms** that process the emotional and wellbeing status of the user with the aim of **knowing the context surrounding the user**;
- Contextual information is used by the different **recommender systems** implemented in WellCo to provide **personalized recommendations** that ensure the adoption, follow-up and maintenance of the proposed behaviour change actions for as long as possible.
- To address the **motivational dimension** of the user during this process of change of habits, WellCo offers:

  Social Incentives that generate a sense of belonging to WellCo. "Goals" are the main element around which social incentives emerge.
  Immediate Rewards that increase the positive experience of the action, with important outcomes for motivation and persistence.
  Progress Monitoring and Continuous Support. The user has a clear roadmap for personalised guidance and follow-up. These elements are:

- **Affective-Aware Coach** that provides recommendations to the user and offers support in case of needed. The coach leverages information of the user available in the database to personalize interactions. Also, information derived from the emotional status of the user is used with the purpose of showing empathy. The coach implements:

  (a) **Tips** shared by experts in each of the different wellbeing areas: physical activity, nutrition, mental and general wellbeing.
  (b) **Video-call events** arranged by coordinators or GPs about the main topics of interest or areas of behaviour in WellCo.
  (c) **Validation of recommendations** by experts providing the observers outcomes and feedback loop into the system.

8.4 *The Expected Impact of the WellCO Affective-Aware Coach*

The foreseen impact of the system proposed by WellCO project is at three levels:

- **Societal Impact**

Proper dissemination and exploitation actions have been performed during and after the project with the purpose of transferring to general population the results derived from WellCo. The more important societal impact expected for WellCo is the contribution to the improvement of well-being on population thanks to WellCo virtual coach and the awareness raised on prevention through ICT technologies promoting behaviour change towards well-being.

- **Economic Impact**

WellCo training will allow individual users to self-manage their own health, so the consequence of WellCo could be the delivery of an approach that help to spread the culture of health prevention and population health management (PMH). This culture will have significant impact on the sustainable future of healthcare in Europe.

- **Scientific Impact**

Proper dissemination actions will be essential to ensure that the knowledge gained in WellCo is transferred to the scientific community. In quantitative terms: 8 scientific papers have been published in conferences and 2 as an article in scientific journal. Being 3 of these papers provided for open access in OpenAire. In addition, the project has brought possibilities to 2 Ph.D. students that were involved along since the project beginning till the end.

8.5 *Exploitation Model for WellCo Coaching System*

WellCo allows multiple exploitation models, through the individual exploitation of their modules as well as through the whole exploitation of the business solution.

Individual models developed along WellCo are mostly related with the monitoring of users' behaviour and how this behaviour could be modified. On this area we have developments like mental health assessment, activity monitoring, risk estimation, bite counting, energy expenditure, social interaction assessment, etc. Moreover, inside the project other exploitation assets like emotional assessment via visual and speech analysis have been developed as well as recommendations engines. All these developments have been based on innovative technologies like IoT, big data, machine learning and deep learning technologies. Being all of them important exploitable outcomes of the project.

Finally, WellCo as a complete application, has established a minimum viable product to be used in the initial exploitation steps on the prevention domain, focusing on public health, private health and insurance companies, all of them mostly motivated, after pandemic, on health prevention through ICT technologies.

9 Conclusions

A European community of project dedicated to the design and test of solutions for Active and Healthy Ageing, have been built around the PM-15 H2020 call. This is important because a common research framework is being shared and joint initiatives support the construction of a common vision, interoperable tools and mutual development to encourage a true exploitation of research outcomes. Only through such initiatives, research findings and innovative technological solutions could land among citizens. All projects recognize the importance of the elderly empowerment through the leverage of existing mobile and ICT tools as basic and key strategy. The digital acquaintance and "stability" are crucial for this category of subjects. Thus, the innovation should stay "behind the curtain" of the existing object by increasing their intelligence and the capability to support, to remind, to stimulate elderly in activities aimed at keeping or improving their health status. In this perspective, the perceived importance of the new solutions and related applications, stays in the "how better I feel" but with minor (apparently) and incremental changes in my habits.

This also represents the reward that is necessary to support the motivational dimension of people. All projects also recognize the importance of such actions both at short-time and local level, with immediate rewards through local stakeholder and policy makers (community, town, …) like social incentives small economic revenues in the form of discounts for certain products (for healthcare, food and nutrition, …), and in the long-term by increasing the level of the intervention at a wider community (regional, national, European). The rewards represent the strategic tools for perceiving the positive experience of the action so that motivation and persistence is continuously maintained.

The expected exploitation is envisioned in the frame of eHealth or Digital Therapeutic solutions. Their recent introduction and the possibility to be included in the welfare systems at national level could represent the key point for the actual deployment of these solution in the healthcare sector.

Acknowledgements All projects are funded under the Horizon 2020 SC1-PM-15-2017 call Personalised coaching for well-being and care of people as they age (RIA).

For further details and information please visit the projects' websites:

- CAPTAIN—Coach Assistant via Projected and Tangible Interface, G.A. No. 769830, https://www.captain-eu.org/.
- COUCH—Council of Coaches, G.A. No. 769553, https://www.council-of-coaches.eu/.
- EMPATHIC—Empathic, Expressive, Advanced Virtual Coach to Improve Independent Healthy-Life-Years of the Elderly, G.A. No. 769872, http://www.empathic-project.eu/.

– HOLOBALANCE—HOLOgrams for personalised virtual coaching and motivation in an ageing population with BALANCE disorders, G.A. No.769574, https://holobalance.eu/.

– SAAM—Supporting Active Ageing through Multimodal coaching, G.A. No. 769661, https://saam2020.eu/.

– vCare—Virtual Coaching Activities for Rehabilitation in Elderly, G.A. No.769807, https://vcare-project.eu/.

– WellCO—Wellbeing and Health Virtual Coach, G.A. No.769765, http://wellco-project.eu/.

– NESTORE—Novel Empowering Solutions and Technologies for Older people to Retain Everyday life activities, G.A. No. 769643, https://nestore-coach.eu/home.

References

1. Eckert, J. K., Morgan, L. A., & Swamy, N. (2004). Preferences for receipt of care among community-dwelling adults. *Journal of Aging & Social Policy, 16*(2), 49–65. https://doi.org/10.1300/J031v16n02_04.
2. Matsumoto, H., Naruse, T., Sakai, M., & Nagata, S. (2016). Who prefers to age in place? Cross-sectional survey of middle-aged people in Japan. *Geriatrics & Gerontology International, 16*(5), 631–637. https://doi.org/10.1111/ggi.12503.
3. Boldy, D., Grenade, L., Lewin, G., Karol, E., & Burton, E. (2011). Older people's decisions regarding 'ageing in place': A Western Australian case study. *Australasian Journal on Ageing, 30*(3), 136–142. https://doi.org/10.1111/j.1741-6612.2010.00469.x.
4. Mynatt, E. D., & Rogers, W. A. (2001). Developing technology to support the functional independence of older adults. *Ageing International, 27*(1), 24–41. https://doi.org/10.1007/s12126-001-1014-5.
5. Bowles, K. H., Dykes, P., & Demiris, G. (2015). The use of health information technology to improve care and outcomes for older adults. *Research in Gerontological Nursing, 8*(1), 5–10. https://doi.org/10.3928/19404921-20121222-01.
6. Hoque, R., & Sorwar, G. (2017). Understanding factors influencing the adoption of mHealth by the elderly: An extension of the UTAUT model. *International Journal of Medical Informatics, 101,* 75–84. https://doi.org/10.1016/j.ijmedinf.2017.02.002.
7. Cho, J. (2016). The impact of post-adoption beliefs on the continued use of health apps. *International Journal of Medical Informatics, 87,* 75–83. https://doi.org/10.1016/j.ijmedinf.2015.12.016.
8. Wildenbos, G. A., Jaspers, M. W. M., Schijven, M. P., & Dusseljee-Peute, L. W. (2019). Mobile health for older adult patients: Using an aging barriers framework to classify usability problems. *International Journal of Medical Informatics, 124*, 68–77. https://doi.org/10.1016/j.ijmedinf.2019.01.006.
9. Lee, E., Han, S., & Jo, S. H. (2017). Consumer choice of on-demand mHealth app services: Context and contents values using structural equation modeling. *International Journal of Medical Informatics, 97,* 229–238. https://doi.org/10.1016/j.ijmedinf.2016.10.016.
10. Wang, S., et al. (2019). Technology to support aging in place: Older adults' perspectives. *Healthcare, 7*(2) (Art. no. 2). https://doi.org/10.3390/healthcare7020060.
11. Konstantinidis, E., et al. (2019). A new approach for ageing at home: The CAPTAIN system. In *MedInfo.* https://doi.org/10.3233/SHTI190606.
12. de Vries, H. (2017). An integrated approach for understanding health behavior; The I-change model as an example. *PBSIJ, 2*(2) (2017). https://doi.org/10.19080/pbsij.2017.02.555585.
13. Beristain Iraola, A., Álvarez Sánchez, R., Petsani, D., Hors-Fraile, S., Bamidis, P., & Konstantinidis, E. (2020). Virtual coaching for older adults at home using SMART goal supported behavior change. In *Companion Publication of the 2020 International Conference on Multimodal Interaction*, New York, NY, USA, Oct. 2020 (pp. 251–255). https://doi.org/10.1145/3395035.3425311.

14. Peek, S. T. M., Wouters, E. J., Luijkx, K. G., & Vrijhoef, H. J. (2016). What it takes to successfully implement technology for aging in place: focus groups with stakeholders. *Journal of Medical Internet Research, 18*(5), https://doi.org/10.2196/jmir.5253.
15. Tessarolo, F., et al. (2019). User-centered co-design and AGILE methodology for developing ambient assisting technologies: Study plan and methodological framework of the CAPTAIN project. In *2019 IEEE 23rd International Symposium on Consumer Technologies (ISCT)*, Jun. 2019 (pp. 283–286). https://doi.org/10.1109/isce.2019.8901003.
16. Petsani, D., et al. (2020). Creating a feedback loop between persona development and user research towards better technology acceptance. In *HCI International 2020—Late Breaking Papers: User Experience Design and Case Studies*, Cham, 2020 (pp. 282–298). https://doi.org/10.1007/978-3-030-60114-0_19.
17. op den Akker, H., op den Akker, R., Beinema, T., Banos, O., Heylen, D., Bedsted, B., Pease. A., Pelachaud, C., Traver-Salcedo, V., Kyriazakos, S., & Hermens, H. (2018). Council of coaches—A novel holistic behavior change coaching approach. In *Proceedings of the 4th International Conference on Information and Communication Technologies for Ageing Well and e-Health—Volume 1: ICT4AWE* (pp. 219–226), Funchal Madeira, Portugal, March 2018.
18. Kantharaju, R. B., de Franco, D., Pease, A., & Pelachaud, C. (2018). Is two better than one? Effects of multiple agents on user persuasion. In *Proceedings of the 18th International Conference on Intelligent Virtual Agents (IVA2018)* (pp. 255–262), November 2018.
19. *Ageing populations in Europe: Challenges and opportunities for the CEB* (Council of Europe development Bank), 2014. https://coebank.org/media/documents/Study_Ageing.pdf.
20. Cordasco, G., Esposito, M., Masucci, F., Riviello, M. T., Esposito, A., Chollet, G., Schlögl, S., Milhorat, P., & Pelosi, G. (2014) Assessing voice user interfaces: the assist system prototype. In: *Proceedings of 5th IEEE international Conference on Cognitive Info Communications*, Vietri sul Mare, 5–7 Nov (pp. 91–96).
21. Esposito, A., Esposito, A. M., LikformanSulem, L., Maldonato, M. N., & Vinciarelli, A. (2016). On the significance of speech pauses in depressive disorders: Results on read and spontaneous narratives. In: A. Esposito et al. (Eds.), *Springer SIST series on Recent Advances in Nonlinear Speech Processing* (Vol. 48, pp. 73–82).
22. Esposito, A., Esposito, A. M., & Vogel, C. (2015). Needs and challenges in human computer interaction for processing social emotional information. *Pattern Recognition Letters, 66,* 41–51.
23. Troncone, A., Palumbo, D., & Esposito, A. (2014). Mood effects on the decoding of emotional voices. In S. Bassis, A. Esposito, & F. C. Morabito (Eds.), *Recent advances of neural network models and applications* (Vol. 26, pp. 325–332). Springer International Publishing.
24. Montenegro, C., López Zorrilla, A., Olaso, J. M., Santana, R., Justo, R., Lozano, J. A., et al. (2019). A dialogue-act taxonomy for a virtual coach designed to improve the life of elderly. *Multimodal Technologies and Interaction, 3*(3), 1–19.
25. Justo, R., Ben Letaifa, L., Palmero, C., Gonzalez-Fraile, E., Torp Johansen, A., Vázquez, A., et al. (2020). Analysis of the interaction between elderly people and a simulated virtual coach. *Journal of Ambient Intelligence and Humanized Computing, 11*(12), 6125–6140.
26. Tenorio-Laranga, J., Fernandez Ruanova, B., Torres, M. I., Justo; R., Alday, A., & Llano Hernaiz, J. X. (2019). Designing a virtual coach: Involvement of end-users from early design to prototype. *International Journal of Integrated Care (IJIC). 2019 Annual Conference Supplement, 19*(S1), 1–8.
27. Esposito, A., Amorese, T., Maldonato, N., Vinciarelli, A., Torres, M. I., Escalera, S., & Cordasco, G. (2020) Seniors' ability to decode differently aged facial emotional expressions In: *Faces and Gestures in E-health and Welfare (FaGEW), 15th IEEE International Conference on Automatic Face and Gesture Recognition.* Buenos Aires.
28. Torres, M. I., Olaso, J. M., Glackin, C., Justo, R., & Chollet, G. (2020). An spoken dialog system for the empathic virtual coach. In *Lecture Notes in Electrical Engineering* (Vol. 579, pp. 259–265).
29. Esposito, A., Amorese, T., Cuciniello, M., Esposito, A. M., Troncone, A., Torres, M. I., Schlögl, A., & Cordasco, G. (2019) Seniors' acceptance of virtual humanoid agents. In *Ambient Assisted Living*. Lecture Notes in Electrical Engineering (Vol. 544, pp. 429–443).

30. Torres, M. I., Olaso, J. M., Montenegro, C., Santana, R., Vázquez, A., Justo, R., Lozano, J. A., Schlögl, S., Chollet, G., Dugan, N., Irvine, M., Glackin, N., Pickard, C., Esposito, A., Cordasco, G., Troncone, A., Petrovska-Delacretaz, D., Mtibaa, A., Hmani, M. A., Korsnes, M. S., Martinussen, J. L., Escalera, S., Palmero Cantariño, C., Deroo, O., Gordeeva, O., Tenorio-Laranga, J., Gonzalez-Fraile, J. E., Fernandez-Ruanova, B., & Gonzalez-Pinto, A. (2019). The EMPATHIC project: Mid-term achievements. In *Proceedings of COACH Workshop: Personalized Coaching for the Wellbeing of an Ageing Society @ PETRA PErva-sive Technologies Related to Assistive Environments (PETRA) Conference* (pp. 629–638). ACM Digital Library.
31. Fernandez Ruanova, B., Tenorio-Laranga, J., Alday, A., Llano Hernaiz, J. X., Justo, R., & Torres, M. I. (2019). Innovation on home-based care services. *International Journal of Integrated Care (IJIC), 2019 Annual Conference Supplement, 19*(S1), A22, 1–8.
32. Dodge, R., Daly, A. P., Huyton, J., & Sanders, L. D. (2012). The challenge of defining wellbeing. *International Journal of Wellbeing,* 222–235. https://doi.org/10.5502/ijw.v2i3.4.
33. Clifford, J. (2011). The UN disability convention and its impact on European equality law. *The Equal Rights Review, 6*, 11–25. https://www.equalrightstrust.org/ertdocumentbank/ERR06_jarlath_article.pdf.
34. Tropea, P., Schlieter, H., Sterpi, I., Judica, E., Gand, K., Caprino, M., Gabilondo, I., Gomez-Esteban, J. C., Busnatu, S., Sinescu, C., Kyriazakos, S., Anwar, S., & Corbo, M. (2019). Rehabilitation, the great absentee of virtual coaching in medical care: Scoping review. *Journal of Medical Internet Research, 21*(10), e12805.
35. https://www.frontiersin.org/articles/10.3389/fdgth.2020.546562/.
36. The 2021 Ageing Report (2021–2070), *European Economy, 142* (2020).
37. Digital Transformation. *Shaping the future of European healthcare.* Deloitte Center for Health Solutions (September 2020).
38. *Italy: Town pays people to cycle to work.* https://www.bbc.com/news/blogs-news-from-elsewhere-34831650#:~:text=An%20Italian%20town%20will%20pay,Il%20Tirreno%20news%20website%20reports.
39. Michie, S., Atkins, L., & West, R. (2014). *The behaviour change wheel. A guide to designing interventions* (1st ed., pp. 1003–1010). Great Britain: Silverback Publishing.

Conclusions

Giuseppe Andreoni and Cinzia Mambretti

Abstract Based on the lessons learnt from the co-design, development and integration processes, the research findings and the outputs from the engagement with a network of stakeholders over the course of the EU funded initiatives, this chapter is providing a set of reflections about the future directions of the Active and Healthy Ageing challenge. From the demographic perspective, to research considerations and data management directions we have tried to identify some keywords aim to help sketching the future policies and research directions for ageing well in Europe.

1 The Demographic Perspective

Ageing is strongly impacting our lives and several aspects need to be considered in this challenge.

Through this book we have tried to present, to describe, and to explain the most recent strategies and solutions that applied European research has put in place to try to match the needs for Active and Healthy Ageing.

Even recently, through its Green paper on Ageing [1], the European Union has stated this urgent priority as an intergenerational action of solidarity and responsibility, as a major topic for development of innovative technologies and integrated services, under a new perspective of technological humanism.

A first interesting consideration is related to this strange but actual parallelism between global Ageing and technology development and innovation. Well, scientific advances are often dedicated at improving our health and life, so that the ore lifespan and life expectancy at birth have significantly increased in the last decades. We are observing a similarity between the curve of Moore's Law—that describes the technology development and miniaturization—and the demographic curve describing

G. Andreoni (✉)
Department of Design, Politecnico di Milano, Via G. Durando 10, 20158 Milan, Italy
e-mail: giuseppe.andreoni@polimi.it

C. Mambretti
Fondazione Politecnico di Milano, P.zza L. Da Vinci, 32, 20133, Milan, Italy

G. Andreoni and C. Mambretti (eds.), *Digital Health Technology for Better Aging*, Research for Development, https://doi.org/10.1007/978-3-030-72663-8_21

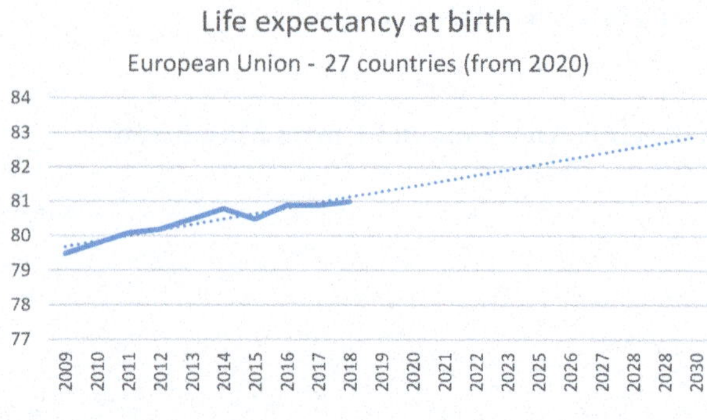

Fig. 1 Projection of life expectancy at birth in the Eurozone at 2030

the Ageing effect in our societies. In twenty years about a global 5% increase in lifespan is expected (3.5 years more on 80 years of age) and this is an extraordinary datum processed through a very simple linear extrapolation on the data provided by Eurostat (Fig. 1).

However, elderly people of today are the last not digital native population but they greatly benefit from technologies' adoption even and for only the last part of their lives. From a certain point of view, this fact is demonstrating the huge impact the new technologies could have in a strategic and large action dedicated to AHA and the benefits for people, for their and our health (so including familiar caregiver), and for our welfare systems that are affected by a dramatic increase of costs for the management of chronic diseases.

From the long journey of the European projects dedicated to innovative solutions to promote the improvement of quality of life, social inclusion and independent living of elderly several considerations arise.

2 The Research Perspective

Firstly, the *4P Medicine* concept (Preventive Predictive Personalized and Participatory) even so recent but so physiologically based seems to be an old approach with respect to the new challenges that the developments in the cited projects emphasized. The patient-centered approach, the codesign methodology is no more successful if not accompanied by the new fifth P, the *psychocognitive medicine* [2, 3]. This new dimension emphasizes the impact on quality of life as an additional fundamental marker of effectiveness beyond the evidence-based medicine approach as the results of clinical trials. Clinical outcomes without quality of life and functioning are meaningless. In this vision, we need to look at the subject more that the patient, and he/she is to be considered not simply as an end-point of care intervention but, and specifically, in his/her global dimension including emotions, attitudes, and cognitive processes which have specific relations with his/her own care process. We have seen and understood how much the psychological and cognitive profile of the elderly have strong impact on different aspects of the care interventions from the clinical outcome to the acceptance of methods and tools so to impact on therapy adherence in a very significant way.

This empathic approach is very important in all healthcare services and it is even more than necessary for prevention. *Prevention* means to avoid things happens, both continuous or progressive processes and traumatic sudden events. It is quite an invisible enemy to fight against, and for this reason even more dangerous: we do not know if, when and how it will come. Preventive actions need a strong commitment, engagement and motivation and it is for this reason that the psychocognitive domain becomes fundamental. We have experienced several behavior change theories to support these preventive intervention: the Capability, Opportunity Motivation (COM-B) model or the Health Action Process Approach (HAPA) have demonstrated a good impact for the adoption of healthy strategies in elderly lives, but the short duration of pilots (at the moment of writing this chapter) still needs further application for a long-term demonstration of effectiveness.

Surely all projects, and NESTORE specifically, demonstrated the interesting pivotal role of the exploitation of personal interests as motivational triggers. In this case, it is not just for prevention but for the immediate positive feeling and even pleasure that the suggested coaching activity is then followed up by subjects. The proposed concept of "pathways of interest", i.e. a structured coaching strategy developed and exploiting the personal interests of individuals, demonstrated to be promising. The COVID epidemy and the related recursive lockdowns—it can be also remarked that the pilot countries for the NESTORE project were Italy, Spain and The Netherlands, i.e. 2 out of 3 countries with the major impact on social life and physical activity of elderly in Europe due the SARS-COV-2 virus—significantly affected the piloting activities so limiting the application of the intervention and related outcomes and new studies at national level are under development to test this method. We will follow these initiatives to monitor further evolutions.

In any case, it is important to underline the double change of paradigm that all the PM-15 projects are proposing. The first change is represented by passing from the situation that "if I'm ill they will cure me" to the "I change my habits to prevent to be ill or the decline of my conditions": it represents a first monumental milestone in the mind of elderly people. *Elderly people are asked, encouraged and considered a partner for taking an active role in all the phase of health management, not just and simply as end-users*, i.e. people to take care of, a passive category. Their participation, however, requires empowerment, i.e. making them available and ready systems and services to implement this participative action. The ubiquitous healthcare is made possible through technologies for sensing, monitoring, delivering feedbacks and suggestions, to sustain motivation, in one world to implement a true and actual telemedicine, or better remote health care. Here is the second change requested to all the actors, including elderly: the adoption and use of technological systems that elderly are not ready or acquainted in their operations. This is also said *empowerment* of users. Empowerment is not just making them available technological devices but requires usability, acceptance, naturalness of interaction, seamless integration with daily activities, long term adoption and use to be effective. This is why empowerment is so difficult. It requires a multidisciplinary polytechnic, psychocognitive and social approach to make technology be effective in their lives, and, above all, a participatory approach in co-design the solutions they need to adopt.

We can speak of a new *Usability-by-design approach* that is needed to make systems usable and effective, to make a real transition and translation of technological tools and devices *from Design to Life.* Today the community of designers should include users, relatives and/or intergenerational actors, user experts, psychologists, interaction experts, domain experts, clinicians, technologists, economists, health technology assessment experts, ethics and RRI representative, politicians and policy makers, companies (technology, materials, services…) representative, i.e. a complex structure of stakeholders. They are all important if not necessary, and the co-design approach should the anticipated by a proper educational intervention to open minds, to prepare to listen each other needs and requests, to understand the different languages of the different discipline around the same project or system, to recapitulate and synthetize the different perspective in a single complex element. Designers often follow the Double Diamond model as methodological approach in design and development of new systems. But a diamond has several facets that are the different points of view or perspectives we need to win this apparently simple but incredibly difficult challenge of mHealth services design and implementation. *Multifacets Design is the approach for achieving Usability by Design.*

3 The European Perspective

This is also relevant when we are addressing a complex, unique but different, European population. Europe is building its unique soul but several and unavoidable differences will remain forever: culture, education, anthropometric phenotypes, climate, food and nutrition, social structure, economies and several other factors are featuring nations, regions and even towns. Therefore, *adaptability and modularity* in products, system and systems should become intrinsic while the technology could become a homogenization factor. Avatars, companions, coaching strategies needs a robust clinical reference and knowledge but the capability to intercept the personal needs and requirements and cultural models.

On the analogies and differences across European population in active healthy ageing the NESTORE experience demonstrated how these factors are essential to suitably tackle the AHA challenge at local and even individual level.

But these differences should also drive policies and interventions and welfare and healthcare system level. We think that a global approach is neither effective nor respectful of territorial differences. Personalised Medicine is then to be considered as having a wider ambition, at single individual but also at community or territorial level.

4 The Data Perspective

Last but not least, a special mention goes to data and their management. We are living in the data era, someone is speaking about *Datism* as the philosophical approach of our age.

Today we continuously produce and store large amount of personal and sensitive data. Photos, economical transactions, social activities and messages (chats), position and its change over time, places visited, friends, personal interests profiling through internet navigation chronologies and cookies, lifestyle data, nutrition, activity and posture, health related data, phone calls, voice and verbal vocabulary, we are auto-generating huge datasets whose relevance is very high in order to setup personalized services. Only innovative data mining techniques and *Artificial Intelligence algorithms* could become effective and efficient tools to manage such a large dataset to extract relevant and personal indicators.

But the same techniques are necessary for passing from the individual dimension to general knowledge that is so important in the evidence-based medicine, without forgetting the personalization that drives the best outcome.

This autogenerated *Data Portfolio* needs to be made properly structured and interoperable but in the respect of the *privacy by design paradigm*. On this point the GDPR regulation has started to operate but a long way is still in front of us.

Acknowledgements NESTORE—Novel Empowering Solutions and Technologies for Older people is funded under the Horizon 2020 SC1-PM-15-2017 call Personalised coaching for well-being and care of people as they age, G.A. No. 769643, https://nestore-coach.eu/home.

References

1. Green Paper on Ageing. (2021, January 27). *Fostering solidarity and responsibility between generations*. EU Commission.
2. Pravettoni, G., & Triberti S. (2020). A "P5" approach to healthcare and health technology. In G. Pravettoni & S. Triberti (Eds.), *P5 eHealth: An agenda for the health technologies of the future*. Springer, Cham. https://doi.org/10.1007/978-3-030-27994-3_1.
3. Gorini, A., Caiani, E.G., and Pravettoni G. (2020). Chapter 7 - Psycho-cognitive factors orienting eHealth development and evaluation. In: Pravettoni G., Triberti S. (eds) P5 eHealth: An agenda for the health technologies of the future. Springer, Cham. https://doi.org/10.1007/978-3-030-27994-3_7.

The manufacturer's authorised representative in the EU is Springer Nature Customer Service Centre GmbH, Europaplatz 3, 69115 Heidelberg, Germany. If you have any concerns regarding our products, please contact ProductSafety@springernature.com

Printed and bound by CPI Group (UK) Ltd, Croydon, CR0 4YY
22/09/2026
02221056-0002